How to Be Good
with Money

About the author

Eoin McGee is a financial planner, the founder of Prosperous Financial Services and the host of RTÉ's *How to Be Good with Money*.

How to Be Good with Money

Eoin McGee

Gill Books

Gill Books
Hume Avenue
Park West
Dublin 12
www.gillbooks.ie

Gill Books is an imprint of M.H. Gill and Co.

© Eoin McGee 2020

With thanks to Indiepics and RTÉ.

978 07171 8670 9

Print origination by O'K Graphic Design, Dublin
Edited by Djinn von Noorden
Proofread by Esther Ní Dhonnacha

Printed by ScandBook AB, Sweden

This book is typeset in Brocha Light 11pt/17pt.

The paper used in this book comes from the wood pulp of managed forests.
For every tree felled, at least one tree is planted, thereby renewing natural
resources.

All rights reserved.
No part of this publication may be copied, reproduced or transmitted in any
form or by any means, without written permission of the publishers.

A CIP catalogue record for this book is available from the British Library.

5 4 3 2

ACKNOWLEDGEMENTS

When I met Conor Nagle, from Gill Books, and he asked me if I would consider writing a book, I was scared. I had always wanted to write a book, and had always hoped that someday I would. However, when someday became today, it was a daunting task. And as I started writing this book, it did prove to be very challenging. When I finished the first draft, edits were made, and the entire Gill team worked with me. It was then I started to realise just how rewarding the process was. The support from Seán, Avril, Teresa and Conor was and continues to be superb.

Writing requires time and, for me, that means time away from my private practice. This results in more pressure on the team, who, as always, picked up the slack and worked tirelessly. Thank you so much to Colleen, Karl, Mary, Sheenagh and Sue.

To Ciara, Rachael and the rest of the team at indiepics. As a result of my workload, you had to put up with me being tired on set, while also reviewing briefs for the TV show, *How to Be Good with Money*, during all hours.

To the financial planning community here in Ireland and the UK for being so willing to share their ideas, their stories and to discuss concepts.

Thanks to my best mate Seán. The support you give, in your unique way, is always appreciated. However, a special mention to you for spending those days in Portugal by yourself while I wrote the book.

To those who help me be my best self. You give your constructive criticism but, just as importantly, offer the support and encouragement to just keep going.

To Clare. I still talk to you and you are still guiding me.

To my brothers David, Conor and Mick. You all added to this in different ways and it is really appreciated.

To my kids for understanding 'I am working on the book' but, more importantly, for being who you are. Sadhbh, Darragh, Fionn and Rian, I love you.

To my mother for the phone calls, chats and discussions that helped me balance everything throughout my life, and even more so since I started writing this book.

To Dad, for surviving this long! You are a miracle. You've inspired my career, my profession and led me down a path that results in the fact that I love doing what I do every single day. Thanks, Dad.

CONTENTS

INTRODUCTION

I would say I was six. It was 1986. I was walking towards the village of Blanchardstown, holding my dad's hand. I asked him, 'Could you have died?' He looked down at me, still walking along, and said, 'Yes, I could have.' I burst into tears as I realised that my dad was not invincible, and life doesn't last forever. My dad had a quadruple bypass when I was two. He had three stents put in when I was six and a quintuple bypass when I was eight. He was only 48.

As he recovered after the quintuple bypass, he asked his doctor how this had happened. 'I am 48 years old and I have had three major heart incidences in the last six years. Why?' he asked. His consultant explained that there were two reasons. He explained that it was hereditary, which was outside of his control. But it was also stress. 'What is the biggest stress you have in your life?' It didn't take Dad long to admit that his biggest stressor was likely work. Equally it didn't take the doctor long to ask, 'Can you afford to give up work?'

My dad never had anything to do with the financial services industry. He was a civil servant. But he did engage with the industry at one point and he was sold an 'income protection' policy. This meant, because of his health, he was able to give up work and the income protection would pay him 75 per cent of his wage until he returned to work or he retired, whichever happened first. So, he could in fact afford to give up work. It took him two years to get his head around it but at 50 years of age my father stopped working and was in receipt of his income protection until he officially retired.

My father is still alive today. It is not confirmed but some of the people who work in St James's Hospital believe my dad is the longest post-open heart surgery survivor in Ireland. Both my father and I believe he would not have survived this long had it not been for the income protection. The income protection literally kept him alive.

At a very young age I saw the importance of having good cover in place in case things go wrong. But more importantly, I witnessed first-hand the impact it had on the ability to recover and continue to live your best life. I am not saying that when I was ten years old and my father was giving up work to look after his health I sat back and said, 'I want to sell income protection for the rest of my life.' However, when I left college and was offered a job in Irish Life, I was very attracted to it. I started to realise that this industry and the advice my dad had received were the reason I still had a dad. Very quickly I realised that to have the same impact on families' lives that financial services had on my family's life I needed to be client facing: that is, I needed to be giving families and people advice around their money.

This is why I am a financial planner. This is why I am writing this book.

Why should you read this book?

This book is for you if you have ever wondered: am I actually doing the right thing with my money? Will I be OK financially in the future? Could I do better? Am I missing something? How do I get out of crappy debt? How do I get into happy debt? What happens if something goes wrong? How do I make my money last until the end of the month? Is there a right way of investing money? How do you start saving? Basically, this book is for you if you have any money at all and you are wondering how to be good with it.

How to read this book

It is possible that you will be able to jump to a certain section, just read that section and get what you need. But that is not how this book is written. It is intended that you would read it from start to finish. I would strongly suggest that you don't skip sections because you think they are not relevant to you. Financial planning is a dynamic process and looking at all angles, even if they don't apply to you today, will give you a different perspective on things, and there are lots of nuggets in each section that are transferable.

Who am I and why should you bother listening to what I have to say?

I'm just a bloke with four kids who's lucky enough to have found a career that I love. I was doing it for ten years and the only people listening to me were my own private clients. At least I hope they were listening. Then one day I got a break on Newstalk and things went from there. In the last six or seven years I have been doing lots of work with RTÉ, Newstalk, Today

FM and many of the local radio stations. I comment regularly in the printed press and I have been lucky enough to have been involved with an amazing production company who took a leap of faith and put me in *This Crowded House*, a TV show presented by Brendan Courtney that led on to *How to Be Good with Money*, the TV show that I present myself.

I've owned my own private practice for just over ten years and have brilliant colleagues working with me. Like any small-business owner, we've had some incredible times and some really difficult ones. To this book I'm bringing over 20 years of experience of dealing with high-net-worth clients' finances, helping them to use their money to live the lives they want to live. But I'm also bringing to you what I have learnt from them, their attitudes and how they think about things. I'm also bringing my knowledge of running my own business and the ups and downs that entails. But lastly and most importantly, I'm bringing the constant feedback I get from delivering conferences and the real-life stories I hear every day through my work in the media and when I'm approached on the street.

Where do I get the stuff?

Most of what you read in this book I've learnt from other people: I read a ton of books, listen to podcasts every day and have attended countless conferences over the years. I also like to think that I don't just assimilate information, but that I present it in an understandable and accessible way. Having said that, I do sometimes hear people in my industry repeating an original concept of mine! Some of the most inspiring people I've learnt from include the likes of Dave Ramsey, Jesse Mecham, Nick Murray and Carl Richards, to name but a few.

But the people I learn the most from are my clients. They throw up the issues to be solved – sometimes they even throw up the solutions. I watch them go through life and I get a unique insight into how people handle life and handle money.

What you will get from reading this book?

Each section covers a distinct area of personal finance, although all are intertwined with each other. Starting with the basics, we will see how understanding the dos and don'ts of budgeting, setting up spending rules, and managing your day-to-day spending are the foundation of any good financial plan. We will discuss debt – getting into happy debt and how to get out of crappy debt. We will also look at how to save and invest your money and, finally, how best to protect it all – by laying out the strongest financial plans for your retirement and later life.

By reading this book, I hope that you will learn a lot about your own money – how you manage it, how you invest it and, most importantly, how you use it to support the life you want to live. I hope to dispense the tools that will help you be more aware – of your spending and saving – so that, ultimately, you can become good with money.

SECTION 1

DAY-TO-DAY SPENDING

The basics

I t doesn't matter if you have lots of money or struggle to meet every single pay packet. You need to get the basics right. In this section, we look at how to manage your day-to-day spending. These are the foundations: get it right and the wealth creation will be built on solid ground. Get it wrong and you may get away with it for some time but if you hit a bump in the road you will hit serious problems.

Being conscious with your money

People sometimes ask me, 'If I were to change one thing to make me better with money, what should that be?' The answer is being conscious. Being conscious is about spending your money on the things you *want*. In all the TV shows I have been involved in, and in all the client engagements I have had over the last 20+ years, being conscious is the one thing that ties the people together who are having issues with their money: they simply don't know where it's going.

This problem is not salary-level specific. My private clients who earn hundreds of thousands per year can very easily fall into this trap, as can a person who earns minimum wage. Not knowing where your money is going or not having a handle on what you spend means you're blindly walking through your financial life without any real idea of what is going on. You need to take control – and it's much easier than you think.

I want you to try this challenge. For a week don't change a single thing about the way you spend money, but do one thing extra. Every time you spend money, take out your phone – or a notepad, if you prefer – and write down exactly what you spent that money on. There are some serious tools and software out there that can do this for you but for the purpose of this challenge, let's keep it simple. For example:

Sandwich and coffee – €8.50

At the end of the week, take out that notepad or phone list, open a spreadsheet on your computer (or use a clean piece of paper and fill it out as below) and start to analyse your spending. People are often shocked as to where their money is going and just how much of it they spend on certain things. Keep this analysis really simple. Don't get too drawn into categorising every penny. Making two categories, such as 'Had to buy' and 'Wanted to buy', is a really good way of doing it. For example:

Had to buy:	Wanted to buy:
Bus ticket – €3.50	Coffee – €3.00
	Pint – €4.00
	Dress – €22.00

When you've completed week one, repeat the exercise for another week. Again, don't plan changes, just spend as you would normally. At the end of week two, again transfer all your spends from your phone or notepad onto a new spreadsheet or piece of paper.

This week, however, look at the expenditure and *really* think about it. If you were planning your spending for the next two weeks, is this exactly how you would choose to spend your money?

Coffee is always targeted by the media: 'Stop drinking coffee and you'll be rich.' But what if you really like coffee? What if coffee is your reward during downtime, your treat to yourself? How the hell are you supposed to get rich if you have to give up your one, small luxury?

I'm not going to tell you to give up coffee – or beer or crisps or taxis, or whatever your guilty pleasure is – but you might want to have a think about what it means to you.

The Three-Question Challenge

This is where the Three-Question Challenge comes in. I want you to look at your analysis and work out whatever your guilty pleasure is costing you.

Question 1

Let's imagine you spent €30 on coffee, pints, wine, or whatever you enjoy during the week. Ask yourself this: is it worth €30 to you?

If the answer is yes, move on to Question 2.

Question 2

If you had €1,560 in your hand right now and somebody asked you to hand it over to cover the cost of your coffee for the next year, would you hand it over or would you think twice about it? €1,560 is just €30 per week over one year. What else could you do with €1,560? When was the last time you had a weekend away or even a summer holiday? Would you prioritise your treat over a holiday?

If the answer is yes, then you really are showing that this guilty pleasure is worth a lot to you. But let's move onto the next question.

Question 3

I want to think about the tax you pay. If you're a higher-rate taxpayer, then you need to earn roughly €3,120 per year to end up with €1,560 in your pocket after tax in order to pay for your treat. If you're a standard-rate taxpayer, you need to earn around €2,000 to end up with €1,560.

Let's assume you're a 35-year-old paying tax at roughly 50 per cent. If you work until you're 65, you'll be using €93,600 of your future earnings to fund the cost of a treat. That's almost €100,000 between now and retirement that you'll blow on your coffee or whatever it is you spend just over €4 per day on. Not only that, but the cost of your coffee is going to go up between now and when you turn 65. Now if that doesn't piss you off, then you really do love your coffee – but you also need to consider this.

Time is money

Let's stick with our 35-year-old paying higher-rate tax. Let's assume you earn €50,000 per annum, which is significantly above the average wage. During your working life you're going to work 3,893 hours, or 486 days, or almost two years, just to pay for your €30-per-week guilty pleasure.

If you still don't care and you still want to keep the treat, congratulations. I am genuinely happy for you, because you're using your money on something that brings you real joy and you deserve it.

But now do the same maths for all the other stuff in your 'wanted to buy' box above. Too often we spend our money on the things some clever person in a marketing department wants us to spend our money on. Stop that cycle. Be conscious.

Budgets

I hate the idea of budgets: the idea that you scrimp and scrape all month long and then at the end of that month you get to 'reward' yourself by putting extra money in your savings account. It's as depressing as going on a diet and, at the end of the month, getting to look at and smell your favourite full-on take-away and then having to put it away for some time in the distant future.

Budgets are painful but being broke is also painful. Choose your pain.

Whereas 'budget' conjures up feelings of restriction, thinking of it in terms of good spending rules means that you take control of your money and decide how it's going to be spent. The key to setting up good spending rules is to stop all the guessing. Too often when people go to tackle their day-to-day spending, they sit down, they plan all the money they are going to get in and all the ways they are going to spend it. Inevitably what happens next is life. Life happens. You don't get paid what you expected, or the car breaks down, or you're invited to a wedding and your budget is a failure and you give up.

Look at what money you have right now and work out when you next get paid. For the sake of argument, it's Friday; you have €100 and you're getting paid on Tuesday. Now apply the spending rules. What do you want this money to do for you between now and next Tuesday?

You look in the press and find you need to spend €25 on food. You've promised the kids you'd get takeaway on Saturday night and watch a movie – €25. You need diesel but €25 will do until Tuesday and you have to pay for swimming on Monday for the term for one of the kids – that uses up the last €25. Congratulations! You have taken full control of your money. You have allocated a role for every penny you have, and you know what you are going to spend it on.

The alternative here is that you do the opposite and plan nothing and hope you get through. Maybe on your way to get the takeaway you stop off and get yourself a coffee or a pint and, come Monday afternoon, you realise you don't have enough for the swimming and you end up putting it on the credit card and the cycle continues. But you've taken control, and this is what being conscious is all about.

Marketing departments are the enemy

Being conscious has absolutely nothing to do with being tight, but has everything to do with winning the battle against marketing departments. Winning the battle means spending your money on things you want to buy as opposed to spending your money on things some marketing manager wants you to buy.

There are large departments of marketing teams in every major company in the world. Their job is to both directly and indirectly influence how you spend your money. They literally spend their entire working days finding ways to get you to take your money out of your pocket and give it to them. It is their sole purpose during their working hours. They do it consciously so that you spend subconsciously. Why are we willing to pay more for one item than we would for another item of the same quality? Marketing.

Selling water to fish

A perfect example of marketing tactics was when my fourteen-year-old daughter went on a school trip: she and over a hundred other fourteen-year olds headed off with a handful of teachers to the UK for five days. When she came back, she was all about some bottled water everybody was drinking. The interesting thing was when I asked if it was sparkling. It wasn't. Now, there's a slight possibility that two different sparkling waters are different. I always find some brands have smaller bubbles in them than other brands!

But this was still water – with a cool bottle, mind, but still water all the same – and it was the only brand these teenagers were willing to buy during their five-day trip. The craziest thing was the price of this water was about 30 per cent more expensive than an ordinary brand of water. These kids were Irish. It rains in Ireland – it rains a lot. This was literally selling ice to Inuits.

Now why was that? Why were these kids all of a sudden brand conscious when it came to water? Why did they have an affiliation to one water brand over another? It's only still water, after all!

First of all, there was some herding going on. They were following the crowd. They didn't want to be different, and this can be extremely powerful. In a well-known test scenario, three people are in a waiting room, two of them actors and in on the secret and one not. The room starts to fill with smoke (harmless smoke) but the actors don't budge and continue waiting. The poor randomer can be seen on video looking at the others and beginning to panic. But because they don't move, the guy doesn't move either. Why not? Because the urge to belong is more important than the urge to save his life.

At some point one, or more likely two, of these teenagers succumbed to this cool-looking bottle (marketing), with the expensive price tag (marketing) and remained loyal (marketing) to this more expensive brand for the entire trip, thus bringing others along with them on this journey of subconsciously spending almost £2.50 a pop on what started out as a simple thirst-quenching exercise. Would a cheaper brand of still water have done? Of course.

But that's not the point. What happened on that trip was a perfect example of what happens to us each and every day. We buy stuff because we've always bought that brand. Or we buy stuff because somebody else has it or 'it's the best'. But we also buy stuff we don't want or need, but that we buy because we've succumbed to marketing.

Shop marketing tactics

Every time you walk into a shop, you spend money. How often do you come out of the shop with just milk? If you want to save money, stop going into the shops. Shops are designed to get you to spend money. It's in-your-face marketing. All the essentials like milk and bread are at the back so you have to walk by all the promotions to get them. Down to the music played in-store, all is planned: when the shop is quiet, they play relaxing music and you walk slower. When the shop is busy the tempo goes up because they want to push you through.

Smells are another tactic. One supermarket chain (that no longer trades under its original name) is famous for its bakery. This is partly because their bakery genuinely produces lovely goods, but also because it is believed they pumped the smell of the bakery into the car park. You were thinking about bread before you even got into the shop.

Smell is an important one for marketeers because it is believed to be very good at subconsciously stirring up old memories. Have you ever walked by somebody and smelt their perfume or aftershave and thought of an old boyfriend or girlfriend? That's the power of smell. What happens when you smell something that reminds you of something positive is that it opens you up to subconsciously being receptive to buying stuff.

A well-known American retailer, particularly popular with teenagers (probably because they're the only ones with eyesight good enough to see the clothes, the stores are so dark) has patented a smell, which they pump into all their stores. Not only do all their stores look the same, they smell the same, feel the same and, guess what, they also tend to employ young, attractive male and female staff too. None of this is by accident. It is to get your money out of your pocket and into theirs. They have thought the whole thing through. Our problem is we probably haven't. 'I just wandered in for a look and I ended up spending a fortune.' 'They had some great bargains, but I spent a fortune.' 'Every time I go in there, I end up leaving with twice as much as I went in for.'

Remember, this isn't about depriving yourself of the things you really want. This is about being conscious. It's about spending on the things you really want, really need, and putting your money to work providing you with the life you want to have.

Online shopping versus actual shopping

Walking into a shop that smells, looks and feels good is something that you now know will cost you money. The more times you walk in, the more money it will cost you.

But there are some advantages to walking into a physical shop. The marketing department has to work much harder to get that money out of your pocket because you have so many opportunities to stop yourself from buying stuff. Think about it – you'll have to drive, walk, cycle, get the bus – it doesn't matter, you have to get to the shop in the first place. And all the time you can be thinking, what am I looking for? Do I really need it? Can I afford it?

You then get to the shop, you start to look around, you pick something up and start to see what the fabric feels like. You're thinking – is it what I'm looking for? Do I really need it? Can I afford it? These are all your weapons against the marketing departments. You have time to think and consider. Then you walk to another rack and find something else. It throws another conundrum at you. Is this one better? Is the colour what I was looking for? Which one is the better option? Do they have my size? All your weapons against the marketing teams!

You pick the one you like best and go looking for your size. They have it and now you have to queue up to try it on. Weapons.

It fits and you like it. It makes you feel good, but you have to take it off again and queue up at the till. Weapons.

What happens next is really interesting. You go to pay.

A well-known fast food restaurant wanted to test the use of contactless in one of their restaurants before rolling it out across the entire world, so they introduced contactless in only one of the restaurants, then sat back and watched. They found that people who 'tapped' spent between 10 per cent and 15 per cent more than those who were paying in cash.

Why this is? When we physically pay with cash we reach into our pocket and we have to remove the cash. We can touch it, feel it, we can even smell it. But we have some sort of attachment to it. It means something to us. We value it more than we do a piece of plastic that we tap quickly and stick back in our pockets and days later we might notice the transaction on our banking app. There is little or no connection.

This is of particular concern for the younger generation. They are growing up in a cashless society. As a kid I remember doing a job for a neighbour. I had to lift the cobble lock on their driveway and load it up in a van. When I had it all clear I then had to clear the driveway and smooth out the muck beneath before getting a delivery of gravel, which had to be spread across the 'new' driveway. My mate William O'Donnell and I spent a week of our summer holidays in blistering heat doing this job. We worked hard and we were very proud of what we accomplished by the end of the week, then we got paid. Willie and I understood the value of the money we got paid. It was cash. We were about fifteen and there was no way we were going to blow the money frivolously. We had worked so hard to get it.

The unfortunate thing is I am not sure I would have valued the money as much had it just been lodged into my bank account and had I just seen a balance on my smartphone like teenagers today do. I hope that I would have still been somewhat careful with it, but there was a great feeling that Friday afternoon – we got a good job done and we had money in our pockets and there was a disco to go to that night.

Hic and click

Nothing feels more cashless than shopping online. There is a phenomenon called 'hic and click' that I think sums it all up so well. This phenomenon occurs around 9 p.m. on Thursday nights. At this time people, generally women, have had a glass of wine and are thinking about the weekend. They decide they need some new clothes and they get on the laptop and start to browse. A few minutes later they have a little 'hic' and they click on something to buy.

Wham! Just like that, in one click, they have bought something, and it will be delivered tomorrow in time for the weekend. There is no getting to a shop, searching through the rails, trying stuff on, queuing up, reaching for cash, feeling the cash, handing the cash over. All your weapons are gone and what's worse is that you've had a few glasses of wine, so everything looks fabulous!

Online companies have come to the realisation that they can circumvent all your defences when you are online. This 'one-click purchase' is ideal for them. It means you have your card details saved to your account and therefore don't even need to go looking for the card to pay for stuff. It's just one 'hic' and click.

In a TV show I was involved in a few years back we had somebody who had what we'd call a 'shopping habit'. She enjoyed spending money on clothes. My survey isn't very scientific because I was only looking at her habits, but this person would be what I would describe as a professional shopper.

There was one particular store she loved to buy in: she often went to the shop itself, but she also shopped in that particular store online. What surprised me was the difference in her average spend when she bought online compared to when she bought in-store. Even though she was buying from the same shop, my analysis found that she spent three times as much when she shopped online compared to when she shopped in the physical store.

This to me highlights just how easy it is to shop online and how well retailers can do out of us by simply getting around our natural weapons.

Is it all about cutbacks?

Good financial planning and being good with money are not about being thrifty or cutting back on everything. It's all about making sure the money you have is working to provide you with the life you want to live. It is about making sure the future is looked after financially so you can enjoy today more. Being aware – or being conscious – of where your money goes and what you spend time on is a good way to ensure you're making the most of the resources you have available to you. Only you can identify the things that are important to you. Only you can decide how you want to spend your time and your money. Don't be fooled by marketing departments that get you to spend your money on the things they want you to buy.

Yes, the process may involve cutting back on things, but remember this is about cutting back on things that you identify as not adding value to your life, things that others (marketing departments) are getting you to spend your money on and not things you consciously decide to spend your money on. It is about using your money to live your best life.

I make loads of money. I don't need to worry about day to day.

You do.

Don't fool yourself that if you have plenty of money coming in, then this section on spending rules just doesn't apply to you. It does. Every client I have ever had who is not conscious of their spending can benefit from these rules. Remember it is not about being thrifty. It is about spending your money on the things you actually want. Being crap with money is classless and is not specific to any income category.

I once advised a couple who were earning more than €500,0000 per annum between them when one of them lost their job. They struggled as much as, if not more than, any other couple I have seen going through an income shift like that. And guess what? The salary they lost was the lower of the two. They still had over €30,000 per month coming into the household. Don't underestimate how real their pain was to lose one of their incomes. It meant a serious shift in their lifestyle. But how could this be?

It is because of Parkinson's law. Parkinson's law relates to time, or more specifically it states that a task will take as long to do as the time you have to do it. So, if you have an hour to cut the grass it will take an hour. But if you have three hours to cut the grass it will take three hours. Parkinson's law, I believe, applies to your income. If you earn €60,000 a year you will spend €60,000 a year. But if you earn €600,000 a year you will spend €600,000.

My clients had been succumbing to Parkinson's law for years. They had the massive house with lots of acreage, a gardener, staff around the house, college and secondary-school fees, seriously expensive hobbies and pastimes. They enjoyed a good life – and why shouldn't they? They had worked hard to get to where they were, both of them. They had also accumulated large amounts of debt, which the banks had been happy to facilitate. The difference when you are a higher earner is that the stakes are higher. High earners, as well as having more money, also have something that other people don't, and that is access to big loans. Big loans for cars, holidays, houses, boats – whatever.

The banks were all over my couple when the two salaries were flowing in, and although I won't claim it to be national policy of this particular bank, at a local level they could not get themselves further away from my clients when things started to go wrong. In fact, it was how the banks started treating them that resulted in them reaching out to me to become clients.

We sometimes have clients who are struggling with the concept of Parkinson's law, so we ask them when they got their last pay rise. If they reply that it was around a year ago, we ask them how they feel about that pay rise now. Answers vary, but can usually be summarised as: what pay rise? Parkinson's law is sometimes referred to as lifestyle creep. Honestly, do you think you suffer with lifestyle creep? How do you feel about your last pay rise? In reality, if you earn a really strong salary you are not immune to financial mistakes. The stakes can be much higher and if Parkinson's law kicks in you are just as likely to fall into the trap of your money not lasting until the end of the month as the person on minimum wage.

Being crap with money affects us all in different ways. Having lots of it can be painful and having very little of it, in some instances, can actually be OK. There are people I know who proclaim themselves to be broke but happy and I definitely know some people who have loads of money but are miserable.

Does money make you happy?

'I don't know if I would be any happier if I were rich, but I am willing to give it a try.'

In 2010, Harvard University carried out a study where they sought the answer to this very question. They approached people on the street and gave them $5. There was one rule: they had to spend it now and they had to spend it on themselves. They followed people as they bought things like coffee for themselves and then asked them how they felt right now, on a scale of 1–10, with 1 being sad and 10 being happy. The answers centred around the 4s, 5s and 6s. In other words, people were just kind of meh.

Buying something for themselves didn't make them sad. It just didn't make them any happier. This is probably because people buy things for themselves all the time. You have to buy shoes and socks and bread and milk and all sorts of things for yourself all the time. So, buying one more thing for yourself doesn't really make a difference to your level of happiness.

Next, they went on to different people and again gave them $5. This time, however, the rules changed. This time the people had to spend their money on somebody or give it to somebody else. Some people simply gave it away or bought things and gave them to random people. What was very interesting was, afterwards, when these people were asked how happy they were, they were in the 8s, 9s and 10s. They were much happier giving the money away than the people who spent it on themselves. You could draw a conclusion that money does, in fact, make you happy – provided you give it to somebody else.

But I believe that the study needs to be broadened. Firstly, it is possible that one of the reasons giving money makes you happy is because, unlike spending on yourself, you don't do it all the time. I wonder how the results would differ if you made somebody gift money every day for a month and then asked them at the end of the month how giving made them feel. Would it have the same impact?

But more importantly I think they missed a trick completely. In private practice when we meet with a new client for the first time, we spend a huge amount of the first meeting talking to clients about their goals, objectives and values. Sometimes it takes a while for clients to get into it because they are there expecting to be talking about the charging structures on pensions and we are firing questions at them about what they want to achieve with their life.

To drill into their core values and objectives there are lots of different questions we use but there are two that we describe internally as the pillar questions. The first is straightforward. We ask the client to imagine that it is some time in the future. We ask them to imagine they are 75 years old and they are looking back on their life and then we ask, 'You are 75 looking back on your life. What stuff, if you haven't done it between now and then, would you regret that you didn't do?'

The answers are often slow to come, but there are some very common threads. Educating the kids is often high on the list, but even this can cause some funny exchanges between couples. One person can say college is an absolute must and the other says, 'It's grand, sure. But if college isn't for them ...' Next up people often talk about financial security. People don't want to be worrying about money at the age of 75. Beyond that it can go anywhere. Granted, we deal with clients who have wealth and earn good money, but if our clients are anything to go by, there are going to be a lot of Irish people in their fifties and sixties in the coming years driving across the US in RVs or hotel-hopping around Europe.

But it is our second pillar question that really gets to what people really want out of life. Our business is built on confidentiality. Yes, we sometimes discuss client situations with other clients provided there is no possible way of identifying who those clients are. But there are two people who have agreed that we can use their stories even though they are identifiable as a result. Those people are my dad, who I have already spoken about, and Clare.

Clare

I didn't know Clare when she got cancer at 30 years of age. She had a mastectomy but unfortunately the cancer had spread to the lymph nodes and it was stage four. Three years later the cancer was gone. Clare never said, 'I beat the cancer.' She always felt it was treated and it was gone. When Clare's cancer had been treated, she made some decisions. She knew herself that it was going to come back, and she felt that, because she had had stage four before, when it did come back the outcome wasn't going to be as positive.

She put her list together. She married her long-term boyfriend Ciarán, with whom she had two beautiful kids, but with whom she had never actually walked up the aisle. She did Glastonbury with Ciarán and some pals. She tried a tent but then progressed to an RV. She did Disney with the kids and a cruise with Ciarán. She did a rave on a beach in Ibiza with the girls and lots of other things along the way.

I remember when the cancer did come back, I was sitting on the end of her bed chatting to her. For some peculiar reason that I can't recall both my kids and her kids left us alone for two or three hours and we got to really talk. I learnt so much from Clare that day, but one thing really struck me. Clare said, 'I am really lucky.'

Now, I was sitting there thinking to myself, Clare, you have had stage four cancer. It is now back and I am worried the outcome isn't good. But rather than utter those words I simply asked, 'Why?'

Clare explained that when she got better the last time, she knew the cancer was coming back and so she sat back and made a few decisions. The first was that she could either wallow in self-pity or decide to enjoy her health. She chose the latter. Then she started to make a list of the big stuff and the little stuff she wanted to do, a bucket list effectively. That is where Ibiza and Disney and all the other stuff came from.

What Clare said to me next will stick with me forever. She said, 'I have lived more life in the last three years than I would have in the next thirty.' She went on to explain that she was present in the years of health she had in between. We talked about how I should be telling clients her story in order to get them to start thinking in a similar way.

Clare passed away a few months later but she lives on in her kids, her family, her friends and through Climb4Clare, the charity she established before she passed away. But also, in a very small way, she lives on through my private practice, doing what she always did best, which was getting the best out of people.

The 'Clare question' often follows the '75 and looking back' question and it is this: if you had two years to live, if everything was OK financially, what would you do for the next two years?

It's astonishing to watch how clients react to the question once they have heard Clare's story. Sometimes, the answers are along the same lines of the 75 and looking back question, and sometimes they are wildly different. Somebody who initially might have said that at 75 they wanted to have achieved a list of things in their career might now say they would give up work. But what is incredible to watch is how focused people become on experiences and spending time with the people in their lives who are most important to them. They want to do things, but they want those things to be done with the people they love. This is where I think the Harvard study fell short. When you get into it, most people at their core want to experience things with the people they love, and money often allows them to do this.

For example, we often explain to new clients who have just sold their business, inherited a large sum of money or won the lotto that the important thing to remember is that you are still you.

The things that made you happy before are still the things that will make you happy now. The only difference is, you now have enough money and you have the time to enjoy those things. So, in this way, I do believe money makes you happy.

I had a perfect example of money making me happy recently with my twelve-year-old son. I won a trip to Italy to watch Leinster play Zebre in Parma. We flew with the team, went to the game and spent two nights in Parma before getting a speed train to Rome and seeing the sights for two days. We added Rome to the prize – so it did cost me something – but this was a great use of money.

When you organise experiences such as trips abroad or sporting events with people you love, you're multiplying the enjoyment. There's the planning and anticipation: what will it be like? Where will we stay? Will the weather be good? There's the experience itself, and your enjoyment of it.

And then there's the memories.

Experiences, and your memories of those experiences, last much longer than stuff. I'm fairly sure that 20 years from now I'll have no idea what model of smartphone I owned in 2019 but I will remember the time I went to Italy with Darragh. And even if an experience goes wrong, it can still be a positive. For example, had it rained during those two days in Italy, I probably would have come back saying, 'We spent a lot of time indoors and really got to bond with each other.' Yet when things go wrong with something you've bought yourself, it doesn't work the same. I don't think anyone, sitting at their new laptop and watching the little loading thing spinning around and around, would consider themselves to be bonding with their MacBook.

Some stuff did go wrong on our trip. We wanted to take the train from Parma in northern Italy down to Rome because we wanted to see the country, albeit from a train travelling at 249 k/ph. But we also wanted to try and get a full day in Rome, so we decided to take a 6 a.m. train out of Parma on the Sunday morning.

When we were planning the train trip, we looked forward to the mountainous views on the way down. The reality, however, was that the Italian engineers had decided to go under the mountains for much of our journey down, so we were in complete darkness and got to see no mountainous landscapes. And yet the shock, surprise and realisation of our stupidity will probably be one of the lasting memories of that trip.

Money can make you happy. If you give it away, buy experiences and in some circumstances even if you buy things. But what lots of money does, more than anything else, is give you time. When you have large amounts of money, you can afford to spend time on the things you enjoy. But strip it down to its core and whether you have loads of money and loads of time or not, my experience from dealing with all types of clients is that it's all about the people you surround yourself with. This is the most important thing in your life, and you can't buy true friends and good family.

But what do you do to make the most of your money? Where do you start? What is the key to learning how to be good with money?

Daily spending rules

You start with daily spending rules. Get the foundations right and build from there.

Rule 1: Don't keep up with the Joneses

Being loaded and being broke is entirely relative. I take three fifteen-minute phone calls per day from prospective clients in my private practice. We call these initial calls, and they usually book out months in advance, but the idea behind them is to find out what the client hopes to achieve by engaging with us, and to give them an idea of how we operate and to see if the fit is right.

These phone calls give me a unique insight into lots of things, including people's perception of wealth.

People often start off by telling me how they are just not sure if they are doing things right. They don't want to wake up in ten years' time and find they should have taken advice earlier and that they've made mistakes. Believe me, lots of people talk about earning good money but are struggling to make ends meet – classic Parkinson's law. We've found that about 85 per cent of our clients suffer from Parkinson's law regardless of their level of earnings. The 15 per cent who've cracked it all have the common trait of being conscious with their money.

What's really interesting during these calls is how people convey information about themselves, and the language they use. I've learnt that that when people say, 'We make really good money' or 'We're high earners' or 'We're good savers' or 'We have significant amount of money in the bank' or 'We've accumulated large amounts of wealth,' it tells me nothing about how much money they *actually* have.

You see, wealth, savings and earnings are all personal things. I have clients telling me they have accumulated large amounts of money and when I ask how much they'll tell me they have €1,000. That is a large amount of money to them. It's relative. But €1,000 is not a large amount of money to the person who answers the same question with 'I have €12 million in liquid assets.'

Your 'loaded' is another man's broke and, guess what, that's perfectly fine. Remember what we said earlier? Most people, when brought back to basics, back to their core wants and needs, when asked the Clare question, will talk about spending time with the people they love.

Comparing yourself to others is a pointless exercise because all you can compare are the physical things. The things you can see. You have no idea if that person is actually happy. The fact that they're driving a brand-spanking-new car tells you nothing of their happiness. In fact, the brand-new car is more likely a sign of Parkinson's law than it is of true wealth or happiness.

The car finance industry, and specifically personal contract plans (PCPs), are an unregulated activity. We'll talk more about PCPs later (page 45) but for now – did you know that approximately 80 per cent of new cars are sold with some sort of loan on them? So next time you see a neighbour or friend or some bloke down the GAA club in a new car, don't think to yourself, 'I like the new car.' Instead think, 'I like the new loan,' because you're probably spot on with the latter observation.

Wealth is relative. Remember most of us could probably reach financial independence today if we sold everything we owned and moved to outer Mongolia and lived in a shack. But there are things, people and places we feel associated with and therefore something else drives us to keep going as we are.

Rule 2: Spend less than you earn

I deliver a programme in second- and third-level schools and colleges and when I tell a 16-year-old to 'spend less than you earn' I'm often met with the response 'But that's stupid, sir. How could you spend more than you earn?' Yet I would suggest that within ten years that young man, who thinks I am stupid, will have a car loan, personal loan, credit card or some other form of crappy debt and will indeed be spending more than he earns.

Nobody sees borrowing money as paying for today by robbing from the future. They see it as 'I need this now' or, if they're more honest, 'I want this now.'

We talk more about crappy debt in Section 2 (page 43) but needless to say we live in a society where we have access to credit, and we like to avail of it. It is a treadmill and I would suggest that it is almost impossible, regardless of how much you earn, to create real wealth without first tackling your crappy debt. But spending less than you earn goes beyond just avoiding debt. It is also about creating wealth. It is about ensuring that some of what you earn today is allocated to the future. Not just the distant long-term future but also the medium- and short-term goals you have.

Rule 3: The rocks and the sand

A college lecturer started his lecture one day with a large glass container, some rocks and some sand. He then asked students to come up and attempt to fit the rocks and the sand into the container. Some students started by putting the sand into the container first, trying to squeeze the rocks in on top, but they wouldn't fit.

The lecturer then asked everyone to sit down. He told the students to imagine that the rocks were mortgage repayments, car loans, groceries and other essentials. The sand, however, was things like socialising, takeaway coffees, dinners out and other discretionary items. As he spoke, the lecturer started placing the rocks in the glass container, followed by the sand. Not all the sand would fit in, but that was OK. Sand is discretionary spending. It will fill the gaps the rocks didn't fill but you know when to stop, when the budget is full.

You see, the glass container represents your monthly budget, the total income you have for the month. The rocks and the sand are the things you need and the things you want to do in the month. Most people do the stuff they want to do first and then get hit during the month with bills and essentials. And then they find there's no space left in their budget. Doing it the other way around, with the rocks first, means you still have the same amount of money, but it also means you know when to stop. You know when all the money runs out. You won't overrun the budget creating problems for the future.

When you start doing this, start simple, by just making the rocks the things that come out by direct debit; your loan repayments, for example, and other essentials like the electricity bill. But real financial planning, creating real wealth, comes when your rocks every month start to have headings like saving for back to school, Christmas, a holiday, changing the car in three years' time, the kids' college and even retirement. Some of this stuff you can work out yourself. For example, most parents who have kids already in school know how much it costs to send their child back to school. If you don't have a child in school, I would suggest you are probably surrounded by parents and teachers who would be more than willing to tell you all about it if you asked.

Find out how much it will cost. Let's say it is going to cost €400 and you will need that money in four months' time. Then you need to create a 'school rock' of €100 per month. If you don't, then in four months you will either be dipping into savings, if you have them, or like 11 per cent of primary school parents and 21 per cent of secondary school parents, according to a Barnardos survey, you will have to borrow to get your child back to school.

> *Top tip: If you do end up having to borrow for something like school, promise yourself this is the last time it's going to happen. If you take the loan over 12 months, guess what, when the loan finishes it will be back to school time again and you won't have been in a position to save anything because you were paying back a loan! Try and get the loan over six or even nine months and, when it is finished, diverting the loan repayments into savings specifically for back to school. You may not break the cycle next year, but each year reduce the term of the loan until eventually you do. This goes for everything that is cyclical like school or Christmas or holidays.*

The costs of back to school, holidays and Christmas can be worked out relatively easily. They are usually the amount of money you need divided by the number of months you have until they happen. But other things that need to become your rocks may require a little more calculation. How much should you put into your pension? How much should you be investing in the college fund? When you start to invest in the long term, the calculations become a little more complex, but they are not to be feared. This is because it is not just a straight-line calculation – you can start to take advantage of compound interest, and take on a little more risk to get better returns. We cover this in much more detail in Section 3 (page 93) but, needless to say, short-term goals require short-term vehicles while long-term goals require long-term vehicles.

Rule 4: Life isn't full of surprises

People often talk about the fact that they can't budget or create spending rules because of the fact that every time they do life happens and the budget goes out the window. But actually when you start to talk to them about what 'life' did to them, most things are predictable and can therefore be budgeted for. Christmas costs money and happens every year. Plan for it. So too does back to school and going on holiday. These are the easy things to identify.

Other things that are identifiable as rocks are the car breaking down. Or the fact that the average household spends €120 per annum on repair or replacement of appliances. Maintenance in the house is also something that you can, if you look, see coming. You don't walk outside one day and realise the house needs to be painted. You can also prepare for situations: if you are of a certain age, expect to be invited to weddings. A little older? There'll be christenings, communions, confirmations. It goes on.

These things are only a surprise if you have not planned for them, but with a little thought and preparation, they won't become catastrophes.

Rule 5: Pay yourself first

Back in the 1960s, Ireland followed the US and introduced

Pay As You Earn, or PAYE. PAYE is literally that – you pay your taxes as you earn, at the source. When we get paid, our taxes get taken out of our payslips straight away. When you look at your payslip usually the left-hand column describes how much you get paid and the right-hand column describes how much is being taken off you in taxes and other deductions. The only way to take money out of the left-hand column and pay yourself first (before you pay your taxes) is through putting money into a pension. We will talk more about this later (page 152).

Rule 6: Don't do this for yourself

If you don't think that taking money out regularly and putting it away is worth doing, think about this for a minute. The average person saves in excess of €300,000 during their working life, yet the average pension pot at retirement is about €100,000. How can the average person save over €300,000 yet their pension pots are one-third the size of that and nobody has €300,000+ to show for it?

That's because we save this money for somebody else – the banks. Our average mortgage is about €200,000. The repayments on a €200,000 loan over 25 years at 3.5 per cent are €1,001 per month, so over 25 years you would make total repayments of €300,300 for the bank. In other words, you can save over €300,000 in your working life, if you save it for somebody else. The thing about the mortgage is we see it as other people's money. It is one of our rocks because we see it as a commitment and would often go without to ensure it gets paid. It also happens regularly and automatically, which are all attributes we associate with being a good saver.

Interestingly, in a heterosexual couple, the woman is generally better with money. I don't actually have figures or stats on same-sex relationships, but you could imagine one person will always be better with money than the other! The reason, it is believed, is that on average women are better with money than men because when it comes to the family finances women don't see the 'family' money as 'their' money. Women believe the money belongs to the family and so they mind it better.

This is the same when it comes to saving over €300,000 for a bank during your working life. We do it because we see it as somebody else's money and not ours and therefore we do it. If only we treated ourselves as well as we treat our banks. But this looking after others goes even deeper. Right now, fewer than 50 per cent of Irish working people are paying into pensions. Strip out public sector workers and that number drops to 1 in 3 people paying into a pension.

There may be lots of reasons for this but one I find really interesting is the idea that we don't believe our older self to be us. There was some research carried out where brain activity was being measured. When the subject thought about themselves a certain part of their brain lit up. When they thought about somebody else a different part of the brain lit up. But when they thought about themselves 20, 30 or 40 years from now, the part of the brain used to think about other people lit up. In other words, our brain thinks that our future self is somebody else. Why would you decide not to go out this weekend, or go on holiday this year or change the car, because you want to put money away for somebody else to enjoy 30 years from now?

Perhaps you're reading this and thinking, 'Yeah but I'm not married so I don't have "family" money. I get the whole saving for the bank thing but I have a mortgage so I have no option and I understand that I don't think I am who I will be in 20+ years, but it is just not motivating enough to get me going.'

Maybe this will help you. If you have kids now or if some day you hope to, one thing is sure to happen and that is that you will get old and they will grow up.

According to recent research carried out for Bank of Ireland by Red C, 51 per cent of 25–45-year-olds expect their parents to help them get on the property ladder. If you have two kids, one of them is going to expect help from you to get them on the property ladder. So don't get your finances in order for yourself. Do it for future you, when you become Bank of Mam and Dad.

Rule 7: Never wipe out your savings

Savings are hard got. We will discuss this later (page 158), but while it's difficult to build up a lump of cash for something big such as buying a house or even a holiday, there is nothing more demotivating than wiping it all out in one go. So many of our clients find that, usually three or four years after they have moved into their first home, they're still making good money, were once really good at saving and now struggle to save.

Often this can be put down to the fact that they saved really hard to get their first house. They had their goal and they achieved it. Then they used all their savings in one go to pay the deposit and for all the other things that come with buying a house. Their savings were gone; they were tight for cash and often they start to accumulate credit-card debt and other short-term facilities like overdrafts. The cycle starts. They had planned for the couch and the cooker and all that big stuff but nobody told them about the cost of the first supermarket shop, or the cost of toilet roll holders, or the fact that the car is going to break down six weeks after they move in.

But even if they haven't accumulated debt they still haven't got back on the savings wagon. Why? This is because it was so hard to do it in the first place. It took sacrifice and then even though they had the house, they had no bank balance to show for all that work. It can often feel like somebody else, i.e. the builder, got the benefit of your savings. You made all the sacrifice and somebody else got all the gain.

Often people find it difficult to motivate themselves again. My suggestions is, other than in exceptional circumstances, never spend more than half your savings. This means once you spend half there is still a reasonable amount to get you going again. Exceptional expenses include, for example, buying a house – but even then I would try to keep it that you are left with a decent pot after you pay for everything. Holidays, cars, Christmas are not exceptional. Don't spend more than half your savings on them. If you need to spend more than half your savings then you don't have enough savings and shouldn't be spending the money anyway.

Rule 8: Don't save your credit card details

We've talked about consciousness. Saving your credit card details is one of the marketing departments' strongest tools; it's why 'hic and click' exists. If you don't save your credit card details at least you have to get up from the computer or sofa to go get the card to type in the details.

I was explaining this during a seminar to a couple of hundred employees in a large multinational. When I saw a woman at the front frowning, I asked her what was wrong. She said, 'Sure that's silly – it's too much hassle to go get the card, I prefer to save it.' I asked her whether she saved it for all her sites, to which she replied, 'Oh no, only the ones I use all the time.' I think this proves my point. Put up some barriers during online shopping. Force yourself to get off the couch to buy that dress.

Rule 9: The 72-hour rule

If you are definitely going to buy, whether it's online or in a physical shop, do yourself one last favour. Wait 72 hours. By waiting 72 hours all the marketing departments' big guns fade away and the decision becomes much closer to what you actually want versus what the marketing departments want. If you don't make an effort 72 hours later to either collect it or go back online, don't just buy it the next time you come across it a month later. If it didn't mean enough to you to go back 72 hours later, it's not something you need and most likely isn't even something you want.

> Top tip: stick it in the online basket and come back 72 hours later. If you're in a physical shop, ask them to hold it for a day or two.

Rule 10: Think of money in terms of time

When I am in with students delivering these programmes, one of the things they seem to latch on to is the idea of treating money as time.

Imagine you're paid €10 per hour. Imagine you see a lovely pair of shoes for €80 that you really want. Instead of thinking about the shoes as a lovely pair of shoes, or thinking of them as a quick tap of your card, or thinking of them as a €50, €10 and a €20 in notes, I want you to think of the shoes as an eight-hour shift at work. Think about getting up in the morning, dragging yourself out of bed, washing, dressing, feeding yourself before getting to work. Working all day and then getting yourself home again. Are the shoes worth that much of your time? Really?

In theory, money is limitless. It may not be easy, but we all have ways of making more money. What is not limitless is time. Thinking of items like shoes in terms of time instead of money changes your perspective. You can never get back the time spent at work. You can, however, get €80 back.

Working out how much you get paid per hour is easy. Don't get too caught in the minute details. The easiest way is to look at your payslip. Look at the bottom right hand corner, where it says 'net pay' and divide it by the number of hours you worked during that pay period. This will give you your take-home pay per hour. For example, if your take-home pay is €800 and you worked 40 hours for that, it means you get paid €20 per hour after tax. Working this out once starts to put purchases in perspective. You start to appreciate your own time more.

This can get scary when you look at bigger stuff. I remember at one point figuring out for a guy who was earning €25,000 per annum that he had worked 18 months out of the last five years just to pay for his smoking habit. Imagine getting out of bed every day for 18 months to pay for smokes.

Sometimes we also need to think about what value we add to other people, people like our bosses. An interesting exercise I used to do when I wasn't working for myself was to look at the top left-hand corner of my payslip where the gross pay is and then see what my before-tax wages were. I would then divide this by the number of days I worked that month. This would give a rough idea of the cost I was to my boss, on a daily basis. I would think to myself driving home, 'Did I add that much value to the business today?' If not, I was costing the business money. When you are an income-generating asset of a business and you cost the business money, the road is going to be short.

You can do this very easily for yourself. For the purposes of keeping this simple let's ignore other benefits and things like pay-related social insurance (PRSI). Let's say for every €10,000 of salary you have per year you cost the company about €40 per day. So, if you are on €20,000 a year, you cost the company about €80 per day. If you are on €50,000, you cost the company about €200 per day. So next time you're making your way home from work, think to yourself: did I cost the business money today or did I make the business money today?

Golden rule: Get back up again

You're going to fail. In fact, if you do this right you are going to fail over and over and over again. The measure of the success or failure of this change you are about to bring about in your finances is not how many times you fail but how many times you successfully start again.

Remember life happens, things go wrong, washing machines break down and cars need fixing. But things also go right: you get invited to a wedding, you become pregnant. When you're not planning your money properly these things can be seen as a failure of your money management. But the more you get into this the more you find that the things that were once surprises are no longer surprises. Or maybe they are, like the pregnancy one, but you are now able to cope with them so much better.

I recently asked a good pal of mine, Shane, how he got on in his hurling match. He said, 'We didn't lose,' and I said, 'So you won,' and he said, 'There's no win or lose – there's only win or learn.' He's a genius, our Shane, but I suspect he robbed that from somewhere. But it does prove a point. The more times things go wrong, provided you get back up again, the more you will learn. Only you can fix your finances, only you can get the most out of your money and only you can decide the best way to do it.

Financial independence

There's a lot of work in sorting out the day-to-day stuff, getting yourself into good debt like mortgages and out of crappy debt like credit cards and car loans. But it's also about getting your investments set up correctly and knowing that you are investing enough in the right type of pension. Remember the end goal – financial independence.

Financial independence is the day in your life when you have created enough wealth that you don't have to work again, and you don't have to worry about money. We strive to get our private clients there as early as possible by making the most out of the money they have. But reaching financial independence does not mean you have to give up work. It means that beyond that point in your life you work because you want to and not because you need to.

I once had a new client come into our office for a first meeting. I asked her why she had come to see us. She explained that she was making good money and had created good wealth but that she absolutely hated her job. She had done some of her own maths and had worked out that she could stop working in ten years' time at the age of 59. She wanted to know how she could improve her date of financial independence so that she could stop working earlier than in ten years' time.

Work had lost its appeal and just felt like a slog, and now she was facing down another decade of it. When we asked her what did make her happy, she lit up. She started talking about walking. But not just any old walking – she liked to walk very long distances in mountain ranges all across the world. We are talking about weeks of walking at a time. Think more Phileas Fogg than Usain Bolt here.

But this lady knew that she only had so long before her body would eventually say *enough*. She might be able to stop working at 59, but she might also find that her body just didn't want to do the long-distance stuff. She was stuck.

We talked to her about the nuevo retirement plan. The traditional plan we all think of when we think of retirement is that we accumulate as much money as possible, we reach financial independence as early as possible and then we stop working. But research has shown that this is not exactly healthy: in fact, one study from the University of Zurich found that, among blue-collar workers, for every extra year of early retirement, they lost about two months of life expectancy.

The nuevo retirement plan is where you take lots of mini retirements. They need to be planned, but basically you go to your boss and ask for two months off sometime in the future – perhaps in 18 months' time. This is usually unpaid, although some workplaces allow you to carry over holidays. We have suggested this to hundreds of clients. At the start we were surprised with how many bosses accommodate it. Now we're just surprised at how surprised our clients are that their bosses said yes.

> *Top tip: If you're the boss, then this is an absolute must for you for so many reasons. Firstly, your business probably runs better without you in it. Secondly, most people who own their own business are so devoted to it that if they don't practise for retirement then when they actually do retire, they are bored silly. But most importantly, getting the people who work with you to run the business with you gone for two months is great practice for a time when you might get sick and can't work for a protracted period. You dramatically improve the chances of there being a business to come back to by doing dry runs every couple of years.*

It was only our first meeting and we had not yet checked her projection of financial independence, but the client was stressing over her predicament, so we suggested that a nuevo retirement, at this stage, was the right thing to do. She loved the idea. We explained that it would probably push back her ten-year projection – assuming it was correct in the first place – but she wanted us to build it into her plan.

We started to crunch the numbers, building a financial plan that would allow her money to support the life she wanted to lead, but the twist in the story is what we realised when we started to build out the financial plan: the client was six months away from financial independence. In fact, she had probably already reached it but couldn't access certain investments until after her fiftieth birthday, which was six months away.

A couple of weeks later we brought the client in and delivered the news. She asked to go through the numbers. We pulled them apart and put them back together and then that lovely moment came, when she sat back in her chair and realised she could give up work.

A couple of weeks later I rang her to see how she was. She explained that she was really enjoying work. When I asked her why, she replied that it was the simple fact that she was working because she wanted to, and not because she had to. When she was having a bad day, she could simply decide not to go in the next morning.

She then went on to say that she was being super-productive and getting on with everyone. And not only that, but her bosses, thinking that she was leaving, had given her a pay rise for the first time in ten years! When I did ask her if she was leaving, she laughed. Not a chance, she said. In fact, she'd organised two months off the following year and told me she'd leave only if they refused a future request for two months' leave down the line.

Even if you have plenty of money, there's always room for improvement. Financial planning is all about sorting the long-term stuff in order for you to enjoy today. And you can't sort the long-term stuff if you're making consistent mistakes today.

Start with little steps to become more conscious of your spending. That doesn't mean you have to become tight — it means you start spending on the things you want to buy, and not what some marketing department wants you to buy. Work on your rocks and your sand, identify your goals and your big expenses, and make sure you are not being hit with the same surprises, like Christmas or back to school, year after year.

Getting on top of your day-to-day money management helps to build the foundation you need to really get ahead financially, to plan for the future but also to live for today.

SECTION 2

LOANS AND BORROWING

Getting into debt

There are two types of debt: happy debt and crappy debt. Happy debt is when you borrow money, usually at a reasonably good rate, for things that appreciate in value, like a house. Crappy debt is expensive loans (compared to a mortgage, for example) for things like cars that depreciate in value.

Crappy debt also covers loans for things you consume. These are the worst of all. You borrow money from the future to pay for something today, such as holidays or clothes or even essentials like food. You use or experience the things today and then you use your future income to pay for them. Credit cards or personal loans facilitate this robbing of your future self.

When the economy is doing well it can feel like these loans are being thrown at you. You walk into the bank and there are signs up, you walk down the street and see cheap rates being advertised. You're doing your grocery shopping and even the supermarkets themselves have got in on the act by offering you store cards and credit cards.

I hate crappy debt. I don't love happy debt but at least, used properly, it can add to your future wealth. I can honestly say I've never had a client who has done well financially once they've become accustomed to short-term crappy debt. Even clients who appear to be extremely wealthy, enjoying high salaries and a jet-set lifestyle, can often crash and burn because they're laden with debt. In fact, unless they realise it quick enough it is actually inevitable.

Servicing commitments

I've never seen a client sustain maintaining total commitments of greater than 50 per cent of income over any reasonable amount of time. Some may be able to do it in short bursts for specific reasons but not with any type of longevity. When I say commitments of 50 per cent of income, I mean that all your commitments towards things like mortgage/rent, car loans, personal loans and credit cards do not exceed 50 per cent of your monthly take-home pay. In simple terms, if you take home €1,000 per month your commitments, if they are over €500, are not sustainable.

It's important to realise that I'm not talking about the cost of food and clothes. I'm talking about loans and essentials such as rent. Financial planning rules and even mortgage lending guidelines would suggest that 35 per cent of take-home pay is sustainable. In my experience the clients I see with 25 per cent of their income going on commitments really start to get ahead.

The 15 per cent sweet spot

But it is the clients who are using less than 15 per cent of their income to service their commitments who really create long-term wealth. 15 per cent is the sweet spot. When you are paying out less than this you can afford to maximise things like pensions and long-term savings. When investment opportunities come your way, you have the financial ability to take advantage. But you also just manage better on a day-to-day basis. You have reserves so you don't need to borrow money for big things like cars and you pay for things like car insurance and car tax up front instead of in instalments, where you get creamed with interest. You are always ahead.

The treadmill of debt

Debt, particularly crappy debt, is like a treadmill. You get on and you start off slow. It's easy. It increases gradually and the repayments start to take a bit of a nip out of you. Then you hit a rough patch and you find that you just need to put this bill on the credit card. You always clear the credit card but this time you don't, you make the minimum repayment, next month will be better and sure you have your bonus coming or that big job is due in. The treadmill is moving faster. You need to keep up your payments, but you're tired. You get a personal loan and clear the credit card. That was clever, cheaper interest rate. You know it's not right, paying off a credit card over five years, but you were getting nowhere fast. You don't cancel the credit card, just in case. You know if you can just get through this month it will get better. Then you throw another bill on the card. Life at home is tough, you're fighting over stuff you never fought about before – a weekend away is suggested, and although you're worried about money, you're more worried about the marriage, so you pay for it with the credit card. You feel a little bit resentful of the fact that your partner doesn't share the burden of this debt – after all they helped you accumulate it. You are making good money, life should not be this hard, you deserve some treats. The treadmill keeps turning faster, and faster, you add more and more debt. School is back. How much for a Halloween party? The incline keeps getting higher and higher ... and then Christmas.

Then one day something snaps. You realise you can only do what you can do and no more. You only have so much income. You have moved on from trying to hold on to any type of social life, you entered survival mode long ago and it is really only about feeding your family and keeping them safe and warm. You have missed a few payments, so you have given up trying to protect your credit rating, but more importantly you don't want a good credit rating because you never ever want to borrow again. You hate your debt. You want it all to go away and go back to the way it was.

I see this change in people and it is very recognisable. But I also see others who have a lot of debt, say they hate it, say they want out of it, but when they clear a credit card, they tell me they still want to hold on to it 'just in case'. These people have yet to hit rock bottom. They are still on the treadmill and potentially may never get to the point of hating their debt and therefore will never eliminate it. I have met people about to retire who have never got off the treadmill, life always threw stuff at them. These people often have household incomes of €200,000+. They have no assets except their home and are now wondering how they are going to service their debt in retirement without a decent pension pot.

Crappy debt is so easy to get into. But once you are, it's difficult to get off that treadmill. And the first step is to recognise just how much damage it's doing to you.

The real cost of crappy debt

Life is never as good as you expected it was going to be, but equally it's never as bad as you thought it was going to be either. When it comes to money, we always think to ourselves that the future is going to be bright. I have a bonus coming, I am due a pay rise, I will get that new job. Everything will be much better then. The reality is not everything works out as expected. But crappy debt providers prey on the fact that the one thing we learn from history is that we don't learn from history.

How much does crappy debt cost you? Let's imagine you're buying a second-hand car for €10,000. You plan on keeping it for five years. The road tax is €570 per year and the insurance for this size of engine is €800.

You have savings to buy the car. You're trying to decide whether to use your savings or borrow the money. If you borrow the money with a rate of 9 per cent it means you'll repay €207 per month – in total you'll pay back €12,454 in repayments to clear the loan.

Then you consider the car tax. If you pay the tax quarterly it costs you €161 per quarter, which equates to €644. This is €74 more expensive than if you just paid the full year upfront at €570, and also mounts up over five years.

Lastly, car insurance, if you pay upfront, will cost you €800. But paying for it monthly can cost as much as 20 per cent extra once the insurer puts their interest on. This means you could be paying out as much as €960 per year.

Between the €2,454 in interest on the loan, the €370 extra you pay in quarterly car tax and the €800 (which equates to a whole year of car insurance!) extra you pay for the car insurance over the five years, the total cost of spreading the cost of your car using crappy debt is actually €3,624. Do you wonder why you haven't been on holiday in years?

Credit cards are worse. Let's imagine you decide to go on holiday. Strangely enough, if you've been on holiday before it's likely you'll want to go again. The holiday is going to cost €3,000 for the family and you will need €1,000 spending money. If you don't have the savings to pay for this and the holiday is ten months away, then you need to save €400 per month for the next ten months.

If you can't afford to put aside €400 per month then you need to ask yourself what will be so different when you come back that you'll be able to afford to pay back the money you put on the credit card. You book the holiday and plan to save, but you don't save. The holiday must be paid for and you stick it on the credit card. The future is bright, you'll sort it out when you get the pay rise/bonus/new job/lotto win. Three years later, your credit card balance isn't coming down. You make the minimum repayments every month, but you just don't understand why the balance is stagnant.

Minimum payments on your credit card feel like minimum pain for you, but it's maximum gain for the credit card company. And they encourage you by suggesting that anything between 2 per cent and 5 per cent of the balance outstanding each month is the minimum they require.

On your €4,000 holiday, paying the 2 per cent would equate to €80 per month. If your credit card is up at 22 per cent interest, then paying the 2 per cent minimum per month will mean it will take you over 11 years to pay off the holiday. You'll end up paying back a total of €10,960 in repayments. In fact, you could have gone on holidays almost two more times for the interest you will have paid.

But here's the rub. This assumes that you pay the €80 per month every month – but remember, the suggested two per cent is based on last month's closing balance. This means that every month, if the balance goes down at all, the suggested two per cent will be less. You'll be getting nowhere, just like on a treadmill.

You could be reading this thinking that this is a ridiculous example. Nobody pays the minimum. I want to be clear: you are wrong. I have met lots of people who not only pay the minimum, but actually think the minimum is what you are supposed to pay. 'Why else would they put it down on the statement like that then?' Credit card companies prey on your positive outlook on life and on your positive outlook on money. They also lead you astray. Suggested minimum payments are one thing but they also often choose to display their interest rates in what to me are very unfair ways.

The devil is in the detail

I was at dinner with a group of people. (It is important to state that there was little or no alcohol involved that night.) I started talking to the man sitting next to me about credit cards and mentioned to him that in Ireland money lenders are regulated differently to other lenders. The Central Bank – rightly so – has a different set of rules for high-interest lenders, and considers a lender to be a money lender if they charge 23 per cent or more.

That is why so many credit card companies charge 22.9 per cent on their cards and no more. It is because they don't want to fall into the category of being a money lender.

When I mentioned this to my companion, he was shocked. He could not believe there were credit card companies charging almost 23 per cent. He went on to explain that he was only charged 1.5 per cent on his credit card and it was the cheapest debt he could access. He had been buying stuff for work using the credit card and using it for cashflow purposes as it was so cheap. This guy was an educated guy; he was very clued into his profession and I had respect for him professionally, so I was confused. I immediately thought he must be on an introductory offer and I quizzed him on this. He said he'd been with the same provider for years and had never asked them to reduce the rate, so I discounted that idea.

By this stage I was really gobsmacked. He said he could even show me the statement, and that's when the penny dropped –he was indeed being charged 1.5 per cent, but it was 1.5 per cent *per month*. His card company, like many others, wasn't sticking it in his face that he was being charged 18 per cent per annum. Instead he was being told what he was being charged per month and because of what he believed to be cheap credit he was funding his life and work on this card. We joked about the fact that he should really try move his mortgage on to the credit card, but I must say it has to have hurt him when he realised the mistake he had been making. He never did come back afterwards to me and confirm that I was right, but to me that says it all.

Credit card debt is expensive. The average asking price for a house in Ireland, according to Daft.ie, is €263,000. Assuming an

80 per cent mortgage on this it means the average mortgage is probably somewhere close to €210,000. We have an average mortgage rate in Ireland of around 3 per cent. The repayments on a €210,000 loan over 25 years at a rate of 3.04 per cent would be €1,000.21 per month. In total you would repay €300,063. In other words, the bank would make just over €90,000 in interest on you.

If, like my dinner companion joked, you could stick the mortgage on the credit card, and assuming you had to pay 22 per cent interest, your repayments would go up to €3,866 per month and over the 25 years you would pay the credit card company total interest of €949,800. It is an incredibly expensive way of borrowing money.

Credit cards can be useful. For example, did you know that when you use them correctly you can get up to 56 days of interest-free credit from a credit card company? If you didn't know this then you're definitely not one of the miniscule amount of people who are actually using their card to their own advantage and I am going to strongly suggest – in fact I am going to warn you – not to start thinking that you can fool the system and be good with credit cards.

I could explain how you get the 56 days interest free, but I won't. It would only encourage you. It is a trap. In my experience fewer than 5 per cent of people I have come across in private practice actually use this unique 56-day interest-free period to their benefit and I believe they are always walking a thin line.

There are other 'positive' things about credit cards, such as the fact that you get insurance on things you buy and can cancel flights more easily. Again, let me be clear, the credit card companies don't offer these things or provide these services out of the kindness of their souls. They do it to make money and the cost to you is temptation. What price are you willing to pay to avoid temptation? If you're using a credit card to book flights so you have some type of cancellation cover then cancel the credit card and pay for travel insurance.

I don't like credit cards.

Payday loans

Another form of expensive credit is payday loans. There are more payday loan 'shops' in the US than there are McDonald's restaurants. Thankfully we don't have a massive payday loan industry here in Ireland, but it does exist and the fact that is isn't prevalent here isn't any consolation if you are one of the people who is caught in that trap.

A payday loan is a word used to describe a small loan that is expected to be paid back over a short period. They started as loans that you got mid-month while you were waiting for payday and which you then repaid on payday. However, they have developed, and the word 'payday' loan is now widely accepted as any short-term loan for a smaller amount of money. Although in Ireland they are not officially banned, these loans thrive on extortionate interest rates, and therefore because they are charging more than the 23 per cent threshold imposed by the Central Bank they are regulated as money lenders.

The UK had a very large industry of payday lenders. However, new legislation, which basically capped interest rates at 0.8 per cent per day with a maximum interest rate of 100 per cent of the loan amount during the term (i.e. you won't pay back more than twice the loan amount), has resulted in the industry struggling. These caps, combined with fines imposed in the UK by the regulator in relation to collection practices, amongst other things, has resulted in firms like Wonga, who were at one point valued at over £1 billion and had over one million customers, going into administration.

These lenders thrive on the fact that people often struggle to get to the end of the month, and with 85 per cent of people getting paid monthly the problem is spread wide, allowing for more customers. They also tend to use technology such as apps or fancy websites to approve your loan very quickly and then have it lodged into your bank account often within hours. Some years ago I saw interest rates in the UK of almost 6,000 per cent. Although I don't see that anywhere today, you can get a payday loan in Ireland today that has an annual percentage rate (APR) of 187.2 per cent.

Companies that give out these loans can argue that the loan amount is very low, so the interest rate only represents a small amount of money. For example, you borrow €100 and you pay back a total of €130; that is 187.2 per cent APR. They also argue that APR isn't fair as it's representative of a full year and these loans are shorter terms. However, what people need to realise is that, according to the US organisation Center for Responsible Lending, 75 per cent of people use a payday loan to clear off a payday loan, compounding an already extortionate interest rate.

In the UK and particularly the US, the typical method of distributing the product is to have small 'stores' in neighbourhoods. People walk in on payday and clear their loan and then 75 per cent of people take out another one. In Ireland I actually believe it is a little more sinister; I was speaking to somebody recently who had one of these loans and had no idea what interest rate they were paying or just how bad these things were. They told me that these 'Jimmy loans' weren't nearly as bad as I made them out to be. Apparently, Jimmy is a sound local lad who everyone's known for years. This approach, whether intentional or not by the moneylenders operating in Ireland, is dangerous. People buy from people. I have no doubt that Jimmy probably feels he is serving the community well with these loans. Jimmy, you are not.

If times are tough and you need to borrow money to get you to your next payday, I suggest you try anything but these types of loans. First port of call for short-term emergencies must be family and friends. If you can't go there, try the credit union, the bank, get an overdraft – even a credit card is better than these loans. Once you get on the payday loan treadmill it is very hard to get off. Avoid! Avoid! Avoid!

Equity release

Sometimes when you're looking at a loan product the interest can seem reasonable but the way in which it is applied is incredibly expensive. This could not apply more than in the case of equity release loans. Equity release loans, sometimes referred to as seniors' loans or senior equity release loans, are loans you get on the strength of your house and they are given out to people who are already in the second half of their lives.

They're offered mainly to people from 50–60 onwards and the idea behind them is that you are sitting on an asset, i.e., your home. It has no mortgage on it and the money tied up in this asset is useless to you unless you sell the house.

The problem is you are either already retired or you are close to retirement and therefore your income is often ignored by the banks when it comes to working out whether you can afford the repayments on an ordinary loan. Equity release loans don't care what your income is because there are no loan repayments. You borrow the money and the loan is paid off, either whenever you have the money to pay it off, or after you die and either your family come up with the money or the house is sold to clear off the loan.

The interest that is to be paid back gets added to the loan each month. Then next month the interest you owe gets added to the loan amount and the interest from last month. Then the next month your interest gets added to the loan amount, the first month's interest, the second month's interest … you can see where this goes. You pay interest on interest and the loan outstanding can start to grow very quickly.

I met somebody in a shopping centre in Drogheda a few months ago. She was an amazing character who I'm guessing was in her mid-70s and she was what I would describe as a proper lady. She asked me what she should do. She had a concern about her finances. I asked her to explain. She told me that ten years ago she had wanted to give all her kids some money. They hadn't asked for it. It was just something she wanted to do. She wanted to watch them enjoy the money.

She took out an equity release loan of €50,000 and divided it up amongst the kids. Ten years later she discovered the total amount she now owed was over €130,000. She was worried how she would ever be able to pay the money back. I assured her of a few things.

Firstly, these loans have changed a lot over the years. There was a storyline in *Coronation Street* a few years back when Gail Platt's boyfriend was giving out loans to all the old people in the area. But every time he was short of cash he would kill them off one by one to get his money out of their houses. Thankfully my Drogheda pal didn't need to be worried about this.

Nowadays, different rules apply to these sorts of loans. Lenders will only give you a small percentage of the house value as a loan. The exact amount is determined by your age: the older you are the higher percent they'll give you. But it would be typical that it would not exceed 25 per cent of the value of the house. So, if your house is worth €400,000 then you won't get any more than €100,000. The main reason for this is that the loan provider provides a guarantee that when you die and the loan has to be paid back, the loan amount will not be greater than the value of the house. If it is then they take the hit and there is no recourse to any of your other assets.

But secondly and something of interest to my friend in Drogheda is the fact that you can, if you wish, make repayments on these loans. You can pay it all back in one go, you can pay the interest and some capital each month, or you can basically pay whatever you want.

Paying something off each month is very helpful in reducing the compounding of the interest but it does call into question whether this loan was for you in the first place. As we got deeper into conversation, I asked her about the fact she was losing sleep over the loan. I asked her how her kids felt about the loan. The reality was her kids didn't worry about it at all. They knew whenever she passed away the house would be sold and the loan would be cleared.

Yes, it was frustrating that the lender was going to make a bucket of money on the back of their mother's house, but the reality was that this was not for the lady to worry about. I suggested she go to the kids and explain that the loan was now standing at €130,000. She should explain that there was a promise on the loan that the house would cover the full repayment and that anything left over would go to the estate. She should ask them if they were worried about the loan. If they were then they could start making repayments on the loan. But if not, then she needed to stop worrying about it. After all, this wasn't actually her problem to worry about. It was theirs. She will be somewhere else when this loan has to be paid back.

These loans are an expensive way of borrowing money. Not because of the interest rates, which are often only a couple of per cent points above an ordinary mortgage, but because of the way interest is charged on interest and how it compounds. The loan providers are transparent on this: they do give you a schedule at the start, which shows year after year how the loan amount will increase and exactly how much you will owe them at any given time.

There are certain circumstances where I think these loans can be useful. There is a problem with housing right now in Ireland. There are people who are starting to slow the pace of life down a little, whose kids have fled the nest, who are sitting in houses that are too big for them. They could trade down but often times there is the short-term cash flow issue. I regularly get calls from people saying they are building a more suitable home. They have the planning but they need some money for a short period until the sale of the house goes through. They can't put the sale through because the new house isn't built and they will have nowhere to live. This gap would traditionally have been filled by a bridging loan, but banks these days tend not to be keen on them. An equity release loan would be ideal in this circumstance because it would have no repayments and because it will be cleared quickly. The compounding would have little time to do real damage.

Good financial planning

Another scenario where these loans are really useful is where you have no dependents (or you have dependents but don't want to leave them any of your money). Good financial planning is about spending your money on yourself, gifting it to others in a tax-efficient way and not leaving a big inheritance tax bill behind you.

We explain this to all our private clients. Over the years I have witnessed a real split of attitudes. Some people have a really strong desire to leave lots of money to their kids or loved ones. Other people feel their sole purpose in life is to get through their own money themselves and leave nothing behind. Both attitudes are perfectly valid. It is only an issue if we discover during our meeting that each person in the couple has opposing views. If you are of the opinion that you spend it on yourself and feck the rest of them, then one of these loans may be right up your street. Why shouldn't you take the equity out of your home and enjoy it on whatever you want? Alternatively, if you're looking at your parents and you feel they could do with a few quid and you personally aren't worried about your inheritance then you could talk to them about this.

There were a number of banks involved in this market from 2005 onwards, which disappeared with the crash of 2008. At the time of writing there are no providers in the market but I have spoken recently to one from years ago who said they were months away from opening up the option again. And although there have been no providers of these loans over the last few years, the demand was still there.

We had a particular client who needed money, was already retired and wanted one of these loans. In his circumstance we did something different. We sold 25 per cent of his house to one of his sons. He had three kids and luckily one of them could afford to come up with the cash to buy the quarter of the house. It was agreed with his two siblings that when the father passed away, the 75 per cent remaining would be split three ways between all three of them. This means that when the father passes away the son will already own 25 per cent and will inherit another 25 per cent. The siblings still get their 25 per cent each. This case was fortunate in that the son had the money. He did not need to borrow it.

You might think that you can do the same, and just borrow from a bank in your own name and give the money to your dad. But first you'll need to put the house in your name. This may be an issue for your siblings but it should be an issue for your father. He needs security of tenure, i.e., he needs to know you can't legally throw him out. He gets this by you giving him a right of residency. This is a legal document that says he can live there until he dies, if he wants to. This is great for your father but crap for a bank. They now would have a mortgage out to you on a house where there is somebody who is not party to the mortgage who has a right to live there. If you stop paying the mortgage and they try and take the house back and sell it they can't because your father has a right of residency. Banks don't like this so they don't do it.

Equity release has a place, and its place is limited. But if you're single with no dependents and you don't have anybody to leave your money to, then it's a no-brainer. Take the money if you need it and blow it on whatever life experience you want. If you're not in this position, tread carefully with these loans. But most importantly, talk to the people who are most likely going to be responsible for paying the bill – your kids.

Non-recourse lending

The way equity release loans are set up is on a non-recourse basis. This means that if things go wrong or when the lender wants their money back, they can only get it from the house itself. They can't go after any of your other assets or, in the case of equity release, your estate.

Non-recourse loans are much more prevalent in the US, where it's not unusual for mortgage loans to be given on this basis. This is why, in the US, you can have what is called a strategic defaulter. This is where an individual is perfectly able to make their loan repayments but chooses not to. They have done the maths and figured out that the house has lost so much money it will never come good again and they choose to stop making repayments because all the bank can do is take the keys back, sell the house and walk away. They cannot be pursued for any more money. If their maths are correct, they have walked away from a loss-making investment. All it has cost them is their credit score.

As things started to get really bad in Ireland after the crash this mantra started to come from our banks. They said we had strategic defaulters here in Ireland. This, in my opinion, is laughable. Unlike the US we do not have non-recourse loans (or at least we didn't then, and have one provider in the market now). But the fact we didn't then means that if you decided to strategically stop paying your loans the bank could sell the house and then still chase you for whatever was left on the mortgage plus all their costs. The debt would follow you like a bad smell for years. You'd have damaged your credit history; you'd have lost the house; and you'd still be paying back the money for years to come.

It suited the banks to have people thinking they were paying more for their mortgage than they had to because their neighbour was a strategic defaulter. We have rules imposed by the Central Bank about how much a person can borrow based on their earnings but also limits to how much can be borrowed. The idea behind these rules is to ensure that we are not given so much money that we drive house prices up and that we end up back where we were with mortgages so high that we can't afford to pay them back. They are also there to protect the banks from themselves, so the banks don't lend out so much money that when the next crash comes, the bank fails and needs the taxpayer to bail them out again. The banks often give out that the rules are too tight and they can't give out the money people need. The Central Bank does allow the banks to 'break' the rules in 10 or 20 per cent of cases per year, which are called exceptions. Exceptions are designed to try and remove the 'unfairness' of how rigid the Central Bank rules are.

A perfect example of the rules being unfair is a case I had recently where the individual had put her name on a mortgage years ago with her sister. She did this to get the mortgage across the line so her sister could buy a house. She never benefitted financially from the transaction and the house has since been sold. But with the Central Bank rules my client and her husband are now considered to be 'second-time buyers'. Being second-time buyers means that within the Central Bank rules they must come up with a 20 per cent deposit for the house whereas if they were first-time buyers they would only have to come up with a 10 per cent deposit.

They want to buy a house for about €300,000. The difference in the deposit is €30,000 for a first-time buyer or €60,000 as a second-time buyer. When I delved into their finances, I figured out that for them the difference was being able to buy a house eight years from now versus being able to buy a house five years from now. It was going to take them three years more to save the extra €30,000 and they were good savers. The only way they can be treated as first-time buyers is if a bank gives them an exception and gives them 90 per cent of the purchase price instead of the 80 per cent second-time buyers ordinarily get.

The exceptions are interesting because getting one is a bit of lottery. Banks tend to save them for people who are 'good' customers, whatever that means. But you also find that the time of year you apply for a mortgage can have an impact on your success or failure to get an exception. For example, if you apply towards the end of the year then it is likely all the exceptions will be used up. Whereas if you apply in December and tell them you won't be actually drawing down the loan until the new year, you are then using up an exception from next year's allocation.

I have anecdotal evidence that this is also affecting house sales. Builders are holding off putting new houses on the market until the new year when more people have exceptions available to them. Auctioneers tell me that the end of the year is much quieter and they now expect a rush each January. But getting an exception can also come down to not only what bank you go to but what branch you walk into. If you walk into a bank in Dublin and they happen to have used up the branch's allocation for exceptions then you won't get one. But if you walk into a bank in Cork and they have exceptions left, your case could be approved one. And yet it's the same bank!

So why not apply directly to head office, I hear you ask? Well, the way a bank works is that if you're a customer of a certain bank branch and you apply centrally for something, the 'sale' will be given to your branch anyway. And head office has the same limits as the branches do, so again, if they've used up their allowance of exceptions, you're snookered.

Exceptions serve a purpose, but they are not without their faults. Another solution the Central Bank could look at would be telling the banks they can lend under whatever criteria they want if they do so on a non-recourse basis. This would put manners on the banks and make them less likely to engage in reckless lending.

One bank in Ireland does give out mortgages on a non-recourse basis, but only for people buying investment properties. But they will only lend a maximum of 65 per cent of the value of the house. So, if the house costs €300,000, the most they will give you is €180,000. You see? Non-recourse results in the banks having manners.

Getting a mortgage is a difficult task but understanding what the rules are and how they can be pushed helps you to navigate the process better and improves your chances of getting a mortgage. Exceptions are available, and one thing I have learned from watching clients apply for loans is to not stop at the first no. You need to keep trying, even with the same bank. Go back and ask again a few months later. Exceptions are a real case of 'it's not you, it's me', so don't give up.

Happy debt and crappy debt

As we have already discussed, there is happy debt and crappy debt. Crappy debt is dangerous and in some cases life-threatening. Happy debt is never actually happy – OK, so nobody wakes up in the morning delighted at owing the bank €210,000, but happy debt can be used for good. Getting into debt is easy. In fact, the higher the interest rate the easier it is to get the loan.

There are times in your life you will want to get into debt. When you want to buy your first house, move to a new house or buy a second property are all the obvious ones. But less obvious is when you don't think you need a new mortgage, but you actually do. This is when you're paying over the odds for your mortgage and could get a cheaper rate elsewhere. It's estimated that over 100,000 people in Ireland are paying more for their mortgage than they could be. Since 2018 new rules have come into effect where now your mortgage provider must tell you if there is a cheaper rate available to you with them. But no legislation, rules or common sense exists that creates a situation where your bank is going to write to you and tell you that other banks out there are cheaper than themselves.

Applying for a loan

Whether you're a first-time buyer, you're moving house or you simply want to get a better rate on your mortgage, how you prepare yourself to apply for the loan is really important. Add in complications like wanting an exception or to be treated as a first-time buyer when you're technically a second-time buyer and it becomes crucial. So what steps should you take to present your financial self in the best possible light?

If you're a straightforward case, have no loans, a good credit history, plenty of savings, a good pensionable job and you don't need to break the Central Bank rules then what you need to do is shop around and see who has the cheapest rates and start there. Of course, there are other considerations when it comes to choosing a mortgage than just the rate. A good mortgage broker will tell you that the bank's rate today is really important but so too is the bank's rate in the past. Are they just cheap right now? Have they always been consistently the cheapest in the market?

But what about other stuff that makes one bank more attractive than another? Will you need to go interest only, which is reduced repayments, at some point? Or maybe you might want to take a break altogether (a moratorium) from the mortgage, for example when you have kids and one of you is on leave? How does the bank you are applying to treat such applications? And what if stuff goes wrong? During our recent downturn, different banks behaved very differently when people got into trouble. Some were compassionate, some had decent amounts of support staff and some had support staff who were trained better than others.

I honestly don't know how anybody ends up with the most suitable mortgage for themselves without using an independent broker (he would say that, I can hear you think). But there is so much to choose from and so much history to know about the bank you are applying to that if you arranged the perfect mortgage by walking into a bank and arranging it yourself, then it was by pure chance. When it comes to applying for a mortgage, I think Donald Rumsfeld said it best when he said, 'There are known unknowns and unknown unknowns. That is to say there are things you know you don't know and things you don't know you don't know.'

Applying for a mortgage is a stressful time. There's so much you won't know about the process and then there's a whole pile of emotion thrown in on top for good measure. I've also found that the stress is not twice as bad for a couple, it's three or four times worse. This is because a single person applying gets their stuff together: they apply for the loan, they deal directly with one person, whether that's someone in the bank or a broker. The communication is direct. Introduce a partner into the mix and then there is a need to relay information quickly amongst three parties at a time that one member of the couple is probably dealing with the auctioneer and the moving company. The bank or the broker isn't ringing back and the third party starts to get frustrated because they feel outside the loop.

Then stuff goes wrong. A perfect example of this was when I had a client applying for a mortgage to buy an investment property. He was dealing directly with the bank. His case was perfect: strong income, good savings even after putting down the required deposit. He had solid tenants lined up to move into the property, but even without the rent his income was strong enough that he could pay the mortgage from his salary and still be OK financially. He was also independently wealthy outside of his property portfolio. To be honest, he could have bought the house with or without the mortgage but for various reasons was getting a mortgage.

The bank said no. They said they were happy with the financials but didn't like the town he was buying in. It was a small town in the midlands and they had bad experiences in that area with people refusing to make their mortgage repayments and therefore they had made the decision not to lend any more money in that area until the situation improved. I was gobsmacked. I actually think this is financial prejudice. This client lived in and loved his town so they really added insult to injury when they then asked him would he be willing to buy something 'inside the M50' because they would be happy to support such an application.

As mortgages tightened post-crash, there were other things that came as surprises to people in the mortgage business. For example, there was a time when the only thing that damaged an application from a credit history point of view was if you had missed other loan repayments. But I had a loan declined for a client years ago because they had missed a direct debit for their health insurance. Things are getting a little better though – a sure sign that banks are looking to give out money is when you see billboards advertising that they want you to switch your mortgage from your bank to their bank because 'We have the lowest rate on the market.'

Pre-crash of 2008, almost 20 per cent of all mortgages were 'switchers' – that is, where you move from one bank to another for a better rate. Post-crash, this went down by almost 90 per cent to just under 3 per cent. Banks had their own problems and did not want to take on your mortgage, thus increasing their problems and reducing the burden on the competitor they just took the mortgage over from.

At the height of the Celtic Tiger era I attended a financial conference. The room was full of independent advisors and mortgage brokers, including an underwriter from one of the big mortgage providers. (In case you don't know, an underwriter is the person who pulls your file apart and decides if they are going to give you your mortgage or not.) The underwriter spoke to the room about how to get mortgages with his bank across the line. He went into detail about the clients they like to lend to and the ones they are less keen on. But there was one comment he made that summarised his entire presentation, which threw everything he'd been talking about for the previous 40 minutes out of the window. He told us to send in our clients' applications because if they didn't give our clients the money, *some other bank would instead*.

At that time credit was readily available and banks were out in their droves filling people's boots with it. Roll on a few years and things were very different. Banks were in hiding. They were not giving out money and they had battened down the hatches. In 2006 as a country we borrowed just under €40 billion in mortgages. By 2011 this had dropped to just over €2.4 billion. This was partly because no one wanted to take out a mortgage, but also because none of the banks were giving out money.

Closed for business

Nothing summed it up for me more than another conference I attended four or five years later. Topics were varied and more on the financial planning side than on mortgages, which is why I was surprised to see a presentation from one of the big mortgage lenders on the agenda – remember they were still in hiding at this stage.

The topic was a dual one about helping your client in financial difficulties engage with his bank and also what type of lending they are doing and to whom. I had not realised it from his name but was intrigued to see my underwriter from a few years previous take to the podium. He gave a good presentation on how his bank was actively engaging with people in difficulty. He showed empathy and compassion and did a really good job of trying to convince the audience that his bank cared.

His time was ticking by and we hadn't started talking about who they were looking to give money to and how best to apply for a mortgage with them. That's when he dropped another line: there was no point in going through their lending process at the moment because they were looking for reasons not to give out money to our clients.

That was pure madness on many fronts. The fact that this was the same underwriter from the same bank giving a completely different message was one thing. The fact that he accepted the invitation to come and speak was another. But the fact that things were so bad in his bank that some group of executives sat around a table and signed him off to go out and tell the independent advice community that effectively this bank was closed for business just shows where they were at that point.

But what difference does it make to you? We'll go through these cycles again and again. Right now, we're in a phase where banks are increasingly willing to give out money but are constrained by Central Bank rules. But we will get back to a point where the banks shut the doors again and the Central Bank won't need to impose rules. My point is you cannot control what stage of the cycle the banks are going to be in when you decide you want to buy, switch or move house. You can only control how your finances look, so what do you do to prepare yourself financially for applying for a mortgage?

Realise the preparation starts a long time out

Getting mortgage ready isn't something you should start thinking about the week before you apply. It is something you should be thinking about, in some cases, years in advance. In fact, we did some research in May 2018 that showed it can take the average person, earning the average wage, who wants to buy the average house in Dublin, 21 years to save the deposit.

We used numbers from Daft.ie, cost-of-living figures and average income government sources. The reality was if you are single, living in Dublin, paying average prices for your cost of living and paying rent, then there is very little left over to save for a deposit. This means making yourself better than average any way you can, like having your bank accounts looking strong. Banks will look at three-month bank statements, but they might ask for six months and sometimes even twelve months. When it comes to car and personal loans, they will ask for a year's worth of statements.

If you're self-employed they will request two years' worth of accounts, sometimes even three, before they will consider your application. This is difficult for somebody who has recently gone out on their own because they not only need three years' worth of accounts – they need three years of consistently good accounts because they will take an average of the three years to work out what you make.

We have had people who were thinking of going out on their own and we have had to suggest they get their mortgage first because it will add two to three years to them being mortgage ready. We have also had self-employed people who took a job with somebody else because when you work for somebody else the bank will consider your application once you are out of probation, which is usually six months but can be as little as three months.

If you're in a new job and you are applying for a mortgage, don't stress too much. If things are going well and you are in probation but want to apply for a mortgage, it's always worth asking your employer how comfortable they would be about considering an early end to your probation in order for you to apply for a mortgage. By phrasing it this way you are offering to become a better employee in return for your probation being finished sooner. They get something and you get something, which is the way these things should work. (Take the same approach when asking for a pay rise!)

Most employers love to hear employees say the words, 'I'm applying for a mortgage.' Having a mortgage means that you need financial stability. If you are good at what you do then your employer knows you won't be going anywhere for a while. So you might find they help you get out of that probation. If they do say no to your request, don't take it personally. You could be the absolute best employee the company has ever had but sometimes, particularly in larger companies, doing this for you sets a precedent that they then feel they have to fulfil for others. They may be happy to do it for you but it just leaves them too exposed in the future or creates an issue for people they have said no to in the past.

Whether it is three months, six months, twelve months or 21 years, you need to become mortgage-ready sooner than you might think. And mistakes can be costly. If you missed a payment on a loan it can follow you around for five years after that loan is fully complete. That is a long time!

The one thing that is a tell-tale sign of your overall finances is your bank statements.

Your bank statements need to be clean

Every financial transaction you do goes through your bank statements. Very few people still get paid in cash so this means most of us have our salaries paid into our bank accounts. Even if you're one of those people who gets paid in cash, tax paid of course, then I would suggest you lodge your wages in full every time you get paid. This gives real clarity to a bank about what you are bringing in.

But whether you are lodging it yourself or it is lodged directly by your employer, our bank statements show our financial trail to the bankers and lenders of this world. Even when you spend in cash you still have to take the cash out of the bank first. When I look at clients' bank statements now, there is less and less cash being used. Even trivial stuff like coffees or a Coke are now paid for by tapping. This gives the banks a real idea of how you spend your money. This is a good thing if you are coping financially and can afford this loan but can be a negative too.

The most important thing for me is that your bank statements show you have an ability to repay. The easiest way to prove this is by showing that you can put away each month more than the mortgage repayment is going to be. I would suggest you use an online mortgage calculator like the one on www.ccpc.ie and you work out how much your mortgage repayments are going to be, then you multiply that by 1.3, so if the loan repayment is €1,000 per month your target is €1,300 per month.

You should be able to show over a long period of time (12 months+) that you can put away €1,300 per month. When I say put away, I mean between rent, loan repayments (on loans that will be cleared when you get the mortgage) and savings, they should total €1,300 in our example. If you have been paying rent of €1,000 per month and saving €300 per month and you walk into a bank and say, 'Look, I have been forking out 1.3 times your mortgage repayment for a long time now,' it gives them great comfort.

But there is also rationale behind you doing this. When the bank looks at your application, they will look at their current interest rates and what the loan repayments will be costing you. But they will also add a few per cent to their current rates to see how your finances would cope with a rate increase. This is what is called a stress test.

Banks don't just want to know you can afford the loan today. They know interest rates go up and down and therefore the Central Bank gets them to check how it would impact you. If you are trying to squeeze as much as you can from a mortgage, some banks offer fixed rates of seven years or more. When they do this, they don't stress test to see what impact an increase would have. This is because in seven years from now your financial situation will have changed anyway and I assume they are hoping you will have got at least one pay rise between now and then.

My argument is that if you can afford to meet all your financial commitments as they fall due and you are saving money for the short, medium and long term then you are perfectly entitled to spend what is left over, guilt free, on whatever you like. It is your money. You worked for it and who are they to judge? But there are certain things that are red flags when it comes to banks deciding if they want to give you a mortgage or not. They are things like:

Betting

If you bet with your own money the bank can take a leap and assume you would be willing to bet with their money too. If you do want to bet, don't do it via your bank account. Do it the old-fashioned way and walk into the bookie's. This has the added advantage that it is a barrier to you actually being able to bet and you will be more mindful about whether you really want to place this bet. I once had a client refused a mortgage because they had betting transactions on their accounts. The client was gobsmacked – and offered to show the bank his very healthy bookie's account statement.

Let me say this clearly: a bank doesn't care that you do well. I'm not going to judge you on whether you should or should not be betting. I am just saying that, if you want to get a mortgage, don't do it through your bank account.

Missed payments

If you can't meet payments as they fall due, then it shows you are struggling financially and even if there is plenty of money coming in it shows a lack of organisation.

Banks are in the business of making profits. Every time you miss a repayment it creates work for them. The perfect mortgage for them is one where the payments come in like clockwork and they just have to write you a letter once a year telling you how much you still owe them. Anything outside of that costs them money. So even if you are really strong financially, if you are not on top of things from an organisational point of view then you are not attractive to them. The worst thing to miss is loan repayments, but missing bills and even optional things like your online TV streaming just shows up your lack of organisation.

What should be happening is all your repayments should come out of your account when they are due. You can take control of this. I am always surprised when I explain to clients that you can choose when a direct debit or standing order hits your account.

A client might say, 'I often miss the car loan repayment because it comes out at the end of the month.' Well, then you need to change the time the car loan repayment comes out of your account or address the underlying issue, which is why you are running out of money before the end of the month.

Take control of your direct debits and standing orders. Sit down and look at the dates they all come out on. And if the dates don't suit, change them.

The overdraft

How much you consistently have in your bank account is very important. Overdrafts are expensive: they are used for things we consume and are therefore crappy debt. But they are awful crappy debt because they are pre-approved – and so easy to get into but really difficult to get out of. Overdrafts are for emergencies. If you are constantly in your overdraft then the bank can quite fairly look at you and say you are constantly in a state of financial emergency. To me overdrafts are actually quite psychological. You just have a new floor.

I dealt with a couple whose finances were in reasonable shape but he was constantly in overdraft and she never dropped below a €500 positive bank balance. Her floor was €500; his floor was –€750, which was his overdraft limit. Every month without fail they would both reach their floor. I took a two-pronged approach to moving his floor. Firstly, we worked out an amount he could 'save' each month. For him this was €250 a month. We took the €250 from his account each month for three months and put it into a savings account separate to his bank account.

Three months later we lodged the €750 to his current account and wrote to the bank and asked them to cancel the overdraft. It worked. But better still, he still saves the €250 per month and uses it for other things throughout the year like car insurance, Christmas, etc. If you are stuck in overdraft, get yourself out of a constant state of financial emergency well in advance of applying for a mortgage.

Shared history

When you find 'the one', you might consider buying somewhere to live together. How you feel about discussing your partner's past relationships is entirely up to you, but discussing your partner's financial history is a must. I am not suggesting it's first-date stuff, but as things get more serious you need to figure out if there are any issues hiding in the closet. I have seen it so many times: somebody applies for a mortgage and they find out that there is an issue from years ago with a credit card that never got cleared when the person went to Australia for a year or missed repayments on a loan that finished three, four or even five years ago.

A cheeky way of finding out about somebody's attitudes to money is to ask them what their parents were like with it. I remember I was doing a piece on Newstalk one time. It was Dr Ciara Kelly presenting, a counsellor, David Kavanagh, and myself. So, we had a doc, a shrink and a financial planner on air together. The topic was around couples and money.

My ears perked up when David mentioned that we marry one of our parents and, if we're lucky, we marry the parent we like. This interested me because the same is said about money. We will either become exactly like or exactly the opposite to our parents when it comes to money. That is of course unless we consciously take action to learn how to do it 'properly'. Asking your partner about their parents' attitude to money can give you an insight into how they might behave with money. But you need to go further. What you really want to know is if there are any skeletons in the closet that might come back to haunt you right at the moment you find your perfect house.

Their financial history is now yours, and vice versa. If you have stuff you need to tell them about your financial past, do it well before you start applying for a mortgage together. You'll dramatically improve your chances of getting the mortgage across the line if you go with your hands up at the outset. If the underwriter has to come to you querying something, then you are immediately on the back foot. That is of course if you are lucky enough that they come back and query it at all. Often times you will get refused and you may not know why.

If it's possible either of you has an issue, then before you apply for a loan, request your report from both the Irish Credit Bureau and the Central Credit Register. The reports will tell you what the banks know about your financial past. The report is free to get and you just need to fill in some simple details about yourself on both www.icb.ie and www.centralcreditregister.ie.

Your shared history does go beyond loans and possible missed payments. If you are following all the rules, staying out of overdraft and not gambling through your account and they are not, then you need to get them in shape too before applying.

Don't go too hard if they are a spender and you are not. There is research that suggests men and women actually spend the same amount of money as each other over the course of the year. Women tend to spend little and often and men tend to spend on bigger-ticket items like gadgets, but over time the amounts are similar.

Remember if you have everything covered including long- and short-term savings and are meeting your commitments, then let your partner spend, guilt free.

Loans

If you have personal or car loans it would be usual to clear them before you get your mortgage. Lots of people don't realise the impact a loan has on your ability to borrow.

One of the calculations a bank does when assessing whether or not you can afford the mortgage is what's called 'nets' in the industry. This is your net income and typically people cannot afford to spend more than 35 per cent of their take-home pay in servicing debt. If you are already using 12 per cent of your income to service a car loan it only leaves 23 per cent to service the mortgage, which reduces your borrowing capacity by roughly a third.

People often ask me if they need to clear the loan before they apply for the mortgage. The answer is no. You might even get the mortgage you need and keep the loan. But I would always suggest you offer to clear the loan 'prior to drawdown'. This means you are basically telling the mortgage provider, 'I have this loan here, I want a mortgage of X. I would like to keep my savings and not clear the loan but if you want me to clear it then give me approval with a condition on it to prove I have cleared the loan before you give me the cheque to buy my house.'

NDIR

NDIR is net disposable income requirement. When the bank looks at you, as mentioned above, they often use 35 per cent of your take-home pay, sometimes less for lower earners, as an acceptable amount of money that can be used to service the mortgage.

But then they look at this figure and take it out of your wages; there is a further calculation that needs to be taken into account and that is that they have to be satisfied that after you use 35 per cent of your wages to pay the mortgage you still have enough money left over to live on.

The more people there are in your house the more money needs to be left over. This is often the reason why lower-income earners struggle to get a mortgage. It is because once the 35 per cent is taken away from their take-home pay, they do not have enough money left over to live on.

If at first you don't succeed ...

There is lots of stuff to consider when it comes to applying for a mortgage. The important thing to remember is that you present yourself in the best possible light. If there are issues, don't try and hide them. Flag them instead, so your honesty is noted when they are found anyway. Be aware that you are the customer. I know it often feels like you are going cap in hand but remember the average bank makes a little over €100,000 in interest off the average mortgage. Don't shove that in their face but there will be moments during the process that you feel annoyed, upset, anxious, all of the above, and this can help you because you can think to yourself, if they don't want my €100,000 interest, I will go somewhere else. The Central Bank rules have to be applied by all the banks but all their calculators don't work exactly the same, so if you aren't having much luck then try a different bank or, better still, start with a mortgage broker in the first place. If you find a good one, they are invaluable. But do remember there is lots outside of their control and they are often pulling their hair out just as much as you are when the banks are slow to respond on queries and questions.

The Central Bank rules

The Central Bank introduced rules in 2016 that basically created the ground rules for all banks in terms of how they work out how much they could give somebody looking for a mortgage. The idea behind them was that the Central Bank wanted to ensure that all banks lent money in a responsible way.

The rules centre around two things: loan to value limits and loan to income limits.

Loan to value limits

This is a restriction on what amount a bank can lend as a per cent of the value of that house. The rule states that a first-time buyer cannot borrow more than 90 per cent of the value of a home, second-time buyers can't get more than 80 per cent and a person who is buying a property to rent it out cannot get more than 70 per cent. This means a first-time buyer has to come up with a deposit of 10 per cent of the purchase price of the house. So, for a €300,000 they need a deposit of €30,000

– but a second-time buyer who wants to buy the same house would have to come up with €60,000 and an investor would need €90,000.

Banks can use what is called an exception, which I have already explained in greater detail (page 59). This is where in a small number of cases banks break the Central Bank rules and give you more money. The number of times they can break the rules is based on the amount of loans they give out. For first-time buyers they can give more than 90 per cent in 5 per cent of cases, 20 per cent of the time for second-time buyers and 10 per cent for investors.

The per cent is based on the total loan amount. If a bank issues €1,000,000 of loans to first-time buyers in a calendar year, €200,000 of these loans can break the rules. It is done by the total loan amount as opposed to the number of customers. This means if you are getting a big mortgage of, let's say, €600,000, you use up twice as much of their available exceptions as a person borrowing €300,000.

Loan to income limits

The other rule is around loan to income. What this means is that the amount of money you can borrow is based on how much you earn. Notwithstanding the other rules I mention above about NDIR and nets, the Central Bank rules state you cannot borrow more than 3.5 times your income or, in the case of a couple, 3.5 times the combined income.

If together you earn €100,000 in total, the most you can borrow is €350,000. It is important to realise that this is an additional test to the others, not an overriding rule. Therefore, if you can't afford the mortgage or the repayment is greater than 35 per cent of your income, then you may still be refused the loan, even though the loan amount is less than 3.5 times. For example, a 62-year-old is unlikely to get 3.5 times their income because most banks will want the loan cleared back by the time they turn 65, or 70 with some banks or in certain cases. Paying back a loan over eight years or even three means the repayments increase substantially, meaning it may become unaffordable.

Again, the banks can use exceptions based on the total loan amount they issue in a calendar year. For first-time buyers they can break the rules in 20 per cent of cases and 10 per cent of cases for both second-time buyers and investors. The rules are interesting, and it has been suggested they are the Central Bank's way of interfering with house prices. Perhaps – but we were in a bad place during the last crash. This measure is supposed to protect the country from having to bail banks out again. It's hard when the rules aren't working in our favour but not as hard as it is on the other side, in a house in negative equity and a mortgage we can't afford to repay.

Rebuilding Ireland

There is one 'bank' out there that breaks all the Central Bank rules whenever they want, and that's the government initiative called Rebuilding Ireland Home Loans. This is an effort by the government to help people get on the property ladder and the product is, in my opinion, brilliant. Basically, if you earn less than €50,000 a year, or as a couple you earn less than €75,000, and you are a first-time buyer, then you would be mad not to get your mortgage through Rebuilding Ireland. Their rates are much cheaper than the banks and they will give you more money than the banks will because the rates are fixed for the entire mortgage. There is a variable rate but I struggle in the case of Rebuilding

Ireland to see any good reason why anybody would be better off taking the variable rate when the fixed rates are so good.

To qualify for Rebuilding Ireland you must be a first-time buyer and *you must have had an insufficient offer from at least two banks*. This is really important and a common misconception. You need an insufficient offer, not a refusal from two banks. So if you want to buy a house in a certain area and you can't get a mortgage big enough from any of the banks to buy in that area, then you get two insufficient offers and head off to Rebuilding Ireland. I have seen people get approved for as much as €50,000 more with Rebuilding Ireland than they could with an ordinary bank.

There is another misconception, that it can only be used for new builds. It doesn't have to be a new build and it can even be used if you are building your own home, provided it isn't massive. The house you are building or buying cannot be bigger than 175 metres^2.

Help to buy

This is another initiative that the government introduced and this one is only for first-time buyers buying new houses. It is often overlooked by people probably because they don't know they are entitled to it. In simple terms you can get up to 5 per cent of the purchase price of the house and you can use it as part of the deposit. Rebuilding Ireland and the banks will accept it as part of your savings.

The amount you get is restricted by the value of the house and the maximum you can get is €20,000. The money is actually a refund of the tax you have paid in the last four years, so if you haven't paid enough tax you won't get the full amount. This can be problematic for people who left Ireland during the recession and now want to move home, because they haven't paid tax here and so won't get the refund.

Getting out of debt

Getting your mortgage for your first home or switching your mortgage to get a cheaper rate is often something that you feel good about. But when you are stuck in a spiral of crappy debt and you are on that treadmill you need to come up with a plan for how to get out of it.

It is important to note that I am going to describe two ways you can tackle your debt, but these are for people who can afford their debt and just feel they are getting nowhere in tackling them. If you are in a position where you feel your debt is completely unaffordable then you are best talking to a personal insolvency practitioner (PIP).

A PIP will review your situation and if they find your debt is in fact at a level that is not sustainable, they will put a plan together and present it to your banks. If it is accepted you will pay the agreed amount on a monthly basis for up to six years or sometimes up to seven years and whatever is left on the loans at the end is typically written off and you become debt free. This is with the exception of your mortgage. There may be something written off the mortgage but you will usually continue to pay the loan back over an agreed period. The important thing is that when you engage with a PIP, in most cases – in fact practically in all cases – the family home will be protected. You will not lose your house.

If this does not sound like the route you need to go down, you have a good income and you are just finding that you can't get out from under the debt, then I have two approaches to suggest: the traditional route and what is called the snowball route.

Regardless of which route you decide to take, the first step is to identify some extra cash from your daily spending. You're already making the required repayments on the loans so you will need to accelerate these repayments by paying more towards the loans on a month-to-month basis. Cut back on something; or better still, if you're about to get a pay rise, decide now not to let Parkinson's law kick in and use the extra take-home pay to tackle your debt.

Top tip: the first step to getting out of debt is identifying where to find the funds to pay off more of your loans every month.

People often feel that because they only have a small amount of money there is no point. If you feel like that you are totally wrong. Even €5 per month extra off your loans helps – anything helps. You're forming a habit, and, as you'll see from the methods below, even a small amount compounds over time. Another word of warning: if you are a couple and you aren't both 100 per cent together on this then you are completely wasting your time. It will cause arguments because you want to cut back and they don't. You will start to succeed only to find the credit card has been used. You both need to work towards the goal together.

The traditional route

Once you've identified money from your budget to put towards your loans, the next thing you need to do is to list all your loans in one place. I always find that when I get clients to write the numbers down with pen and paper it is more impactful than entering them into a spreadsheet. You can of course use a spreadsheet as well, but make sure you write them down on paper first.

You should have seven columns on your page and when you are done it might look something like this:

Liabilities						
	Amount O/S	Repayments	Interest Rates	Months Remaining	Years remaining	Total Repayments
Credit Card	€4,000.00	€105.00	20%	61	5.1	€6,400.89
Car Hire Purchase	€12,000.00	€330.00	8%	42	3.5	€13,788.53
Credit Union	€16,000.00	€424.00	8%	44	3.6	€18,491.42
Credit Union	€1,752.00	€136.00	6.75%	13	1.1	€1,823.83
Total Liabilities	€33,752.00	€995.00	10.69%			€40,504.67

You will notice that I have not included the mortgage in this. Mortgages are happy debt. That doesn't mean I don't want to get rid of them, but we handle them differently and we need to clear all our crappy debt before we touch the happy stuff.

It never fails to amaze me, when showing this to a client, that almost always their attention is drawn to the total repayments figure, which is €40,504.67. But then I cruelly draw their attention to the total amount outstanding – in this case €33,752. This couple is going to pay the best part of €7,000 in interest over the next five-and-a-bit years if they keep paying their loans back as they are. I then hit them harder with the fact that this is just what they will pay from now to the end, ignoring the interest they have already paid.

Remember I want them and you to hate your debt. Paying off debt by the agreed terms is painful, tackling your debt quicker is painful, so choose your pain. If you don't hate your debt you have significantly less chance that you will be successful clearing it off quicker and you are much more likely to relapse into debt in the future.

You'll notice in my previous table that the loans are listed randomly. The traditional route of tackling debt is to reorganise your debts from the most expensive repayment down to the cheapest:

Liabilities						
	Amount O/S	Repayments	Interest Rates	Months Remaining	Years remaining	Total Repayments
Credit Union	€16,000.00	€424.00	8%	44	3.6	€18,491.42
Car Hire Purchase	€12,000.00	€330.00	8%	42	3.5	€13,788.53
Credit Union	€1,752.00	€136.00	6.75%	13	1.1	€1,823.83
Credit Card	€4,000.00	€105.00	20%	61	5.1	€6,400.89
Total Liabilities	€33,752.00	€995.00	10.69%			€40,504.67

Then, while continuing to make the scheduled repayments on all your loans, you take your extra money and start putting it towards the most expensive loan first and when that's gone take the extra money and move it to the second most expensive loan and so on until all your debts are gone.

Let me be really clear: this is absolutely the best way to clear off the loans in the cheapest way possible. But it doesn't always work for everyone. It is a long game and it can be hard to stick with it. Going after the most financially sensible way is pointless if you fall off the wagon and don't get to the finish line at all.

If you think this is something you can stick to, great. Go for it. I usually judge it on a case-by-case basis. I get a feel for the client and I understand what the chances of their success will be. I also have a good indication of how much they hate their debt. Only you can judge this for yourself. But if you want to improve your chances of succeeding then let's look at the snowball route together.

The snowball effect

I'm not sure who came up with it first, but US businessman and broadcaster Dave Ramsey is a big advocate of this route and has helped thousands of people clear their debt with it. The idea behind the snowball route is not dissimilar to the traditional route. Starting with the same loans as mentioned above, instead of listing them in the order of most expensive to cheapest repayment, this time we list them with the lowest loan amount up to highest loan amount outstanding:

Liabilities						
	Amount O/S	Repayments	Interest Rates	Months Remaining	Years remaining	Total Repayments
Credit Union	€1,752.00	€136.00	6.75%	13	1.1	€1,823.83
Credit Card	€4,000.00	€105.00	20%	61	5.1	€6,400.89
Car Hire Purchase	€12,000.00	€330.00	8%	42	3.5	€13,788.53
Credit Union	€16,000.00	€424.00	8.00%	44	3.6	€18,491.42
Total Liabilities	€33,752.00	€995.00	10.69%			€40,504.67

With the snowball route you once again make the scheduled payments on all loans but this time you take the extra money you've identified and you put it towards the loan with the least amount outstanding *first*. This doesn't actually make a whole pile of financial sense because as you can see in our example the €1,752 left on the credit union loan is the lowest-interest loan this person has and we are about to throw our extra money at getting rid of our cheapest debt first.

But what it does is it gets this person a quick win. Clearing debt is hard and it is a long road. By tackling the lowest loan amount first, what happens is that you are rewarded early on and it keeps you engaged and motivated. This may be a slightly more expensive route to clearing your loans but I have found over the years that when clients are set on this path, they are much more likely to succeed than with the traditional route.

When the first loan is cleared, you take the extra money you were paying towards this loan – in this case, the €136 you were paying towards the credit union loan – and add it to the repayments for the next-lowest loan amount. In our example above this is the credit card, which is the most expensive debt.

Again, when the credit card is cleared, you get the extra money. What was going towards the credit union and what was going towards the credit card you add together and start paying off the next loan, which is car hire purchase. When that loan has gone you repeat the process again and again until all the loans are gone. Like a snowball.

In the above example this couple, instead of being in debt for the next 61 months, are on a schedule to be crappy-debt free in 26 months. But not only that, instead of paying over €41,000 in repayments they will pay €36,000. That is a saving of €5,000 because they got hard on their debt. It's not all plain sailing. Sometimes you'll get knocked off track, but that's OK. The important thing is to start again and not lose sight of the end goal.

Things can get thrown at you: you ring the bank to increase the repayments and, in what is often the case, they are fixed loans and you can't pay extra, you can only clear them in full. If that is the case you move to the next loan and when everything is clear you build savings to wipe out the rogue loan. Don't waver – you're on a plan. Clearing that first loan feels amazing and really spurs you on, but nothing feels better than clearing the last one. You know you are debt free and you never have to go back there and not only that, you have loads of extra cash every month now to use towards your next goal.

If you're in a relationship it is an incredible journey to go through together. Watching couples do it over the years, I have seen them become much more aware of their finances, much more appreciative of what they have, but most importantly they both end up once they have succeeded vowing that no matter how shiny that new car looks, or how crystal clear the picture quality is on that TV, they will do without it unless they can pay for it upfront.

Tackling the mortgage

I purposefully did not include the happy debt that is your mortgage in the snowball and traditional methods. That is because I think you need to take a different approach to this.

I have often come across new clients who are paying extra each month off their mortgage, and when I ask them, why they say because they had extra cash and didn't know what else to do with it. In my experience in most cases paying extra off the mortgage is the wrong thing to do. There are limited circumstances in which it makes financial sense but the problem from a financial planning perspective is that there is whole pile of emotion tied up in a mortgage.

People feel they could cope if things went wrong if they had no mortgage, or they need the mortgage clear in time to pay for college fees. Or their parents cleared the mortgage young and it did them no harm. As a financial planner I completely respect the emotion. There is one time in particular where I will completely bow down to it and that is if a client has enough money to clear the mortgage in full and they want to do it even after I have shown them it doesn't make financial sense in their circumstances.

Let me be clear, if you are not maxing out your pension contributions each year and you are not maxing out all other investment options available to you such as share purchase in work, then using your spare cash to clear the mortgage quicker is the wrong thing to do. If you have loads of spare cash then by all means go for it but I still think there is a better way.

When you give the bank extra money each month for your mortgage you need to remember two things. Firstly, it is a long-term investment, in fact it is as long as is left on your mortgage. So if you have 20 years left on the mortgage, then putting an extra few quid each month towards the mortgage is a 20-year investment. We will talk about this more in the next section (page 93) but long-term investment needs a long-term vehicle. When a client tells me they want to put money towards their mortgage because interest rates are so low, I ask them why they're using a short-term vehicle for a long-term goal.

Secondly, remember that putting extra money towards the mortgage means it's gone. You're not getting it back unless you remortgage. You might wonder why you would need it back, but the reality is the most likely time you will need it back is when you are having some sort of emergency, such as illness or redundancy. In both cases, the bank are not going to be very receptive to you sticking in an application to remortgage even when you have been overpaying every month for years.

Mortgage versus savings

I believe there's a happy medium to be found. If you've maxed out the pension contributions and you still have extra cash, rather than putting it towards the mortgage, why not set up a separate savings account? Use a long-term vehicle (which we'll look at in the next section in detail, page 93) but don't stick those savings in a regular bank account. This is because a mortgage is a long-term thing, so saving the extra money should be for the long term, too. Don't use a short-term vehicle (a bank account) for a long-term goal. As you pay into the savings they will start to accumulate and grow. At the same time, you will be making your scheduled repayments on your mortgage and it will be coming down. As the savings accumulate and the mortgage comes down, at some point in the future you will have the same amount in savings as there is left on the mortgage. You then have a decision to make – to keep your savings or clear the mortgage. It is interesting to watch people at this point. They have been saving for years to clear the mortgage early but when they get there, they feel an attachment to the savings and the mortgage doesn't bother them anymore.

> *Top tip: People often argue that you save more interest by paying it off monthly, but there is little or no difference between paying a loan back three, five or seven years early, whether you do it in one swoop or gradually over the years.*

The massive advantage to building up a savings account instead of overpaying into your mortgage every month is that you have the savings available to you at any time. If you get sick or lose your job, you have your savings.

Good financial planning is about creating options for yourself today and into the future. Leave as many options as possible open for as long as possible.

SECTION 3

GETTING YOUR MONEY TO WORK FOR YOU

W hy should you invest instead of just leaving your money on deposit in the bank, post office or credit union? How do you invest? How do you build up money to be able to invest? Why are pensions better than just savings?

Let's start with why you should invest your money.

If you're going to spend money you have today in the next five years then it belongs in your bank, post office or credit union account. Let's just call them deposit accounts. If you are not, then the money does not belong in your bank, post office or credit union account.

It's that simple. I call it the five-year rule.

The five-year rule

The five-year rule exists because of inflation. Deposit accounts are a short-term vehicle. Five years or more is not short term. If you have a long-term goal like college for the kids, retirement, or a midlife-crisis spending spree, don't use a short-term vehicle for a long-term goal.

Inflation eats away at your money. There is some comfort in the idea that, let's say, you deposit €10,000 into the bank today and in five years' time there will still be €10,000 plus a little interest on it. You feel like you're making money. But let me be clear: you're losing money. You will lose money sitting on deposit if it sits there long term.

Let's look at an example. You have just changed your car. You really like your new car but you are disciplined so you decide now you are going to keep the new car for only five years. Your car cost you €10,000 today and you are sure you will buy the exact same car in five years' time. You think it might be a good idea to do a deal with the garage now for the car you want to buy. You have €10,000 today and you offer it to the garage and tell them you will be back in five years' time to collect your car. Not surprisingly they say no.

Now you need to put away the €10,000 so that in five years' time you can use it to buy the car.

Not including other factors such as any increase the car manufacturer is going to put on the car to increase their profits, just imagine for the purposes of this exercise that the cost of the car will only increase in line with inflation. How much will the car cost, allowing for inflation, in five years' time?

Anybody who tells you what house prices, share prices, pork belly prices or anything like that are going to do in the short term is either guessing or lying. We don't know. Nobody knows. If they did, they wouldn't be telling me or you. When it comes to longer term predictions there is a bit more predictability with what certain things like shares and houses are going to do, but not in the short term.

Inflation

The main mandate for the bankers at the European Central Bank (ECB) is to use interest rates to control inflation. They have a target inflation rate of 2 per cent per annum. In other words, they want inflation to be close to 2 per cent to keep things ticking over but want to make sure it doesn't rise too high above or dip too far below that figure. (Interestingly, in the US the Federal Reserve (the Fed), which is the US equivalent of the European Central Bank, has a dual mandate. The Fed can use interest rates to not just control inflation but also to spur or curb growth of the economy.)

Our single mandate in Europe did prove troublesome for the ECB when things were difficult during the global financial crisis in 2008. They could not change interest rates to spur the economy – they could only change them if there was evidence that hitting their 2 per cent target of inflation was at risk. That 2 per cent inflation margin gives us a solid basis to use when working out how much your €10,000 car will be worth in five years' time. So, ignoring manufacturer increases and just taking inflation into account, the cost of the car would go from €10,000 to €11,040.

Now if you put your money in a deposit account and somehow managed to get a rate of 0.5 per cent per annum, after Deposit

Interest Retention Tax (DIRT) – the tax you pay on the growth of money sitting in bank accounts – your €10,000 will have grown to €10,252. You lost money; in fact you lost almost €800. You cannot afford to buy the car without adding money to it from somewhere else.

But inflation might not do that, and you may get a better return on your deposit account because again we are back to guessing (or lying) about what those rates will be.

The real cost of a deposit account

As of September 2019 the per cent change in the consumer price index between September 2014 and September 2019 was 1.7 per cent per annum. This means that unless you have been getting 1.7 per cent interest after DIRT on your deposit account for the last five years you have lost money. We are only looking at five years, but when you start to look at longer periods the problem compounds.

For example, let's look at saving money for college for your kids. Imagine their grandparents decided the day they were born to put €12,000 on deposit for them towards college. It costs around €12,000 for one year in college for a child who lives away from home so we're assuming that their grandparents are offering to pay one child's first-year college costs.

Let's say your child goes to college exactly 18 years later. Most people will argue that college costs will increase above inflation, but let's stick to our 2 per cent inflation rate for now. For every €12,000 that college will cost, between now and 18 years from now that will increase to €17,138 just using inflation of 2 per cent. (Using higher inflation of let's say 4 per cent increases this €12,000 cost to €24,309!)

A deposit account getting a whopping 1 per cent per annum will mean your grandparent money will only grow to €14,353. Granny and grandad are planning on covering a full year in college. Inflation has different ideas and it will mean that at best, by using a deposit account, they will cover 84 per cent of the first year in college or until around the end of March or early April. Granny and Grandad's good intention could fall short by as much as €2,785 against inflation or about €10,000 based in above-inflation cost rises.

An 18-year time frame is one thing but the longer you stretch these things the bigger the gap becomes. For example, if you are 35 today, something that costs €10,000 now will cost you almost €20,000, double the amount, by the time you reach 70 years of age. Leave €10,000 on deposit and even getting 1 per cent after tax it will have grown to €14,166. Your savings might still look better than they were when you started but the real value, the purchasing power of your money, will go down.

But what else can you do? What's the alternative? The reality is you need to turn up the risk volume if you want to beat inflation. Turning up the volume on risk does not mean gambling your money. It is about taking a measured approach to investing properly.

Invest and forget

Every person in the investment world has a different view of what 'investing properly' actually involves. I'm going to give you my opinion and lots of people will disagree with it. That's fine. I believe the investment world has been made overly complex to create jobs for the boys, but it's really not that complicated. There are a few things you need to get right but once you do, it is about 'invest and forget'.

Asset allocation

The biggest decision you must make is what is called asset allocation. In simple terms, this means what percentage you put into each type of investment: how much do you put in shares, how much in bonds, how much goes into property and so on. For lots of reasons, in private practice we tend to use shares and bonds. This is because lots of Irish people are already heavily exposed to property and because we want to keep things simple. We don't see the need to introduce absolute return or hedge funds, commodities, or derivatives or alternatives ... the list is endless.

Chasing after this stuff often feels to me like trying to chase the next big thing. I believe there is no next big thing, there is only the last big thing. Trying to chase the next big thing is a pointless exercise because once you have heard about it then it is generally not the next big thing – it has had its day. There are some exceptions, but trying to find them is down to sheer luck. The amount of different crap investments you would have to do to be able to find that one whopper of a winner would often mean the loss negates the gain. Not always but extremely often.

Shares and bonds

There is no such a thing as a perfect, low-risk, high-return investment. You don't need to be fancy in your investments. Keep it simple. Investing properly is boring. Set it up right with simple, reliable, proven asset classes and then forget about it. You can build a perfectly good portfolio using just shares and bonds. What are shares and bonds? Let me explain.

In 1979 my parents bought a house in Dublin. Let's just say it cost the equivalent in punts of €10,000. They borrowed €8,000 from the bank – meaning the bank became the bondholder – and they put in €2,000 themselves – meaning they became the shareholder.

The difference between my parents and the bank was that my parents owned the property and therefore they became the shareholders. The bank, however, did not own the property; they just loaned their money to my parents in order for them to buy it. They did get some promises from my parents – for example that they would pay the money back and if things went wrong my parents would agree to sell their assets and then pay the bank back.

Throughout the mortgage but particularly during the 80s I have no doubt my parents felt the bank were making much more money off the deal than they were. This is very typical; markets are cyclical. There are times when a bondholder does better than a shareholder. But 40 years later, who do you think did better out of the deal? I don't even need to tell you how much the house is worth today for you to see that the bondholder, i.e. the bank, got their interest. But the shareholders, who in this example were my parents, in the long run did better out of owning the asset (the house) itself. This is tried and tested over time. The longer the period the more probability there is that the shareholder will do better out of a deal.

Bondholders make money by lending their money to companies in the form of corporate bonds and to governments in the form of government bonds, a little like banks do when they lend families money to buy homes in the form of mortgages. Each year a bondholder will get interest off the government or company they lent the money to and when the bond matures, they get all their money back, provided everything goes smoothly. If things go wrong, then sometimes the bondholder gets back less than the original amount they gave as a loan. This is often called a haircut. Interestingly, though, when things go very wrong, bondholders get paid before shareholders do. So bonds are considered less risky than shares.

When things go as planned the bondholder collects their coupon (interest) each year and gets all their money back in the end. This is not an unusual occurrence. Sometimes people don't want to keep their bond until maturity and are free to sell it on the open market to whoever wants to buy it.

Being a shareholder or owning shares means you own a little bit of that company. You get fewer promises; in fact the only promise you get is that when you sell the shares you will get for them whatever somebody is willing to pay for them. Most times you get paid a dividend each year. This means the company of which you are now a part owner as a shareholder shares some of the profits with you. But that isn't even promised. Sometimes the dividend is turned off completely, particularly if the company is going through a difficult time. But then some companies, particularly the big tech companies, make a blanket decision that they don't pay dividends. It is a just a choice they make. Possibly because they believe by not paying a dividend all their growth will be reflected in the share price but also because by not paying a dividend these rapidly expanding companies have more money to reinvest in the business itself rather than giving it out to shareholders.

When I say 'shares' people always get that worried look on their faces. Images of their parents, holding their heads in their hands because they had lost money on the shares the bank manager told them to invest in, come flooding back.

Learning from data

There is one thing we have in abundance when it comes to investing, particularly when you stick to the simple stuff like shares and bonds, and that is data. We have data over very long periods of time. We also know that markets are cyclical, repeating patterns over and over again. This gives me great confidence when advising clients. I can show them what has happened before when things go wrong but also when things go right.

I pay for a powerful piece of software that allows me, when required, to step a client through any period in history they want. If my client has a memory of 1989 when their parents got wiped out financially, I can show them how their investments would fare if 1989 happened next year. The data gives us an abundance of knowledge to learn from. However, we as humans have an issue and I think Warren Buffett, amongst others, sums it up best: 'The one thing man learns from history is that man doesn't learn from history.'

For me this quote tells two stories. The first one is that markets are going to repeat the mistakes of the past. It is inevitable. Think about the fact that the 22-year-old who is starting in the big investment bank somewhere in Manhattan was only 11 in 2008; they didn't watch the global financial world collapse. More importantly, they didn't feel the pain, the stress or the suffering of the people who lost money as a result. They will, I hope, have studied it in college but they won't have personally learnt from it so therefore it is inevitable that when they become senior managers in the next ten or 20 years they may consider taking, once more, some of those risks that led to the crash.

But this isn't a problem for my private clients and should not be a problem for you. We know things will go wrong; we expect markets to fall, and so we're not scared when they do. When building out a portfolio for clients, one of the things we do is to test it against the most recent and worst crash on the stock markets. Currently that is 2008, which we will continue to use until the next one comes along ... and then we'll use that.

Leave it alone

Something that often surprises our clients is that when you leave the investment alone (invest and forget) then over long periods of time the crash has little impact on the overall financial plan. Clients soon realise that markets are constantly on an upward trend: despite some bumps they stay on an upward trajectory. This makes sense when you sit back and think about it. As a whole, the world is constantly progressing. Companies are getting bigger and are making more money. At times businesses will fail but others will thrive, and when you are invested across many companies, it all levels out. If things are set up right from the start, and you leave it alone, then over time you will see your investment increase. It will be hit from time to time, but that is OK.

In some cases, a crash can even benefit a client financially over the long term. These are clients who are earning and putting fresh money into the market. If you are putting fresh money into your bonds and shares each month or year, the right thing to do when a market crash happens is to keep doing it. It can often feel counterintuitive.

I get it. The whole world, the newspapers, the news and the radio are all telling you the world is falling apart and you are taking your hard-earned cash and investing it in the 'world', but it can dramatically improve your finances over the long term if you just stick to the plan. The media is not a friend of the long-term investor. The media tends to be backward-looking, telling you what happened yesterday. The markets are forward-looking. You cannot look backwards when moving forwards and expect to succeed.

Never in my working life have the financial markets and the financial world become more mainstream than during the global financial crisis of 2008. This was difficult for clients, but even more difficult for people with no advisor. They had nobody to call and vent their worries to. I think the banks did an incredible disservice to their clients during this period. It is anecdotal evidence – I accept that – but we picked up an incredible number of ex-banking clients after the global financial crisis.

These ex-banking clients were worried about how much their investment was falling and went into the bank that sold them the investment to speak to their advisor – to find that their advisor was no longer there. It was not that the advisors had left. It appears that there was a culture within some of the banks to rotate advisors around branches. (I worked in one bank back in the early 2000s and it wasn't unusual to move from branch to branch.)

However, I do think the timing on this was incredibly poor from some of the banks and quite opportune for advisors who were worried about talking to clients who were losing money because of an investment they had advised them to go into. The reality is this: if the bank's intention was to free their advisors from the 'stress' of having to look somebody in the eye who had invested money with them that subsequently went down in value, then they completely missed the point of the role of the advisor.

A good advisor sets up an investment properly, has conviction in how the money is invested and expects things to go up and down. They then hold the client's hand when – not if – the market has what is best described as a temporary decline. A temporary decline on markets happens every 3–5 years on average. Some people call these market crashes, but I think that is misleading. Something that crashes tend not to do is move forwards again. Markets are constantly on an upward trend; they do go up and down but over long periods of time they stay on an upward trend.

The no-brainer 60/40 portfolio

It is widely accepted in the investments community that, if a client has no advisor, the no-brainer 60/40 portfolio is the way to go. A 60/40 portfolio is an investment made up of 60 per cent global shares and 40 per cent bonds.

I like to use this portfolio as a benchmark. It is also useful when looking at what happens with investments. Temporary declines, or market crashes if you want to call them that (and I don't), happen every three to five years and a 100 per cent share portfolio will decline by 31 per cent on average.

A 60/40 portfolio shouldn't fall by as much – it could, but the reality is that if you invest in a 60/40 portfolio today, a year from now there is a 17 per cent chance that it will be down. We tell clients this all the time. And then we go on to ask them whether, in three years' time when there's a seven per cent chance that their investment will be worth less than it is today, they are OK with those odds. And lastly we explain that in five years' time there's a 0.4 per cent of us having a negative conversation but if the client waits for seven years or more, there has never been a seven-plus-year period when a 60/40 portfolio was down.

Rolling Performance							
	6 Month	1 Year	3 Year	5 Year	7 Year	10 Year	14 Year
No. of Periods	14,883	14,702	13,971	13,241	12,510	11,414	9953
Frequency of Loss	3,745	2,504	958	53	–	–	–
Frequency of Loss per cent	**25.2 per cent**	**17.0 per cent**	**6.9 per cent**	**0.4 per cent**	**0.0 per cent**	**0.0 per cent**	**0.0 per cent**

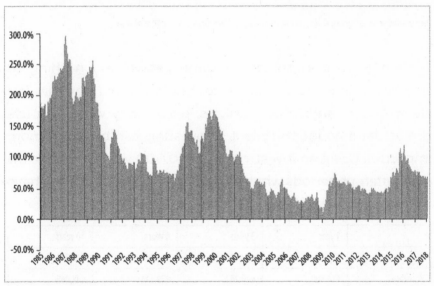

Data encompasses rolling seven-year periods over 40 years (1978–2018).

Sometimes, if a client is struggling with the concept, we show them what the worst-case scenario is over one, three, five and seven years. Looking at the future in monetary terms can often change perspective.

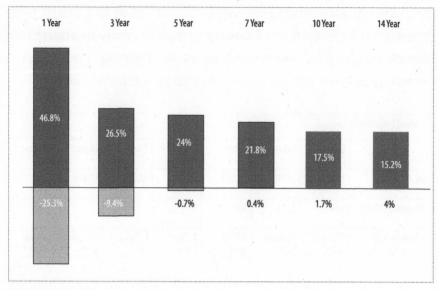

The best- and worst-case scenarios for your investments if you invest it over 1, 3, 5, 6, 10 or 14 years.

Percentages mean things to some people and nothing to others. It is important that we communicate in a way that the client understands. But numbers, particularly when you use the actual amount the client is investing, can be much more impactful. Using an investment of €10,000 you can see below over different periods what the best and worst outcomes have been over the last 41 years:

	1 year	3 years	5 years	10 years
Worst case	€7,596	€7,412	€9,366	€10,511
Best case	€14,680	€20,242	€29,316	€48,068

Once the client has grasped this, we ask them – taking into account that they now know the odds over one, three, five and 10 years – what they think the odds are of having a positive daily outlook on their investment. There is a 44 per cent chance that if you look at a 60/40 portfolio and compare it to yesterday, it will be down. The problem is the pain of that loss is four times greater than any joy you get from the 56 per cent chance of a positive return compared to yesterday.

We spend years trying to teach our clients to invest and forget. This requires having faith in the investment they've made, not to react to market movements and, most importantly, not to be checking their investment values online regularly.

Time, not timing

Even though crashes will happen again and again and again, we need to learn from what happens afterwards. People think they can time the market; that they can pick out when it has bottomed out, invest their money and then ride it to the top and withdraw their money. They then think they can safely leave it in cash until the market bottoms out again. Anybody who successfully does this repeatedly is, in my opinion, either from the future and has travelled back in time or is lying about their investment success.

> Top tip: timing the market is an absolute fools' game: the best time to invest your money is when you have it and the best time to take out your money is when you need it. Beyond that you should try and have as long a time as possible between the two.

Even if you get it horribly wrong, the reality is that time is an amazing healer when it comes to investment choices. Imagine that on 30 October 2007 you invested your life savings – let's say it was €100,000. Eighteen months later it was down the tubes. You took a serious hit. In fact your €100,000 would have been worth €66,035.

The journey to the bottom.

You go down to the bank because you're worried about your money and when you arrive in you're told that the advisor who sold you the investment has now moved to a new branch. But don't worry, Gerry works here now and he's great. You meet with Gerry and he explains although he's sorry your money is down by 33.96 per cent in the time since you invested, he doesn't know what conversation was had at the point of sale and he does things very differently. He suggests you move it to their new fund, which hasn't lost nearly as much money in the past 18 months and is a much safer bet (this is, of course, the last thing you should to be doing).

You don't know what to do. You worry that leaving it where it is means you will lose more money but moving it into Gerry's new fund doesn't feel right either. You ask Gerry to switch it to cash to give you time to think and to avoid losing any more money. Gerry obliges. You go home to think about things and decide to wait until the bottom of the market before moving it out of cash and reinvesting it. Another bad idea.

The thing is, no bell rings at the bottom of the market. Moving money out of your current investment and into cash means you double down on your risks. You now must be right on three different fronts:

1. That where you are is the wrong place to be;
2. That where you are moving the money to is the right place to go; and
3. That you are timing it correctly and you aren't currently already sitting on the bottom.

What you're doing here is trying to time the market. Think about this for a minute. There are people in the investment world who do this 'timing' stuff for a living. They are paid extremely well, they have teams around them from the best universities, they have what feels like endless resources and most of them who try to time the market fail miserably. What hope do you think you have? If they work 50 hours a week, 48 weeks a year they spend 2,400 hours per year using their brains and their teams' brains thinking about how and when to invest your money, and you probably spend two hours a year at most thinking about this stuff; what are the chances you're going to get it right?

After your chat with Gerry, you move the money to cash. You then sit waiting for the bottom-of-the-market bell to ring so you can invest again. Life goes on and you start to forget about 'keeping an eye on things'. And ten years later you wake up and you are still in cash.

At the start of this particular ten-year period, banks were actually in need of cash and offering really decent deposit rates, but in the latter years you were lucky to be getting 0.25 per cent

– in fact, really lucky. But let's assume you average a whopping 1 per cent per annum on deposit in the ten years. Over the ten-year period your deposit account would recover somewhat, climbing from €66,035 when you moved it out to €72,942 (remember that, in all these scenarios, we're ignoring taxes and charges so as to keep it simple).

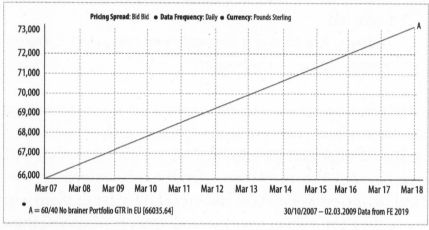

The growth of a bank account earning 1 per cent interest.

The recovery after the fall.

But what journey would you have taken if you had left it in the investment? What if you'd done what every long-term investor should do when they set up an investment properly, one they have faith in, which is to invest and forget? OK, so you met with Gerry the day that the market bottomed out. Your timing was awful and you picked the worst time ever to move to cash. You took the entire hit and then you sat on the sidelines as the market went into recovery mode.

Not only would your investment have recouped all the losses, but it would also have broken through your original investment and ten years later it would have been worth €176,225. Look at the chart above: the money went up and down. You may still have had some scary days but the less often you looked, the more positive an experience you would have had.

Remember: invest and forget!

The power of perception

I have a huge amount of respect for the way Carl Richards, the financial planner and *New York Times* columnist, communicates complex financial ideas in an easy-to-understand way. He uses simple sketches to explain things. One of the best I have ever seen is one he wrote when a friend called him and asked him to address his staff because the stock market was tanking. It had dropped by 500 points, which is a lot, and was now sitting at 17,537, and they were worried about the money they had invested in their pensions (401ks in the US).

In simple terms, investing in a stock market – in this case they were talking about the Dow Jones Industrial Average (DJIA) – is an easy way to invest in a collection of companies. The DJIA is made up of 30 companies based in the US. The S&P 500, for example, is made up of 500 companies listed in the US – they are in the top 500 based on their financial size. When each company share price moves it affects the movement of the index. When Carl received the call, the companies in the DJIA had tanked the previous day and had lost something close to 3 per cent of their value, thus dragging the index down by 500 points. In general, fluctuations of up to 1.5 per cent, maybe slightly more, are considered a normal day on a stock market.

Carl replied, 'The Dow Jones is over 17,000?' He was so surprised because a few years earlier, when the market was at about 12,000, he had made a conscious decision to stop listening to the daily news about stock markets, so when he heard it was sitting at over 17,000, he was genuinely shocked. This is the perfect example of invest and forget. He had missed everything that had gone on. He had a perception in his head that the market sat around the 12,000 mark and missed all the 'noise' between 12,000 and 17,537.

His perception of 17,000 was different because he was looking up at 17,000 whereas his friend's staff were looking down at it and so it was a huge cause for concern for them. But it was the way he communicated it to the staff members that blew me away. When he went to see them, he drew two simple charts on the whiteboard:

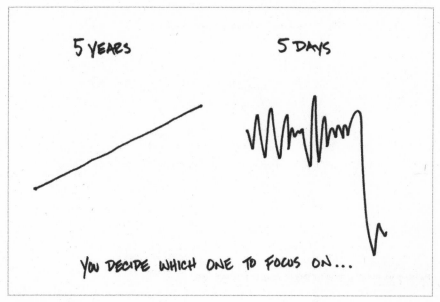

5 YEARS 5 DAYS

YOU DECIDE WHICH ONE TO FOCUS ON...

Courtesy of Behavior Gap

He had a straight-line experience. He started at one point and finished at another. His friend's employees had a squiggle experience. Yet they also started at one point and finished at another.

The person who experiences the squiggle on the right will start and ultimately finish in the same place, but their experience of the journey is completely different. It is volatile, emotional and head-wrecking. Checking your investments all the time means subjecting yourself to far too much pain.

Predictably unpredictable

Markets go up and down, but they are always on an upward trend. Declines happen – they are expected, and they are temporary. The next graph shows the same portfolio over different periods of time: one month, one year, ten years and twenty years:

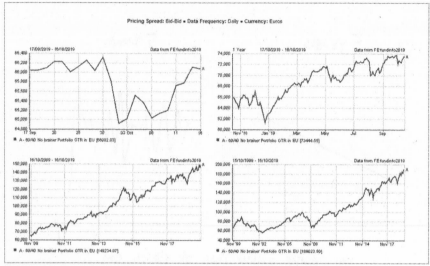

Markets go up, markets go down, but they are always on an upward trend.

But notice how the ups and downs get smoother the longer out you go. You have a choice when you invest: you can look at it regularly and drive yourself around the bend or you can leave it alone, not check on it and get the same financial result. Less is more.

Investing with confidence

To be able to invest and forget, however, you need to have absolute confidence in your investment. You can build confidence in your investment portfolio by having it set up right in the first place. Here are some of the ways you can do that.

'Time in' not 'timing'

Time, as seen above, seriously dilutes the risk of any investment. The longer you leave it the more it smooths the returns out over time. Put the money in when you have it and take it out when you need it and hope there is a long time in between. Even people with practically unlimited resources also struggle to pick the perfect time to get into and out of the market, so what chance do you have? Don't go there.

Sometimes I bring clients through a full financial planning process and we spend considerable time going through our investment philosophy. They get it – or at least we think they do. They accept they have too much money sitting in cash, that it needs to be invested long term. But invariably, they ask if we shouldn't wait. Perhaps the markets are a little too volatile right now? We tell them they want to time the markets, which is not a good idea. They don't see it as such, but that's exactly what it is. No bell is going to ring at the bottom.

I remember being at an advisor conference a few years ago when the speaker asked the audience to write down what the biggest threats to the world stock markets were going to be that year. The answers were if Brexit happened and if Trump got elected. Guess what? Both happened and the markets did fine.

The speaker then explained that they had asked a group of advisors the same questions the previous year at a similar conference and at that time the top answer was – Crimea. Now what was going on in Crimea at the time was scary, with potential for it to become a serious global political issue. If you were planning on investing your life savings, you may have been spooked by the thoughts of a world war looming and you may have held back.

By attempting to time the markets, you're also betting against the odds. An investment portfolio that is 100 per cent in shares will go up 75 per cent of the time in a calendar year. So if you wait for 12 months there is a 75 per cent chance you are going to be wrong. As well as this, you now know that with a 60/40 no-brainer portfolio there is a 99.6 per cent chance that five years from today your investment is going to be positive. That is regardless of what is going on today. They are just the odds.

The five-year rule, revisited

The five-year rule is the rule that I mentioned earlier (see page 94). It says if you're going to spend the money in your bank account in the next five years then it belongs in your bank account. But if you are not going to spend the money in the next five years then it does not belong in your bank account.

To have confidence in your investment portfolio make sure you have an investment time horizon of at least five years. Yes, you can do well in shorter periods but as we detailed above there is a 99.6 per cent chance of getting a positive result on a 60/40 portfolio over a five-year time horizon. I am happy with those odds versus the near-certainty that inflation will eat your money over the same time period if you leave the money on deposit.

Be wary of any advisor who is suggesting they can get you good results in less time than this. You need to be prepared for the long haul. Applying the five-year rule regularly is a key element to becoming good with money. You need to look at the money you have sitting on deposit at least annually, but ideally every quarter, and decide how much you have in your bank account right now and how much of it you'll realistically spend over the next five years. If any of that money won't be spent in the next five years, get it out of there and invest it long term.

Passive versus active

When deciding to invest, one key thing to consider is if you will go active or passive. Passive, in this context, does not mean sitting back and doing nothing. It simply means are you going to buy the benchmark. Active, on the other hand, means you are going to pay a fund manager to beat the benchmark.

Having confidence in how your money is invested can be helped by minimising the risk as much as possible. One of the things I have learnt as I get older is that no one can let us down if we expect nothing from them. It's quite a cynical view to take on life but it's the perfect perspective to have when deciding how to invest your money.

At a conference a few years ago one of the exhibitors' stands had a jar of jellybeans on the table beside the pens and phone chargers and other branded merchandise. Jellybeans are typical of these events; you end up eating them all day because every stand seems to slip you a few as you walk by. But this exhibitor was doing something different with their jar of jellybeans. They were raffling off an iPad for whoever could guess how many jellybeans were in the jar.

What was interesting is that this wasn't just another way of gathering attendees' business cards, although attendees didn't know this yet. The fund house that was doing this raffle were out to prove a point: that is, don't try and beat the market. They did prove something very interesting. After the conference was over, the results came back from the guesses. They found that one person guessed there were 409 jellybeans in the jar and somebody else guessed there were 5,365. The average guess, however, was 1,653 jellybeans in the jar. The actual answer was that there were 1670. The average *was only 17 jellybeans* away from the real answer.

Now take this lesson and apply it to investing. According to Dimensional Fund Advisors, who carried out the jellybean survey and manage about $600 billion of people's money worldwide, there is €328 billion transacted every day on stock markets. That is across 82.7 million transactions.

I don't know how many people took part in the jellybean survey, but I would argue that there were not 82.7 million people in the raffle for the iPad and they still got close to the correct answer. We know that there are 82.7 million transactions per day on stock markets. That is a lot of guesses as to what the right answer is for a share price. When you have the power of 82.7 million decisions to harness, then I think you are getting close to the right answer.

Fund managers

Something you have to decide when thinking about how to invest your money is whether or not to use a fund manager. A fund manager's job is to try and beat the benchmark. They go to work each day and decide what shares they want to buy and what shares they want to sell in the hope and expectation that when all their decisions flush through they will do better after charges than the benchmark.

They choose their benchmark, for example, the S&P (Standard & Poor) 500, the Eurostoxx 50, the ISEQ, the FTSE or the Dow Jones. These are the representatives of the international financial markets you hear about on the radio. The S&P 500 is the top 500 companies in the US based on their financial size, the FTSE 100 is the top 100 in the UK, the ISEQ is the top in Ireland and so on. As an investor you have two options: you can buy the market by investing in one or all of the indices or you can pay a fund manager to try and beat the benchmark.

I believe it is possible to pick a good fund manager, but it is not probable, so in private practice we don't do it. The odds are stacked against you if do decide to use a fund manager. Lots of people dispute how numbers are calculated and the reality is you can use numbers to prove anything you want. Having said that, one piece of research using data from Morningstar (a fund analytics company widely used by professionals) found that out of 2,414 US-domiciled mutual funds, between the time they started looking at them in 1998 to the end of 2018 20 years later, 58 per cent of them had disappeared altogether. This doesn't mean they disappeared with people's money. Disappearing might mean they merged with another fund or morphed into something else or it might mean they went out of business. But when a fund goes out of business the assets are usually protected and so too are the investors.

Worse still was that out of all the initial funds, only 23 per cent survived and beat their benchmark. Taking all this into consideration it would suggest to me, based on this one study, that you have a 77 per cent chance of picking a fund manager who does not beat their benchmark. Those odds are not great.

Most fund managers would completely dispute the findings – and so they should, their livelihoods depend on it. Yet those managers are the ones with a good track record. Logically, those with a poor track record would tend to stay quiet.

But even a good past fund performance wouldn't be enough to convince me to invest with them. I once attended a conference in Switzerland, where the Nobel laureate Kenneth French spoke via video link. He was working on numbers at the time that suggested a fund manager needed a track record of over 70 years to prove that their fund performance was down to skill and not luck. Most careers don't last that long, particularly in the fund management world, so that's kind of hard for a fund manager to prove.

There are exceptions to this. For example, Warren Buffett has been around a while and has become incredibly wealthy on the back of his own fund management. Yet it could be argued that Warren Buffett created his wealth and track record at a different time for the fund management industry and that it could never be repeated. At this stage his fund has so much power that it doesn't just invest by buying shares in companies; it buys shares in companies and often takes a seat on the board as well, which means his fund can influence change and drive up share prices.

As well as Buffett, there are a few other fund managers who are believed to be able to consistently beat the market. This puts incredible pressure on them to perform. One example is Neil Woodford, who was lauded by the UK media for years. His fund performance backed it up. However, he made some decisions that have resulted in him stepping down completely and in investors not being able to access their money. It's still unclear what they will get back.

Don't take a bet

A fund manager is a little like a Premiership football team. But no club wins every year and no club can tell you with certainty where they will finish in the table next season. Now take this to another level and imagine you had to try and predict for the next 20, 30 or even 50 years where Liverpool would finish in the Premiership. Then take everything you have in your pension and savings and place it on your prediction. To me that is what you are doing when selecting a fund manager: you're taking a bet that the one you picked will consistently win the Premiership or at the very least qualify for Champions League football. If you choose a club and they finish further down the table, you would have been better served deciding to support every club instead of one club. In other words, buying the index.

Why should you hang your financial future on one individual? Why invest with somebody who would guess that there are 406 jellybeans in a jar that has 1,670? Why take the risk that they are having a bad day, month or year?

The world moves markets: every day, every transaction moves share prices up and down. No different than anything else that is for sale in the world, demand pushes prices up and lack of demand brings prices down – shares work in the same way. If lots of people try to buy a share in a company, then the share price of that company will go up. If lots of people try to sell shares in a company, then the price will go down. Millions of transactions a day means that share prices are going up and down all the time, but the result of all those transactions is what nobody can argue to be a fair price at that moment, for that share.

And you can piggyback on all those decisions. How? By investing in the index – a fund that tracks all those companies. You can buy the index and capture all the decisions in one purchase.

Buying the index

Buying the index is often called passive investing. This is not to be confused with doing nothing. Passive simply means you invest and let the market determine what is bought and sold. (This is opposed to active management, where a fund manager decides what is bought and sold.)

If a fund manager is not for you then you might decide to invest in an index. But which one? Should you buy the US, UK or European index? What about emerging markets?

We use historical data when guiding our clients through our investment process. What I am about to explain is how we decide where to allocate the shares portion of an investment portfolio. In about two-thirds of cases, the shares element represents 60 per cent of a client's portfolio. Since shares are the driver of the returns, this decision is crucial.

We look at the returns different countries' stock markets have achieved in different years, going back to 1999. For example, in 1999, New Zealand had a return of 32.3 per cent. This means if you invested €100 in the New Zealand stock market on 1 January 1999, by 31 December it would have been worth €132.30. In contrast, if you invested in Belgium that year, your €100 would have grown to €100.40.

When we go through this with private clients, we lay out the stock-market performance of the developed world's countries for the next five years, ending in 2003. We ask them to imagine that it is the end of 2003. They have some money and they're about to invest it for 15 years. Looking back at the previous five years, where would they put that money?

This can be an interesting moment, particularly if the client has an occupation that requires critical thinking and informed decisions. These critical thinkers tend to struggle with this question. We push them to tell us where they would invest, and we assure them we won't judge them.

The thought process can throw up some interesting observations. Some people go for Sweden, because it was on top in the most recent year. Others go for Finland for the opposite reason. Others suffer with what is called home bias and choose Ireland, and then others pick the US, just because. I have had people pick Switzerland because they like the colour of the flag, or Portugal because they've been there. Once they have picked, we show them all the data and we follow the country they've chosen. For simplicity, let's just pick Ireland.

When you look at Ireland's performance relative to other countries over the full 20 years, it was top of the pile sometimes and bottom of the pile at others. It spent a little time in the middle, too. Ireland's performance – and every other country's performance – was random. Nothing about the previous year or years gives any indication of what any country is going to do the following year. It is a random walk. I cannot tell what is going to happen next year based on the past.

If you think the developed world performance is confusing and random, best of luck trying to decipher a pattern from emerging markets.

When we invest clients' money, we do so in both developed and emerging markets. This means we can guarantee to our clients that we will have them invested in the best-performing countries. We can also guarantee that we will have them invested in the worst-performing countries and everything in between. We don't want our clients guessing what is going to happen next year. We don't need to: let the world decide and go with it. We invest our clients' money across the entire world – all the different sectors and countries. It means that they spread their risk, which will reduce the risk they take and smooth out their return.

Market cap

Once we have decided that we are splitting the shares portion of a particular portfolio across all countries we then have to decide how much to put into each country. Below is a map of the world, but this map is not based on landmass, which is the size of a country – it's based on the size of each country's stock market:

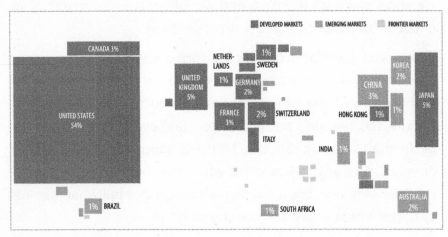

The size of each country's stock market.

Market capitalisation

Every company has a value, called the company's market capitalisation. Simply put, if you bought 100 per cent of the shares in a company, the market 'cap' is the amount of money you have to pay. Every company at any given time has a finite number of shares in existence.

Imagine a company (Prosperous Ltd, for the sake of argument) was listed on the stock market and there was a total of 1,000 shares in existence in the world. If the price per share was €1.50 then the market cap of Prosperous would be

$$1,000 \times €1.50 = €1,500$$

The market cap of Prosperous Ltd would be €1,500, so you could buy 100 per cent of Prosperous for that price. Now if the share price of Prosperous rose to €2 per share then the market cap rises to €2,000 (1000 x €2).

When putting an index together it is often weighted based on a company's market cap that is listed on that stock market. For example, at the end of 2017 it is estimated that there were approximately 3,600 companies listed in US stock exchanges in the United States. When making up an index like the S&P 500, all these companies would be listed based on their market cap. The higher the market cap, the higher up the index they would go. S&P then draws a line at 500 and only invests in them. The FTSE 100 would draw a line after the largest 100, Eurostoxx 50 after the top 50. At one point Allied Irish Bank (AIB) at the height of the boom was big enough to just scrape into the Eurostoxx 50 but they didn't last too long before they fell out again. But it does give you an idea of the size of the companies in these indices.

When you look at the market cap-weighted chart you can see that based on financial size, at the end of 2018, 54 per cent of the world's companies listed on stock markets were in the US. But what also jumps out at me is that 95 per cent of the financial world could not care less about Brexit. The UK only represents 5 per cent of world stock markets. Yes, it is possible that what happens in the UK affects the rest of Europe, but looking at it on this scale shows you that Brexit is not the end of the entire world.

Of course, Ireland is more affected by what happens in the UK than most countries, but this is a good example of how the media bubble we live in here makes the problems we face feel global when in fact they are local.

Occasionally a client might say they want to invest heavily – up to 30 per cent – in one particular country such as India, because they think it's the next China. The financial world, which consists of 82.5 million transactions a day, thinks that India is worth 1 per cent of the share element of your portfolio and yet this client is suggesting it is worth 30 times that. Those 5,436 jellybeans immediately spring to mind. In addition, at the end of 2016, the market cap of the Indian stock exchange was €505 billion. The value of Apple on the same day was €587 billion. Now if I told a client to invest 30 per cent of their share portfolio in one company, I would hope they would think I need my head examined.

The Irish perspective

Another example is when people want to buy a property as an investment. Look how big Ireland is on the map. At the end of 2016 our market cap – again that's the value of all the companies listed on the Irish stock exchange – was €91 billion. This compares to the market cap of all the companies listed on US stock exchanges being valued at €24,109 billion. Now dive deeper and consider the ridiculousness of the idea that the three-bedroom house around the corner from you valued at €282,000 is a better investment than any other investment in the world. 'You can't beat bricks and mortar' is a saying that gets to me, because you can. How is it possible that the best investment in the entire financial world happens to be next door to you?

In Ireland we have an obsession with property. The economist David McWilliams stated in a TV show recently that almost 85 per cent of our wealth in Ireland is tied up in land and property. Don't get me wrong, property does have a place in an investment portfolio, but the balanced sector average in Ireland right now for professional fund managers is to have about 8 per cent in property – not 85 per cent!

We like investing in property because we can see it, touch and feel it. We can drive by it and see that it exists. But I also believe that we're kidding ourselves when it comes to the true cost of holding property. We look at what we pay for it and what we sell it for, and we decide that the difference is what we 'made off it'. We ignore the running costs, the taxes, replacing the boiler and all the other things that go with it. But that's OK, because apparently you can never go wrong with property.

The other issue I have with property is its liquidity. All our investments are liquid. If you need to access money you can usually do so within a few days. Try selling a property in a hurry and see how long it will take to get the money even if the market is booming. But what's worse is if you only need some of the money tied up in a property – you can't just sell one of the bedrooms.

We need to be a little more realistic about what returns we get from property but also the hassle that comes with it. With new clients who have large property portfolios, we are slow to encourage them to sell an existing property and incur costs on that but we are also strong on ensuring they don't add property to a portfolio if they are already overexposed. It's the same principle that we apply if they come to us asking whether they should invest more money in India.

You need to balance where you invest your money around the world and property, in my opinion, is not the solution. Neither is going all in into India. I have yet to come up with a better way of spreading money invested in shares than across a market cap-weighted portfolio. This means that you end up with the shares being split (see chart above) 54 per cent US, 5 per cent UK, 3 per cent France and so on across the world. These balances change each day but by investing in a fund that adjusts for this regularly you don't need to worry about keeping up.

Once you have decided that you're not going to invest using a fund manager and that you are going to go passive with a market cap-weighted portfolio then you can do other things to improve your chances of success.

> *Top tip: stocks and shares are the same thing. Technically 'stocks' is used when referring to a holding of different shares in different companies whereas 'shares' refers to owning a small piece of one company.*

Small and value

When we invest a client's money, we like to tilt some of the shares element of their portfolio towards small and value stocks.

Any stock market can be divided up into four categories: small and large and value and growth.

The difference between small and large is straightforward. Research has proven that over long periods of time small companies outperform large ones. This makes sense: if a company is making €200 million per year and wants to grow by 10 per cent, they need to find €20 million. But if a company is making €2 billion a year, they need to find €200 million, which is harder to do. Smaller companies are also higher risk, so you expect more return.

Value and growth stocks are a little harder to explain. Growth companies are those expected to achieve high or fast levels of growth in the future and tend not to pay out dividends. They are often fast-moving tech companies that use the profits to reinvest in the business rather than paying it out as a dividend. Value companies aren't necessarily the opposite of this, but it is often the case that they are out of favour for some reason. What I mean by this is that the share price has been driven down to the point where you could buy all the shares in that company and it would cost you less than if you were to buy all the assets the company owns.

This is what Richard Gere did in *Pretty Woman*. Julia Roberts asked him to explain what he did, and he described how he buys all the shares in a company and then sells off everything they own and makes money off that transaction. Richard Gere was a value investor in the movie.

Michael O'Leary of Ryanair had a Richard Gere moment a few years ago when he was trying to buy Aer Lingus. The value of all the shares in Aer Lingus at the time was €650 million. In other words, if he went to the stock market and bought up all the shares in Aer Lingus, he would own it – or rather Ryanair would – at a cost of €650 million. But if he immediately sold all the assets Aer Lingus had (the Heathrow slots, the buildings at Dublin and Shannon airports, the aircraft they owned, everything), Ryanair could have gained €750 million. They could have made €100 million on the transaction. Ultimately Ryanair was prevented from buying Aer Lingus because it was deemed that they could hold an unfair advantage by controlling too much of the industry, and could potentially use that to their advantage.

A company often becomes a value stock when the stock market overreacts to something like negative news about that company. Stock markets overreact to stuff all the time, both on the positive and the negative side, driving share prices too high or driving them too low. This presents an opportunity. When we invest client funds, we buy a market cap-weighted index along similar lines to the MSCI World index with 80 per cent of their shares allocation and then we tilt the rest of the shares 10 per cent each into small and value.

It's important, however, to realise that this tilt towards small and value is not active management. The chioce of funds we use to select the small and value stocks is based purely on evidence. You can see the size of one company in a market relative to another using the information that is provided publicly to everyone. You also have access to the value of a company's assets versus the value of all its shares when making the call on how to invest in value stocks. This is factual investing. There is no bloke sitting in a corner trying to figure out which CEO they like best and picking between companies. Empirical evidence has shown this type of investing works over time. But it does not work *all* the time. For example, between 2009 and 2018 growth stocks have outperformed value stocks:

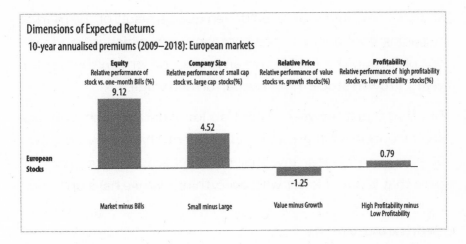

Dimensions of Expected Returns
10-year annualised premiums (2009–2018): European markets

There is evidence that suggests this is because of where growth and value stocks were ten years ago. Other evidence suggests that it is related to dividends.

Value stocks are shares that are out of favour with the market and so the market drives the share price down. Imagine the share price was €100 and the company was paying a dividend of €2. Then the market drives the share price down to €50 for some reason.

Now if you were the CEO of that company, you'd want to show that your company is strong, that the market is overreacting and that your share price is too low. The last thing you're going to do is reduce the dividend you pay out, so what was €2 on €100, or a 2 per cent dividend, is now €2 on €50, or a 4 per cent dividend. In the last ten years bond yields and deposit rates have been so low that people have been using high dividend stocks for income. This has distorted the market for these types of stocks. People bought them because the yield was high, driving the share price up and the dividend yield down, thus making them less attractive to the investor chasing the dividend. If, however, ordinary market conditions had prevailed, then the share price would have been driven up as a result of the market regaining confidence in the company with which it had fallen out of favour. This could have an impact on why, in the last ten years, growth stocks have outperformed value.

But that is just ten years. There is a lot of data that shows value stocks outperform growth and I am not changing a 20-, 30-, 50-, or even 75-year investment plan because of ten years of data that is out of kilter with everything else we have on hand.

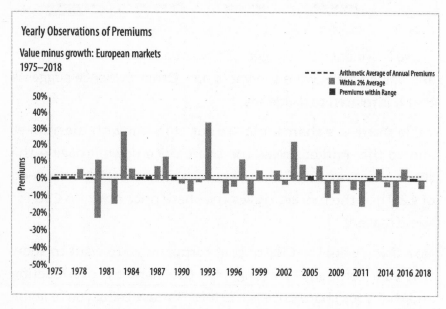

Yearly Observations of Premiums

Value minus growth: European markets
1975–2018

In fact, the longer you look at it over time, the more convincing it becomes that this way of investing works and that recent years were a blip, particularly when you consider the theory that the starting point ten years ago of value versus growth stocks was skewed. In the next chart you can see that value stocks outperformed growth stocks over a five-year period two-thirds of the time:

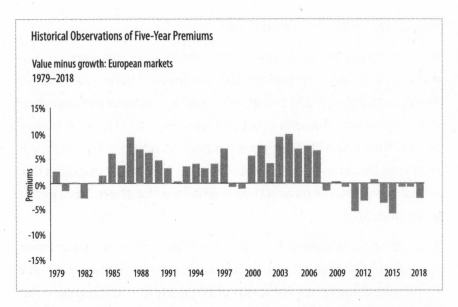

Historical Observations of Five-Year Premiums

Value minus growth: European markets
1979–2018

Top tip: shares give you the returns and bonds provide the balance.

Keep it simple

When you invest there are lots of things that you need to consider but keeping it simple, at a level that is understandable to you, is always a great option. As I have outlined in this book, buying shares in a company, owning a little bit of the world's biggest and most successful firms, is a simple concept to grasp. Alternatively, the idea of giving these companies a loan of your money in the form of a bond is also straightforward to understand provided you don't get too caught up in the minutiae.

I don't feel the need to invest a client's money beyond shares and bonds. Why would I, when shares give you the returns and bonds provide the balance? You don't need complicated, you need functional. You need an investment that's going to give you the returns to achieve your goals.

Asset allocation, revisited

We often get caught up in the intricacies of getting our investment right. Where should we invest? When should we invest? How much will the charges be? Is the fund manager the right manager? What is the tax treatment of this investment versus that one? The list goes on and on and on. The reality is that one decision over everything else has more impact than any of these decisions and that is what is what the industry calls asset allocation.

Asset allocation means how you divide your money up between, for example, shares, bonds, commodities (commodities, in simple terms, are things that come out of the ground such as gold, silver or oil), absolute returns and all the other things you can invest in. This list goes on and on. There is some dispute about the impact of asset allocation but the figure that comes up more often than any other is that 92 per cent of the return you will get from any investment is determined by the asset allocation.

What this means is that if your investment returns 10 per cent, then 9.2 per cent of that return came from how you split your money between the asset classes and 0.8 per cent came from factors such as when you put the money in and when you took it out (timing), whether you went with a fund manager and which one you chose, whether you just bought the index (passive versus active) and all the other decisions you made after you made the asset allocation decision.

New clients who have made investment decisions in the past tend to completely flip their investment decision process. They spend 92 per cent of their time trying to pick who to invest their money with and when to invest their money and 8 per cent of their time on the really important decision which is, in a simple portfolio, how much are they going to put into shares and how much they are going put into bonds.

Attitude to risk

Remember that shares drive your returns over a long period of time. The other stuff, like bonds, is only there to provide ballast. Even though there will be periods when our clients will make money on their allocation to bonds, there will also be times when they will lose money from being invested in those bonds. However, one of the main reasons why we don't put all of a client's money into shares and do allocate to bonds is to steady the ship. Investing is a rocky road, and we want to ensure that our clients stick with the plan.

If you accept that over long periods of time the shares element of your portfolio will be the driver of your returns, then you can think about it a little like drinking a glass or two of pure Irish whiskey. Some of our clients can drink neat whiskey and never have a hangover. But other clients have to dilute their whiskey (shares) with water (bonds) in order to avoid feeling sick.

If the goal is to feel happy and relaxed, then drinking straight whiskey – or investing 100 per cent in shares – will get you there quicker, but with a higher probability of something going wrong. If you dilute the whiskey with a little water – split your investment between shares and bonds – then it might take more time to get there but you are less likely to fall over along the way.

For example, if you invested 100 per cent of your money in shares on 12 September 2000, you were then hit with two major but temporary declines over the next ten years. If, however, you added 40 per cent bonds to your shares, then you broke even again just over five years later, in February 2006.

Pricing Spread: Bid Bid ● Data Frequency: Daily ● Currency: Euro

A = 60/40 No brainer Portfolio GTR in EU [33.55%]   12/09/2000 – 29/10/2013 Data from FE 2019
B = MSCI Word GTR in EU [0.14%]

However, you can see why investing in 100 per cent shares can be rewarding. For example, between March 2009 and April 2015, €1,000 invested in a 60/40 portfolio turned into €2,393, yet if you were invested 100 per cent in world stock markets over the same time period then you would have turned your €1,000 into €3,623.

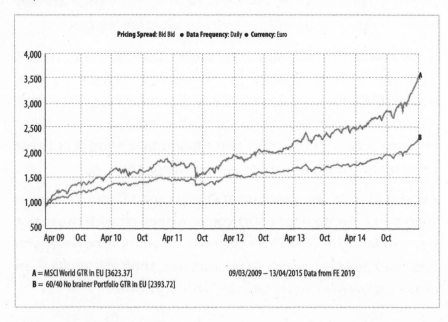

Pricing Spread: Bid Bid ● Data Frequency: Daily ● Currency: Euro

A = MSCI World GTR in EU [3623.37]   09/03/2009 – 13/04/2015 Data from FE 2019
B = 60/40 No brainer Portfolio GTR in EU [2393.72]

Over even longer periods, for example the type of time horizons we use when building a financial plan for private clients, shares can be even more rewarding. We build financial plans until 100 years of age. That means our 75-year-old client still has 25 years to go, our 50-year-old client has a 50-year time horizon and when you go down to clients younger than that they have a ridiculous length of time they will be invested for. The longer the time period the more you expect shares to reward you. But that is at a cost: the reality is the ride is going to be an awful lot choppier. I am not for one minute suggesting people should be going 100 per cent in shares; it is not for everyone.

In fact, based purely on people's attitude to risk surveys, according to Finametrica, who have carried out more than 1 million of these tests, only 1 per cent of people have an appetite for investing 100 per cent of their money in shares. And 38 per cent of people fall into the 60/40 portfolio bracket.

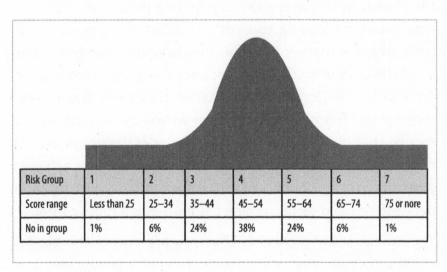

Risk Group	1	2	3	4	5	6	7
Score range	Less than 25	25–34	35–44	45–54	55–64	65–74	75 or nore
No in group	1%	6%	24%	38%	24%	6%	1%

The most overwhelming reason why most people should not invest all their money in just shares is not the risk of the investment itself but rather the investor themselves, i.e. you.

My belief is backed up by observing client behaviour over the years but also by an annual study carried out by Dalbar, in which they look at the difference between the performance of a fund versus the performance of an investor in those funds over time.

In this study, investors lag the market by around 5 per cent. In other words, if the market achieves 8 per cent the investor gets a return of 3 per cent. When I discuss this with clients, they immediately jump to the assumption that it is charges that kill the returns, but the difference is typically put down to investor behaviour, particularly hopping in and out of the market at the wrong times. The Dalbar study has been running for 25 years and consistently shows the same results, which is that investors don't do as well as the funds they are invested in.

The 2018 study really highlighted that investor timing is a major factor in damaging their returns. Investors got into and out of the market at the wrong times, meaning they tried to protect themselves by moving to cash and didn't move enough into cash when the market fell. Then they were too heavily invested in cash when the market rebounded and so missed the bounce. For example, in October, when markets did badly, the average investor lost more than the market whereas in August, a good month, they didn't gain as much as a result of their position. The net result was that in 2018 alone the average investor achieved a net return of -9.42 per cent versus the market, which lost 4.38 per cent. As I said earlier, timing the market is a fool's game.

The Dalbar study highlights that you are one of the biggest threats to your own investment. How much you invest in shares versus bonds and the mixture of the two is a great way of ensuring you protect yourself by not taking on so much risk that you stay up at night. Sleepless nights over investments should not be part of your life and end up with you waking the next morning and deciding to pull your money out of your investment because you are scared. Having enough exposure to bonds, although it may reduce your long-term returns, does often mean that you stick it out with your investment. Sticking it out to the end always trumps pulling the plug early and sitting on the sideline.

However, one of the things that scares me is that in the financial services industry, in general, attitude-to-risk surveys are what professional advisors use to decide how much in shares a client should have. If the client does one of these surveys they come out with a score typically between 1 and 7, with 1 being the safest, i.e., a cautious or no-risk investor, and 7 a high-risk investor. Using these tests as a roadmap to design a portfolio would mean somebody with a score of 7 would end up with a concentrated portfolio of 100 per cent invested in shares.

The advisor often then uses this score to determine how much of your portfolio to invest in shares and how much in bonds and so on. These surveys, which are actually more akin to psychometric tests, ask the right questions to find out how much are you willing to watch your money go up and down or, put more precisely, the test works out exactly how much pain you are willing to take. Once the survey knows your pain threshold it then creates the perfect portfolio for you, a portfolio that inflicts that pain on you repeatedly. It is daft, in my opinion.

To me, attitude-to-risk surveys are simply a starting point when it comes to investing a client's money. There are two other things that I believe need to be considered when building an investment portfolio, and they are capacity for loss and required rate of return.

Capacity for loss

Capacity for loss is where you test to see what would happen to your investment – or even better to your entire finances – in a temporary decline. When we do this for clients we take all their finances into account and run a simulation of the crash of 2008. (And yes, there will be a time when markets will go through what they went through in 2008 and the five years after. That's how markets work, they go up and down, but they're always on an upward trend. We expect them and we build them into a financial plan and most importantly we don't react when they do happen. We invest and forget.) In most cases the decline damages their long-term wealth. If it damages it to a detrimental point then we take this into consideration in conjunction with the other two factors (attitude to risk and required rate of return) and it is likely to influence us to reduce the amount of shares in the portfolio.

But what can often happen when we run the simulation is that a temporary decline of the magnitude of 2008 happening again would improve our client's financial future. This can be confusing – try and explain to a client that a major financial crash would be great for their finances! The reason for this has to do with where in the investment cycle a client happens to be at the time of a crash. If you are investing fresh money from your wages into pensions or your investments, or even moving from cash to investments before during and after these events, it means you pick up cheaper shares and when they recover, which they do, you benefit from the cheaper shares you bought when those shares bounce.

Think about it another way. Imagine going into a car showroom and seeing a car you really like. It costs €50,000. You go home to think about it and decide it's definitely the car for you. You get up the next morning, head for the car dealer and when you get there the salesperson you spoke to yesterday says that the same car is now on sale for €40,000. You were going to buy it at €50,000 so you're delighted to get the same car for €40,000. You're going to buy the car, right?

Why then, when you are about to buy into a portfolio that has you spread across somewhere north of 3,000 companies, and the value of them drops overnight, would you decide to wait until the price goes back up again? That makes no sense. I struggle to find another rational example where people want to buy things because the cost of them is going up and don't want to buy them if the cost is going down.

Some people argue that running a simulation like 2008 is pointless because provided you stay invested it doesn't matter how low the market goes. If you just stay in the game then it will always recover over time. I agree with that. But I still think it is a good idea. To me it's like getting on a plane. I will watch what I will have to do in case of an emergency because I feel more comfortable knowing what I must do if something goes wrong. I believe if you know that temporary declines do happen, and you can see how your finances are going to react when they do that, you then will know what to do when they do happen. Which is?

Invest and forget. Do nothing.

Required rate of return

This, to me, is the most important thing when it comes to constructing an investment portfolio. It is also the most difficult calculation to work out. It is relatively easy if you are working out one thing, for example, I have pot of cash X today and I need to grow to Y over the next ten years. You run the maths and you find out what growth you need after tax. But when you're taking a more holistic approach to your finances then there are many more moving parts and how they interact with each other needs to be considered. We do this calculation using a powerful piece of software but ten years ago I was doing it through Excel. Ultimately you could also do it yourself if you have a handle on how Excel works and what you are trying to measure.

The reason I believe required rate of return is the most important – over capacity for loss and attitude to risk – is because it determines, while ignoring the other two, what return you need to get on your investments for the financial plan to work. In simple terms it is accepted that the more risk you take the more return you expect. Note I said the more risk you take the more return you expect – that doesn't mean taking more risk means you *get* more return, it just means you *expect* more return.

If, when you run the calculations, you find you need a high rate of return, then if you want your plan to work regardless of your attitude to risk or your capacity for loss you may have to take on more risk than you expected. Otherwise you must change your plan to accommodate the fact you are not going to achieve the required rate of return.

Alternatively, if you find that you don't need to take as much risk as you have an appetite for, then you can reduce the risk. Reducing the risk, simply put, is reducing the amount of exposure you have to shares and increasing what you have going into bonds. If you don't need to take risk, why would you take it on? The only reason is greed, and greed can be healthy. But increasing the risk because of greed can often result in regret and then when markets do hit a temporary decline you are more likely to question your decision and pull the plug on your investment. Or at the very least you'll move it to a safer asset split at precisely the wrong time.

Required rate of return when combined with capacity for loss and your attitude to risk should lead you to create a portfolio that is tested for when stuff goes wrong, is in line with your limitations of pain and, most importantly, is designed to achieve your goals.

Rebalancing

Timing the markets is for people who think they can make quick money by getting in and out of the markets – that's not investing, that is betting. The problem with trying to time the markets is that what you want to do and what you should be doing are two completely different things.

Most of the time we want to buy shares that are going up in value in the hope that they will continue to go up and we want to sell shares or bonds that are going down in value because we are worried they are going to continue to go down. We make our investment decisions based on fear, greed and panic. The reality is that doing the opposite, which is selling our winners to buy our losers, is something that has been proven to work well, particularly at times when the markets are going through a rough patch.

That is why a rebalancing strategy is essential. It forces and even automates the decision to sell your winners and buy your losers. How it works is, if you start with a 60/40 portfolio and the 60 per cent in shares grows and the 40 per cent in bonds loses money over time then the split could drift to 70/30. When you rebalance, you sell the 'extra' shares and buy the bonds and bring things back to 60/40.

This also has the added advantage that it means it keeps your investment in the same risk band you started out with. If, having reviewed your attitude to risk, your capacity for loss and your required rate of return, you found that the ideal portfolio for you was in fact a 60/40 portfolio, just because markets move you to 70/30 does not mean that your entire outlook for this investment has changed. Markets don't change your goals; they get you to them.

How often you rebalance and how you do it is an interesting debate. Some people like to do it on a drift basis, in other words if the portfolio moves by 2.5 per cent or 3 per cent in any direction it automatically gets rebalanced back to the original split. This is hard to achieve because unless the fund you invest in does it automatically then the product providers in Ireland, with one exception, struggle to do this from a technology perspective.

The other option is to do it monthly, quarterly or annually. You can find lots of research to suggest which way is best or the optimum frequency. Just make sure it happens regularly and don't get caught up in it. Automate it so you don't let emotion stop you from doing what is right.

There are lots of things you can do to set up your investment to give it the best chance of success: asset allocation, passive or active management, tilting towards small and value stocks, not timing the market, rebalancing and when you have it all set up then remembering to do nothing when things go wrong. But you can also help your investment success by not picking an investment based on its volatility, controlling costs or even trying to chase the next big thing.

Volatility

Volatility is a fancy word for how risky an investment is: how much an investment goes up and down by, how rough the ride is. It was around the time of the global financial crisis, when the financial world was in turmoil and investors were trying to flee the market, that investment professionals started the mantra of 'control the volatility'. It sounded like they knew what they were talking about; it made the investment world seem sophisticated and complex.

But markets go up and down, all the time. An investment professional should not be trying to control the markets. There are 82.7 million transactions on markets every day – how is anybody going to control that? What the investment professional should be doing is trying to control the investors' behaviour in regard to markets. They should be preparing their clients for the inevitable ups and downs, helping them to learn what to expect.

Volatility became mainstream in the investment world because people were scared and unprepared for the turmoil around the global financial crisis. The reaction to that was to give people assurances that that turmoil was now being controlled. Volatility is a measure of the 'riskiness' of an investment. It is backward-looking and allows you to compare one fund to another and to see how much risk it took in the past. When clients are putting their money into an investment, they want to know how risky it is. But I have never had a client come to me and say, 'Eoin, how well managed was the risk on that investment?' All they want to know is what the return was.

Volatility has its uses in that it can tell you, when comparing two different funds, which one took more risk to achieve its returns. As for funds that are marketed on the basis that they are controlling the volatility? Caveat emptor.

Costs

The only thing that is certain to detract from your investments is costs. If you're weighing up two identical investments and one is more expensive than the other, then hands down the best thing to do is to go with the cheaper one. Cheaper, when it comes to investments, isn't always better, but it usually is. In Ireland, the two ways you're usually charged when you invest in a pension, long-term savings plan or investment are the allocation rate and annual management fee.

Allocation rate

Allocation rate is a charge on the way in. A 100 per cent allocation means that all your money is invested. It's not unusual for an investment to get 97 per cent allocation – this means that 3 per cent of the amount you invest is taken as a charge at the start of your investment. If you're investing €100,000 then €3,000 is taken out and only €97,000 is invested. This is typically either paid to the financial advisor or kept by the product provider.

Sometimes the charge can be 5 per cent and you only get 95 per cent allocation. Our starting point for our clients is that they get 100 per cent, i.e. there is no upfront charge, but we have the advantage that we charge a fee, so we have our base costs covered.

The government now hits most long-term investments and savings plans with a 1 per cent levy. This was introduced during the financial crisis; most investment houses do offer to cover this 1 per cent levy and also give you 100 per cent allocation after the levy is paid for. When they do, they usually protect themselves by making sure that, if you take the money out in the first three, four or five years, they hit you with a penalty to recoup their costs. Penalties can also be used when the allocation rate is lower than 100 per cent but the product provider pays commissions to the advisor, and therefore wants to ensure that if you decide to pull the plug they won't lose out financially.

Pensions can also incur fees. In fact, you'd think that if you're in a large corporate pension scheme this wouldn't be the case, but some of the most shocking cases I have seen were in big schemes. I came across one client in his sixties, who was single, approaching retirement and earning €65,000 p.a. He realised he needed to really try and boost his pension pot and had started paying in €1,000 per month into his pension. He was planning on paying an extra €1,000 per month to bring it up to €2,000 per month – so this was on top of what he was paying into his main scheme, bringing him close to the maximum allowable contributions to his pension.

I was disgusted to see how much he was being charged. Every month the pension provider was deducting €120 from his €1,000. He was getting 88 per cent allocation with a 12 per cent charge being taken off every contribution.

When I started in this industry it was not unusual for 50 per cent of the first year's payments to disappear in charges and then, from year two onwards, 5 per cent to be taken. But 12 per cent every year was ridiculous in this day and age. Had he increased his premium to €2,000 he would be paying €240 per month in charges before his money was even invested. I moved his pension and he started getting 100 per cent allocation on the €2,000 per month.

To put that in perspective, let's say I have two clients, Client A and Client B. Client B is paying €2,000 per month into their pension and getting 100 per cent allocation (let's ignore the other charges) and manages to get 4 per cent per annum growth on their pension. Over five years, their pot will grow to €132,598.

If Client A is getting 88 per cent allocation on their €2,000 per month and they too get 4 per cent per annum growth, their pot will be €15,912 less than Client B's will be in five years' time. In fact, just to break even with Client B, Client A would need 9 per cent growth per annum. That's 5 per cent more than Client B, per annum, over five years.

Annual management fee

This is another charge you might get hit with where, instead of it coming off the money you pay in, it comes out of the value of the accumulated fund. It doesn't matter if the fund is going up or down – the charge is a percentage of whatever is in the fund. It is usually deducted daily but some companies have part of it come out daily and part of it taken at different intervals during the year. Typically, it is not unusual for you to pay in the region of 1.5 per cent per annum in annual management fees.

Yet it is widely accepted in Ireland to quote fees by way of the 'annual management fee' – this despite legislation that requires fees to be also quoted by their OCF (ongoing charges figure). OCF takes into account the transaction costs associated with investing. It is considered more transparent and more inclusive of all costs and therefore I would have a preference for looking at it over the annual management fee. Essentially they both reflect the costs of a owning a fund, it is just OCF includes more of the costs than the annual management fee would.

There are some issues around the OCF and how it is calculated, one of which being that it assumes the highest levels of commissions are being taken and exit penalties apply even though they may not in your particular contract. But in general the OCF is a more transparent reflection of all the costs associated with an investment and is certainly a useful way of comparing two options, even if you take into account that some of the fees reflected may not apply to you.

Other charges might include policy fees, which are usually €3 or €4 a month, so over a 40-year pension this will account for somewhere between €1,440 and €1,920. You also may be hit with a pensions board levy or other administrative costs.

It's important to have a frank discussion with the person you engage with. Accept they need to be paid and find out who is paying them and how much. From March 2020 all advisors regulated by the Central Bank will be required to discuss commissions with their clients when talking about new products. This is something you should welcome and is another layer of transparency. I don't believe there is a problem with commissions provided the client knows how much the advisor is being paid and by whom.

The next big thing

People sometimes ask me about cryptocurrencies or another new trading platform that will help you buy and sell the best shares on the market – complete with an algorithm to make you millions. The reality is that there is no next big thing. When your colleague at work is talking about the next stock or you get an email about something incredible that is going to change the world, sit back and think to yourself, if this is a sure thing and we're all going to get rich quick, then why isn't the person who told me about this just keeping it all for themselves?

There are two factors at play when you are being offered a chance to get into an investment at the ground floor. One is that it's just an all-out sales pitch – the company is trying to offload shares or pieces of this investment and usually they're doing it because they're getting paid well to do so. The other is that if somebody you know has already invested in this next big thing it makes them feel less stupid if they can convince other people within their peer group to do the same. This is not malice on their part – they're simply looking for confirmation bias. Unfortunately you're probably doing it because they signed up to it and so you felt they must be right.

Investing properly is all about being boring. You don't need shiny new things all the time. You need a strategy, conviction about what you're doing and an expectation that things go up and down all the time. You should, where you can, tilt the portfolio towards investments that are proven to work over a long period of time, such as investing in small and value stocks.

But most of all you need to have enough confidence in your investment or pension that you can sleep at night – and know for sure that you are going to invest and forget.

Building the pot

It's great to have money in investments, or a pension pot you need to invest more wisely, but what if you need to create that pot in the first place, or you've started but need to give it a bit of a lift? There are two reasons we don't invest as wisely for the long term as we should. The first is that most people don't want to engage with financial advisors. The second is that most people don't know how to invest properly. The two are very much connected. There are methods to investing properly and the government also gives you a helping hand along the way. But before we go there, we should look at why people don't like to engage with advisors. I take several calls a day from potential clients whose past experiences all have a similar theme. (Granted, I only hear about negative past experiences because if I was hearing about the good ones then the client would not be ringing me – they would be meeting their existing advisor).

When I first started advising clients early in my career, it was less about financial planning and more about, well, just trying to sell products. Don't get me wrong; selling products has come under the spotlight in recent years and is being painted as an absolute negative in the financial services industry. It isn't just the products themselves, it's also the pushy salespeople. It's the client feeling they're 'just being sold to'. This does not serve us well as an industry and is certainly not a pleasant experience for the client.

In my practice we don't 'sell' products, but we do 'buy' products on behalf of our clients. When I say products, I mean things like investments, pensions, life cover and specified illness cover. The process we have set up and the fact that we charge fees means that nobody in my office can or would feel the need to 'sell' a product to a client. The client's financial plan is at the heart of everything we do. If it says the client needs to buy a product then we go to the market and find the absolute best product to meet that need. Conversely, if it says the client does not need a product then we will also tell them that.

When we do buy products, we get paid by the product providers. We are transparent about how much and by whom we get paid. But here's the thing: I have set the fees in my private practice to a level that there is zero pressure on anybody in my office to generate more than just the fee from a client engagement. Product sales, done the right way, do have a place.

Pensions

Pensions get a bad rap. Back in the day I worked for a large life company with over 300 salespeople. One thing I learnt very early on was not to mention the 'p' word on the phone. When making calls to prospective clients, instead of asking if I could come and chat to them about pensions, I'd get a much better reaction if I phrased it like, 'I want to show you how to extract wealth from your business in a tax-efficient way.'

There is no better place to invest your money than into a pension.

Your mind might be jumping right now to stories you've heard about people who had their pensions wiped out, or were ripped off in charges. They are all true. But those stories are more about the crap advice they were given and nothing to do with the pensions themselves.

Saying you don't want to invest in a pension because your friend had a bad experience is a bit like saying you don't want to eat ever again because your friend had food poisoning. Getting good advice from somebody you trust when setting up your pension is key to getting it right. Every story I have ever heard about pensions that blew up had one thing in common – they lacked diversification. Typically, they were invested in one share, like a bank share, or in one property. Then there are the stories of people who didn't blow up completely but lost loads of money and then pulled the plug and moved the pension pot to cash, never to recover. That is a crap idea. Don't do it.

Let's look at the simple maths. If you are a higher-rate taxpayer, then every time you put money into a pension it costs you €6 to put €10 in – in other words, you pay €4 less in tax. That is a 66 per cent rise on your €6 investment. If you are on the lower rate of tax, then you are turning €8 into €10.

Another way of looking at this is imagining you are on the higher rate of tax. Imagine you took home €1000 per month after tax. You decide to invest €100 into a pension. The €100 comes out of your wages but your take-home pay does not drop by €100. Your take-home pay goes from €1,000 down to €940 – a drop of €60 – and yet you got €100 into your pension. It cost you €60 to invest €100 into your pension. The reason is because you paid €40 less in tax.

As the money goes in there's another bonus, because you won't pay any tax as your investment grows. Every few years we hear of people who move abroad just before selling their company in Ireland, in order to avoid paying tax on their business profits. You can do that without the need to move – just start a pension! (And don't think for one second that the person who moved abroad before selling their business didn't bring a ridiculous pension pot with them too.) And the best bit is, when you stop working and you retire, you get some of the money out tax free too. That's all you need to know about pensions. You get tax relief on the way in, they grow tax free and you get a tax-free lump sum at the end. It's that simple. You won't beat it doing other things because in most cases whatever else you want to do with your money can probably be done inside your pension anyway.

For example, I remember sitting with a client who said to me he didn't like 'investing in funds and stuff', that he had his own share portfolio where he chose his own shares and it was absolutely kicking the ass of his pension returns. He prefers to do it himself. Now without getting into all that's wrong with almost everything he said there, I was able to get to the root of his issue regarding pensions with one question. I simply asked him why he wasn't buying the shares inside his pension rather than outside of it. His answer was the classic I don't-like-pensions-because-my-friend-lost-money-on-his response.

I stepped him through the maths. Let's say he wants to buy €10,000 worth of a particular share. He's done his research and he's going in for the kill. He believes it is going to make him a fortune. He uses his after-tax income to buy the share. This means on his level of earnings, taking USC, PRSI and income tax into account (let's just say around 50 per cent), he needs to earn €20,000 of salary so he has €10,000 after tax. He ploughs ahead.

The share does well, and he sells it a year later for €20,000. He pays 33 per cent capital gains tax on the growth and ends up with €16,600 tax paid to roll over into his next investment. Remember, he's going to roll it over because he's making these investments instead of his pension, so he has a long-term view.

The alternative to the above is if he takes his €20,000 and invests it into his pension. He immediately reduces his tax bill by €8,000 but he does still have to pay USC and PRSI. He buys €20,000 worth of shares. They double, but this time the growth is not subject to tax because it is inside the pension. He now has €40,000 inside his pension to roll over into his next investment.

It was a lightbulb moment for the client. He realised he could invest €20,000 for the same cost as €10,000 was currently costing him. I explained that this was the case but the maths were slightly off – you see, what he would be doing is investing using his before-tax income instead of his after-tax income.

But we do need to consider two things: firstly, the USC and PRSI he has to pay, and secondly, the fact that this money is inside his pension and at some point, he will need to get it back into his hands. What we were looking at is two scenarios: on one hand he has €16,600, tax paid, available for him to spend today if he wanted. On the other hand he now has €40,000 sitting inside a pension.

To level the playing field, let's look at what would happen if you were taking that €40,000 out of a pension (25 per cent of your pension fund can be taken out tax free up to a maximum of €200,000). So taking this investment in isolation he would get €10,000 or 25 per cent of the €40,000 out tax free.

The balance of €30,000 can be taken out whenever he wants (subject to one restriction, which I will ignore for now to keep it simple) but when he does take it out it is subject to income tax, USC and PRSI. Using the same 50 per cent rate, after tax he has €15,000 plus €10,000 from the initial lump sum but we do have to allow for the fact that when he invested the €20,000 originally, he got the income tax back but not the rounded-up €2,000 PRSI and USC.

To summarise, my friend paid €23,000 in tax by doing what he did *outside* his pension when he could have paid just €16,600 in tax by keeping the transactions *inside* his pension. In even simpler terms, there is no more tax-efficient way of investing than with your pension.

Planning your pension

When you're planning your pension, you first have to allocate your money to what you might need over the next five years, beyond those five years but before you retire, or not until retirement. You want to try and fill the pension pot first but only after you have satisfied the other two options, which are long-term savings and deposit account.

When the money goes into your pension or into your long-term savings the rules of investing are exactly the same as above. You decide on asset allocation (page 134), passive or active (see page 117). Will you tilt towards small and value? How are you going to rebalance the portfolio?

Having the same strategy across all your investment, savings and pensions pots means you remove the risk of what you are doing right on one side being taken away by what you are doing wrong on the other. As I said at the very start of this section, many people will disagree with my investment philosophy, but I am supported by Nobel laureates and empirical evidence, so I am confident in my suggestions as to how to invest money. You also need to be confident when the markets go through a temporary decline, which they will every 3–5 years.

Investing this way, whether it's through your pension or your long-term savings, does not require large amounts of money. Most savings and pension providers have products that allow you to invest for as little as €100–€200 per month. The rules of investing are applied equally whether you are investing €100 or €10,000,000. If they work for one, they work for the other.

But how do you start, and what are the things you need to look out for when it comes to building up a savings and pension pot?

Obviously the first thing you have to do is to identify what money you can afford to save. When you go through your spending rules and become conscious with your money you'll usually find you have more than you thought. You then look at where the money is going short, which is less than 5 years (deposit account); medium, which is 5 years-plus (long-term savings plan invested in the likes of a 60/40 portfolio); and long, which is for post-retirement (this is your pension pot and is invested in the same way you invested the long term savings, using a 60/40 or 80/20 or whichever portfolio is best suited to your needs).

Once you know where the money is going and how much you are going to save then you must make sure you are mentally prepared to stick with it. It is not unusual for us to come across people who described themselves as brilliant savers but for whatever reason have lost the will to keep going and are now worried about slipping into debt (see the example on page 31).

The typical couple who fall into this are often a couple who are a few years in their new house; before the house they saved like mad to get the deposit together. They then moved in and the first mistake they made was they used up all their savings getting the house, paying the deposit, covering legal costs and all the furnishings. They were wiped out.

Think about what has happened here: they saved for years, it was really hard. But they did it, they built up a huge pot of cash and then in one swoop they wiped it out. Yes, they got their house and the sofa they always wanted and maybe even the good TV. But their experience of savings was that it's hard to do and then it is gone, completely.

The half rule

> *Top tip: I would always suggest that, with some very limited exceptions, you never spend more than half your savings in any one go. This works because it means you never hit zero, but also each time you spend half, the amount you're spending becomes smaller and smaller. It encourages you to build the savings back up so you can spend a decent amount again.*

This is a great rule for kids who come into money as a result of communions, confirmations or big birthdays. Don't let them spend more than half and then get them to leave a gap before they can spend again. It's also an invaluable lesson for an adult. When you don't wipe yourself out you're not starting again from scratch and you also have some left over in case of an emergency, meaning you have less chance of going into debt.

However, the spend–half save–half rule may not always apply, especially for major life purchases such as buying a house. In this scenario you'll need to use common sense. I would suggest you save the deposit, the legal fees, the cost of furnishing the house – including things like the big shop you do when you first move in – and then duvets and soft furnishings that cost a fortune but are often forgotten at planning stage. Once you have calculated all this add 10 per cent in case of overruns and then decide how much extra you need to leave behind in your savings. It has to be a figure that will keep you motivated to continue the savings habit. It needs to be in the thousands, not in the hundreds.

A good way of helping rekindle the savings habit is to give your savings pot a name. When you're saving for a home you can visualise having your own space, furnishing it how you want, painting your kitchen – it's a goal you're excited to work towards. Apply the power of this to anything you are saving for. For example, if you're saving for next year's holidays, then put it in a separate vault, wallet or subfolder of your bank account and call it 'Holiday to Greece' or wherever it is you are going.

What this does is connect you to that goal. You can visualise it. Giving your savings a positive identity has a much better ring to it than just 'savings' or worse still, 'rainy day fund'. This takes on even more importance when you're a couple. You both decide your goals together, name them together and work towards them together.

Imagine your partner says, 'Let's go out', and you say, 'We have no money', and they say, 'Sure just use the rainy day fund, it rained today'. Now imagine they say, 'Let's go out'. You say, 'We have no money', and they say, 'Sure just use the Kids' Christmas Fund/Holiday to Majorca/House Deposit'. Doesn't that have a whole different ring?

Having said all that, when deciding on goals, one thing that is extremely important for a good savings habit is to have lots of little rewards built in. If you have a medium-term goal like saving for a deposit for a house it can be boring putting your life on hold to reach that goal. You need to keep yourself – and your partner, if you have one – motivated in order to have any chance of achieving a long-term savings goal.

Sprinkle your path with little rewards along the way. You might decide that while you are saving for the main goal in three years' time you are not going to go on any big foreign holidays but instead you sprinkle in some weekends away. These mini goals keep you going and dramatically improve your chance of success. And if you're in a couple, they also reduce the chances of you killing each other along the way.

Timing is all

The final tip I have for keeping you on the straight and narrow when it comes to saving money, whether that is for pension, medium- or long-term savings, is to make it part of your essentials – your rocks – and to do it at the start of the month.

The average person in Ireland saves over €300,000 in their working life, yet the average pension pot in Ireland is believed to be only €100,000 and about 66 per cent of people have no pension at all. So where does this €300,000 get saved? Unfortunately, it is saved and given to the banks. The average mortgage is approximately €200,000: add interest to that and you are up over €300,000 in total repayments over a standard term. We treat our mortgage repayments as an essential and we do it every month, without fail (for the most part, for most people), at the start of each month. We get paid and then we pay the mortgage. If only we did the same with our savings.

Too often I speak to people who tell me they can't save any money – they just don't have any left at the end of the month to save. When I delve into it, they tell me their strategy is they get paid, live their life on a tight budget for the month and then they try and save whatever they have left at the end of the month (see page 25).

Save at the start of the month, once you have been paid. And don't just save – pay all your other standing orders, such as the mortgage or rent and utility bills. Then whatever you have left is yours to spend – guilt free – on whatever you want, safe in the knowledge that you can enjoy today because you're looking after tomorrow.

SECTION 4

PROTECTING IT ALL

What happens if I die?

Having a financial plan is wonderful, but the best financial plan in the world is useless in the event of sickness and death. Thankfully, you can hedge a financial plan using what are known as protection products, such as, for example, specified illness cover, income protection and life cover.

Many people are uncomfortable talking about these products, whether it's because they're difficult situations to imagine being in, or because of their cost: they feel they are protecting themselves against something that may not happen during the term of the policy. Strangely enough, these people can feel that if they got to the end of the policy and they haven't claimed then they were hard done by. I look at it differently. To me it means you're not dead. That's a decent result. Protection products are an essential part of your strategy to ensure the success of your future financial plan and to make sure that you don't clean out the family finances in case of sickness or even death.

These policies are quite straightforward. They can be made complex with bells and whistles, but you don't need to get caught up in that stuff. At their core is the principle that if you get one of a list of specified illnesses then the specified-illness cover pays out a lump sum; the same applies if you die. Income protection works on the basis that if you can't work due to illness or injury it pays you a wage until either you return to work or you retire, whichever happens first.

Combining these policies with a financial plan means that if things go well the plan works out; and if things go wrong – provided you have adequate cover – then one, two or all of these policies kick in and the family will survive financially. If a client has a lot of assets then our calculations can often show that they don't need any of these policies but the reality is that it is almost impossible to come through one of these events without doing at least some damage to your wealth, no matter how wealthy you are.

Wealthy or not, you do need to consider how your family are going to survive financially if you were to die. Research by Royal London suggests that 3 out of 10 people in Ireland have made no provision for their families in the event of their death. And of the people surveyed, almost 20 per cent believed that their life cover was how their families would survive financially.

Different life insurance companies have different claims statistics each year. They vary year to year but also from one company to another. One company, relatively new to the life insurance market, had an average payout of €190,000 over the last five years. Yet the claim statistics from one of the largest life insurance companies last year showed that their average payout was just over €75,000. There are also companies with an average payout of €54,786, and a further one with an average payout of €45,639. The average payout out has nothing to do with the claims process of the life insurance company. It is simply a case of the company paying out the amount that the policy holder took out themselves. There are no aggregate figures on the average life cover payout number, and you can see the variance. But, for argument's sake, let's just round the numbers and use a figure of €100,000.

Even if it were as high as €100,000 I don't believe €100,000 is near adequate to provide any decent level of protection. If your partner dies and you were paid out a lump sum of €100,000 and you drew an income off it, you would get €613 per month. This is ignoring taxes and assumes 4 per cent growth, but it also means that at the end of 20 years all the money will be gone. Think about that for a minute. The average wage in Ireland is currently €38,871. A married couple in a one-income household would expect to take home €643 per week after tax – a €100,000 lump sum would provide less than this weekly income for an entire month before tax.

If your partner dies and you are married to each other or in a civil partnership, provided you don't start living with a new partner, social welfare kicks in and you will be paid what is called a widow's, widower's or surviving civil partner's (contributory) pension. You do need to be married or in a civil partnership to qualify. I had a client who was terminally ill and had been with their partner, whom they loved, for a long time. When we discussed how this social welfare benefit worked, they felt, for lots of reasons including the money, that they should get married. When the person did die the family got the social welfare pension and are still in receipt of it today. There is no waiting period. If you are married when you die, and you satisfy the other criteria, then it will be paid.

The amount paid out is based on how many dependents you have, if any. But a young family of one adult and two kids under twelve years of age would get €1,197 per month. There are rules to how you qualify for this but in general if your deceased partner had been working and paying PRSI on a consistent basis the probability is you will qualify.

What if your partner was the sole earner, with €100,000 in life cover and on the average wage of €38,871, and also had the appropriate PRSI contributions for you to qualify for a full widow's, widower's or surviving civil partner's pension? You might think you'd be OK if they were to die. In fact, what happens is that the gross (before tax) household income is going to drop from €3,239 per month down to €1,810 – that is, a reduction of €1,429 or a whopping 44 per cent.

But the reduction also assumes that the €100,000 will be paid to the family. The reality is that in lots of cases the money is paid to the bank to clear the mortgage and the family never gets it. I have had countless amounts of conversations with people about what would happen financially if they died and the response is often 'Sure the mortgage would be cleared, they would be grand.' When you start to talk them through it, they start to realise what the impact of losing an income would be on the family. But it also highlights the fact that in most instances we have life cover to protect the bank if we die but we don't have any cover to protect the family.

Why do we believe the bank is more important, or more vulnerable financially, if we die, than our own families?

The cost of running a household

Let's assume you earn the average wage of €38,871 per year and are 38 years old and you plan on working until the age of 68. Ignoring inflation and pay rises you have yet to earn a total of €1,166,130 – that is, of course, if you don't die between now and then. Having the mortgage cleared off or even getting a life cover payout of €100,000 would not go near replacing that lost income if you did die. Whatever way you look at it, the household is going to suffer financially.

It's accepted that you spend some of your own money on yourself (an estimate suggests we spend about 25 per cent of our money on ourselves). But you cannot take a blanket approach to this. If you're single and earn €200,000 per annum you may well spend 100 per cent of your wages on yourself. If you're married on €200,000 a year you may spend €50,000 per year or 25 per cent of your wages on yourself but if you're married with four kids in a one-income family and you earn €30,000 per year it's unlikely you spend 25 per cent or €7,500 per annum of your income on yourself.

In my opinion if you earn the current average wage of €38,871 and you have a family, 25 per cent is too much. This is where common sense can be used. I would say about €3,000 per annum, which is €250 per month, is a reasonable number to take.

Working out your household's costs

The 25 per cent rule is handy enough, but if you want a true figure then you need to look at your expenses. Identify those that are specific to you – such as clothes, personal entertainment and car-running costs – and deduct them. Then look at the general costs: with four of you in the house, for example, you can take 20 per cent off the food shopping bill. Look at your regular household expenses – gas, electricity, Wi-Fi, bins – and add them up. This is how much it will cost to run the household when you die.

Be conscious that some of the expenditure will go down but some costs may also go up. When we do insurance costings for a couple, we often find, in the first instance, that there is no financial shortfall because they have either enough savings, enough cover or a combination of both. We then go through the findings with them. We outline their financial position and show them that based on the initial findings there is no shortfall, they have enough cover.

Questions you need to ask

But we then delve deeper. What does that person envisage happening to the family after their death? For example, would the surviving partner continue to work? Would they cut their hours? Would the cost of childcare need to be increased in the budget? What about future career progression? Would they be able to travel with work? Would they even want to? Would it hinder their ability or desire to chase bigger jobs and promotion?

These questions are universal, but the answers will be unique to each couple. It is essential to discuss them. A good place to start is to ask yourselves, 'What would life look like for you if I were to die and how would that impact us financially?'

Whatever about trying to work out what costs will be gone or reduced if you die prematurely you need to look at what costs would go up. You can do some simple maths to get to the figure quickly without going through your expenses line by line.

Take your salary, deduct 30 per cent for tax (a blended assumed tax rate to simplify things), deduct your mortgage repayment and then if you are married or in a civil partnership and have been paying PRSI for years, allow for the basic widow's, widower's or surviving civil partner's pension. When you get to the final number add in extra expenses you identified after your chat. The last thing to do is to take this number and multiply it by the number of years you have left in your working life. An example might look like this:

Salary		€60,000.00
Less		
30 per cent tax	€18,000.00	
Mortgage repayments	€14,400.00	
Basic social welfare	€ 10,550.80	€42,950.80
		€17,049.20
Plus		
Extra childcare	€6,000.00	€6,000.00
		€23,049.20
Multiply by years left in work		30
Require minimum level of life cover		€691,476.00

You then work out what other life cover you might have from work, or policies you have taken out, and deduct them from the number you have come up with. Make sure your mortgage has life cover on it – and even if it does, don't take that amount away from your final calculation. You've already allowed for it when you got rid of the mortgage repayments above.

A good financial planner will carry out a more detailed check into your life-cover needs. They'll check the value of your other income sources and what investments you have and build them into the calculations. They'll also assume the money is invested after you die and isn't left being eaten by inflation in a bank account, which reduces the amount of cover required. But if you want a rough idea as to whether you're over- or underinsured, the above calculations are a great starting point.

Human capital

What this calculation highlights is a major factor known as your human capital (see chart above). You start with your salary, do the deductions and add-backs and are left with a number – in our example it is €23,049.

Human capital is the present-day value of all the money you have still left to earn in your career. For example, if you earn €100,000 per annum and you have 20 years left in your career then, ignoring pay rises, you have 20 x €100,000, which is €2,000,000 of income left to earn. In this case you have €2,000,000 of human capital. Human capital is the value of all your future income today, but it is quite different from your net worth. Net worth is the value of all your assets minus any loans you have today. Net worth is the amount of money you would bring with you on a plane to Rio if you sold off everything you owned and cleared off all your debts.

Obviously, the number of years you have left in your career has a huge bearing on how much human capital you have. Typically, the younger you are the more human capital you have. But the older you are, even though you have less human capital, the higher your net worth. Life cover is designed to protect your human capital. Although dying at any stage in your career will result in you damaging your long-term financial future, if you have had an opportunity to build decent net worth this can be used by your family instead of life cover to ensure they survive financially if you die. This means that as you get older, and ideally build net worth, your need for life cover reduces.

It's not unusual for our clients to have built up enough in assets to negate their need for life cover. This is particularly true for young people in their 20s and early 30s who have a huge amount of human capital yet are working in industries like tech and have accumulated large amounts of shares in those companies. It's always incredible to me to sit across from these clients and watch them realise just how valuable the 'free' shares they have been getting are worth to them over their long-term future.

Inheritance tax

Unfortunately, if you do manage to reach this point it often creates a different issue. If you have large amounts of net worth with or without large amounts of human capital then this often indicates to me, as a financial planner, that you will likely have a need for a different type of life cover, called section 72 (page 177). A section 72 plan is used in the event of death so that the people you leave your money to receive it tax paid instead of having to pay the inheritance tax on it.

According to current Capital Acquisitions Tax (CAT) legislation, in your lifetime you and your spouse can leave your kids a total of €335,000; that is a *combined* total from both you and your spouse to *each* of your children. If you have two kids then they can each get €335,000 or a combined total of €670,000 from you and your spouse. At one point this allowance was over €500,000 per child. During the global financial crisis the government reduced it down closer to €200,000. They have committed to bring it back up over €500,000 but they are doing it painfully slowly.

Anything you give your child when you are alive is deducted from the amount you leave them on death and when you go over the €335,000 allowance, they will have to pay tax at 33 per cent. Let's say you leave them a total from you and your spouse of €435,000. They will have to pay tax of just over €33,000. They will start to accumulate interest on any unpaid taxes within 1–12 months depending on what time of the year the assets are passed over to them.

The common misconception is that your home won't be included in this calculation. There are circumstances where the family home is exempt, but on the whole it isn't. If your child lives with you because they never moved out or they moved back in because you have a care need, then it is possible the value of the family home is deducted from the estate before calculating the tax. But what lots of people don't realise and can often get a shock from is that if the child inheriting the family home owns property anywhere else in the world, when they inherit your house the family home does not become exempt. This includes if you give them an investment property on your death at the same time as the family home.

This can seem incredibly unfair: you could have a six-year-old living with their parents and the parents die. The child's life is in turmoil and the taxman can jump in and tax them on their home. This is because if the parents have other properties, and the six-year-old inherits these properties on the death of their parents, then the child will be subject to tax on the family home. It only starts to make sense when you consider why the exemption exists in the first place. My thoughts on this are that Revenue look at it and say if it is your home, we don't want you to be left homeless because you have to sell it to pay tax. But if you have a property anywhere else you can live in, anywhere in the world, then you won't be homeless, so either sell the family home or sell one of the others and clear the tax.

Tax avoidance not tax evasion

There are clever – and entirely legal – ways tax planners get around this. It's tax avoidance, not tax evasion! For example, if you have two properties and two kids, they will give each of the children a property so the one who gets the family home, assuming they are exempt on the residency rule, won't be hit with tax. Of course, the other child will need to be compensated if they are paying taxes and the intention is that both get equal after-tax amounts. Then there are the more complex situations where there are lots of assets and it can be beneficial to incur the cost of setting up a trust or even family office. These structures effectively create a separate legal entity and can be more tax-efficient for passing large amounts of money, but the costs can be prohibitive.

There are other, more straightforward things you can consider that can reduce the tax bill on the people you leave money to. For example, if you have a successful business that is operating and making money, it means the taxman is happy – because when you do well, they do well. That is why there are generous reliefs available if you pass the business to your children, including on death. The rationale, in my opinion, is the same as the home exemption in that Revenue don't want to put a good business that is paying taxes and possibly even giving people jobs out of business because they have to pay a tax bill. This means that if you qualify then you can deduct 90 per cent of the value of the business before working out the tax to be paid. A business can be made up of all different types of businesses. Exemptions apply to farms too; however, some of the boxes you must tick to qualify as a farmer are a little different. These additional checks are there to make sure you are actually a farmer and not pretending to be one to evade paying tax.

There is one very clever avenue open to everybody that lots of people don't know even exists. If you have the money and you are concerned about inheritance taxes on your loved ones then you are allowed to give your children – in fact you can give anybody in the state – up to €3,000 per annum under the small gift tax allowance rules. This means you and your partner in any calendar year can give each of your children €3,000. So from a couple to one child that is €6,000. But not only can you give it to them, you can give another €3,000 to their partner and their kids and whomever else you decide is worthy of getting your money. Provided you don't break the €3,000 limit per person, and you do it within the calendar year, it is exempt.

Some people are aware of this allowance and go about writing a cheque once a year for their – usually adult – children to enjoy. But what many people don't realise is that although you must give it to the person – which means they become the legal owner of the money – they don't have to spend it. We often use specially designed savings policies that accumulate up the €3,000 allowances and then the entire pot gets given to the child sometime in the future. So you and your spouse could be putting €3,000 each, which is a total of €6,000 per annum, for each of your children into a long-term investment like the

60/40 portfolio mentioned earlier, for 10 or 20 years or even more, and when your offspring decide to cash in they will pay tax on any growth but the amount they receive will not come out of their €335,000 allowance.

You do have to be careful on a few fronts. Firstly, the money is their money once you give it to them. It belongs to them from day one. You might think six-year-old Johnny is a lovely little fella and start putting money aside for him for years and years. If at 18 years of age Johnny turns out to be a drug dealer you will not be able to stop him accessing his money. Equally, if you give the money to little Johnny in this way and you run into financial issues, you cannot take it back. Little Johnny may choose to give it to you but if he does then it could well become taxable under capital acquisition tax rules and unfortunately the threshold for little Johnny giving money to his parents isn't €335,000, it is only €32,500. If Johnny is going to give each of you more than this amount, then you will be paying tax of 33 per cent on what possibly feels like your own money.

The second thing you need to be careful about is what will you use the money for. Revenue allow you to pay for the cost of raising your child. Money you give them or use towards ordinary living costs, for example light, heat, food and shelter, is all allowable and does not come out of their €335,000 threshold. This also includes the cost of sending them to college.

But there's no point in putting money into a long-term investment using the €3,000-per-year allowance if the money is going to be used for college, since you're allowed pay for your child's education anyway so there is no benefit in using the allowances. If you haven't got college covered, I would suggest you are not in a position to start using the €3,000 allowance –

unless of course your child is not going to college or if they do, you're not the one paying for it.

'Reasonable' costs

There are things the taxman does not consider to be reasonable costs of upbringing and they are things like giving your child help towards the deposit for their house. Revenue also came out a few years back and declared that you cannot pay unreasonable costs towards your child's wedding. There are different interpretations of what different people have been told by Revenue when they asked for clarification of what 'reasonable' means.

One tax planner said they were told you could only pay for the wedding if it took place in Ireland, since it's customary for the father of the bride to pay for a wedding in Ireland but not if the wedding is abroad. Others have told me that you can pay for the meal but nothing else. I think the idea behind Revenue leaving it loose and describing it as 'reasonable' has intent. I always remind myself that the people who make and enforce these rules are often parents themselves: they don't want to be unfair on what should be a joyous occasion for their family, and they know the rules they make also apply to themselves. I think the idea behind the word 'reasonable' is that some very wealthy parents were paying for exorbitant weddings.

The easiest way to apply this rule is, to put it simply – don't take the piss.

I'm often asked by clients what is considered a 'reasonable' gift they can give their children. How will anybody ever know? The fact is that you can do anything you want in life: break laws, evade tax … whatever. There will be no consequences – provided you don't get caught. Unlike sharing your Netflix subscription password with your auntie, the consequences for not paying taxes are high and often shameful, resulting in heavy fines and public shaming. It's just not worth it. In addition, at some point, at what will already be a difficult time in their lives, your kids will sit in front of a solicitor and have to disclose the gift they got from you: do you really want to put that burden on them? That's your decision.

The other thing people often ask is if they can hand over money as a loan, instead of as a gift. Fair question, but Revenue only deems it to be a loan if it's paid back or at the very least there is evidence of intention to pay it back. But the loan may need to be called in if you die and it's still outstanding – if not, I think it's fair to suggest that whatever is left on the loan will be considered a gift. In other words, if you have €100,000 left on this loan when you die your child will either need to pay it off or the €100,000 comes out of the €335,000 allowance.

Section 72 policy

There's one silver bullet left when you've exhausted all the options to reduce the inheritance tax bill: in private practice we set up what's called a section 72 policy, named thus because it references section 72 of the Taxes Consolidation Act, 1997. This policy is essentially is a life cover policy that pays out a lump sum when you die. The difference is, this lump is used to pay the inheritance tax bill and if set up correctly it means your kids will receive their inheritance tax paid. It can be a tricky exercise getting the amount of cover you need to be exactly the same as whatever the tax bill will be, so the policy needs to be reviewed on a regular basis. The reality is that the policy will always pay out too much or too little. If it's too little then your kids will have to cough up a few quid, god love them. If it's too much the excess is paid into the estate and is, ironically, taxable.

You might think that these policies are expensive, but it's all relative. The cost is typically less than what you would pay for an ordinary couples policy because these policies pay out on the death of the second person: this is because usually on the death of the first person the estate passes to the spouse and there is no tax between spouses. But because the policy pays out on the second death it means that when the life insurance company is doing its assessment, they are looking at how long the healthiest person is going to live, and therefore the amount of time they expect the policy to last is longer. There have been cases in the past where one person of the couple was quite ill and couldn't get ordinary life cover, but because these policies are based on the second death and not the first, being ill does not mean you can't take out a policy like this one.

We do a few different calculations when assessing if this is something that makes financial sense for a client. The first is to look at the cost of the cover as a percentage of the value of their assets. This allows us to work out how much 'drag' the policy is putting on the growth of their assets – in other words, by how much their investments would need to grow to cover the cost of the policy every year. For example, if a married, non-smoking 60-year-old couple had an inheritance tax bill of €100,000, they could get a policy for €199.53 per month. Let's assume their estate is valued at €1,200,000. This means their assets need to grow by just under 2 per cent per annum to cover the cost of the policy. If their assets grow by 4 per cent per annum this policy will drag that back to 2 per cent when you consider the cost of the policy.

Another way of looking at this is that if it costs our couple €199.53 per month to cover a €100,000 tax bill using a section 72 policy we want to work out how many years will they have to pay into the policy to reach the point where they will have paid more than €100,000 into the policy. So, when will they reach the point that they will have paid more in than they will get out? In this case they will have to pay €199.53 for 501 months or almost 42 years to have paid more into the policy in premiums than their beneficiaries would get out in the payout. So, if this couple is expecting to live beyond 100 years of age this policy starts to make less sense.

A few years back there was a bit of a game-changer in the Irish section 72 market when one provider introduced a genius feature. Lots of people quite rightly live in fear of their inheritance tax situation, were they to die today, and plan on gifting the money over the years and more importantly, spending it on themselves. The government has also committed to continue to increase the thresholds, leading people to believe that if they give it a few years there will be no tax to be paid on an estate, rendering the policy pointless. The new feature took this into account and now at the end of every year from the end of year 15 onwards they give you three options. You can keep going as you were; you can stop paying and lock in an amount of life cover that will be paid out whenever you die; or you can take a refund of typically 70 per cent of all the premiums you've paid in so far. This meant that people who have a problem now have a feature that gives them options.

Ultimately you can do whatever you need to reduce your tax bill on your next of kin. Or you can do nothing. I find that clients have two attitudes. Some are anxious to protect their already heavily taxed money and will do anything to avoid extra bills;

others consider their kids to have done very well, and therefore fully able to pay whatever bill is due. But in my opinion, there is no better use of your money than spending it on yourself.

Getting sick

Even if you're not planning on dying anytime soon, don't assume you've no need for cover. The probability of you getting seriously ill during your working life is significantly higher than it is of you dying during that period.

Take a mortgage as an example. Most of us are forced by our bank to take out life cover to protect our mortgage but very few of us consider taking out cover to clear the mortgage if we get seriously ill. Specified-illness cover does just that – it pays out a lump sum if you are diagnosed with a serious illness that is specified on the policy's terms and conditions.

There is a long list of illnesses covered but the big three are cancer, heart attack and stroke. The numbers change each year but, according to New Ireland, approximately 80 per cent of all claims paid are for these three illnesses.

When you consider that the majority of claims are for just three conditions it always amazes me when I see one life company coming out saying they have better cover than the other insurers because they cover 56 illnesses and others only cover 52, or whatever daft number they are all up to now. It doesn't really matter. Some of the illnesses covered are nonsensical and the cynic in me would suggest are only there to make that company have a longer list than the other companies. Size isn't everything. For example, at one point a company started covering mad cow disease. Their competitors argued that the ridiculousness of having that covered was that the test to prove you have mad cow disease is done on the brain and would kill you if you did have it done. Specified-illness cover only pays out if you live for 14 days after diagnosis, so covering mad cow disease meant you could never be diagnosed with the condition and survive long enough for the policy to pay out.

Claim statistics

In general, the claim statistics on these polices are very good, with excellent transparency for the industry. Each provider produces their annual claims, which are widely scrutinised by both the industry and the media. It's different from company to company and year to year but consistently they pay out more claims than they reject. Sometimes new clients come to us because they had an issue trying to claim a policy and it was refused. When we look into it, in most cases, we find that the client never should have expected that claim to be paid and therefore it should not have been submitted.

The kitchen-table test

We like to explain to clients that for one of these policies to pay out the first test is what we call the kitchen-table test. A good starting point is to ask yourself, 'Has my spouse sat at home at the kitchen table wondering if I am going to make it through this?' If they have then it is a good indicator that you should investigate a claim. This isn't exactly scientific, but you get the idea. For it to be something you would claim for, it has to be very serious.

Specified-illness cover was once called serious illness cover but somebody successfully claimed against an insurer on the basis that even though their illness was not specified it was serious and they took out serious illness cover. Your condition can also be very serious – life-threatening, even – and yet not be something you could claim. In May 2018 I had a bad fall and I cracked my skull in two places, resulting in a brain bleed, which required surgery. It was serious, and it was life-threatening. It also passed the kitchen-table test. But I wasn't compensated. In fact, I didn't even submit a claim on my specified-illness cover because I don't believe I deserved a payout.

In contrast, a good friend of mine, Barry, who also runs his own financial planning practice, had a heart condition a couple of weeks after my brain surgery. It was serious, it passed the kitchen table test and he did get a payout on his specified-illness policy. The contrast between Barry and me is that Barry has a condition that will be there for life; he will be constantly monitored and will be back and forth to doctors and hospitals. In my case, although the recovery has been incredibly tough and even now causes me to have issues such as intense headaches, I will make a full recovery. If I had been left in a position where I was left with any debilitation it may have changed the situation as regards getting a claim paid, but thankfully I wasn't. Therefore, quite rightly, I got no payout and Barry did.

You could argue I suffered a financial loss and therefore I should have been paid something but the reality is that specified-illness cover is used more for capital expenditures, As an absolute minimum we want to leave our clients in a position that they can clear the mortgage if they want to in the event of a life-changing diagnosis. But having money for adapting the house and putting in bedrooms downstairs is also useful. Beyond that we want them to have enough money to enjoy life, as much as they can.

If you are diagnosed with a life-limiting specified illness, then one of the things we have seen in our clients is that their mentality shifts. They want more time having experiences with the people they love, and money helps them to fulfil what are often new priorities. But more than anything else specified-illness cover means you don't suffer a financial crisis at the same time as suffering a medical one.

There are situations where specified-illness cover won't pay out but where income protection does. Income protection pays you a wage until either you go back to work or you retire, whichever comes first. It will give you up to 75 per cent of your wage less whatever you get from social welfare. I say 'up to' because it depends how much cover you decide to pay for. Typically, it doesn't pay out for a period, which is usually the first 13 or 26 weeks, but it can be shorter depending on what box you tick when filling out the application forms.

Sometimes you can be sick enough to be out of work long term but not sick enough to get a specified-illness claim. One good example of this is mental health issues. Approximately 25 per cent of income-protection claims are for mental health-related issues; this would not be something you could claim under your specified-illness policy, but it is something you could claim on the income protection. That's because the criteria for successfully claiming income protection are if both your doctor and the insurance company's doctor declares you unfit for work.

Likewise, there are things that would be paid out under specified-illness cover that wouldn't be paid on income protection. I recently had a client who had a stent put in and had the required level of heart disease to get his specified-illness payout in full. But he was back to work, fit and well, before the 13 weeks on his income protection kicked in. He was happy to be back at work and happy with the fact he was recovered so quickly. He felt his recovery went better because he knew he now had money in the bank, and he could take his time if he needed it.

As you now know specified-illness protection pays you a lump sum and income protection pays you a salary until you go back to work or retire, whichever happens first. It is harder to get income protection than specified-illness cover and factors such as what you do for a living are taken into consideration. For example, if you are doing a lot of business mileage it can be harder to get cover because there are more things that can mean you will be out of work. If I work at a desk, I might be able to go to work with a broken arm, but if I am a taxi driver it's unlikely I can work.

Once they start paying a claim the insurance companies can be paying that claim for a very long time, and one of the side benefits to this is that some of them invest heavily in the people they are paying claims to. I know of one case where a person was put through college to retrain as an accountant and supported back into the workforce because they couldn't go back to their original job. I have also heard of cases where they are supported with mental and physical rehabilitation to help them back into the workforce. Don't get me wrong – the companies are doing this because if it works they are off the hook – but we also have to accept the person off work benefits too and when they do go back to work they are often eased into it with their income protection being turned off slowly. If the new job doesn't work out for whatever reason then the benefit gets turned on again immediately without the need to wait the 14 or 26 weeks.

Insurance companies have become much better at working with their customers; they also learn from negative feedback about their policies. For example, one of the things that people hate about the policies and will often laugh at in my office is the 'loss of limb' criteria. It is not good enough that you lose one limb: you need to lose two or more limbs for compensation. Other more contentious reasons are breast and prostate cancer. Breast cancer in situ – meaning it has not spread anywhere else such as the lymph nodes and is contained in one spot – does not get a payout. Neither does prostate cancer if it has not advanced beyond a certain stage. Statistics show the recovery rate is so strong when the cancer is at that level or contained to one spot that the policy does not pay out. This is not something that goes down well and so one of the things that insurance companies have done is to introduce partial payments of perhaps €10,000 or €15,000 – and the criteria for this are not as stringent as for a full payout. Obviously, in all of these cases, if the condition progresses it may mean a full claim is paid out.

Terminal illness benefit

Terminal illness benefit is something we have used with clients in the past. It makes a significant difference and often goes unnoticed. Basically, if you have a life insurance policy, regardless of whether you have specified-illness cover or income protection or not, and you are told you are going to die in the next 12 months, then the full life-cover amount will be paid out now instead of after you die. This allows the person who is dying to sort out their financial affairs and often provides them with the cash they need to enjoy the days they have left. I cannot stress enough the impact a life cover payout or specified-illness cover lump-sum cheque has on a grieving family or a patient who is suffering incredible pain. Taking the financial pain away at least is something that I get to do from time to time in these awful situations.

When it comes to protecting the client and their family, we take our job very seriously. The mantra we have is simple. Did we explain the situation to the client well enough that if they ring us in six months' time and tell us they are sick or their partner has died that we will be comfortable we gave them the right advice? I still don't rest until I have reviewed the file and I know either the client has the cover they need or has decided they didn't need it. I know that if something were to happen to one of my clients and I had not done my job properly it would haunt me. Selfishly, perhaps, I would prefer not to take on that burden, so I make sure the client gets the advice they need to make an informed decision and I put the decision on them, not me.

When a client has a restricted budget, this burden becomes even more of a responsibility. We must decide how to best allocate their budget between life cover, specified-illness cover and income protection. The hierarchy of needs is complex when it comes to specified-illness cover versus income protection but before we do any of that we make sure they have the life cover sorted. You see, when you're dead, you're dead – there's no coming back. Your income will stop – it might be replaced with pensions or other benefits, but you won't have any control over increasing your salary in the future or working harder to earn bonuses. You need to make sure first and foremost that if you die your family are financially secure. Once you have that covered, we look at a balance between income protection and specified-illness cover, and because you get tax relief on the contributions into income protection we often prioritise that. But not everybody will qualify for it and I would much prefer a bit of both than all of one and none of the other.

Getting your protection needs sorted might feel like a waste of money if you don't die or get sick during the term of the policies. But take it from me – I've seen the difference between the people who have this sorted and the people who don't. If you think it is costly to have it, try not having it and something going wrong.

Do you need a planner?

In 2008 when I set up Prosperous Financial, the very first core value we instilled in the business was that we would always do the right thing by the client even if it was not right for us as a business. We instil this value daily and it makes decision-making in the office easy. If somebody in Prosperous is unsure about what to do in a given situation they simply ask, 'What's the best thing for the client?'

Research carried out by Canadian firm Great West Life (who own Irish Life in Ireland) suggests that people who have a financial planner have 2.5 times the net worth of people who don't when they retire. I believe there are three main reasons for this:

The financial planner makes really good decisions to grow their client's wealth.

A good financial planner does much more than just make good financial decisions. A good financial planner is your therapist, career guidance counsellor, talker-downer off big financial cliffs and in many cases, becomes your friend. But do their decisions result in your having 2.5 times the net worth of people who don't use a financial planner? You still have to find, make or win the money on which those good decisions will be made.

People who have a financial planner have a decent net worth to start with – that's why they went looking for the advice.

Let's face it – if you're struggling, and I mean struggling to provide food and water and a roof over your head for you and your family, then your priority is hardly going to be to pay a financial planner over feeding your kids. Therefore, people who have a financial planner having 2.5 times the net worth of people who don't is slightly skewed because wealthy people are more likely to have a financial planner than those who aren't as well off.

The financial planner forces the client to review their finances on a regular basis, compare them to where they were and look at where they are going.

A financial planner gets you to review your finances regularly, ideally every year. A good financial planner won't only show you where you are now compared to last year, a good financial planner will hold you accountable to what you said you wanted to achieve with your finances since you last met. But the best financial planner will hold you accountable to not only what you said you wanted to achieve with your finances but also to what you said you wanted to achieve with life.

Whether you use a financial planner or not is your decision. If you choose not to, do yourself and your finances this one favour: write down what you own, what you owe, what you earn and what you spend. Store it somewhere safe. Then set a reminder for one year from today, and when the alarm goes off next year, do it again. That way you'll be able to see what progress you're making and ultimately, you'll be holding yourself accountable.

SUMMARY

Writing this book was an interesting process for me. I was asked to write down all the things I've learned over the last 20 years about money. What I have learned has come through my own professional experience, from running my own financial planning company and through observing my own clients, but it's also come through my own personal life experiences. The reality is that getting it all down in one book is nearly impossible, but I do hope that what you get from reading this is a better understanding of your own money.

Being good with money is all about getting the foundations right, about ensuring you have spending rules set out and all your rocks in place, so that you can then spend any money you have leftover – guilt free – on whatever it is you want. It's about becoming conscious of your spending, and acknowledging that Christmas, back-to-school time and, hopefully, going on holiday are something that happens every year. By planning ahead these things become something you can enjoy, and they don't need to carry any financial stress with them. It's also about realising that these spending rules and budgeting are not about being tight; they are important so that you learn to spend your money on the things that are important to you – things that you actually want and not things that some person in a marketing department wants you to buy.

I hope that by reading this book you will be able to differentiate the different types of debt. Happy debt, like getting a mortgage, for instance, is inevitable for all of us, and there should be no fear around applying for one or paying one off. Crappy debt, however, like personal loans, car loans and credit cards, is something to be avoided. If you are on that debt treadmill, the reality is that if you don't get off it by getting yourself out of debt, you will struggle to create real financial wealth for the future. You need to get rid of it. If you think you are disciplined enough, and you don't need ongoing encouragement or quick wins, it makes sense to clear your crappy debt using the traditional method. But if, like the rest of us, you are not superhuman and you need little wins along the way, then you might find using the snowball method of clearing debt to be the way that works for you.

By managing your day-to-day spending and tackling your debt, you will then find yourself in a position where you can start saving, investing and paying into your pension. If you are worried about starting, start with small contributions – perhaps so small you'd be embarrassed not to make them each month. The rules for investing are no different for €10 per month than they are for a €10-million investment. Remember, investing is simple, and when it is done right, it is boring. It's as easy as invest and forget.

Set your goals, stay on top of your day-to-day money, start investing in your short, medium- and long-term savings plans and begin to build your financial future. But once you have a financial plan in place, whether you do that by yourself or with the help of a financial planner, don't forget to protect yourself. A financial plan that brings you comfortably into old age with no money worries is not bulletproof if somebody gets sick or dies. You need to consider your life cover, income protection and specified illness needs.

Being broke is painful. Being rich and making a mess of it is painful. Waking up in ten years and wondering if you did the right thing with your money is painful. Becoming good with money is painful. Choose your pain: choose to stay where you are or fix it. I can promise you, though, that when you get to the other side and you have your financial plan set up, when you know that the future is looked after and you can enjoy today, guilt free, it is worth the pain it takes to get there.

GLOSSARY

60/40 portfolio: An investment or pension split between 60 per cent shares and 40 per cent bonds.

Absolute return: A style of investing that aims to give positive returns regardless of whether markets go up or down. It makes money by shorting what goes down in value and investing in what's going up. The objective is to make money off markets moving. The funds don't always achieve their objective!

Allocation rate: How much of your money in your pension, investment or savings plan gets invested. An allocation rate of 95 per cent means that 5 per cent of the amount you invest is taken as a charge at the start of your investment.

Annual management fee: A periodic charge paid from an investment, savings plan or pension to the fund's investment advisor. The charge is a percentage taken from the full pot.

Annual percentage rate (APR): The interest rate charged on a mortgage or a loan for a whole year. It is a great way of comparing loans against each other.

Asset allocation: When you invest long-term, you put money in things like shares and bonds. These are assets. Asset allocation is the term used for how you split your money across the assets.

Attitude-to-risk surveys: These test your ability to accept investment risk. If you have a high attitude to risk, you will be willing to tolerate high fluctuations in your investments. If you have a low attitude to risk, you will lose sleep over the money going up and down.

Bonds: When you invest long-term, one of the asset classes you can use is bonds. Bonds are effectively you giving a loan of your money to companies or governments. In return, they pay you a coupon each year and, if all goes to plan, they will pay you back your money in one payment at the end of the bond term.

Capacity for loss: A test on your finances to see how they would fare if a temporary decline happened in stock markets. It is effectively a stress test to see how your money would cope when a market crash happens.

Capital Acquisitions Tax (CAT): The tax you pay when you receive a gift or inheritance over a certain threshold. The rate is currently 33 per cent.

Central Bank: The regulator for the financial services industry in Ireland. It keeps an eye on what is happening in banks and other financial services firms. It also creates rules for the banks to adhere to when it comes to give out mortgages.

Central Credit Register (CRC): Where all the information about any loan over €500 is held. It is run by the Central Bank. You can get a free report from the Central Credit Register, which details what information the banks have about your credit history.

Commodities: An economic good or service that can be invested in. Commodities are typically natural resources, such as oil, gold or coal.

Compound interest: Interest on interest. The addition of interest to the principal sum of a loan, deposit or investment.

Consumer price index: A measure of inflation. It tracks the price of a basket of goods and checks how much it changes on a year-to-year basis.

Current account: Your everyday bank account. It is what you lodge your wages into, and what all your direct debits and bills are paid from. You have an ATM card for it, too.

Deposit account: A bank account for your short-term savings. You will have money going into and out of this account, but it will not be used for paying bills. It usually pays interest but the interest will probably be very low.

Deposit Interest Retention Tax (DIRT): The tax you pay on the interest you get for leaving money in a bank account.

Dow Jones Industrial Average (DJIA): One of the big US stock market indices. It is a collection of the 30 largest US companies based on their financial size.

Equity release loans: Loans given to people, usually over 50 years of age and often older. The money is paid out on the strength of the value of the house. The person who borrows the money is not required to make loan repayments. The interest accumulates each year. The loan is usually paid back in full when the person dies: the house is either sold or the family steps in to clear it.

European Central Bank (ECB): Like our Central Bank but over all of Europe. The ECB sets our monetary policies and interest rates, which influences how much we can borrow.

Eurostoxx 50: This index tracks the largest 50 companies in Europe.

Exceptions: The Central Bank applies mortgage measures that banks must adhere to when lending. The banks can, however, break the rules from time to time, in what is called an exception.

FTSE: An index tracking companies in the UK. The FTSE 100 tracks the largest 100 companies, while the FTSE 250 tracks the largest 250.

Growth stocks: Shares in companies that are expected to grow very quickly in the future. A good example of growth stocks is tech companies, which are growing very quickly.

Haircut: If you have invested in bonds but the company cannot afford to pay you back the money in full, they may pay you back less than they owed you. This is sometimes referred to as 'burning the bondholders'.

Hedge funds: Aims to make money whether markets go up or down, by shorting stocks as well as investing for growth. It is a style of investing.

Human capital: The present-day value of all the money you have yet to earn in your life. The younger you are, the more income you have yet to earn, and the higher your human capital.

Income protection: An insurance policy that pays you a wage if you are out sick from work. The wage usually continues until you return to work or retire, whichever happens first.

Income tax: The tax taken by the government from your wages.

Inflation: The increase or decrease in the value of goods and services.

Interest: The money you receive from a financial institution if you leave your savings with them, or the money you pay when you borrow money.

Investments: Money put away for the medium to long-term. Investments can relate to anything from buying a house to buying a fund that invests in stocks and shares. The objective of an investment is to grow your money.

Irish Credit Bureau: The predecessor of the Central Credit Register. The banks share details about how your loans are performing with the ICB. Other banks can access this information about you when they assess whether to approve your loan or not.

ISEQ: This index tracks the largest companies in Ireland.

Life cover: This is an insurance policy that pays out in the event of the insured person dying. The amount paid out is based on the amount of cover you choose to take out.

Loan-to-income limits: The Central Bank has mortgage measures around how much banks can lend to people when they are approving mortgages. One of the rules, for example, says that somebody cannot borrow more than 3.5 times their income.

Loan-to-value limits: A rule that states that first-time buyers cannot borrow more than 90 per cent of the value of a house, and that second-time buyers cannot borrow more than 80 per cent. These rules can be broken with an exception.

Long-term savings account/plan: When you put money aside on a regular basis and it accumulates over time. When you are investing long-term, it should be in something other than a bank account and should be invested in shares and bonds.

Market capitalisation: If you take the share price of a company and multiply it by the number of shares that exist for that company, you can calculate its market capitalisation.

Moratorium: Where your lender can give you a break from repayments for a period of time, usually three to six months. This is often done if you are sick or have just had a baby.

Net disposable income requirement (NDIR): This calculation is used when assessing your ability to get a mortgage. It works out how much money you have left to live on after repayments. The number is based around your relationship status and the number of dependents you have.

Net worth: The value of everything you own, financial and non-financial, less the value of all your loans.

Non-recourse loans: A loan that should things go wrong and you cannot repay it, the bank can't chase you for the money. They can only sell the asset (typically an investment property), clear what they can of the loan, and write off the rest.

Ongoing charges figure: This is similar to an annual management fee on pensions, savings and investments, but includes more of the transaction costs. It is a fee taken from the size of the pot.

Overdraft: Pre-approved credit where you can go into minus numbers on your bank account. Once it is approved you don't need to apply each time. You get charged high interest when you stay in it for long periods of time and should only be used in emergencies.

Pay As You Earn (PAYE): A method of paying your income tax. It is the money that is taken out of your wages and paid every time you are paid.

Pay-related social insurance (PRSI): This is taken from your wages and is effectively an insurance policy. It pays for things like sick pay from the government, if you are out sick.

Pension: A tax-efficient savings plan that helps people save for their retirement.

Personal contract plans (PCPs): A form of hire purchase when financing cars. You don't actually own the car when you get on a PCP. You have the option to rent again at the end of the term or to pay a lump sum and buy the car.

Personal insolvency practitioner (PIP): A professional who works with the banks on your behalf if you are in financial difficulty. They will design a plan to help you survive financially and will negotiate with the banks to have the plan approved.

Required rate of return: A calculation used when building a financial plan to see what return your investment needs for it to work. If it is very high, you may need to adjust your expectations of what it is you want to do. If it is very low, then you don't need to take on as much risk.

Savings account: A short-term vehicle (less than five years), which can be in the form of a deposit account or a post-office or Credit Union account.

Section 72 plan: A life-insurance policy where the people you leave your money to receive it tax paid, instead of having to pay the inheritance tax on it.

Shares: Pieces of a company. Companies need to raise money at certain times during their growth. They do this by selling parts of the company to the general public of investors.

Simple interest: A straightforward way of calculating interest. It is useful for quick calculations but rarely used in real life. It can relate to loans or growth on investments.

Small gift tax allowance: An amount of money (currently €3,000) that any person in the state can give to any other person in the state in a calendar year. They will not have to pay tax on it and it will not eat into their group inheritance/gift threshold.

Specified illness cover: An insurance policy that pays out a lump sum if you are diagnosed with a listed specified illness. Typical payouts are for things like cancer, heart attack or stroke. The amount paid out is based on the amount of cover you paid for when taking out the plan.

Standard & Poor 500 (S&P 500): An investment index that tracks the 500 largest companies in the US.

Terminal illness benefit: A feature on life-insurance policies that allows your life cover to be paid out to you before you die if you are deemed to be terminally ill. It usually means you are expected to die in the next twelve months.

Universal social charge (USC): A tax that is taken from your wages. It replaced both the income levy and the health levy.

Value stocks: Shares that for some reason are out of favour. The value of all the shares in the company is less than the value of all the assets in the company.

Volatility: This is a measure of how rough a ride an investment has taken in the past. It can be useful in guessing how much an investment might go up or down in the future.

Notes

Notes

Notes

Notes

This book should be returned to any branch of the
Lancashire County Library on or before the date

1/16

2 5 MAY 2019

0 6 SEP 2016

1 7 AUG 2019

2 5 JUN 2017

0 6 JAN 2018   2 6 OCT 2019

− 7 SEP 2021

2 6 JAN 2018

1 0 AUG 2018

2 9 DEC 2018

Lancashire County Library
Bowran Street
Preston PR1 2UX

Lancashire
County Council

www.lancashire.gov.uk/libraries

IRE COUNTY LIBRARY

011813311241 1

ndiana 46240 USA

Sams Teach Yourself T-SQL in One Hour a Day

Copyright © 2016 by Pearson Education, Inc.

All rights reserved. No part of this book shall be reproduced, stored in a retrieval system, or transmitted by any means, electronic, mechanical, photocopying, recording, or otherwise, without written permission from the publisher. No patent liability is assumed with respect to the use of the information contained herein. Although every precaution has been taken in the preparation of this book, the publisher and author assume no responsibility for errors or omissions. Nor is any liability assumed for damages resulting from the use of the information contained herein.

ISBN-13: 978-0-672-33743-7

ISBN-10: 0-672-33743-6

Library of Congress Cataloging-in-Publication Data: 2015910413

Printed in the United States of America

First Printing October 2015

Trademarks

All terms mentioned in this book that are known to be trademarks or service marks have been appropriately capitalized. Sams Publishing cannot attest to the accuracy of this information. Use of a term in this book should not be regarded as affecting the validity of any trademark or service mark.

Warning and Disclaimer

Every effort has been made to make this book as complete and as accurate as possible, but no warranty or fitness is implied. The information provided is on an "as is" basis. The author and the publisher shall have neither liability nor responsibility to any person or entity with respect to any loss or damages arising from the information contained in this book.

Special Sales

For information about buying this title in bulk quantities, or for special sales opportunities (which may include electronic versions; custom cover designs; and content particular to your business, training goals, marketing focus, or branding interests), please contact our corporate sales department at corpsales@pearsoned.com or (800) 382-3419.

For government sales inquiries, please contact governmentsales@pearsoned.com.

For questions about sales outside the U.S., please contact international@pearsoned.com.

LANCASHIRE COUNTY LIBRARY	
3011813311241 1	
Askews & Holts	19-Jan-2016
005.7585 BAL	£24.99
CPP	

Editor-in-Chief
Greg Wiegand

Acquisitions Editor
Joan Murray

Development Editor
Charlotte Kughen

Managing Editor
Kristy Hart

Project Editor
Andrew Beaster

Copy Editor
Language Logistics LLC, Chrissy White

Indexer
Erika Millen

Proofreader
Sarah Kearns

Technical Editor
David Walker
Theodor Richardson

Publishing Coordinator
Cindy Teeters

Media Producer
Dan Scherf

Interior Designer
Gary Adair

Cover Designer
Mark Shirar

Compositor
codeMantra

Table of Contents

About the Author

Alison Balter is the president of InfoTech Services Group, Inc.,
a computer consulting firm based in Venice Beach, California. Alison is
a highly experienced independent trainer and consultant specializing in
Windows applications training and development. During her 30 years in
the computer industry, she has trained and consulted with many corporations and government agencies. Since Alison founded InfoTech Services
Group, Inc. (formerly InfoTechnology Partners) in 1990, its client base
has expanded to include major corporations and government agencies
such as Cisco, Shell Oil, Accenture, AIG Insurance, Northrop, the
Drug Enforcement Administration, Prudential Insurance, Transamerica
Insurance, Fox Broadcasting, the United States Navy, the United States
Marines, the University of Southern California (USC), Massachusetts
Institute of Technology (MIT), and others.

Alison is the author of more than 300 internationally marketed computer
training videos, including 18 Access 2000 videos, 35 Access 2002 videos,
15 Access 2003 videos, a complete series of both user and developer
videos on Access 2007, and Access 2010 and Access 2013 user videos.
Alison travels throughout North America giving training seminars in
Microsoft Access and Microsoft SQL Server.

Alison is also author of 14 books published by Sams Publishing
including: *Alison Balter's Mastering Access 95 Development*, *Alison
Balter's Mastering Access 97 Development*, *Alison Balter's Mastering
Access 2000 Development*, *Alison Balter's Mastering Access 2002
Desktop Development*, *Alison Balter's Mastering Access 2002 Enterprise
Development*, *Alison Balter's Mastering Microsoft Access Office 2003*,
Teach Yourself Microsoft Office Access 2003 in 24 Hours, *Access Office
2003 in a Snap*, *Alison Balter's Mastering Access 2007 Development*,
a power user book on Microsoft Access 2007, *Using Access 2010*, *Access
2013 Absolute Beginner's Guide*, and *Teach Yourself SQL Express 2005
in 24 Hours*.

An active participant in many user groups and other organizations, Alison
is a past president of the Independent Computer Consultants Association

of Los Angeles and of the Los Angeles Clipper Users' Group. She is also past president of the Ventura County Professional Women's Network. Alison is a Microsoft Access MVP and was selected as Ventura County Woman Business Owner of the Year for 2012/2013.

On a personal note, Alison keeps herself busy skiing, taking yoga classes, running, walking, lifting weights, hiking, and traveling. She most enjoys spending time with her husband, Dan, their daughter Alexis, and their son Brendan.

Contact Alison via Alison@techismything.com or visit InfoTech Services Group's website at www.TechIsMyThing.com.

Dedication

Many people are important in my life, but there is no one as special as my husband Dan. I dedicate this book to Dan. Thank you for your ongoing support, for your dedication to me, for your unconditional love, and for your patience. Without you, I'm not sure how I would make it through life. Thank you for sticking with me through the good times and the bad! There's nobody I'd rather spend forever with than you.

I also want to thank God for giving me the gift of gab, a wonderful career, an incredible husband, two beautiful children, a spectacular area to live in, a very special home, and an awesome life. Through your grace, I am truly blessed.

Acknowledgments

Authoring books is not an easy task. Special thanks go to the following wonderful people who helped make this book possible and, more important, who give my life meaning:

Dan Balter (my incredible husband), for his ongoing support, love, encouragement, friendship, and, as usual, patience with me while I authored this book. Dan, words cannot adequately express the love and appreciation I feel for all that you are and all that you do for me. You treat me like a princess! Thank you for being the phenomenal person you are, and thank you for loving me for who I am and for supporting me during the difficult times. I enjoy not only sharing our career successes, but even more I enjoy sharing the lives of our beautiful children, Alexis and Brendan. I look forward to continuing to reach highs we never dreamed of.

Alexis Balter (my daughter and confidante), for giving life a special meaning. Your intelligence, drive, and excellence in all that you do are truly amazing. Alexis, I know that you will go far in life. I am so proud of you. Even in these difficult teenage years, your wisdom and inner beauty shine through. Finally, thanks for being my walking partner. I love the conversations that we have when we walk together.

Brendan Balter (my wonderful son and amazing athlete), for showing me the power of persistence. Brendan, you are relatively small, but, boy, are you mighty! I have never seen such tenacity and fortitude in a young person. You are able to tackle people twice your size just through your incredible spirit and your remarkable athletic ability. Your imagination and creativity are amazing! Thank you for your sweetness, your sensitivity, and your unconditional love. I really enjoy our times together. Most of all, thank you for reminding me how important it is to have a sense of humor.

Charlotte and Bob Roman (Mom and Dad), for believing in me and sharing in both the good times and the bad. Mom and Dad, without your special love and support, I never would have become who I am today. I want you to know that I think that you both are amazing! I want to be just like you when I grow up and I am 88!

Al Ludington, for giving me a life worth living. You somehow walk the fine line between being there and setting limits, between comforting me and confronting me. Words cannot express how much your unconditional love means to me. Thanks for showing me that a beautiful mind is not such a bad thing after all.

Pam Smith, for being one of the most special people in my life. It didn't take long after we met for me to figure out that you would be someone who would have a deep impact on my life. I love you for your spirit, your brilliance, and your inner beauty. Friends forever!

Sue Lopez, for being an absolutely wonderful friend. You inspire me with your music, your love, your friendship, and your faith in God. Whenever I am having a bad day, I picture you singing "Dear God" or "Make Me Whole," and suddenly my day gets better. Thank you for the gift of friendship.

Roz and Ron Carriere, for supporting my endeavors and for encouraging me to pursue my writing. It means a lot to know that you guys are proud of me for what I do. I enjoy our times together as a family.

Herb and Maureen Balter (my honorary dad and mom), for being such a wonderful father-in-law and mother-in-law. I want you to know how special you are to me. I appreciate your acceptance and your warmth. I also appreciate all you have done for Dan and me. I am grateful to have you in my life.

Mary Forman, for not only being one of the most special clients that I have ever had, but also for being a wonderful friend. You are a ray of sunshine in my day and are a pleasure to work with.

Reverend James, for being an ongoing spiritual inspiration to me. I absolutely love and benefit from your weekly messages. I feel blessed to be an integral part of your congregation.

To all my friends at Federal Defense Industries, Phil, Sharyn, Ross, Randye, Steve, and Elaine, who I have not only enjoyed being with and getting to know through the years, but who have also contributed in many ways to my success in business.

Greggory Peck from Blast Through Learning, for your contribution to my success in this industry. I believe that the opportunities you gave me early on have helped me reach a level in this industry that would have been much more difficult for me to reach on my own. Most of all, Greggory, thanks for your love and friendship. I love you bro!

Joan Murray, Mark Renfrow, and Andy Beaster for making my experience with Sams a positive one. I know that you all worked very hard to ensure that this book came out on time and with the best quality possible. Without you, this book wouldn't have happened. I have *really* enjoyed working with *all* of you over these past several months. I appreciate your thoughtfulness and your sensitivity to my schedule and commitments outside this book. It is nice to work with people who appreciate me as a person, not just as an author.

We Want to Hear from You!

As the reader of this book, *you* are our most important critic and commentator. We value your opinion and want to know what we're doing right, what we could do better, what areas you'd like to see us publish in, and any other words of wisdom you're willing to pass our way.

We welcome your comments. You can email or write to let us know what you did or didn't like about this book—as well as what we can do to make our books better.

Please note that we cannot help you with technical problems related to the topic of this book.

When you write, please be sure to include this book's title and author as well as your name and email address. We will carefully review your comments and share them with the author and editors who worked on the book.

Email: consumer@samspublishing.com

Mail: Sams Publishing
   ATTN: Reader Feedback
   800 East 96th Street
   Indianapolis, IN 46240 USA

Reader Services

Visit our website and register this book at informit.com/register for convenient access to any updates, downloads, or errata that might be available for this book.

Introduction

Many excellent books about T-SQL are available, so how is this one different? In talking to the many people I meet in my travels around the country, I have heard one common complaint. Instead of the host of wonderful books available to expert database administrators (DBAs), most SQL Server readers yearn for a book targeted toward the beginning-to-intermediate DBA or developer. They want a book that starts at the beginning, ensures that they have no gaps in their knowledge, and takes them through some of the more advanced aspects of SQL Server. Along the way, they want to acquire volumes of practical knowledge that they can easily port into their own applications. I wrote *Sams Teach Yourself T-SQL in One Hour a Day* with those requests in mind.

This book begins by providing you with some database basics. In Lesson 1, "Database Basics," you get a summary of all the components that are covered through the remainder of the book.

Lesson 2, "SQL Server Basics," teaches you the basics of working with SQL Server Management Studio. You learn about the versions of SQL Server available. You then find out how to connect with a database server and install the sample files.

In Lesson 3, "Creating a SQL Server Database," you see how to create a new SQL Server database. The SQL Server database is a container within which you will place all the other objects you learn about throughout the book.

Lessons 4 through 18 cover tables, relationships, the T-SQL language, views, stored procedures, functions, and triggers. These objects are at the heart of every SQL Server database. Lesson 4, "Working with SQL Server Tables," explains how to work with tables. Then you move on to Lesson 5, "Working with Table Relationships," which covers how to work with table relationships.

Knowledge of the T-SQL language is an important aspect of SQL Server. Probably the most used keyword used in T-SQL is SELECT. Lesson 6,

"Getting to Know the SELECT Statement," delves into the SELECT statement in quite a bit of detail. Lesson 7, "Taking the SELECT Statement to the Next Level," expands on Lesson 6 by covering some more sophisticated T-SQL techniques. You then move on to Lesson 8, "Building SQL Statements Based on Multiple Tables," where you find out how you can build T-SQL statements based on data from multiple tables. Lesson 9, "Powerful Join Techniques," builds on Lesson 8 to provide you with different techniques you can use to join tables. Not only can you use T-SQL to retrieve data, but you can also use it to modify data. Lesson 10, "Modifying Data with Action Queries," shows you how to modify data with action queries. Lesson 11, "Getting to Know the T-SQL Functions," introduces you to many of the built-in T-SQL functions, such as DataAdd, DateDiff, and Upper. These built-in functions prove invaluable for building database applications.

Another important SQL Server object is the view. Lesson 12, "Working with SQL Server Views," shows you how to build and work with views. Lesson 13, "Using T-SQL to Design SQL Server Stored Procedures," begins the in-depth coverage of stored procedures. Lessons 14, 15, and 16 continue to build on each other, each providing more sophisticated coverage of stored procedures and their uses.

Lesson 17, "Building and Working with User-Defined Functions," provides you with an alternative to stored procedures: user-defined functions. Lesson 18, "Creating and Working with Triggers," shows you how you can use triggers to respond to inserts, updates, and deletes.

The last six lessons cover security and administration. You learn about SQL Server authentication and permissions validation and how you can take advantage of both to properly secure your databases. The lessons in Part III also show you how to configure, maintain, and tune the SQL Servers that you manage. Without proper care, even the fastest hardware could run a database that is abysmally slow!

Finally, this book uses the sample database called AdventureWorks2014. Lesson 2 covers the process of installing the sample database. Also, all the sample code created in this book are available in a script file that you can open and execute from a SQL Server Management Studio query.

SQL Server, and the T-SQL language, are powerful and exciting. With the keys to deliver all that it offers, you can produce applications that provide much satisfaction as well as many financial rewards. After poring over this hands-on guide and keeping it nearby for handy reference, you too can become masterful at working with SQL Server and T-SQL. This book is dedicated to demonstrating how you can fulfill the promise of making SQL Server perform up to its lofty capabilities. As you will see, you have the ability to really make SQL Server shine in the everyday world!

LESSON 1

Database Basics

Before you learn about the T-SQL language, it is important that you understand the basics of server databases and the objects they contain. This lesson explains:

- ▶ What a database is
- ▶ What a table is
- ▶ What database diagrams, views, stored procedures, user-defined functions, and triggers are

What Is a Database?

T-SQL is the language you use when working with Microsoft SQL Server. Microsoft SQL Server is considered a client-server database. It is used along with an application that presents the data. An example of such a database is Microsoft Access. A SQL Server database is a collection of objects. This collection of objects includes all of the tables, views, stored procedures, functions, and other objects necessary to build a database system. The tables, which are explained in the next section, in a database usually relate to each other.

What Is a Table?

Tables are generally the first thing you add to a SQL Server database. Tables contain the data in your SQL Server database. Each table contains information about a subject. For example, one table might contain information about customers, whereas another table might contain information about orders. Each table in a database must have a unique name.

A table is made up of rows and columns. The columns are called *fields*, and each field has a unique name. Each row contains an individual occurrence of the subject modeled by the table. Each field contains a specific piece of information about the item that is being described by the row. A row is most often referred to as a record. For example, within the Customer table, the fields included may be the CustomerID, CompanyName, ContactFirstName, ContactLastName, and so on, and each record in the Customer table contains information about a specific customer. Lesson 4, "Working with SQL Server Tables," covers the details of creating and working with tables.

What Is a Database Diagram?

A database diagram graphically shows the structure of the database (see Figure 1.1), showing how one table is related to another within the database. Using a database diagram, you can modify the tables, columns, relationships, keys, indexes, and constraints that make up the database. For more about database diagrams, see Lesson 5, "Working with Table Relationships," where you find out that database diagrams are very powerful!

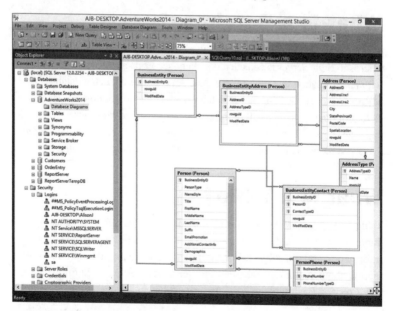

FIGURE 1.1   A database diagram graphically shows the structure of the database.

What Is a View?

A *view* is a virtual table. Its contents are based on a query. Like a table, a view is composed of rows and columns. An example is a view that retrieves data from a customer table and from an order table. It retrieves information from each table for the customers residing in the state of Alaska.

Except in the case of a special type of view called an indexed view, views exist only in memory (their data is not stored on disk). The data in a view comes from one or more tables in the database (see Figure 1.2). It can also come from other views, and even from data in other databases. Whenever you reference a view, SQL Server dynamically retrieves the rows and columns contained in it. There are no restrictions on querying and only a few restrictions on modifying data via views. For more information about views, see Lesson 12, "Working with SQL Server Views."

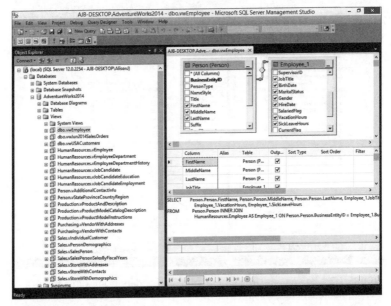

FIGURE 1.2 The View Designer included in SQL Server Management Studio helps you when designing a view.

What Is a Stored Procedure?

A *stored procedure* is a piece of programming code that can accept input parameters and can return one or more output parameters to the calling procedure or batch (see Figure 1.3). Stored procedures generally perform operations on the database, including the process of calling other stored procedures. An example is a stored procedure that updates the city of all customers residing in Westlake Village, changing the city to Venice Beach.

Stored procedures can also return status information to the calling procedure to indicate whether they succeeded or failed. Lesson 13, "Using T-SQL to Design SQL Server Stored Procedures," Lesson 14, "Stored Procedure Techniques Every Developer Should Know," and Lesson 15, "Power Stored Procedure Techniques," cover stored procedures in quite a bit of detail.

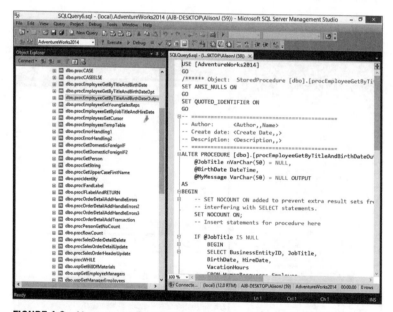

FIGURE 1.3   You can easily create a stored procedure from within the SQL Server Management Studio.

What Is a User-Defined Function?

User-defined functions are procedures that accept parameters, perform some sort of action, and return the result of that action as a value (see Figure 1.4). The return value can be either a single value or a set of values. An example is a user-defined function that combines the contents of the first name, middle initial and last name fields, returning them as a single string.

User-defined functions have many benefits. Like stored procedures, they allow modular programming, meaning that you can call them from anywhere in your program. If you need to modify the function, you can do so in only one place. User-defined functions generally execute quickly. For more about user-defined functions, see Lesson 17, "Building and Working with User-Defined Functions."

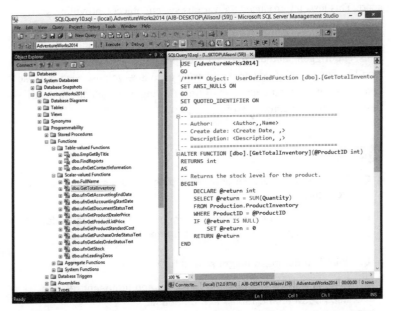

FIGURE 1.4 User-defined functions are procedures that accept parameters, perform some sort of action, and return the result of that action as a value.

What Is a Trigger?

A trigger is a special type of stored procedure that executes when data changes in a database table. There are three events that cause a trigger to execute. They include `Insert`, `Update`, and `Delete` statements that occur when data is modified in a table or view. Triggers have several uses. An example is a trigger that executes when the user tries to delete a customer. The trigger checks to see if the customer is active. If the customer is active, the trigger prohibits the user from deleting that customer. Lesson 18, "Creating and Working with Triggers" covers the intricacies of triggers.

Summary

A database is similar to a house. Without the proper foundation, it will fall apart. This lesson introduced the various system objects, providing you with a sense of what each object does and why it is important. You learned a little about tables, database diagrams, views, stored procedures, functions, and triggers, and the role that each plays in a SQL Server databases. Don't be concerned if you are still unsure as to how you use each of these objects. We will spend quite a bit of time delving into each one in detail throughout the remaining lessons.

Q&A

Q. Describe the difference between a trigger and a standard stored procedure.

A. Triggers execute automatically in response to changes to data; you must explicitly invoke a stored procedure.

Q. What is a database diagram used for?

A. You use a database diagram to define and represent relationships between the tables in a database.

Workshop

Quiz

1. Stored procedures can have both input and output parameters (true/false).

2. You can usually update the results of a view (true/false).

3. How do we refer to a column in a table?

4. What is another name for a row in a table?

Quiz Answers

1. True.

2. True.

3. We refer to a column in a table as a field.

4. Another name for a row in a table is a record.

Activities

Each lesson in this book will provide you with an opportunity to practice the techniques that you have learned in the lesson. The section containing these exercises is referred to as "Activities." Because you don't have enough information yet to build tables or any of the other objects you learned about in the lesson, this lesson does not contain any activities.

LESSON 2

SQL Server Basics

There are some basics you should know when getting started with SQL Server. Knowledge of these basics will help you to make decisions about whether the product is right for you and will help you get started working with it. This lesson covers:

▶ The available versions of SQL Server 2014

▶ Components included with SQL Server

▶ The basics of working with SQL Server Management Studio

▶ How to connect to a database server

▶ How to install the sample files

Versions of SQL Server 2014 Available

Microsoft recognizes that there is a plethora of database users with a large variety of disparate needs and has released the following six versions of SQL Server 2014:

▶ SQL Server 2014 Express Edition

▶ SQL Server 2014 Web Edition

▶ SQL Server 2014 Business Intelligence Edition

▶ SQL Server 2014 Standard Edition

▶ SQL Server 2014 Enterprise Edition

SQL Server 2014 Express Edition

SQL Server 2014 Express provides a great means of getting started with SQL Server. It offers a robust, reliable, stable environment that is free and easy to use. It provides the same protection and information management provided by the more sophisticated versions of SQL Server. Other advantages of SQL Server Express include the following:

- ▶ Is easy to install

- ▶ Has a lightweight management and query editing tool

- ▶ Includes support for Windows authentication

- ▶ Features "Secure by Default" settings

- ▶ Has royalty-free distribution

- ▶ Offers rich database functionality, including triggers, stored procedures, functions, extended indexes, and Transact-SQL support

- ▶ Includes XML support

SQL Server 2014 Express has a few disadvantages that make it unusable in many situations, including the following:

- ▶ Support for only 1GB of RAM

- ▶ Support for a 10GB maximum database size

- ▶ Support for only one CPU

- ▶ Absence of the SQL Agent Job Scheduling Service

- ▶ Absence of the SQL Profiler

- ▶ Absence of the Database Tuning Advisor

SQL Server 2014 Web Edition

SQL Server Web Edition is designed to support the workloads associated with Internet databases. It enables you to easily deploy web pages, applications, websites, and services. Other valuable features include the fact that it supports 64GB of RAM and a 524-petabyte (PB) database size.

The main disadvantage of SQL Server 2014 Web Edition is that it does not include the SQL Profiler.

SQL Server 2014 Business Intelligence Edition

SQL Server 2014 Business Intelligence Edition enables you to deploy secure, scalable, and manageable self-service corporate business intelligence solutions. Valuable features include the fact that it supports 128GB of RAM and a 524PB database size.

SQL Server 2014 Standard Edition

SQL Server Standard Edition provides an affordable option for small- and medium-sized businesses. It includes all functionality required for noncritical e-commerce, data warehousing, and line-of-business solutions. The advantages of SQL Server 2014 Standard Edition include the following:

- ▶ Supports up to 128GB of RAM

- ▶ Supports a database size up to 524PB

- ▶ Has database mirroring

- ▶ Includes failover clustering

- ▶ Includes the Database Tuning Advisor

- ▶ Includes the full-featured Management Studio

- ▶ Ships with the Profiler

- ▶ Includes the SQL Agent Job Scheduling Service

The disadvantages of SQL Server 2014 Standard Edition are that it:

- ▶ Supports only four CPUs

- ▶ Does not support online indexing

- ▶ Does not support online restore

- ▶ Does not support fast recovery

SQL Server 2014 Enterprise Edition

SQL Server 2014 Enterprise Edition includes all of the tools you need to manage an enterprise database management system. It offers a complete set of enterprise management and business intelligence features and provides the highest levels of scalability and availability of all the SQL Server 2014 editions. It supports an unlimited number of CPUs and provides all of the features unavailable in the other versions of SQL Server 2014.

SQL Server Components

SQL Server includes numerous components that facilitate the process of creating, working with, and maintaining SQL Server databases. The components covered in this lesson include the following:

- ► SQL Server Management Studio
- ► SQL Profiler
- ► SQL Server Agent
- ► Database Tuning Advisor

SQL Server Management Studio is covered later in detail in the "Introduction to Microsoft SQL Server Management Studio" section. The other components are covered here.

SQL Profiler

You use the SQL Profiler to create and manage traces and to analyze and replay trace results. Most often, you use the SQL Profiler to troubleshoot database performance issues.

Using the SQL Profiler, you can accomplish the following:

- ► Step through queries.
- ► Diagnose slow-running queries.
- ► Capture the T-SQL statements that are causing the problem.
- ► Monitor performance.

When using the SQL Profiler, you can specify exactly which database events you want to capture. For example, you can trace when TSQL statements start and complete, when stored procedures start and complete, and a plethora of other events (see Figure 2.1). You can save your traces so that you can run them at any time. Lesson 23, "Performance Monitoring," covers the details of working with the SQL Server Profiler.

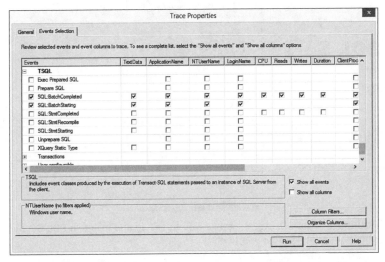

FIGURE 2.1 The SQL Profiler allows you to easily monitor database events.

SQL Server Agent

The SQL Server Agent enables you to easily schedule administrative tasks called jobs. A *job* is a series of actions that the agent performs at specified times, when the agent starts, one time, or when the CPU utilization of the server is considered idle.

You generally use the SQL Server Agent to perform backups, update indexes, or perform other tasks that either protect or maintain your database and its objects. The SQL Server Agent appears as a node of the Object Explorer. When you expand the node, it appears as in Figure 2.2. Using this node, you can view, create, and manage jobs. Lesson 22, "Maintaining the Databases That You Build," covers the details of the SQL Server Agent.

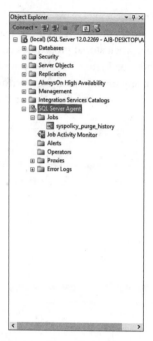

FIGURE 2.2   The SQL Agent enables you to set up and maintain SQL Server jobs that perform a series of tasks.

Database Engine Tuning Advisor

The Database Engine Tuning Advisor enables you to optimize database performance without requiring you to have an expert understanding of the database and SQL Server. The Database Engine Tuning Advisor can perform the following tasks:

► Recommend the best mix of indexes

► Recommend indexed views when applicable

► Analyze the effects of any proposed changes

► Recommend ways to tune the database

► Provide reports that summarize the effects of implementing recommendations

Figure 2.3 shows the Database Tuning Advisor. Lesson 22 covers the Database Tuning Advisor in additional detail.

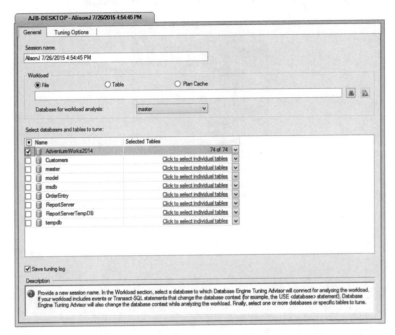

FIGURE 2.3 The Database Engine Tuning Advisor enables you to optimize the performance of your database.

Introduction to Microsoft SQL Server Management Studio

Management Studio is a tool that enables you to create, work with, and manage database objects. In the sections that follow, you explore the various nodes available in Management Studio and find out what is available under each node.

The Databases Node

The Databases node is the first node in SQL Server Management Studio. Within the Databases node are one or more subnodes. The first subnode is

System Databases. There are additional subnodes for each database contained on the server (see Figure 2.4). The sections that follow cover each of the system databases under the System Databases subnode.

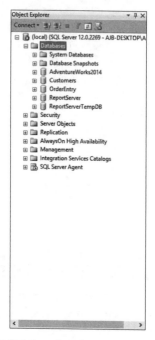

FIGURE 2.4 Within the Databases node are one or more subnodes.

The Master Database

The master database is the "database of all databases." It keeps track of logon accounts, linked servers, system configuration settings, and more. It also contains initialization settings for SQL Server.

The Model Database

Model is a special database. Anything you place in Model is automatically propagated to all the databases you create thereafter. This means that, for example, you can add a State table to Model. That State table then appears in all the new databases you build. You work with Model just as you work with any other database. You can include almost any object in Model. This means that you easily can propagate tables, views, stored procedures, triggers, functions, and more. This not only provides you with standardization between databases, but provides you with a great jump start on creating the databases you need. If you modify Model, you do not affect any existing databases. All new databases will be affected by your changes.

The MSDB Database

The MSDB (stands for Microsoft Database) database is used by SQL Server, SQL Server Management Studio, and SQL Server Agent. All three of them use it to store data, including scheduling information and backup and restore history information. For example, SQL Server maintains a complete backup and restore history in MSDB. There are several ways that you can add to or modify information stored in the MSDB database. They include:

- ▶ Scheduling tasks

- ▶ Maintaining online backup and restore history

- ▶ Replication

The TempDB Database

TempDB is a system database that acts as a resource to all users working with a particular instance of SQL Server. TempDB holds the following objects:

- ▶ Temporary user objects such as temporary tables, temporary stored procedures, temporary table variables, or cursors

- ▶ Internal objects used by the database engine to perform tasks such as sorting

- ▶ Row versions that are generated in data modification transactions

The Security Node

As its name implies, the Security node enables you to manage SQL Server security. Using the Security node, you can work with logins, add to and remove people from server roles, and create credentials. This lesson provides an introduction to security. For more information, see Lesson 19, "Authentication," and Lesson 20, "SQL Server Permissions Validation."

The Logins Node

Logins represent the users and roles that have access to your system. Two types of icons appear under the Logins node. One is granting a role access to the database, and the other is granting a user access to the database.

The Server Roles Node

Server Roles are predefined roles supplied by SQL Server. Each Server Role possesses a pre-defined set of rights. Figure 2.5 shows the available Server Roles. You cannot add or remove Server Roles.

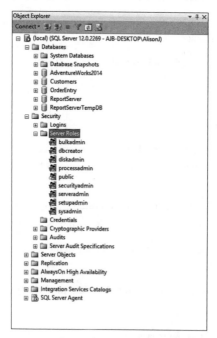

FIGURE 2.5   Each Server Role possesses a predefined set of rights.

The Credentials Node

A credential is a record that contains the authentication information required for SQL Server to connect to an outside resource. Most credentials are made up of a Windows login and password.

Server Objects Node

Server Objects refer to a set of objects used at the server level (not at the database level). These objects include backup devices, linked servers, and server triggers.

Backup Devices

Backup devices include the tapes and disks you use to back up or restore your SQL Server. When creating a backup, you must designate the backup device you want to use (see Figure 2.6). You select from a list of backup devices you have created.

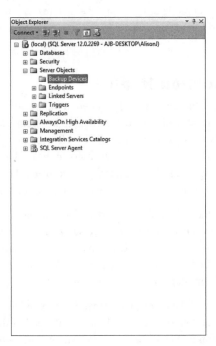

FIGURE 2.6   When creating a backup, you must first designate the backup device you want to use.

Linked Servers

Linked servers enable you to work with other SQL Servers, as well as databases other than SQL Server databases, right from within Management Studio. This offers a few advantages:

- ▶ The capability to get remote server access

- ▶ The capability to issue distributed queries, updates, commands, and transactions on heterogeneous data sources across the enterprise

- ▶ The capability to address diverse data sources in a similar manner

Server Triggers

Server triggers are DDL (Data Definition Language) triggers. They execute in response to changes being made to the structure of the database. They are great for both auditing and regulating database operations. For example, if SQL Server determined that there were more than a specified number of records in a table, it would not allow users to remove fields from the table.

The Replication Node

Data replication is the capability of a system to automatically make copies of its data and application objects in remote locations. You can easily propagate any changes to the original or data changes to the copies to all the other copies. Data replication allows users to make changes to data offline at remote locations. SQL Express synchronizes changes to either the original or the remote data with other instances of the database.

The original database is the *design master*. You can make changes to definitions of tables or other application objects only at the design master. You use the design master to make special copies called *replicas*. Although there is only one design master, replicas can make other replicas. The process of the design master and replicas sharing changes is *synchronization*.

To see an example of data replication at work, say you have a team of salespeople who are out on the road all day. At the end of the day, each salesperson logs on to one of the company's servers through Terminal

Services. The replication process sends each salesperson's transactions to the server. If necessary, the process sends any changes to the server data to the salesperson.

This example illustrates just one of the several valuable uses of replication. In a nutshell, data replication is used to improve the availability and integrity of data throughout an organization or enterprise. The practical uses of data replication are many.

Management Node

The Management node contains tools that help you to manage your SQL Server. These tools include the capability to view both the SQL Server Logs and the Activity Monitor.

SQL Server Logs

SQL Server 2014 adds entries for certain system events to the SQL Server Error Log and to the Microsoft Windows application log. You can use these logs to identify the sources of problems. Using the SQL Server Management Studio Log File Viewer, you can integrate SQL Server, SQL Server Agent, and the Windows logs into a single list, making it easy to review all related events.

Activity Monitor

You use the Activity Monitor component of SQL Server Management Studio to get information about users' connections to the database engine and the locks they hold.

Connecting to a Database Server

Before you can work with a database server and the objects it contains, you must first connect to it. Notice that when you launch Management Studio, the Connect to Server dialog box appears (see Figure 2.7). Generally, all you need to do is to verify that the server name is correct and then click Connect.

Another method you can use to connect to a database server is to click Connect in the Object Explorer and then select Database Engine

(see Figure 2.8). The Connect to Server dialog box appears, enabling you
to modify the Server Name and Authentication mode.

FIGURE 2.7   The Connect to Server dialog box enables you to specify
connection information for the database.

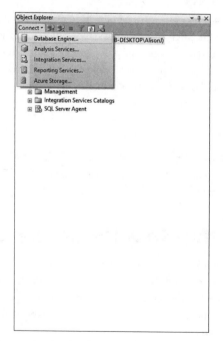

FIGURE 2.8   You can invoke the Connect to Server dialog box from the
Object Explorer.

Installing the Sample Files

This course utilizes the AdventureWorks2014 sample database for almost all its examples. You must install the database before you can work with it.

There are many different websites that provide a link that enables you to download the AdventureWorks2014 database. One of such links is https://msftdbprodsamples.codeplex.com/releases/view/125550. This link downloads a file called Adventure Works 2014 Full Database Backup.zip. Take the following steps to install the AdventureWorks2014 database on your computer:

1. Double-click the zip file to open it. A file called AdventureWorks2014 .bak appears.

2. Place the AdventureWorks2014.bak file in the desired folder on your computer or network (see Figure 2.9).

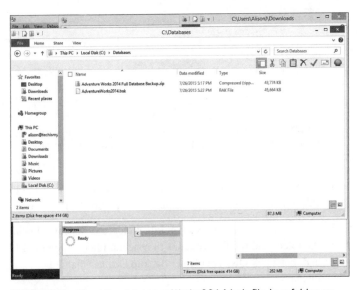

FIGURE 2.9   Place the AdventureWorks2014.bak file in a folder on your computer or network.

3. In Management Studio, right-click the Databases node and select Restore Database. The Restore Database dialog box displays (see Figure 2.10).

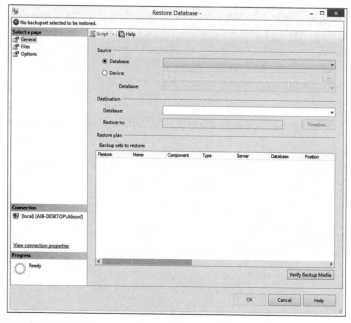

FIGURE 2.10 The Restore Database dialog box enables you to specify information about the database you want to restore.

4. Click to select Device and then click the ellipsis (…). The Select Backup Device dialog box displays (see Figure 2.11).

5. Click Add. The Locate Backup File dialog box displays. Locate the folder and file that contains the backup file (see Figure 2.12) and then click OK. The Select Backup Devices dialog box displays.

6. Click OK.

FIGURE 2.11   The Select Backup Device dialog box enables you to designate the backup you want to restore.

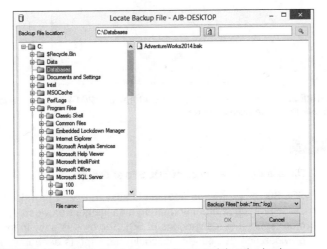

FIGURE 2.12   Locate the folder and file containing the backup.

7. Click OK one more time. You should receive a message that the file restored properly.

8. Right-click the Databases node and select Refresh. You should now see the AdventureWorks2014 database (see Figure 2.13).

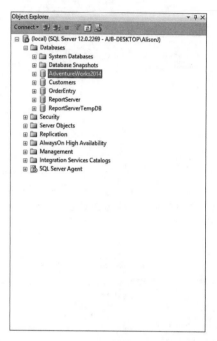

FIGURE 2.13   Once restored, the AdventureWorks2014 database should appear in the Databases node.

Q&A

Q. Discuss the advantages of SQL Server Express.

A. SQL Server Express is free and is easy to use. It provides the same protection and information management provided by more sophisticated versions of SQL Server. It is easy to install, provides rich database functionality, and sports deep integration with Visual Studio 2013.

Q. Name some limitations of SQL Server Express.

A. SQL Server Express limits you to 1GB of RAM, 10GB maximum database size, and support for only one CPU. Furthermore, it does not come with either a job scheduling server or a database tuning advisor.

Workshop

Quiz

1. Name the version of SQL Server designed for small businesses or departments in larger enterprises.

2. What versions of SQL Server support 524PB databases?

3. SQL Server Enterprise Edition enables you to utilize all memory installed on the server (true/false).

4. You are prompted for authentication model during the installation of the SQL Server Express database engine (true/false).

5. Name the management tool you use to manage your databases.

6. Name the tree view that enables you to view the objects managed by your SQL Server.

Quiz Answers

1. SQL Server 2005 Standard Edition.

2. Standard, Business Intelligence, and Enterprise.

3. True.

4. True.

5. SQL Server Management Studio.

6. Object Explorer.

Activities

Download SQL Server Express Edition. Install both the database engine and SQL Server Express Management Studio. Launch Management Studio and practice expanding and contracting the nodes of the Object Explorer. Select different nodes and view the summary information. Finally, take the steps in this lesson to install the sample AdventureWorks2014 database.

LESSON 3

Creating a SQL Server Database

Databases are at the heart of every SQL Server system. They contain the tables, database diagrams, views, stored procedures, functions, and triggers that comprise the system. This lesson covers:

▶ How to create a SQL Server database

▶ How to set database options

▶ How to work with the Transaction Log

▶ How to attach to an existing database

Creating the Database

Before you can build tables, views, stored procedures, triggers, functions, and other objects, you must create the database in which they will reside. A database is a collection of objects that relate to one another. An example would be all the tables and other objects necessary to build a sales order system. To create a SQL Server database, follow these steps:

1. Right-click the Databases node and select New Database. The New Database dialog box appears (see Figure 3.1).

2. Enter a name for the database.

3. Scroll to the right to view the path for the database.

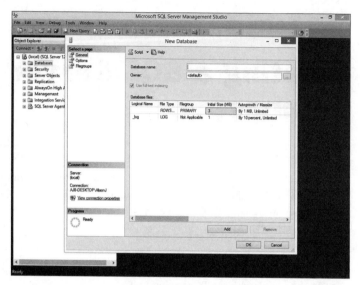

FIGURE 3.1 The New Database dialog box enables you to create a new database.

4. Click the Ellipsis button. The Locate Folder dialog box appears.

5. Select a path for the database (see Figure 3.2).

6. Click OK to close the Locate Folder dialog box.

7. Click to select the Options page and change any options as desired (see Figure 3.3).

8. Click OK to close the New Database dialog box and save the new database. The database now appears under the list of databases (see Figure 3.4) under the Databases node of SQL Server Management Studio. If the database does not appear, right-click the Databases node and select Refresh.

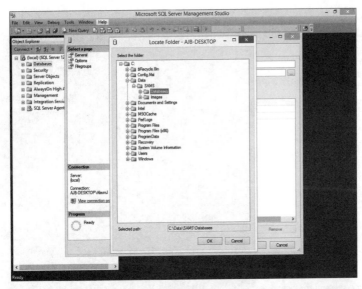

FIGURE 3.2 You can opt to accept the default path, or you can designate a path for the database.

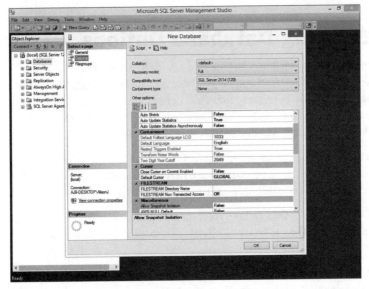

FIGURE 3.3 The Options page of the New Database dialog box enables you to set custom options for the database.

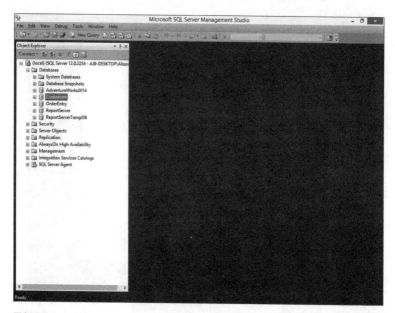

FIGURE 3.4 The new database appears under the list of databases in the Databases node.

Defining Database Options

In the previous section, you created a new SQL Server database. You accepted all the default options available on the General page of the New Database dialog box. Many important options are available on the General page. They include the Logical Name, File Type, Filegroup, Initial Size, Autogrowth, Path, and File Name (see Figure 3.5).

The logical name is the name that SQL Server will use to refer to the database. It is also the name you will use to refer to the database when writing programming code that accesses it.

The File Type is Data or Log. As its name implies, SQL Server stores data in data files. The file type of Log indicates that the file is a transaction log file.

The initial size is *very* important. You use it to designate the amount of space you will allocate initially to the database.

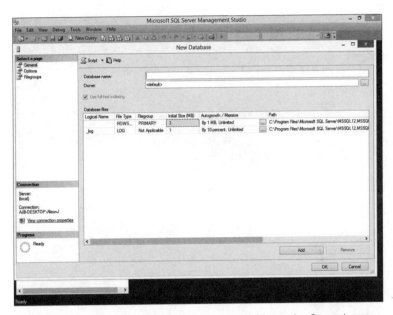

FIGURE 3.5 Several important features are available on the General page of the New Database dialog box.

NOTE: I like to set this number to the largest size that I ever expect the data database and log file to reach. Whereas disk space is very cheap, performance is affected every time that SQL Server needs to resize the database.

Related to the initial size is the Autogrowth option. When you click the build button (ellipsis) to the right of the currently selected Autogrowth option, the Change Autogrowth dialog box appears (see Figure 3.6).

The first question is whether you want to support autogrowth at all. Some database designers initially make their databases larger than they ever think they should be and then set autogrowth to false. They want an error to occur so that they will be notified when the database exceeds the allocated size. The idea is that they want to check things out to make sure everything is okay before allowing the database to grow to a larger size.

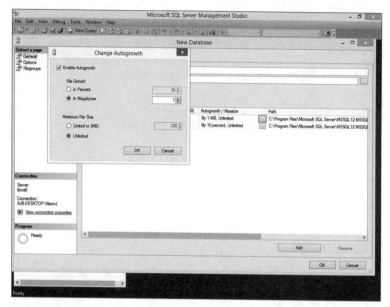

FIGURE 3.6   The Change Autogrowth dialog box enables you to designate options that affect how the database file grows.

The second question is whether you want to grow the file in percentage or in megabytes. For example, you can opt to grow the file 10% at a time. This means that if the database reaches the limit of 5,000 megabytes, then 10% growth would grow the file by 500 megabytes. If instead the file growth were fixed at 1,000 megabytes, the file would grow by that amount regardless of the original size of the file.

The final question is whether you want to restrict the amount of growth that occurs. If you opt to restrict file growth, you designate the restriction in megabytes. Like the Support Autogrowth feature, when you restrict the file size, you essentially assert that you want to be notified if the file exceeds that size. With unrestricted file size, the only limit to file size is the amount of available disk space on the server.

File Groups

One great feature of SQL Server is that you can span a database's objects over several files, all located on separate devices. We refer to this as a file group. By creating a file group, you improve the performance of the database because multiple hardware devices can access the data simultaneously.

The Transaction Log

SQL Server uses the transaction log to record *every* change that is made to the database. In the case of a system crash, you use the transaction log, along with the most recent backup file, to restore the system to the most recent data available. The transaction log supports the recovery of individual transactions, the recovery of all incomplete transactions when SQL Server is once again started, and the rolling back of a restored database, file, filegroup, or page forward to the point of failure. Specifying information about the transaction log is similar to doing so for a database. Follow these steps:

1. While creating a new database, you can also enter information about the log file. To begin, enter a logical name for the database. I recommend you use the logical name of the database along with the suffix _log.

2. Specify the initial size of the log file.

3. Indicate how you want the log file to grow.

4. Designate the path within which you want to store the database.

5. Continue the process of creating the database file.

WARNING: Do not move or delete the transaction log unless you are fully aware of all the possible ramifications of doing so.

Attaching to an Existing Database

There are times when someone will provide you with a database that you want to work with on your own server. To work with an existing database, all you have to do is attach to it. Here's the process:

1. Right-click the Databases node and select Attach. The Attach Databases dialog box appears (see Figure 3.7).

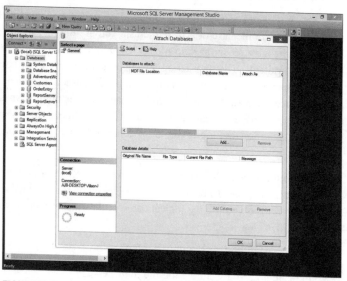

FIGURE 3.7   The Attach Databases dialog box enables you to attach to existing .mdf database files.

2. Click Add. The Locate Database Files dialog box appears (see Figure 3.8).

3. Locate and select the .mdf to which you want to attach.

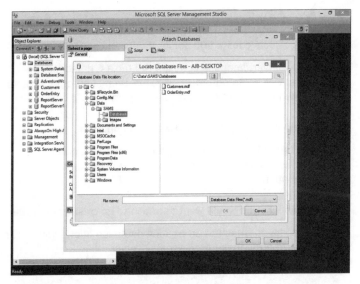

FIGURE 3.8 The Locate Database Files dialog box enables you to select the database to which you want to attach.

4. Click OK to close the Locate Database Files dialog box.

5. Click OK to close the Attach Databases dialog box. The database appears in the list of user databases under the Databases node of SQL Server Management Studio.

Summary

The ability to create a database is fundamental to working with SQL Server. The process of creating a database involves understanding what a log file is and how to configure it. After you have created both the database and the log file, you are ready to create and work with the other database objects.

Q&A

Q. **What objects does a SQL Server database contain?**

A. A SQL Server database contains the tables, database diagrams, views, stored procedures, functions, and other objects required to support the database's operations.

Q. **Explain what a log file is and why it is important.**

A. The log file keeps track of all transactions that occur as the database is used. It is necessary when restoring system information.

Q. **Explain why you would want to attach to an existing database.**

A. The ability to attach to an existing database allows you to easily utilize a database from another server.

Workshop

Quiz

1. What is autogrowth?

2. The autogrowth feature improves the performance of a database (true/false).

3. You attach to a backup file (true/false).

4. It is always okay to delete a log file (true/false).

5. What are the two options for growing a database?

Quiz Answers

1. Autogrowth provides the ability for a database or log file to grow automatically as necessary.

2. False. The autogrowth feature degrades performance. It is best to set the sizes of the database and log files to values larger than you expect you will need.

3. False. You attach to a database file (.mdf).

4. False.

5. By percentage or in megabytes.

Activities

Create a new SQL Server database. Designate sizes for both the database and the log file, indicating you do not want to allow autogrowth. View the database in the Object Explorer. Notice that the database does not yet contain any user objects.

LESSON 4

Working with SQL Server Tables

At the foundation of every SQL Server database are the tables contained within it. The tables store the data in your database. The views, stored procedures, and functions that are covered in this book all manipulate table data. In this lesson, you learn:

- ▶ How to create a SQL Server table
- ▶ How to add fields to a SQL Server table
- ▶ How to set properties of the fields you add
- ▶ How to add and modify table indexes

Creating SQL Server Tables

Tables are made up of rows and columns. We refer to columns as *fields*. Each field has a unique name and contains a specific piece of information about the row. Each table in a SQL Server database must have a unique name.

To create a table:

1. Within Management Studio, right-click the Tables node of the database to which you want to add a table and select New Table. The Table Designer appears (see Figure 4.1).

2. Enter the column names and data types for each field in the table.

3. Designate whether each field allows nulls.

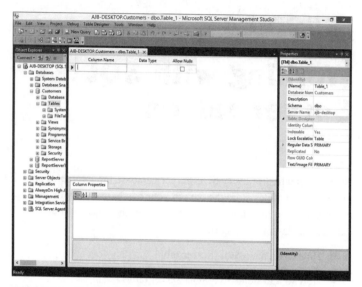

FIGURE 4.1 The Table Designer enables you to enter the column names, data types, length, and other properties for each field in the table.

4. Use the Column Properties tab in the table designer to enter other properties for the table. For example, you use the Length property of a varchar field to designate the maximum length string that the field will hold.

Adding Fields to the Tables You Create

One of the most important properties of a column in a table is the data type. If you do not select the correct data type for a field, the rest of your design efforts will be futile. The data type determines what data you can store in the field. Table 4.1 outlines the available field types and the type of information that each data type can contain.

TABLE 4.1 Field Types and Appropriate Uses

Field Type	Description	Storage
Bigint	Can hold numbers ranging from -2^{63} to 2^{63}.	8 bytes.
Binary	Holds from 1 to 8,000 bytes of fixed-length binary data.	Whatever is in the column, plus 4 additional bytes.
Bit	Can hold a value of either 1, 0, or Null.	1 byte.
Char	Holds from 1 to 8,000 bytes of fixed-length non-Unicode characters.	The number of bytes corresponds to the length of the field (regardless of what is stored in it).
Cursor	A data type for variables or stored procedure OUTPUT parameters that contain a reference to a cursor.	
Date	Defines a date.	3 bytes.
DateTime	Holds valid dates from January 1, 1753 AD to December 31, 9999 or a time value from 00:00:00 through 23:59:59.997.	8 bytes.
DateTime2	Date combined with time of day based on a 24-hour clock. Holds valid dates from January 1, 1 AD to December 31, 9999 and time values from 00:00:00 through 23:59:59.9999999.	6 to 8 bytes based on value contained.
DateTime Offset	Defines a date that is combined with a time of a day that has time zone awareness and is based on a 24-hour clock. Holds valid dates from January 1, 1 AD to December 31, 9999. Time values range from 00:00:00 through 23:59:59.9999999 with a time offset range of −14:00 through +14:00.	10 bytes.

continues

TABLE 4.1   Continued

Field Type	Description	Storage
Decimal	Numeric data type that has fixed precision and scale.	Varies based on the precision.
Float	Approximate-number data type for use with floating point numeric data. Floating point data is approximate; therefore, not all values in the data type range can be represented exactly.	Varies based on the precision.
Geography	Represents data in a round-earth coordinate system.	
Geometry	Represents data in a Euclidean (flat) coordinate system.	
Hierarchyid	A variable length, system data type. Use hierarchyid to represent position in a hierarchy.	5 bytes.
Int	Can hold numbers from -2^{31} to 2^{31}.	4 bytes.
Image	Variable-length binary data from 0 through $2^{31} - 1$ (2,147,483,647) bytes.	Varies.
Money	Can hold numbers from $-922,337,203,685,477.5808$ to $922,337,203,685,477.5807$.	8 bytes.
NChar	Character data type that is fixed-length.	Varies.
NText	Variable-length Unicode data with a maximum string length of $2^{30} - 1$ (1,073,741,823) bytes.	Varies.
Numeric	Numeric data type that has fixed precision and scale. Values can range from -10^{38} to 10^{38}.	Varies based on the precision.
NVarChar	Can contain from 1 to 4,000 Unicode characters.	2 bytes per character stored.

continues

TABLE 4.1 Continued

Field Type	Description	Storage
NVarChar (MAX)	Variable-length Unicode string data. n defines the string length and can be a value from 1 through 4,000. max indicates that the maximum storage size is $2^{31} - 1$ bytes (2 GB).	Varies.
Real	A smaller version of float. Contains a single-precision floating-point number from $-3.40E + 38$ to $3.40E + 38$.	4 bytes.
SmallDate Time	Defines a date that is combined with a time of day. The time is based on a 24-hour day, with seconds always zero (:00) and without fractional seconds. Can store dates only between 1/1/1900 and 6/6/2079.	4 bytes.
SmallInt	A smaller version of int. Can store values between -2^{15} to 2^{15}.	2 bytes.
SmallMoney	A smaller version of money. Can store decimal data scaled to four digits of precision. Can store values from $-214,748.3648$ to $214,748.3647$.	4 bytes.
SQL_Variant	Can store int, binary, and char values. Is a very inefficient data type.	Varies.
Text	Stores up to 2,147,483,647 characters of non-Unicode data.	1 byte for each character of storage.
Time	Defines a time of a day. The time is without time zone awareness and is based on a 24-hour clock.	5 bytes.

continues

TABLE 4.1   Continued

Field Type	Description	Storage
TimeStamp	Exposes automatically generated, unique binary numbers within a database. rowversion is generally used as a mechanism for version-stamping table rows.	8 bytes.
TinyInt	Stores whole numbers from 0 to 255.	1 byte.
Unique Identifier	A globally unique identifier (GUID) that is automatically generated when the NEWID() function is used.	16 bytes.
VarBinary	Can hold variable-length binary data from 1 to 8000 bytes.	Varies from 1 to 8000 bytes.
VarBinary (MAX)	Variable-length binary data. Max indicates that the maximum storage size is $2^{31} - 1$ bytes.	Varies from 1 to 8000 bytes.
VarChar	A variable-length string that can hold 1 to 8,000 non-Unicode characters.	1 byte per character stored.
VarChar (MAX)	Fixed-length non-Unicode string data. Max indicates that the maximum storage size is $2^{31} - 1$ bytes (2GB).	Varies.
XML	Stores XML data. You can store xml instances in a column or a variable of xml type.	Varies.

Working with Constraints

Constraints limit or control the types of data that the user can enter into your tables. There are seven main categories of constraints. They include primary key constraints, foreign key constraints, default constraints, Not Null constraints, check constraints, rules, and unique constraints. The text that follows covers each of these constraint types in detail.

Primary Key Constraints

A primary key constraint is a column or a set of columns that uniquely identify a row in the table. Although you can designate more than one field as the primary key, each table can have only one primary key.

Every table in your database should have a primary key constraint. Furthermore, it is best if your primary key meets the following criteria:

▶ Short

▶ Stable

▶ Simple

Short means that it should be composed of as few fields as possible, and the smaller the field type is, the better. In fact, the optimal primary key is a single int field. *Stable* means that the data within the field never changes. A great candidate for a primary key is an identity column. The "Identity Columns" section of this lesson covers identity columns in detail. *Simple* means that it is easy to remember and deal with. For example, an int field is simple, whereas a char field containing a long string of complex characters is not.

To add a primary key to a table:

1. Use the gray selectors on the left side of the Table Designer to select the fields that compose the primary key (see Figure 4.2).

2. Click the Set Primary Key tool on the toolbar. The columns appear with a Key icon on the record selector (see Figure 4.3).

Foreign Key Constraints

A foreign key constraint consists of a column or of a set of columns that participates in a relationship with a primary key table. The primary key is on the *one side* of the relationship, whereas the foreign key is on the *many side* of the relationship. A table can have only one primary key, but it can have multiple foreign keys. Each foreign key relates to a different primary key in a separate table. SQL Server looks up the foreign key value in the primary key table to ensure that only valid data is included in the table. Lesson 5, "Working with Table Relationships," covers foreign key constraints in additional detail.

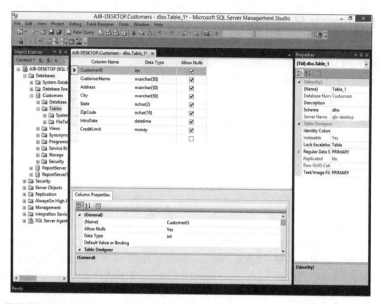

FIGURE 4.2 Use the gray selectors on the left side of the Table Designer to select the fields that compose the primary key.

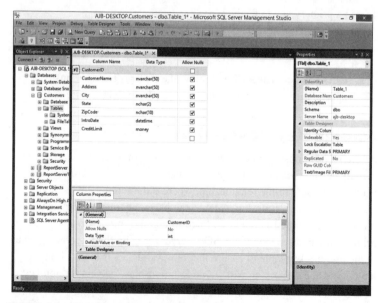

FIGURE 4.3 The columns included in the primary key appear with a key icon on the record selector.

Default Constraints

A default constraint is a value that SQL Server automatically places in a particular field in a table. A default value can be a constant, Null, or a function. All fields except identity and time stamp fields can contain default values. Each column can have one default constraint. You enter the default constraint in the properties for the desired field (see Figure 4.4).

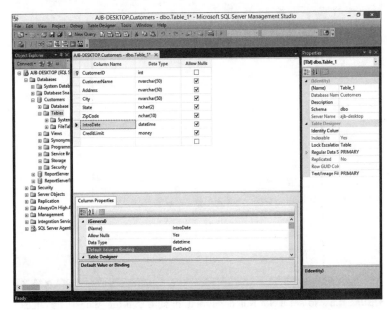

FIGURE 4.4 You enter the default constraint in the properties for the desired field.

Table 4.2 shows examples of default constraints.

TABLE 4.2 Examples of Default Constraints

Expression	Result
GetDate()	Sets the default value to the current date.
Null	Sets the default value to Null.
7	Sets the default value to the number 7.
'Hello'	Sets the default value to the string "Hello".

Not Null Constraints

In certain situations, you may want to require the user to enter data into a field. The Not Null constraint enables you to accomplish this task. To set a Not Null constraint, ensure that you uncheck the Allow Nulls check box (see Figure 4.5).

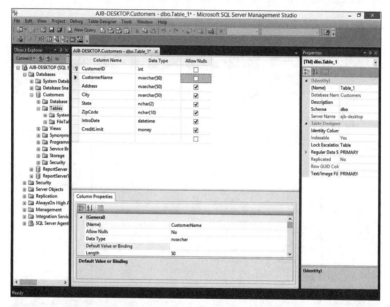

FIGURE 4.5   To set a Not Null constraint, ensure that the Allow Nulls check box is unchecked.

Check Constraints

Check constraints limit the range of values a user can enter into a column. You can enter as many check constraints as you want for a particular column. SQL Server evaluates the check constraints in the order in which you entered them. To enter a check constraint:

1. Click the Manage Check Constraints tool on the toolbar. The Check Constraints dialog box appears.

2. Click Add to add a new constraint.

3. Provide a constraint name and a constraint expression.

4. Designate other options as necessary. The completed dialog box appears as in Figure 4.6.

5. Click Close to close the dialog box and add the constraint.

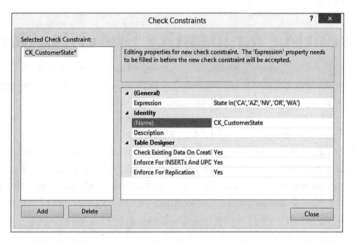

FIGURE 4.6 The Check Constraints dialog box enables you to enter Check constraints for the table.

Table 4.3 shows examples of check constraints.

TABLE 4.3 Examples of Check Constraints

Expression	Result
State In('CA', 'AZ', 'UT', 'CO')	Limits the value entered to CA, AZ, UT, and CO.
DateEntered <= GetDate()	Limits the value entered to a date on or before the current date.
CreditLimit Between 0 and 10000	Limits the value entered to a value between 0 and 10,000.

Rules

Whereas Check constraints apply only to the table for which you enter them, you can apply rules to multiple tables. Microsoft is phasing out their support for rules. They therefore do not allow you to create new rules. Instead of using rules, you should use check constraints and triggers.

Unique Constraints

A unique constraint requires that each entry in a particular column be unique. Each table can have 249 unique constraints. You create a unique constraint by creating a unique index.

Creating an Identity Specification

Identity columns provide an autoincrementing value for a table. You should use an identity column as the primary key field for any table that has no natural primary key that is short, stable, and simple. Identity columns are often of the int data type. You use the properties of the field to designate a column as an identity column (see Figure 4.7). Notice that after you designate a column as an identity column, you can designate both the identity seed and the identity increment. The *identity seed* is the starting value for the field. The *identity increment* is the value by which each automatically assigned value is incremented. For example, an identity field with an identity seed of 100 and an identity increment of 5 assigns the values 100, 105, 110, and so on.

FIGURE 4.7 You use the field's properties to designate a column as an identity column.

Adding Computed Columns

With computed columns, you can create a column that is based on data in other columns. SQL Server automatically updates the computed column when the columns on which it depends are updated. An example is an extended total that you base on the product of the price and quantity columns. To create a computed column, enter the desired formula into the (Formula) property under the Computed Column Specification key of the column (see Figure 4.8).

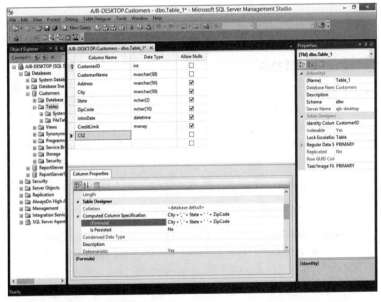

FIGURE 4.8 To create a computed column, enter the formula into the (Formula) property under the Computed Column Specification key of the column.

Table 4.4 shows examples of computed columns.

TABLE 4.4   Examples of Computed Columns

Expression	Result
`Price * Quantity`	Calculates the product of the price times the quantity.
`(Price * Quantity) * (1 - Discount)`	Calculates the discounted price.
`FirstName + ' ' + LastName`	Combines the contents of the first and last name fields and separates them with a space.

Working with User-Defined Data Types

User-defined data types enable you to further refine the data types provided by SQL Server. A user-defined data type is a combination of a data type, length, null constraint, default value, and rule. After you define a user-defined data type, you can use it in any tables that you build. To create a user-defined data type:

1. Expand the Programmability node for the database.

2. Expand the Types node under Programmability.

3. Right-click the User-defined Data Types node and select New User-defined Data Type. The New User-defined Data Type dialog box appears (see Figure 4.9).

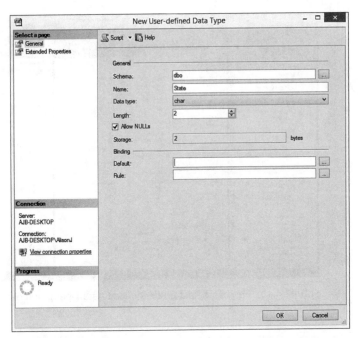

FIGURE 4.9 The User-defined Data Type Properties dialog box enables you to create or modify a user-defined data type.

4. Enter the required information, such as the name, data type, default, and rule associated with the user-defined type (see Figure 4.9) and click OK.

To apply a user-defined data type to a field:

1. Go into the design of the table to whose field you want to apply the data type.

2. Open the Data Type drop-down for the field to which you want to apply the data type (see Figure 4.10).

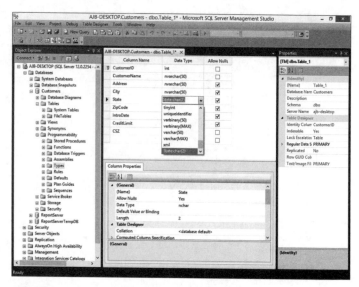

FIGURE 4.10   You can select a user-defined data type as the data type for a field.

3. Select the user-defined data type.

Adding and Modifying Indexes

You use indexes to improve performance when the user searches a field. Although it's generally best to include too many indexes rather than too few, indexes do have downsides. Indexes speed up searching, sorting, and grouping data. The downside is that they take up hard disk space and slow the process of editing, adding, and deleting data. Although the benefits of indexing outweigh the detriments in most cases, you should not index every field in each table. Create indexes only for fields or combinations of fields by which the user will search, sort, or group. Do not create indexes for fields that contain highly repetitive data. A general rule is to provide indexes for all fields regularly used in searching and sorting and as criteria for queries.

To create and modify indexes:

1. Modify the design of the table.

2. Select the Manage Indexes and Keys tool on the toolbar. The Indexes/Keys dialog box appears (see Figure 4.11).

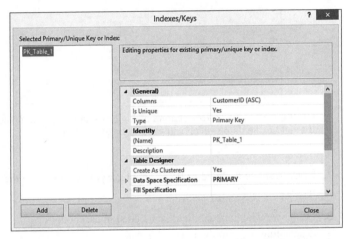

FIGURE 4.11 The Indexes/Keys dialog box enables you to determine the properties of the index.

3. Enter a name for the index.

4. Select the type of index you want to create. Select Clustered to designate the index as clustered. You can have only one clustered index per table. The data is stored physically based on the order of the clustered index.

5. Click Add.

6. Click within Columns and then click the ellipsis (...). You see the Index Columns dialog box (see Figure 4.12).

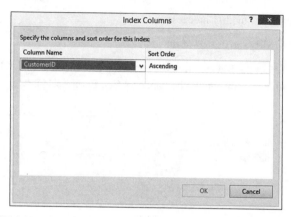

FIGURE 4.12 The Index Columns dialog box enables you to select the field or fields on which you want to base the index.

7. Click to select the field or fields on which you want to base the index.

8. Designate whether each field is included in ascending or descending order in the index.

9. Click OK to close the dialog box. You return to the Indexes/Keys dialog box.

10. If desired, click Create Unique to designate the index as a unique constraint.

11. The completed Indexes/Keys dialog box appears as in Figure 4.13. Click OK to close the dialog box and create the index.

To view all indexes associated with a table, you must first save your table (see the next section, "Saving Your Table"):

1. Click to expand the Indexes node for a table (see Figure 4.14).

2. Right-click the index you want to modify and click Properties. The Index Properties dialog box appears.

3. Make the desired changes to the index.

4. Click OK when you are finished.

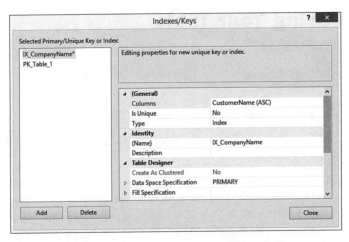

FIGURE 4.13 The Indexes/Keys dialog box enables you to manage table indexes.

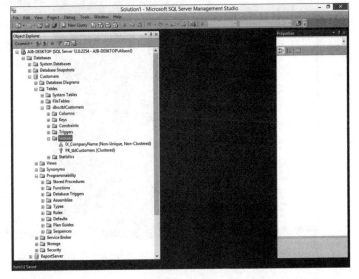

FIGURE 4.14 The Indexes node for a table allows you to view the indexes associated with that table.

Saving Your Table

To save your table:

1. Click the Save button on the toolbar. The Choose Name dialog box appears.

2. Select a name for your table and click OK.

3. Close the table design, if desired, by clicking the "x" on the tab for the table.

4. You may notice that the table does not immediately appear in the Object Explorer. To make it appear, right-click the Tables table and select refresh. Your table shows up in the list in the Object Explorer (see Figure 4.15).

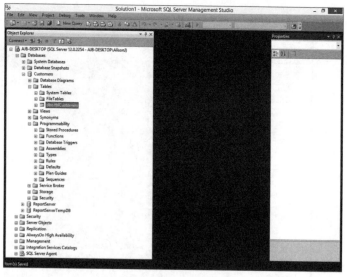

FIGURE 4.15   After refreshing the list of tables in the Object Explorer, the new table appears.

Summary

Tables and the relationships between them are the foundation for any application you build. It is therefore important that you set up your tables with all the necessary properties and then establish the proper relationships between them. This lesson began by covering all the important aspects of designing database tables. You then learned about important topics such as constraints, identity columns, and indexes. Now that you have explored the various ways you can refine the tables you build, in the next lesson you see how to use database diagrams to relate the tables in your database.

Q&A

Q. What is the difference between a check constraint and a rule?

A. Both check constraints and rules limit the range of values that a user can enter into a column. Whereas check constraints apply only to the table for which you enter them, you can apply rules to multiple tables.

Q. Explain what a primary key is and describe the ideal criteria for a primary key.

A. A primary key is a column or a set of columns that uniquely identify a row in a table. A primary key should be short, stable, and simple.

Q. Describe a foreign key and indicate how many foreign keys each table can contain.

A. A foreign key constraint consists of a column or a set of columns that participate in a relationship with a primary key table. The primary key is on the one side of the relationship, whereas the foreign key is on the many side of the relationship. A table can have multiple foreign keys.

Workshop

Quiz

1. What is a default constraint?

2. What is a Not Null constraint?

3. Provide an example of a computed column.

4. A column can have only one check constraint (true/false).

5. Why is the data type you select for a field important?

6. What is an identity column?

7. What is the best use of an identity column?

Quiz Answers

1. A default constraint is a value that SQL Server automatically places in a particular field in a table.

2. A Not Null constraint enables you to require that the user enter data into a field.

3. An extended price that is equal to the price times the quantity.

4. False.

5. The data type determines what data you can store in a field.

6. Identity columns provide an autoincrementing value for a table.

7. The best use of an identity column is as the primary key for a table. This is because it is short, stable, and simple.

Activities

Create a table that will store customer information. Add a field called CustomerID that will be the primary key of the table. Make it an identity field. Add a field called CompanyName. Make it VarChar(40). Add a Not Null constraint to the field. Add a field called Address and another field called City. Make them both VarChar(35). Add a field called State. Make it Char(2). Add a check constraint to ensure that the state is CA, UT, AZ, WY, OR, or WA. Give it a default value of CA. Add a field called IntroDate. Make it a DateTime field and give it a default value of today's date. Add a check constraint to ensure that the date entered is on or after today's date. Finally, add a field called CreditLimit. Make it a Money field. Give it a default value of $5,000. Add a check constraint to ensure that the amount entered is between zero and $10,000. Save the table and try entering data into it. Test the various defaults and constraints that you added to the table's structure.

LESSON 5

Working with Table Relationships

After you add the tables to your database, you next establish relationships between them. This helps to ensure the integrity of the data that users enter into the system. In this lesson, you learn:

- ▶ What relationships are and why you would want to use them
- ▶ How to work with database diagrams
- ▶ How to work with table relationships
- ▶ How to designate table and column specifications
- ▶ How to add a relationship name and description
- ▶ How to determine when foreign key relationships constrain the data entered in a column
- ▶ How to designate INSERT and UPDATE specifications

An Introduction to Relationships

Three types of relationships can exist between tables in a database: one-to-many, one-to-one, and many-to-many. Setting up the proper type of relationship between two tables in your database is imperative. The right type of relationship between two tables ensures:

- ▶ Data integrity
- ▶ Optimal performance
- ▶ Ease of use in designing system objects

This lesson discusses many reasons for these benefits. Before you can understand the benefits of relationships, though, you must understand the types of relationships available.

One-to-Many

A *one-to-many relationship* is by far the most common type of relationship. In a one-to-many relationship, a record in one table can have many related records in another table. A common example is a relationship set up between a Customers table and an Orders table. For each customer in the Customers table, you want to have more than one order in the Orders table. On the other hand, each order in the Orders table can belong to only one customer. The Customers table is on the *one side* of the relationship, and the Orders table is on the *many side*. For this relationship to be implemented, the field joining the two tables on the one side of the relationship must be unique.

In the Customers and Orders tables example, the CustomerID field that joins the two tables must be unique within the Customers table. If more than one customer in the Customers table has the same customer ID, it is not clear which customer belongs to an order in the Orders table. For this reason, the field that joins the two tables on the one side of the one-to-many relationship must be a primary key or must have a unique index. In almost all cases, the field relating the two tables is the primary key of the table on the one side of the relationship. The field relating the two tables on the many side of the relationship is called a *foreign key*.

One-to-One

In a *one-to-one relationship*, each record in the table on the one side of the relationship can have only one matching record in the table on the other side of the relationship. This relationship is not common and is used only in special circumstances. Usually, if you have set up a one-to-one relationship, you should have combined the fields from both tables into one table. The following are the most common reasons why you should create a one-to-one relationship:

▶ The number of fields required for a table exceeds the number of fields allowed in a SQL Server table.

▶ Certain fields that are included in a table need to be much more secure than other fields included in the same table.

▶ Several fields in a table are required for only a subset of records in the table.

The maximum number of fields allowed in a SQL Server table is 1,024. There are very few reasons (if any) why a table should ever have more than 1,024 fields. In fact, before you even get close to 1,024 fields, you should take a close look at the design of your system. On the *very* rare occasion when having more than 1,024 fields is appropriate, you can simulate a single table by moving some of the fields to a second table and creating a one-to-one relationship between the two tables.

The second reason to separate data that logically would belong in the same table into two tables involves security. An example is a table containing employee information. Many users of the system might need to access certain information, such as employee name, address, city, state, ZIP code, home phone, and office extension. Other fields, including the hire date, salary, birth date, and salary level, might be highly confidential. Although you can easily solve this problem with views, in which you create a view with only those fields that all the users can see, you may opt instead to store the secure fields in a table separate from the less-secure fields.

The last situation in which you would want to define one-to-one relationships occurs when certain fields in a table will be used for only a relatively small subset of records. An example is an Employee table and a Vesting table. Certain fields are required only for vested employees. If only a small percentage of a company's employees are vested, it is not efficient in terms of performance or disk space to place all the fields containing information about vesting in the Employee table. This is especially true if the vesting information requires a large volume of fields. By breaking the information into two tables and creating a one-to-one relationship between them, you can reduce disk-space requirements and improve performance. This improvement is particularly pronounced if the Employee table is large.

Many-to-Many

In a *many-to-many relationship*, records in both tables have matching records in the other table. You cannot directly define a many-to-many relationship; you must develop this type of relationship by adding a table called a *junction table*. You relate the junction table to each of the two tables in one-to-many relationships. An example is an Orders table and a Products table. Each order probably contains multiple products, and each product is found on many different orders. The solution is to create a third table called Order Details. You relate the Order Details table to the Orders table in a one-to-many relationship based on the OrderID field. You relate the Order Details table to the Products table in a one-to-many relationship based on the ProductID field.

Creating and Working with Database Diagrams

One way that you can establish and maintain relationships between SQL Server tables is to create a database diagram. It is important to understand how to create, add tables to, edit, and remove tables from a database diagram. The sections that follow cover these topics.

Creating a Database Diagram

To create a database diagram:

1. Right-click the Database Diagrams node and select New Database Diagram. You see the dialog box in Figure 5.1.

2. Click Yes to proceed. The Add Table dialog box opens (see Figure 5.2).

3. Designate the tables you want to add to the database diagram and click Add. Click Close. The diagram appears as in Figure 5.3.

4. Click and drag from the field(s) in the Primary Key table that you want to relate to the field(s) in the Foreign Key table. The Tables and Columns dialog box displays (see Figure 5.4).

FIGURE 5.1 If you haven't yet created any database diagrams for a database, you are prompted as to whether you want to create one.

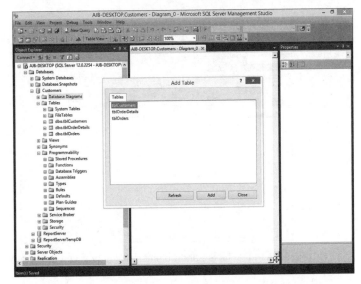

FIGURE 5.2 In the Add Table dialog box, you select the tables you want to include in the database diagram.

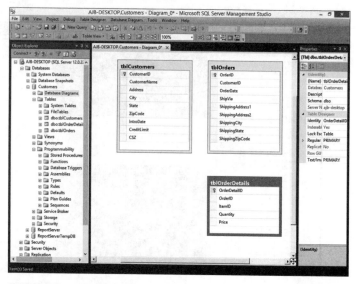

FIGURE 5.3 After adding tables to the database diagram, they appear in the Database Diagram window.

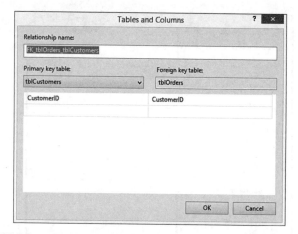

FIGURE 5.4 In the Tables and Columns dialog box, you designate which tables and columns will participate in the relationship.

5. Provide a relationship name and verify that the desired relationship has been established. Click OK to close the dialog box. The Foreign Key Relationship dialog box opens (see Figure 5.5).

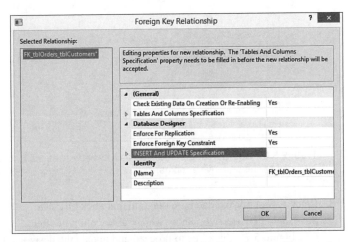

FIGURE 5.5 The Foreign Key Relationship dialog box enables you to designate properties for the relationship.

6. This dialog box contains several important options, which are covered throughout the remainder of the lesson. Designate any properties for the relationship and click OK. You are returned to the database diagram.

7. When you close the database diagram, SQL Server first prompts you as to whether you want to save your changes (see Figure 5.6). Click Yes to commit the changes to the underlying tables. The Choose Name dialog box displays.

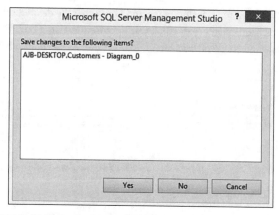

FIGURE 5.6   SQL Server prompts you as to whether you want to save changes to the underlying tables.

8. Enter a name for the database diagram and click OK. The Save dialog box lets you know which tables you will affect (see Figure 5.7). Click Yes to proceed and update the designated tables. The database diagram should now appear under the Database Diagrams node of SQL Server Management Studio.

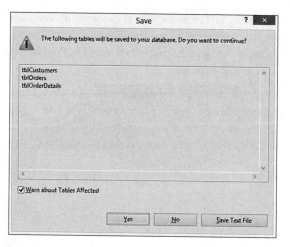

FIGURE 5.7   The Save dialog lets you know which tables your changes will affect.

Editing a Database Diagram

To edit a database diagram, you must first open it:

1. If you just created the database diagram and it does not appear in the list of existing database diagrams, right-click the Database Diagrams node and select Refresh.

2. After the diagram appears, right-click the diagram and select Modify. The Relationships dialog box appears.

To edit the relationship between two tables in a database diagram:

1. Right-click a table in the database diagram whose relationships you want to modify and select Relationships (see Figure 5.8). The Foreign Key Relationships dialog box opens (see Figure 5.9).

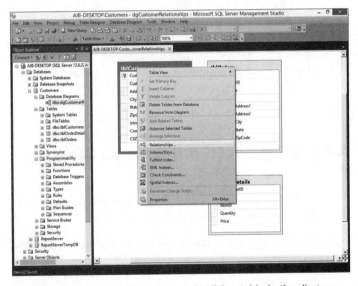

FIGURE 5.8   To edit a relationship, right-click a table in the diagram and select Relationships.

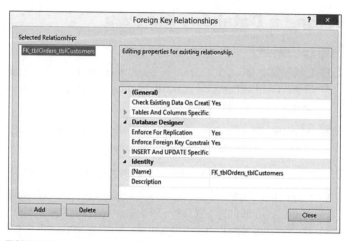

FIGURE 5.9 In the Foreign Key Relationships dialog box, you indicate the relationship you want to modify.

2. Click to select the relationship you want to modify.

3. Modify any of the desired properties (the remaining sections in this lesson cover these properties in detail).

4. Click Close.

Adding Tables to a Database Diagram

To add tables to the database diagram:

1. Right-click anywhere in the Relationships window and select Add Table. The Add Table dialog box opens.

2. Select the tables you want to add to the diagram and click Add.

3. Click Close. SQL Server adds the requested tables to the diagram.

Removing Tables from a Database Diagram

To remove tables from the database diagram:

1. Right-click the table you want to remove and select Remove from Diagram.

2. It is important to note that SQL Server removes the table from the diagram but does not remove the relationship from the database.

> NOTE: It is important to understand the correlation between the database diagram and the actual relationships you have established within the database. A database can contain multiple database diagrams. Each database diagram lets you view and modify the existing relationships. When you establish relationships, SQL Server creates the actual relationship between the tables. You can delete the tables from the database diagram (by right-clicking and selecting Remove Table from Diagram), but the relationships still exist (permanently removing relationships is covered in the section, "Deleting a Foreign Key Relationship," later in this lesson). The Database Diagram window provides a visual blueprint of the relationships you have established. If you modify the layout of the diagram by moving around tables, adding tables to the diagram, or removing tables from the diagram without changing any relationships, SQL Server *still* prompts you to save the changes to the diagram when you close the diagram window. In that case, SQL Server is not asking whether you want to save the relationships you have established; it is simply asking whether you want to save the visual layout of the window.

Working with Table Relationships

It is easy to view all the foreign key relationships in which a table is participating. Follow these steps:

1. Right-click the table and select Design. The design of the table appears (see Figure 5.10).

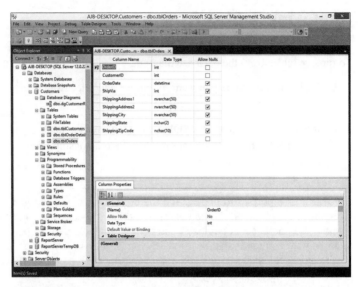

FIGURE 5.10 While the design of the table is visible, you are able to select the Relationships tool on the toolbar.

2. Click the Relationships tool on the toolbar. You then see the Foreign Key Relationships dialog box (see Figure 5.11).

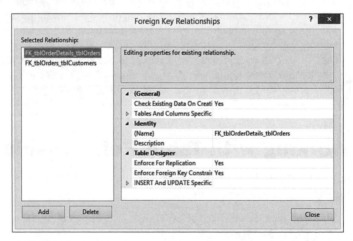

FIGURE 5.11 The Foreign Key Relationships dialog box enables you to work with the relationships associated with a table.

3. Click a relationship to select it. The properties of that relationship appear.

Adding a Foreign Key Relationship

With the Foreign Key Relationships dialog box, you can also add an index. Simply click the Add button. A new relationship appears with a default name and without a description. Before you take any further action, you should supply the Tables and Columns Specification covered in the section "Designating Table and Column Specifications." You must designate the table and column specification before SQL Server will accept the new relationship.

Deleting a Foreign Key Relationship

Deleting a foreign key relationship is easy. Follow these steps:

1. While in the Foreign Key Relationships dialog box, select the relationship you want to remove.

2. Click the Delete button. SQL Server removes the relationship without warning.

> WARNING: When you remove a foreign key relationship, you are removing the data integrity protection it affords you. This means, for example, that after you have removed the foreign key relationship between customers and orders, the user can add orders for customers that do not exist.

Designating Table and Column Specifications

By entering a Tables and Columns specification, you designate the foreign key table that will participate in the relationship, the field in the foreign key table that will participate in the relationship, and the field

in the current table that will participate in the relationship. To work
with the Tables and Columns Specification, follow these steps:

1. In the Foreign Key Relationships dialog box, click the right
   arrow to expand the Tables and Columns Specification property.

2. Click the Build button (...) that appears to the right of the Tables
   and Columns Specification property. The Tables and Columns
   dialog box opens (see Figure 5.12).

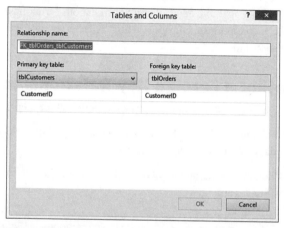

FIGURE 5.12   The Tables and Columns dialog box, showing the
relationship between the Customers table and the Orders table.

3. If you want, modify the relationship name. You generally want to
   rename the relationship to more accurately reflect the relationship
   you are creating (for example, FK_tblOrders_tblCustomers).

4. Click to select the primary key table that will participate in the
   relationship. For example, if you are creating foreign keys for the
   Orders table, you would designate the Customer table as the primary key table.

5. Use the drop-down on the left (under the primary key table) to
   select the field(s) that will participate in the relationship. For
   example, in the foreign key relationship between Orders and
   Customers, the CustomerID in the Customers table participates in
   the relationship.

6. Use the drop-down on the right (under the foreign key table) to select the field(s) in the current table that will participate in the relationship. In the relationship between the Orders table and the Customers table, the foreign key field participating in the relationship would be the CustomerID field.

7. Click OK to complete the process. SQL Server returns you to the Foreign Key Relationships dialog box.

Adding a Relationship Name and Description

It is helpful to provide a descriptive name for each relationship you add, as well as a brief description. This way when you are viewing a relationship in the Foreign Key Relationships dialog box, you can easily see the nature of the relationship you have selected.

To enter or change a name for the relationship, simply click the (Name) property for the relationship. Enter or change the name as you desire.

To enter a description for the relationship, click the Description property for the index. Enter a short description of your choice.

Determining When Foreign Key Relationships Constrain the Data Entered in a Column

As you can see establishing a relationship is quite easy. Establishing the right kind of relationship is a little more difficult. When you attempt to establish a relationship between two tables, SQL Server makes some decisions based on a few predefined factors:

- ▶ It establishes a one-to-many relationship if one of the related fields is a primary key or has a unique index.

- ▶ It establishes a one-to-one relationship if both the related fields are primary keys or have unique indexes.

- ▶ It cannot create a relationship if neither of the related fields is a primary key and neither has a unique index.

As covered earlier in this lesson, *referential integrity* consists of a series of rules that SQL Server applies to ensure that the relationships between tables are maintained properly. At the most basic level, referential integrity rules prevent the creation of orphan records in the table on the many side of the one-to-many relationship. After establishing a relationship between a Customers table and an Orders table, for example, all orders in the Orders table must be related to a particular customer in the Customers table. Before you can establish referential integrity between two tables, the following conditions must be met:

▶ The matching field on the one side of the relationship must be a primary key field or must have a unique index.

▶ The matching fields must have the same data types. They also must have the same size. Number fields on both sides of the relationship must have the same size (int, for example).

▶ Both tables must be part of the same database.

▶ If you opt to set the Check Existing Data on Creation option to Yes, existing data within the two tables cannot violate any referential integrity rules. All orders in the Orders table must relate to existing customers in the Customers table, for example.

After you establish referential integrity between two tables, SQL Server applies the following rules:

▶ You cannot enter a value in the foreign key of the related table that does not exist in the primary key of the primary table. For example, you cannot enter a value in the CustomerID field of the Orders table that does not exist in the CustomerID field of the Customers table.

▶ You cannot delete a record from the primary table if corresponding records exist in the related table. For example, you cannot delete a customer from the Customers table if related records exist in the Orders table (records with the same value in the CustomerID field) unless you designate a Delete Rule (see the section that follows).

▶ You cannot change the value of a primary key on the one side of a
relationship if corresponding records exist in the related table. For
example, you cannot change the value in the CustomerID field of
the Customers table if corresponding orders exist in the Orders
table unless you designate an Update rule in the Foreign Key
Relationships dialog box for the relationship (see the "Designating
Insert and Update Specifications" section that follows).

If any of the previous three rules is violated and referential integrity
is being enforced between the tables, an appropriate error message is
displayed, as shown in Figure 5.13.

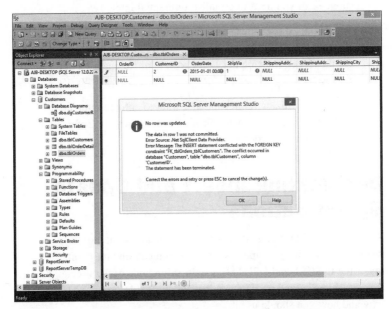

FIGURE 5.13   An appropriate error message appears if referential integrity
is violated.

SQL Server's default behavior is to prohibit the deletion of parent records that have associated child records and to prohibit the change of a primary key value of a parent record when that parent has associated child records. You can override these restrictions by using the INSERT and UPDATE specification, covered in the next section.

For now, let's see how you can establish referential integrity between the tables in your database. The process is as follows:

1. From the Foreign Key Relationships dialog box, select the relationship for which you want to establish referential integrity.

2. Set the Enforce Foreign Key Constraint property to Yes. This step alone is all you need to establish referential integrity.

3. If you want to check existing data when you save your changes to ensure that they do not violate the referential integrity rules, set the Check Existing Data on Creation or Re-enabling option to Yes.

4. If you are utilizing replication and want to enforce referential integrity during the synchronization process, set the Enforce for Replication property to Yes.

Designating Insert and Update Specifications

SQL Server enables you to define rules that dictate what will happen when the user deletes or updates a record. You can find these rules under the INSERT and UPDATE Specification node of the Foreign Key Relationships dialog box. The text that follows explores this node and why and how you should use it.

The Delete Rule

By setting the Delete rule, you determine what happens when the user deletes a record on the one side of a one-to-many relationship. For example, by setting the Delete rule to Cascade, you establish the rule so that the user can delete a record on the one side of a one-to-many relationship, even if related records exist in the table on the many side of the relationship. The user can delete a customer even if the customer has existing orders, for example. Referential integrity is maintained between the tables because SQL Server automatically deletes all related records in the child table.

If you attempt to delete a record from the table on the one side of a one-to-many relationship and no related records exist in the table on the many side of the relationship, you are able to delete the record. On the other hand, if you attempt to delete a record from the table on the one side of a one-to-many relationship and related records exist in the child table, you will delete the record from the parent table as well as any related records in the child table.

> TIP: Setting the Delete rule to Cascade is not always appropriate. It is an excellent feature, but you should use it prudently. Although it is usually appropriate to cascade delete from an Orders table to an Order Details table, for example, it generally is not appropriate to cascade delete from a Customers table to an Orders table. This is because you generally do not want all your order history deleted from the Orders table if for some reason you want to delete a customer. Deleting the order history causes important information, such as your profit and loss history, to change. It therefore is appropriate to prohibit this type of deletion and handle the customer in some other way, such as marking him as inactive or archiving his data. On the other hand, if you delete an order because it was canceled, you probably want the corresponding order detail information to be removed as well. In this case, the Cascade option is appropriate. You need to make the appropriate decision in each situation based on business needs. The important thing is to carefully consider the implications of each option before making your decision.

The Update Rule

With the Update rule set to Cascade, the user can change the primary key value of the record on the one side of the relationship. When the user makes an attempt to modify the field joining the two tables on the one side of the relationship, the change is cascaded down to the foreign key field on the many side of the relationship. This is useful if the primary key field is modifiable. For example, a purchase number on a purchase order master record may be updateable. If the user modifies the purchase order number of the parent record, you would want to cascade the change to the associated detail records in the purchase order detail table.

> NOTE: There is no need to select the Cascade option when the related field on the one side of the relationship is an identity field. An identity field can never be modified. The Cascade option has no effect on identity fields.

> NOTE: Other options for the Delete and Update rules include No Action, Set Null, and Set Default. No Action, the default value, does nothing and therefore does not allow the deletion of parent records that have children or the modification of the key field(s) of parent records that have children. Set Null sets the value of the foreign key field to Null. Finally, Set Default sets the value of the foreign key field to its default value.

Summary

Even if your table design is sound, a database set up without proper relationships compromises both data integrity and application performance. It is therefore important that you establish the proper relationships between the tables in your database. This lesson began with a discussion of the types of relationships available. You then learned about important topics such as how to establish relationships, how to designate table and column specifications, how to determine when foreign key relationships constrain the data entered in a column, and how to designate INSERT and UPDATE specifications.

Q&A

Q. What is the Tables and Columns specification?

A. The Tables and Columns specification enables you to designate the foreign key table that will participate in the relationship, the field in the foreign key table that will participate in the relationship, and the field in the current table that will participate in the relationship.

Q. **Describe three uses of a one-to-one relationship.**

A. You use a one-to-one join when the number of fields required for a table exceeds the number of fields allowed in a SQL Server table, when certain fields that are included in a table need to be much more secure than other fields included in the same table or when several fields in a table are required for only a subset of records in the table.

Q. **Describe a many-to-many relationship and how you create one.**

A. With a many-to-many relationship, records in both tables have matching records in the other table. You cannot create a many-to-many relationship directly. You must develop a junction table and relate the junction table to each of the two tables in one-to-many relationships.

Workshop

Quiz

1. Name the three types of relationships.

2. What is the most common type of relationship?

3. To create a relationship, matching fields must have the same data type (true/false).

4. By setting the Delete rule to Cascade, when a user deletes a row on the one side of the relationship, SQL Server deletes the corresponding rows on the many side of the relationship (true/false).

5. The UPDATE rule is very useful when working with Identity columns (true/false).

6. List three advantages of establishing relationships between database tables.

Quiz Answers

1. One-to-one, one-to-many, and many-to-many.

2. One-to-many.

3. True.

4. True.

5. False. Because you cannot change the value of an identity column, the UPDATE rule is not applicable to an identity column.

6. Data integrity, optimal performance, and ease of use in designing system objects.

Activities

Create a table that will store order information. Add a field called OrderID that will be the primary key field of the table. Make its data type Int and make it an identity field. Add a field called CustomerID. Give it the data type of Int. Add a Not Null constraint to the field. Add a field called OrderDate. Make it a DateTime field. Add another field called ShippedBy. Make it an Int field. Finally, add a field called FreightAmount. Make it a Money field. Now that you have created the table, establish a relationship between it and the Customers table created in Lesson 4, "Working with SQL Server Tables." Base the relationship on the CustomerID field from each table. Make sure you set the Enforce Foreign Key Constraint property of the relationship to Yes. Add some customers to the Customers table. Make note of their CustomerIDs. Add orders to the Orders table for those customers. You should be able to add those orders without a problem. Try adding orders for customers that do not exist. You should not be able to do so because of the referential integrity you applied. Try deleting customers who have orders. Once again, you should fail because of referential integrity. If you are feeling really ambitious, set the Delete Rule of the relationship to Cascade. Then try deleting a Customer with orders. The process should delete the customer and its corresponding orders.

LESSON 6

Getting to Know the SELECT Statement

Knowledge of the T-SQL language is vital to your success as a SQL Server administrator or developer. You use the T-SQL language to manipulate the data in your database. Using T-SQL, you can select, insert, update, and delete data. In this lesson, you learn:

▶ What T-SQL is

▶ How to build a SELECT statement

▶ How to work with a WHERE clause

▶ How to order your output

Introducing T-SQL

T-SQL, or Transact-SQL, is the dialect of the Structured Query Language (SQL) incorporated in SQL Server. To work effectively as a SQL Server developer, you must have a strong grasp of T-SQL. Fortunately, T-SQL is easy to learn. When retrieving data, you simply build a SELECT statement. SELECT statements are composed of clauses that determine the specifics of how the data is selected. When they're executed, SELECT statements select rows of data and return them as a recordset.

NOTE: In the examples that follow, keywords appear in uppercase. Values that you supply appear italicized. Optional parts of the statement appear in square brackets. Curly braces, combined with vertical bars, indicate a choice. Finally, ellipses are used to indicate a repeating sequence.

Working with the SELECT Statement

The SELECT statement is at the heart of the SQL language. You use the SELECT statement to retrieve data from one or more tables. Its basic syntax is the following:

```
SELECT column-list FROM table-list WHERE where-clause
ORDER BY order-by-clause
```

The SELECT clause specifies what columns you want to retrieve from the table that SQL Server returns to the result set. The basic syntax for a SELECT clause is as follows:

```
SELECT column-list
```

Selecting All Fields

The simplest SELECT clause looks like this:

```
SELECT * FROM Person.Person
```

This SELECT clause, combined with the FROM clause covered in the next section, retrieves all columns from a table.

Selecting Specific Fields

You will not always want to retrieve all fields from a table. In fact, most often you need to retrieve data only from specific fields.

The example that follows retrieves only the BusinessEntityID and FirstName columns from a table:

```
SELECT BusinessEntityID, FirstName FROM Person.Person
```

Adding an Expression

Not only can you include columns that exist in your table, but you also can include expressions in a SELECT clause. Here's an example:

```
SELECT BusinessEntityID, Title, FirstName + ' ' +
➡ MiddleName + ' ' +
   LastName AS FullName FROM Person.Person
```

This SELECT clause retrieves the BusinessEntityID column, the Title column, and an alias called FullName, which includes an expression that concatenates the FirstName, MiddleName, and LastName columns (see Figure 6.1).

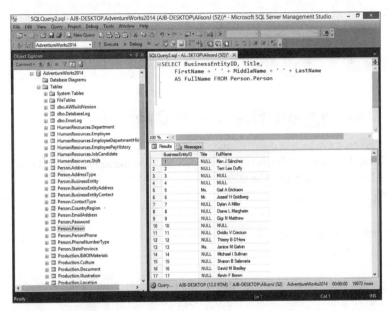

FIGURE 6.1 A SELECT clause that includes an expression that concatenates the FirstName, MiddleName, and LastName columns.

NOTE: The examples throughout this book are based on the AdventureWorks sample database. A backup of this database is available at http://msftdbprodsamples.codeplex.com/releases/view/125550. After you download the file, you must restore the database so that you can follow along with the examples. Lesson 22, "Maintaining the Databases You Build," covers the process of restoring a database.

NOTE: After installing the AdventureWorks database, you will probably notice that all the table names appear in the format *schema-name.table-name*. All objects in databases are contained in schemas. There are many advantages to placing database objects in schemas. Throughout the book, you will see examples such as Person.Address, with Person being the schema name and Address being the table name. When an object is associated with a schema, you must refer to the object along with its schema name.

Adding on the FROM Clause

The FROM clause specifies the tables or views from which the records should be selected. It can include an alias that you use to refer to the table. The FROM clause looks like this:

```
FROM table-list [AS alias]
```

Here's an example of a basic FROM clause:

```
FROM Person.Address
```

In this case, the name of the table is Address. If you combine the SELECT clause with the FROM clause, the SQL statement looks like this:

```
SELECT AddressID, AddressLine1 FROM Person.Address
```

This SELECT statement retrieves the AddressID and AddressLine1 columns from the Address table, which is part of Person schema.

Using Table Aliases

Just as you can alias the fields included in a SELECT clause, you can also alias the tables included in the FROM clause. The alias is used to shorten the name and to simplify a cryptic name, as well as for a variety of other reasons. Here's an example:

```
SELECT BusinessEntityID, FirstName FROM Person.Person AS Clients
```

Including the WHERE Clause

The WHERE clause limits the records retrieved by the SELECT statement. A WHERE clause can include columns combined by the keywords AND and OR. The syntax for a WHERE clause looks like this:

```
WHERE expression1 [{AND|OR} expression2 [...]]
```

A simple WHERE clause looks like this:

```
WHERE PersonType = 'EM'
```

Using an AND to further limit the criteria, the WHERE clause looks like this:

```
WHERE PersonType = 'EM' AND LastName Like 'Ma%'
```

This WHERE clause limits the records returned to those in which the PersonType is equal to EM and the LastName begins with Ma. Notice that T-SQL uses the percent (%) sign as a wildcard. Using an OR, the SELECT statement looks like this:

```
WHERE PersonType = 'EM' OR PersonType = 'SC'
```

This WHERE clause returns all records in which the PersonType is equal to either EM or SC. Compare that with the following example:

```
WHERE PersonType = 'EM' OR LastName Like 'Ma%'
```

This WHERE clause returns all records in which the PersonType is equal to EM or the LastName begins with Ma. For example, the people with EM as their PersonType are returned from this WHERE clause, as are the people whose LastName begins with Ma. The WHERE clause combined with the SELECT and FROM clauses looks like this (see Figure 6.2):

```
SELECT BusinessEntityID, PersonType, LastName FROM Person.Person
    WHERE PersonType = 'EM' OR LastName Like 'MA%'
```

Notice in Figure 6.2 that records with a PersonType of 'MA' appear regardless of their last name. Records of people whose last names begin with 'MA' appear regardless of their PersonType.

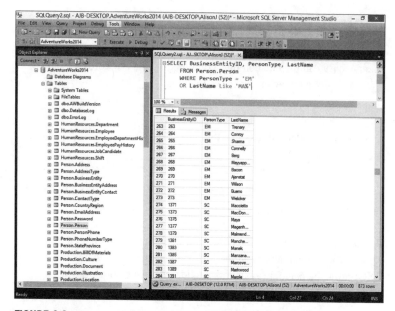

FIGURE 6.2 A SELECT clause that retrieves the BusinessEntityID, PersonType, and LastName columns for all the people with either the PersonType 'EM', or a LastName that begins with 'MA'.

Contrast this example to the following example:

```
SELECT BusinessEntityID, PersonType, LastName FROM Person.Person
    WHERE PersonType = 'EM' AND LastName Like 'MA%'
```

The results appear in Figure 6.3.

If you look at the records returned in Figure 6.3, you see that all records that appear in the result have *both* a PersonType of 'EM' and a last name that begins with 'MA'.

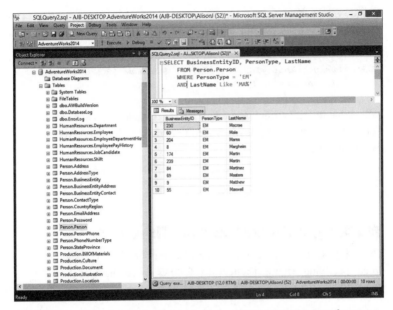

FIGURE 6.3 Using the keyword AND, both conditions must be true for a row to appear in the result set.

Rules When Filtering Data

You must follow several rules when building a WHERE clause. You must enclose the text strings for which you are searching in apostrophes. You must also surround dates with apostrophes. Unlike text strings and dates, you do not delimit numeric fields. Finally, you must include the keyword LIKE when utilizing wildcard characters. Remember that T-SQL uses the percent symbol as the wildcard for zero or more characters. The underscore (_) is the wildcard for a single character. Let's take a look at some examples:

```
SELECT BusinessEntityID, PersonType, LastName FROM Person.Person
    WHERE BusinessEntityID >= 200
```

In this example, because BusinessEntityID is a numeric field with the `int` data type, the criteria for BusinessEntityID contains no apostrophes. With character (string) data, the process is different:

```
SELECT BusinessEntityID, PersonType, LastName FROM Person.Person
    WHERE LastName = 'Martin'
```

Notice that the text string we are looking for is enclosed in apostrophes. You might be surprised that when specifying criteria for dates, you also use apostrophes:

```
SELECT BusinessEntityID, PersonType, LastName, ModifiedDate FROM
➥ Person.Person
    WHERE ModifiedDate >= '1/1/2013'
```

Working with Dates and Times

The T-SQL language is rich with date and time functions you can use when specifying criteria. The text that follows covers many of these powerful functions.

The `GetDate()` function returns the current date and time. Take a look at the simplest example:

```
SELECT GetDate()
```

This example returns one column containing the current date and time. A more complex example of using the `GetDate()` function looks like this:

```
SELECT ModifiedDate, CONVERT(int. ModifiedDate - GetDate())
    FROM Person.Person
```

The T-SQL in this example returns the ModifiedDate from the Person table, along with the number of days between the current date and the ModifiedDate. The results appear in Figure 6.4.

Another T-SQL date function is DAY. Its counterparts are the MONTH and YEAR functions. These functions return the day, month, and year associated with a date. They look like this:

```
SELECT DAY(GetDate()), MONTH(GetDate()), YEAR(GetDate())
```

The results of executing this statement appear in Figure 6.5.

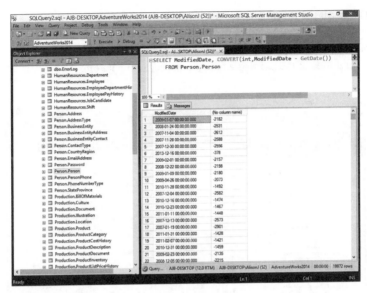

FIGURE 6.4 The GetDate() function returns the current date and time.

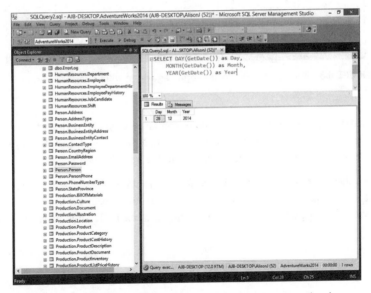

FIGURE 6.5 Use the DAY, MONTH, and YEAR functions to return the day, month, and year associated with a date.

The `DATEPART` function extracts a part of a date. You use it to determine the day of the month, month of the year, year of a date, day of the year, day of the week, week of the year, and other parts of a date. An example of several uses of the `DATEPART` function appear in Figure 6.6.

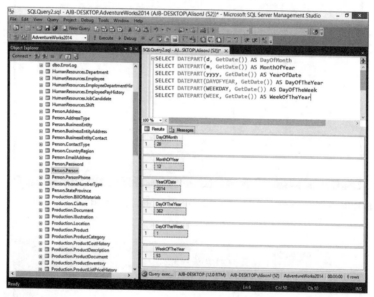

FIGURE 6.6   The `DATEPART` function enables you to return various parts of a date.

With the `DATEADD` function, you add or subtract a specified period of time from a date. For example, you can add a quarter to a date. Examples of the uses of the DATEADD function appear in Figure 6.7.

Another powerful date-related T-SQL function is DATEDIFF. It allows you to determine the number of days, months, years, or other time increments between two dates. Figure 6.8 illustrates some examples of the DATEDIFF function.

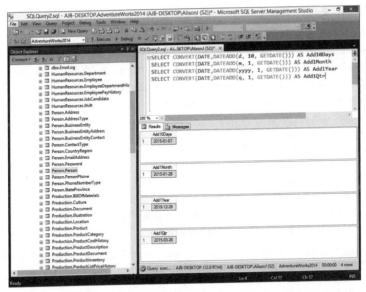

FIGURE 6.7 The DATEADD function enables you to add or subtract periods of time to or from a date.

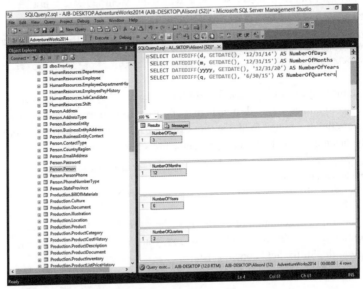

FIGURE 6.8 With the DATEDIFF function, you can determine the interval of time between two dates.

Using IN **and** NOT

The IN and NOT keywords facilitate the process of determining what rows appear in the result of your SELECT statement. The IN keyword allows you to select a series of values that will appear in the result. The NOT keyword allows you to exclude what appears in the result. The following is an example of the use of the IN keyword:

```
SELECT BusinessEntityID, PersonType, LastName, ModifiedDate FROM
➡ Person.Person
   WHERE PersonType IN('EM','IN','VC')
```

This SELECT statement returns the designated fields from the Person table for all records where the PersonType is 'EM', 'IN', or 'VC'. If you want to retrieve all rows where the PersonType is not 'EM', 'IN', or 'VC', you simply add the keyword NOT to the statement:

```
SELECT BusinessEntityID, PersonType, LastName, ModifiedDate FROM
➡ Person.Person
   WHERE PersonType NOT IN('EM','IN','VC')
```

Another example of the use of the NOT keyword is where you want to return all rows from the Person table where the ModifiedDate is not between 1/1/2013 and 12/31/14. It looks like this:

```
SELECT BusinessEntityID, PersonType, LastName, ModifiedDate FROM
➡ Person.Person
   WHERE ModifiedDate NOT BETWEEN '1/1/2013' AND '12/31/2014'
```

Another keyword you might find useful is the NULL keyword. The NULL keyword allows you to designate that you want to retrieve only those rows where the designated field does not contain data or only those rows where the designated field does contain data. Here's how it works:

```
SELECT BusinessEntityID, PersonType, LastName, ModifiedDate FROM
➡ Person.Person
   WHERE Suffix IS NULL
```

This SELECT statement returns all rows where the Suffix field does not contain data. By adding the keyword NOT, you can return only those rows where the Suffix field contains data.

```
SELECT BusinessEntityID, PersonType, LastName, ModifiedDate FROM
➥ Person.Person
    WHERE Suffix IS NOT NULL
```

As you can see, by combining everything you have learned in this section, you can retrieve only the data you want and need.

Using the ORDER BY Clause

The ORDER BY clause determines the order in which SQL Server sorts the returned rows. It's an optional clause and looks like this:

```
ORDER BY column1 [{ASC|DESC}], column2 [{ASC|DESC}] [,…]]
```

Here's an example:

```
ORDER BY BusinessEntityID
```

The ORDER BY clause can include more than one field:

```
ORDER BY LastName, FirstName
```

When you specify more than one field, SQL Server uses the leftmost field as the primary level of sort. Any additional fields are the lower sort levels. Combined with the rest of the SELECT statement, the ORDER BY clause looks like this:

```
SELECT BusinessEntityID, FirstName, LastName, ModifiedDate FROM
➥ Person.Person
    WHERE ModifiedDate Between '1/1/2013' AND '12/31/2014'
    ORDER BY ModifiedDate
```

The results appear in order by ModifiedDate (see Figure 6.9).

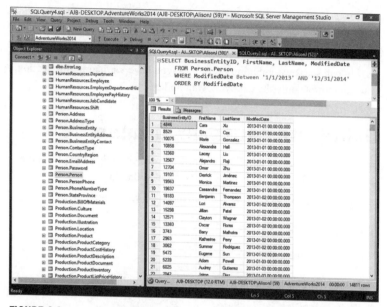

FIGURE 6.9 A `SELECT` clause that retrieves the BusinessEntityID, FirstName, LastName, and ModifiedDate columns for all the people whose ModifiedDate is between 1/1/2013 and 12/31/2014. SQL Server orders the results by ModifiedDate.

Changing the Sort Direction

The `ORDER BY` clause enables you to determine whether the sorted output appears in ascending or descending order. By default, output appears in ascending order. To switch to descending order, use the optional keyword `DESC`. Here's an example:

```
SELECT BusinessEntityID, FirstName, LastName, ModifiedDate FROM
➥ Person.Person
  WHERE ModifiedDate Between '1/1/2013' AND '12/31/2014'
  ORDER BY ModifiedDate DESC
```

This example selects the BusinessEntityID, FirstName, LastName, and ModifiedDate fields from the Person table, ordering the output in descending order by the ModifiedDate field (see Figure 6.10).

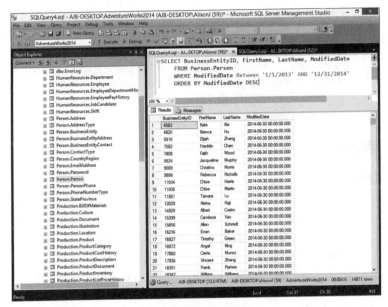

FIGURE 6.10 A SELECT clause that retrieves the BusinessEntityID, FirstName, LastName, and ModifiedDate columns for all the people with a ModifiedDate between 1/1/2013 and 12/31/2014. SQL Server orders the results in descending order by ModifiedDate.

Summary

The T-SQL language is the foundation for most of what you do in SQL Server. It is therefore necessary to have a strong understanding of the T-SQL language constructs. This lesson covered many of the basics of the T-SQL language. You learned about the SELECT statement, the FROM keyword, the WHERE clause, and the ORDER BY clause. We cover T-SQL in additional detail throughout the remainder of the book.

Q&A

Q. Why do you use a SELECT statement?

A. To retrieve data from one or more tables.

Q. Name the wildcard characters you can use when searching and explain the differences between them.

A. The two wildcard characters are the percent (%) sign and the underscore (_). T-SQL uses the percent symbol (%) as the wildcard for zero or more characters. The underscore (_) is the wildcard for a single character.

Workshop

Quiz

1. Which keyword do you use to designate the tables you will include in the query?

2. You use an alias to permanently rename a field in a table (true/false).

3. What is the keyword you use if you want the data to appear in descending order?

Quiz Answers

1. You use `FROM` to designate the tables you will include in the query.

2. False. `ALIAS` provides only an alias for the field in the query output.

3. If you want the query output to appear in descending order, use the `DESC` keyword.

Activities

Build a simple `SELECT` statement based on the Person.Address table in the AdventureWorks2014 sample database. Include the AddressID, AddressLine1, AddressLine2, City, StateProvinceID, and PostalCode fields. Add a `WHERE` clause to limit the records returned in the result to those where the City is Seattle, Redmond, or Newport Hills. Order the data in descending order by City.

LESSON 7

Taking the SELECT Statement to the Next Level

Lesson 6, "Getting to Know the SELECT Statement," provided you with an introduction to the SQL SELECT statement. This lesson takes your knowledge of the SELECT statement to the next level. In this lesson, you learn:

▶ What the DISTINCT keyword is and why it's valuable

▶ How to use the FOR XML clause to return data as an XML document

▶ How to group and summarize data

▶ How to apply criteria to summarized data

▶ Limit the number of rows returned in the output

Adding the DISTINCT Keyword

The DISTINCT keyword ensures uniqueness of values in the column or combination of columns included in the query result. Consider the following SQL statement:

```
SELECT City FROM Person.Address ORDER BY City
```

This statement returns one row for each address record (see Figure 7.1). The same city appears multiple times in the output.

Contrast the statement used in the previous example with this:

```
SELECT DISTINCT City FROM Person.Address ORDER By City
```

This statement returns a list of unique cities from the list of addresses (see Figure 7.2).

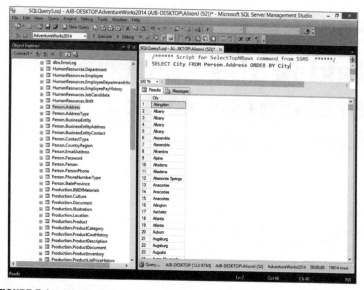

FIGURE 7.1 A SELECT statement that returns one row for each address record. The same city appears multiple times in the output.

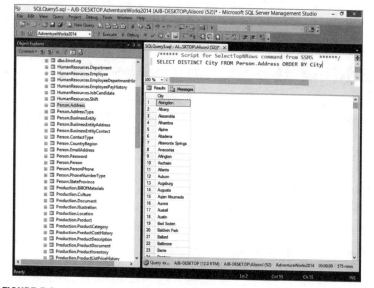

FIGURE 7.2 A SELECT statement that returns a list of unique cities from the list of addresses.

The statement that follows returns a unique list of city and modified date combinations (see Figure 7.3):

```
SELECT DISTINCT City, ModifiedDate FROM Person.Address ORDER BY
➡ City
```

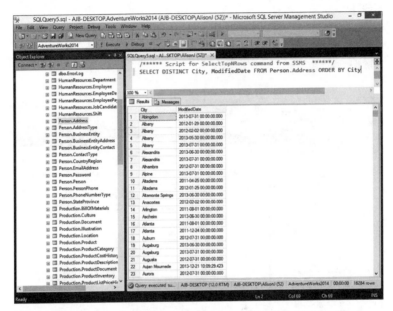

FIGURE 7.3 A SELECT statement that returns a list of city and modified date combinations from the list of addresses.

Working with the FOR XML **Clause**

You use the FOR XML clause to return data as an XML document. When using the FOR XML clause, you must specify the mode as RAW, AUTO, or EXPLICIT. With the RAW option, SQL Server takes the result of the query and transforms each row in the result set into an XML element with a generic identifier. Here's an example:

```
SELECT BusinessEntityID, FirstName, MiddleName, LastName
FROM Person.Person
ORDER BY LastName, FirstName
FOR XML RAW
```

After you click the resulting link, the results appear as in Figure 7.4 (notice the generic *row* identifier). With the AUTO option, SQL Server returns a simple nested XML tree. SQL Server represents each field in each table specified in the SELECT clause as an XML element. Here's an example:

```
SELECT BusinessEntityID, FirstName, MiddleName, LastName
FROM Person.Person
ORDER BY LastName, FirstName
FOR XML AUTO
```

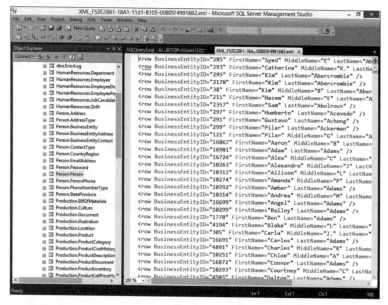

FIGURE 7.4 The result of using the FOR XML RAW clause to return data.

When you click the resulting link, the results appear as in Figure 7.5 (notice the Person.Person identifier). Finally, with the EXPLICIT option, you explicitly define the shape of the tree. You must write your queries so that the columns listed in the SELECT clause are mapped to the appropriate element attributes.

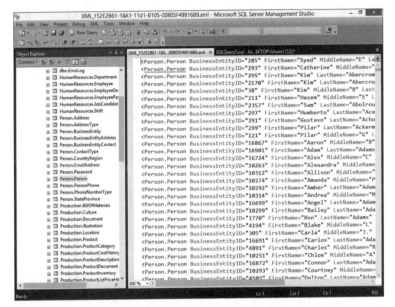

FIGURE 7.5 The result of using the FOR XML AUTO clause to return data.

Working with the GROUP BY Clause

You can use the GROUP BY clause to calculate summary statistics. The syntax of the GROUP BY clause is:

```
GROUP BY group-by-expression1 [,group-by-expression2 [,…]]
```

You use the GROUP BY clause to dictate the fields on which SQL Server groups the query result. When you include multiple fields in a GROUP BY clause, they are grouped from left to right. SQL Server automatically outputs the fields in the order designated in the GROUP BY clause. In the following example, the SELECT statement returns the product number, color, and total safety stock level for each product number/color combination. The results are displayed in order by product number and color (see Figure 7.3):

```
SELECT ProductNumber, Color,
    Sum(SaftetyStockLevel) AS TotalSafetyStock
    FROM Production.Product
    GROUP BY ProductNumber, Color
```

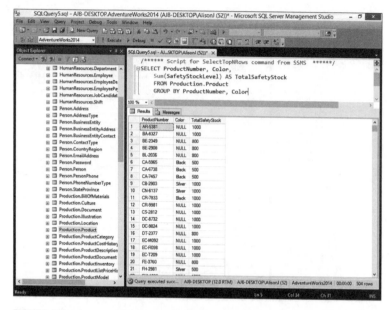

FIGURE 7.6   A SELECT statement that returns the product number, color, and total safety stock level for each product number/color combination.

The GROUP BY clause indicates that SQL Server doesn't display the detail for the selected records. Instead, it displays the fields indicated in the GROUP BY uniquely. One of the fields in the SELECT statement must include an aggregate function. SQL Server displays the result of the aggregate function along with the fields specified in the GROUP BY clause.

Including Aggregate Functions in Your SQL Statements

You use aggregate functions to summarize table data. The aggregate functions available include COUNT, COUNT_BIG, SUM, AVG, MIN, and MAX. The following sections discuss each of these aggregate functions. You can find additional aggregate functions in the Books Online for SQL Server. You can access Books Online by selecting View Help from the Help menu in SQL Server Management Studio.

Using the COUNT **Function**

You use the COUNT function to count the number of rows in a table. It looks like this:

```
SELECT COUNT(*) AS CountOfProducts FROM Production.Product
```

The example counts the number of rows in the Product table (see Figure 7.7).

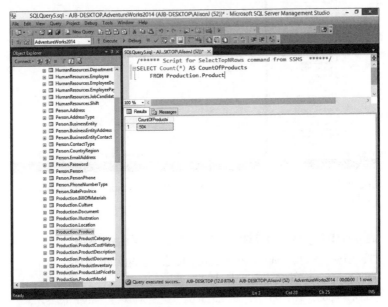

FIGURE 7.7 A SELECT statement that counts the number of rows in the Product table.

As an alternative, you can count values in a particular column. The SQL statement looks like this:

```
SELECT COUNT(Color) AS CountOfColors FROM Production.Product
```

This example counts the number of colors found in the Product table (see Figure 7.8).

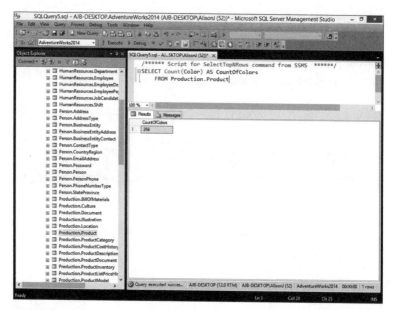

FIGURE 7.8 A SELECT statement that counts the number of colors found in the Product table.

Working with the COUNT_BIG Function

The COUNT_BIG function is identical to the COUNT function, except that it returns a bigint data type. It looks like this:

```
SELECT COUNT_BIG(Color) AS CountOfColors FROM Production.Product
```

Exploring the SUM Function

The SUM function is available only for numeric columns. It adds the data in the columns. Here's an example:

```
SELECT SUM(Weight) AS TotalWeight FROM Production.Product
```

The example totals the Weight column for all rows in the Product table. When used with the GROUP BY clause, the SUM function can easily total values for each grouping:

```
SELECT Color, SUM(Weight) AS TotalWeight FROM Production.Product
➥ GROUP BY Color
```

The example totals the weight for each color (see Figure 7.9).

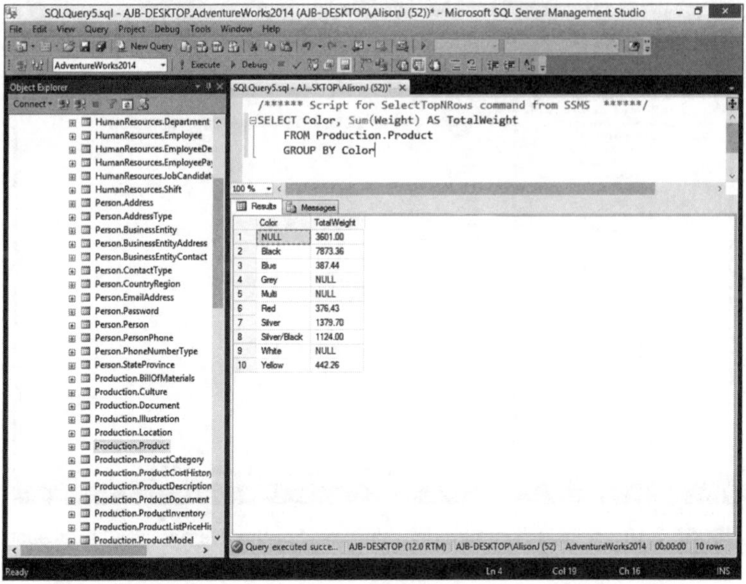

FIGURE 7.9   A SELECT statement that totals the weight for each color found in the Product table.

Working with the AVG **Function**

Just as you can easily total data, you can average data. The following statement finds the average freight for all orders in the Orders table:

```
SELECT AVG(Weight) AS AvgWeight FROM Production.Product
```

When used with the GROUP BY clause, the AVG function can easily average values in each grouping:

```
SELECT Color, AVG(Weight) AS AvgWeight FROM Production.Product
➥ GROUP BY Color
```

The result provides the average weight for each color (see Figure 7.10).

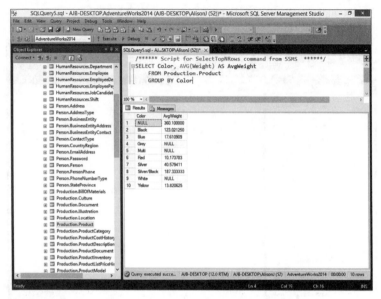

FIGURE 7.10 A SELECT statement that provides the average weight for each color found in the Product table.

Using the MIN **Function**

Another important aggregate function is MIN. You use the MIN function to find the minimum value in a column. This statement finds the minimum weight in the Product table:

```
SELECT MIN(Weight) FROM Production.Product
```

When used with the GROUP BY clause, the MIN function can easily find the minimum values in each grouping:

```
SELECT Color, MIN(Weight) FROM Production.Product GROUP BY Color
```

The result provides the minimum weight for each color (see Figure 7.11).

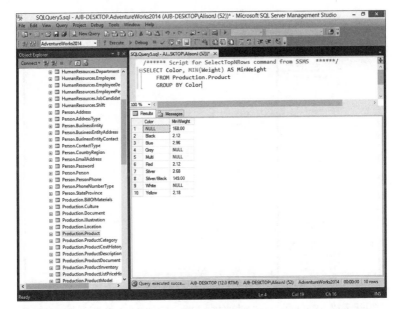

FIGURE 7.11 A SELECT statement that provides the minimum weight for each color found in the Product table.

Using the MAX **Function**

A related aggregate function is MAX. You use the MAX function to find the maximum value in a column. This statement finds the maximum weight in the Product table (see Figure 7.12):

```
SELECT MAX(Weight) FROM Production.Product
```

When used with the GROUP BY clause, the MAX function can easily find the maximum values in each grouping:

```
SELECT Color, MAX(Weight) FROM Production.Product GROUP BY Color
```

The result provides the maximum weight for each color (see Figure 7.13).

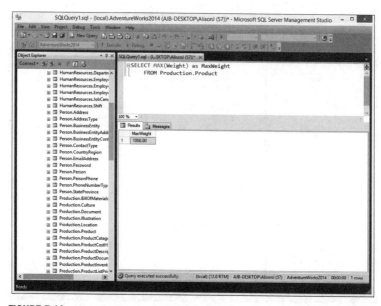

FIGURE 7.12 You use the MAX function to find the maximum value in a column.

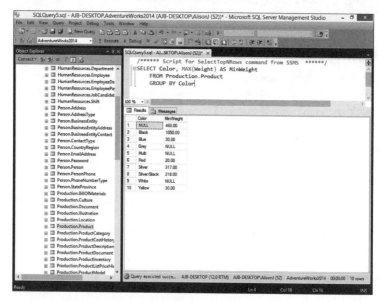

FIGURE 7.13 When used with the GROUP BY clause, the MAX function can easily find the maximum value in each grouping.

Taking Advantage of the HAVING Clause

A HAVING clause is similar to a WHERE clause, but it differs in one major respect: SQL Server applies it *after* it summarizes the data rather than beforehand. In other words, the WHERE clause is used to determine which rows are grouped. The HAVING clause determines which groups are included in the output. A HAVING clause looks like this:

```
HAVING expression1 [{AND|OR} expression2[…]]
```

In the following example, SQL Server applies the criteria > 1000 after it applies the aggregate function SUM to the grouping. Therefore, SQL Server includes only colors with total weight greater than 1000 in the output (see Figure 7.14).

```
SELECT Color,
    Sum(Weight) AS TotalWeight
    FROM Production.Product
    GROUP BY Color
    HAVING Sum(Weight)>1000
```

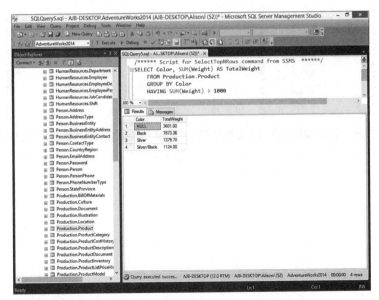

FIGURE 7.14 A SELECT statement that includes colors with total weight greater than 1000 in the output.

Creating Top Values Queries

You use the TOP clause to limit the number of rows that SQL Server includes in the output. Here's an example:

```
SELECT TOP 10 Color, Weight FROM Production.Product
    ORDER BY Weight DESC
```

This example shows the 10 highest weight amounts along with their corresponding colors (see Figure 7.15).

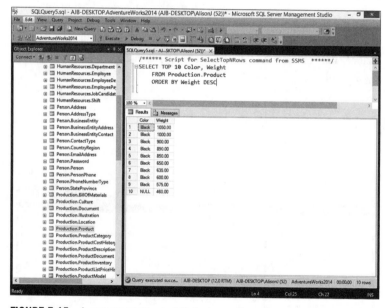

FIGURE 7.15 A SELECT statement that shows the colors associated with the highest 10 weight amounts.

In addition to enabling you to select the top number of rows, T-SQL also enables you to select the top percent of rows. Here's an example:

```
SELECT TOP 10 PERCENT Color, Weight FROM Production.Product
    ORDER BY Weight DESC
```

Here the top 10% of weight amounts appear in the query result.

Summary

As mentioned in Lesson 6, the T-SQL language is integral to your success as a SQL Server administrator or developer. This lesson started where Lesson 6 left off. It covered many important T-SQL language constructs. You learned about the DISTINCT keyword and how to output XML. You also learned how to group and aggregate data, producing counts, totals, averages, minimum values, and maximum values in a grouping. The lesson also covered how to use HAVING to apply criteria to aggregated data. Finally, you learned how to return only the top values from a result set.

Q&A

Q. Explain the difference between the HAVING clause and the WHERE clause.

A. SQL Server applies the HAVING clause *after* it summarizes the data; it applies the WHERE clause *before* it summarizes the data.

Q. Explain the DISTINCT keyword.

A. The DISTINCT keyword ensures uniqueness of values in the column or combination of columns included in the query result.

Q. Why would you use a Top Values query?

A. You use a Top Values query to limit the number of rows that appear in the output.

Workshop

Quiz

1. List the three modes of the FOR XML statement.

2. What is the purpose of aggregate functions?

3. Name four aggregate functions.

4. One of the aggregate functions is COUNT LARGE (true/false).

5. PERCENT is a valid keyword when the TOP clause is used (true/false).

Quiz Answers

1. The three modes of the FOR XML statement are RAW, AUTO, and EXPLICIT.

2. They summarize table data.

3. Sum, Count, Min, Max, Avg.

4. False. It is called COUNT BIG.

5. True.

Activities

Build a SELECT statement that counts, totals, averages, and finds the minimum and maximum SalesLastYear by TerritoryID from the Sales.SalesPerson table. Modify the statement to return only the territories where the total SalesLastYear is greater than 1 million. Finally, return the 100 highest SalesLastYear and associated TerritoryID from the Sales.SalesPerson table.

LESSON 8

Building SQL Statements Based on Multiple Tables

Now that you've learned the basics of the T-SQL language, you're ready to move on to more advanced techniques. To really take advantage of what T-SQL has to offer, you must know how to return recordsets that contain data based on multiple tables. In this lesson, you learn:

- ▶ What inner joins are and how to implement them
- ▶ What outer joins are and how they differ from inner joins
- ▶ How to output data based on multiple tables

Working with Join Types

When you build a system based on normalized table structures, you must join the tables back together to see the data in a useable format. For example, if you have separated customers, orders, and order details, you need to join these tables in a query to see the name of the customer who placed an order for a particular item. Several types of joins are available. They include inner joins, outer joins, full joins, and self-joins. This lesson covers the inner and outer join types. The next lesson, "Powerful Join Techniques," covers full joins and self-joins.

Using Inner Joins

An inner join is the most common type of join. When you use an inner join, only rows on the one side of the relationship that have matching rows on the many side of the relationship are included in the output. Here's an example:

```
SELECT Person.BusinessEntityID,
    FirstName, LastName, PhoneNumber
    FROM Person.Person
    INNER JOIN Person.PersonPhone
    ON Person.BusinessEntityID = PersonPhone.BusinessEntityID
```

This example includes only those people who have phone numbers. The results appear in Figure 8.1.

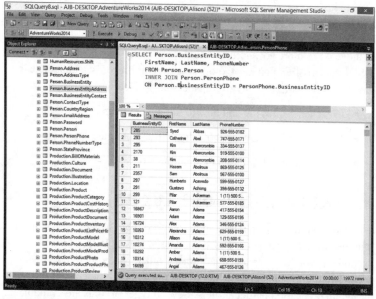

FIGURE 8.1 An inner join that includes all people who have phone numbers.

At times, you need to join more than two tables in a SQL statement. The most common syntax is as follows:

```
FROM table1 JOIN table2 ON condition1 JOIN table3 ON condition2
```

The following example joins the Person, PersonPhone, and PhoneNumberType tables:

```
SELECT Person.BusinessEntityID,
    FirstName, LastName, PhoneNumber, Name as PhoneNumberType
    FROM Person.Person
    INNER JOIN Person.PersonPhone
    ON Person.BusinessEntityID = PersonPhone.BusinessEntityID
    INNER JOIN Person.PhoneNumberType
    ON PersonPhone.PhoneNumberTypeID = PhoneNumberType.
    ➥ PhoneNumberTypeID
```

The results appear in Figure 8.2. Notice that data appears from all three tables.

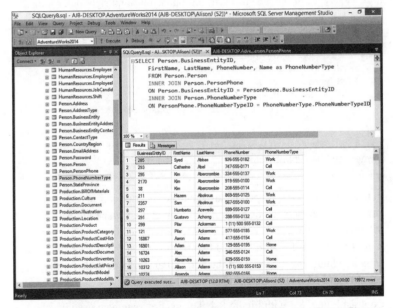

FIGURE 8.2 An inner join that includes data from the Person, PersonPhone, and PhoneNumberType tables.

In the example, the order of the joins is unimportant. The exception to this is when you combine inner and outer joins. When you combine inner and outer joins, the SQL Server engine applies two specific rules. First, the nonpreserved table in an outer join cannot participate in an inner join. The nonpreserved table is the one whose rows may not appear. In the case of a left outer join from Customers to Orders, the Orders table is considered the nonpreserved table. Therefore, it cannot participate in an inner join with OrderDetails. The second rule is that the nonpreserved table in an outer join cannot participate with another nonpreserved table in another outer join.

Creating Outer Joins

An outer join enables you to include rows from one side of the join in the output, regardless of whether matching rows exist on the other side of the join. Two types of outer joins exist: left outer joins and right outer joins. With a left outer join, SQL Server includes in the output all rows in the first table specified in the SELECT statement. Here's an example:

```
SELECT Person.BusinessEntityID,
    FirstName, LastName, PhoneNumber
    FROM Person.Person
    LEFT OUTER JOIN Person.PersonPhone
    ON Person.BusinessEntityID = PersonPhone.BusinessEntityID
```

> NOTE: The word OUTER is assumed in the LEFT JOIN clause used when building a left outer join.

In the previous example, people are included regardless of whether they have phone numbers. Notice that if you look at the lower-right corner of Figure 8.3, you see that 19974 rows were returned from the SELECT statement. This is because I added two records to the Person.Person table *without* adding any records into the Person.PersonPhone table for the people that I added.

Contrast Figure 8.3 with Figure 8.4. The SELECT statement used in Figure 8.4 looks like this:

```
SELECT Person.BusinessEntityID,
    FirstName, LastName, PhoneNumber
    FROM Person.Person
    INNER JOIN Person.PersonPhone
    ON Person.BusinessEntityID = PersonPhone.BusinessEntityID
```

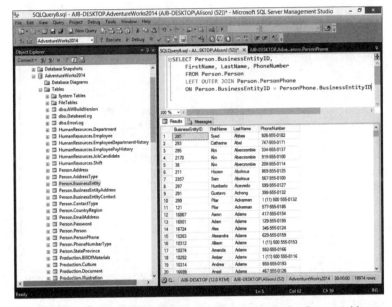

FIGURE 8.3 A left outer join that includes records from the Person table regardless of whether they have phone numbers.

Because the SELECT statement contains an inner join, the two people without phone numbers in Person.PersonPhone do not appear in the result set. Therefore, only 19972 rows appear in the result.

With the right outer join shown next, phone numbers are included whether or not they have associated people. If you have properly enforced referential integrity, this scenario should never exist.

```
SELECT Person.BusinessEntityID,
    FirstName, LastName, PhoneNumber
    FROM Person.Person
    RIGHT OUTER JOIN Person.PersonPhone
    ON Person.BusinessEntityID = PersonPhone.BusinessEntityID
```

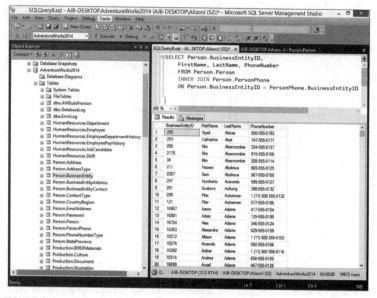

FIGURE 8.4 An inner join that excludes records from the Person table if those records don't have associated phone numbers.

Summary

In a world of normalized data, it is important that you understand how to use queries to join your tables back together. This lesson showed you how to join table data. You learned about both inner and outer joins. The examples provided clearly illustrated the differences between them.

Q&A

Q. Why must you join tables together in a query?

A. When you build a system based on normalized table structures, you must join the tables back together to see the data in a useable format.

Q. Explain what an inner join is.

A. An inner join outputs just those rows on the one side of the join that have matching rows on the many side of the join.

Q. Explain what an outer join is.

A. An outer join outputs rows on the one side of the join regardless of whether they have matching rows on the many side of the join.

Q. What is the difference between a left outer join and a right outer join?

A. With a left outer join, SQL Server includes all rows in the output for the first table in the SELECT statement. With a right outer join, SQL Server includes all rows in the output for the second table in the SELECT statement.

Workshop

Quiz

1. When joining a Customer table and an Order table, all customers will always appear (true/false).

2. When joining a Customer table and an Order table with a left outer join, all customers will always appear (true/false).

Quiz Answers

1. False. Only the customers who have associated orders appear.

2. False. This is true if the Customer table appears in the SELECT statement before the Order table.

Activities

Practice joining the Person and EmailAddress tables in the AdventureWorks sample database with an inner join, a left outer join, and a right outer join. Add a few people without email addresses. Note that the number of rows in the output differs for the various join types.

LESSON 9

Powerful Join Techniques

Now that you understand the mechanics of inner and outer joins, you are ready to delve into more advanced join techniques. In this lesson, you learn:

- ▶ What full joins are and why you might need them
- ▶ The power of self-joins
- ▶ How to utilize union queries
- ▶ What subqueries are and how to take advantage of them
- ▶ How to utilize the INTERSECT operator
- ▶ What the EXCEPT operator can accomplish for you

Utilizing Full Joins

A full join combines the behavior of the left and right outer joins. It looks like this:

```
SELECT Person.BusinessEntityID,
    FirstName, LastName, PhoneNumber
    FROM Person.Person
    FULL JOIN Person.PersonPhone
ON Person. BusinessEntityID = PersonPhone.BusinessEntityID
```

In this example, all people appear in the output regardless of whether they have phone numbers, and all phone numbers appear in the output whether or not they are associated with people. The results appear in Figure 9.1.

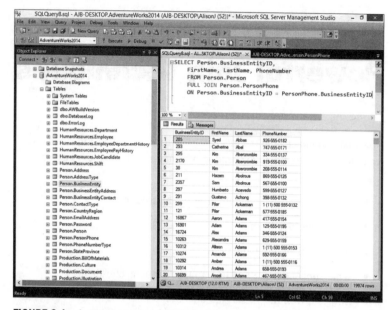

FIGURE 9.1 A `SELECT` statement that shows the result of joining the Person table to the PersonPhone table using a full join.

Taking Advantage of Self-Joins

A self-join involves joining a table to itself. Although it is not the most common type of join, it valuable. Imagine the scenario in which an Employee table contains a field called EmployeeID and another field called SupervisorID. The SupervisorID field must contain a valid EmployeeID. It would not make sense to have separate Employee and Supervisor tables because supervisors are employees. This is where the self-join comes in. A self-join looks like this:

```
SELECT Employee.BusinessEntityID,
    EmployeeInfo.FirstName AS EmployeeFName,
    EmployeeInfo.LastName AS EmployeeLName,
    SupervisorInfo.FirstName AS SupervisorFName,
    SupervisorInfo.LastName AS SupervisorLName
FROM HumanResources.Employee AS Supervisor INNER JOIN
    HumanResources.Employee AS Employee
    ON Supervisor.BusinessEntityID = Employee.SupervisorID INNER
➡ JOIN
```

```
Person.Person AS EmployeeInfo
ON Employee.BusinessEntityID = EmployeeInfo.BusinessEntityID
➡ INNER JOIN
Person.Person AS SupervisorInfo
ON Supervisor.BusinessEntityID = SupervisorInfo.
➡ BusinessEntityID
```

In this example, the SupervisorID from the Employee table is joined
to the BusinessEntityID field in an alias of the Employee table (called
Supervisor). The resulting employee and supervisor information is output
from the query (see Figure 9.2).

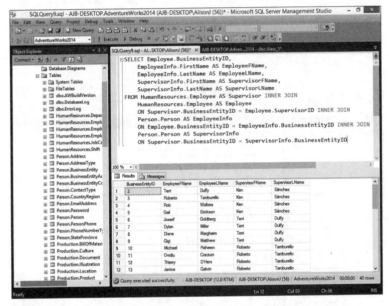

FIGURE 9.2 A SELECT statement that shows the result of joining the
Employee table to itself.

If you take a close look at the results in Figure 9.2, you see that only
employees who have supervisors appear in the result. This is because our
self-join is an inner join. The example that follows uses a right outer join
rather than an inner join to link the Person table to itself.

```
SELECT Employee.BusinessEntityID,
    EmployeeInfo.FirstName AS EmployeeFName,
    EmployeeInfo.LastName AS EmployeeLName,
    SupervisorInfo.FirstName AS SupervisorFName,
    SupervisorInfo.LastName AS SupervisorLName
FROM Person.Person AS SupervisorInfo INNER JOIN
    HumanResources.Employee AS Supervisor
    ON SupervisorInfo.BusinessEntityID = Supervisor.
    ➥ BusinessEntityID
    RIGHT OUTER JOIN Person.Person AS EmployeeInfo
    INNER JOIN HumanResources.Employee AS Employee
    ON EmployeeInfo.BusinessEntityID = Employee.BusinessEntityID
    ON Supervisor.BusinessEntityID = Employee.SupervisorID
```

The results appear in Figure 9.3. Notice that the employee with a
BusinessEntityID of 1 has no supervisor but does appear in the result.

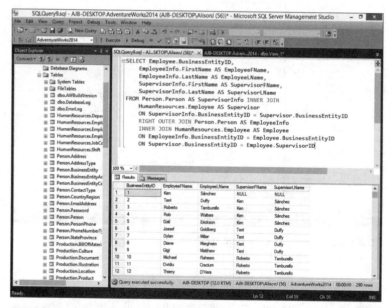

FIGURE 9.3 A `SELECT` statement that uses an outer join when joining the
Employee table to itself.

Exploring the Power of Union Queries

Union queries enable you to combine rather than join data from more than one table. A typical example of a union query is one that combines data from a Product table and a DiscontinuedProduct table. Another example is a query that combines data from a Customer table and a CustomerArchive table. Here's an example of a union query:

```
SELECT TransactionID, ProductID, TransactionDate, Quantity
FROM Production.TransactionHistory
UNION
SELECT TransactionID, ProductID, TransactionDate, Quantity
FROM Production.TransactionHistoryArchive
```

This example outputs all rows from the TransactionHistory table as well as from the TransactionHistoryArchive table (see Figure 9.4).

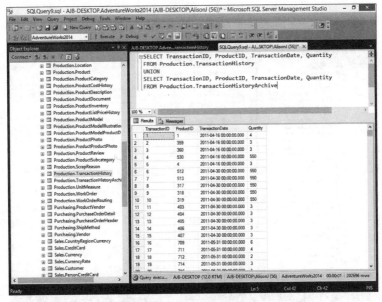

FIGURE 9.4 A `SELECT` statement that outputs all rows from the TransactionHistory table as well as from the TransactionHistoryArchive table.

If you want to order the results, you must place the ORDER BY statement after the second SELECT statement:

```
SELECT TransactionID, ProductID, TransactionDate, Quantity
FROM Production.TransactionHistory
UNION
SELECT TransactionID, ProductID, TransactionDate, Quantity
FROM Production.TransactionHistoryArchive
ORDER BY Quantity DESC
```

In this example, SQL Server combines the results of both SELECT statements in descending order by Quantity. The results appear in Figure 9.5.

It is often helpful to be able to identify the source table for each row in the output. The SQL statement that follows identifies how to accomplish this task.

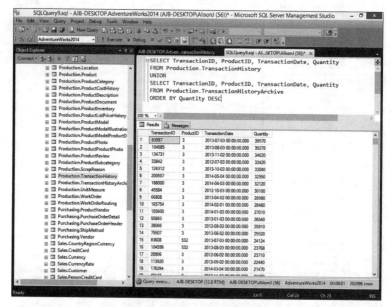

FIGURE 9.5 A SELECT statement that outputs the results of a UNION query in descending order by Quantity.

```
SELECT TransactionID, ProductID, TransactionDate,
Quantity, 'C' as RecordSource
FROM Production.TransactionHistory
UNION
SELECT TransactionID, ProductID, TransactionDate,
Quantity, 'A' as Recordsource
FROM Production.TransactionHistoryArchive
ORDER BY Quantity DESC
```

Notice that in the example, the SQL statement adds a column called RecordSource. It sets the value of the column to a different value within each SELECT statement. The results appear in Figure 9.6.

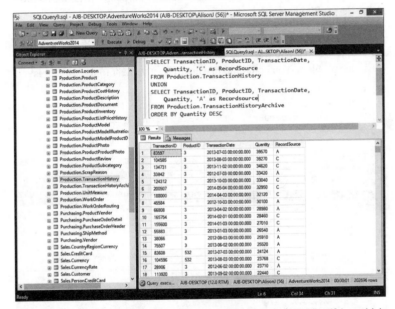

FIGURE 9.6 A SELECT statement that includes an indicator identifying which table that record came from.

Notice in the figure that some rows contain 'C' in the RecordSource column, indicating that they come from the TransactionHistory table. Other rows contain 'A' in the RecordSource column, indicating that they come from the TransactionHistoryArchive table.

Working with Subqueries

A *subquery* is a query that SQL Server evaluates before it evaluates the main query. Here's an example:

```
SELECT BusinessEntityID, FirstName, LastName FROM Person.Person
➥ WHERE
    BusinessEntityID Not In(Select BusinessEntityID FROM Person.
    ➥ PersonPhone)
```

In this example, SQL Server executes the statement that selects data from the PersonPhone table *before* it evaluates the statement that selects data from the Person table (see Figure 9.7). It returns all people without records in the PersonPhone table.

This is *not* a very efficient method of accomplishing the task of finding all the people without phones. A better solution would be to use an outer join to solve this problem. You could modify the SQL statement to look like this:

```
SELECT Person.BusinessEntityID, FirstName, LastName
    FROM Person.Person LEFT OUTER JOIN Person.PersonPhone
    ON Person.BusinessEntityID = PersonPhone.BusinessEntityID
    WHERE PersonPhone.BusinessEntityID Is Null
```

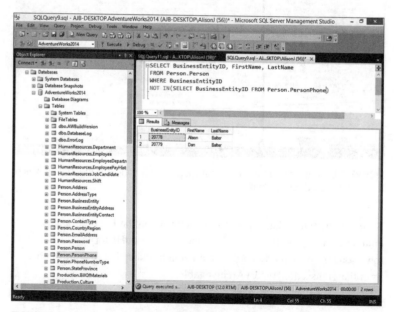

FIGURE 9.7 A SELECT statement that returns all people without phones.

This example uses a left outer join to select all people who do not have phones. Because this uses a left outer join, people are included whether or not they have phone records. Because the criteria designate that only rows with a null BusinessEntityID appear in the output, only people without phone records are included.

Using the INTERSECT **Operator**

An alternative technique to use when you want to only return rows in one table that have corresponding rows in another table is to use the INTERSECT operator. The INTERSECT operator looks like this:

```
SELECT ProductID
FROM Production.Product
INTERSECT
SELECT ProductID
FROM Production.WorkOrder
ORDER BY ProductID
```

The results show only products that have work orders (see Figure 9.8).

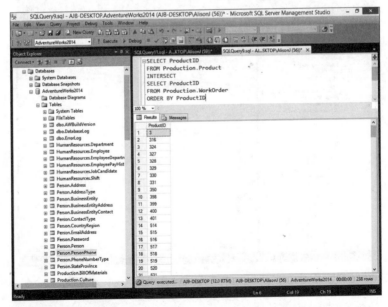

FIGURE 9.8 A SELECT statement that returns all products with associated work orders.

Working with the EXCEPT **Operator**

The INTERSECT operator's counterpart is the EXCEPT operator. The EXCEPT operator returns rows from the first SELECT statement that are not returned by the second SELECT statement. This means EXCEPT returns only rows, which are not available in the second SELECT statement. The EXCEPT clause looks like this:

```
SELECT ProductID
FROM Production.Product
EXCEPT
SELECT ProductID
FROM Production.WorkOrder
ORDER BY ProductID
```

This example returns all Products that do *not* have associated work orders. The results appear in Figure 9.9.

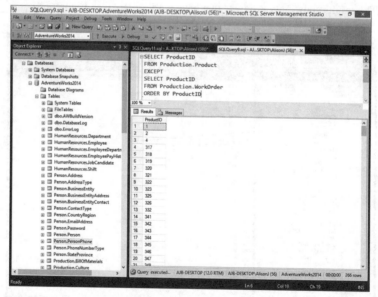

FIGURE 9.9 A SELECT statement that returns all products without associated work orders.

Swapping the order of the tables returns a totally different result. The example that follows returns the work orders that aren't associated with a product. With referential integrity in place, this statement will never return any rows.

```
SELECT ProductID
FROM Production.WorkOrder
EXCEPT
SELECT ProductID
FROM Production.Product
ORDER BY ProductID
```

Summary

This lesson began with a discussion of full joins. You then learned how to create self joins, which allow you to join a table to itself. The lesson moved on to union queries, which allow you to combine data from two tables as if they were within one table. After exploring subqueries, you learned about the INTERSECT and EXCEPT operators that enable you to build queries that mimic the behavior of inner and outer joins.

Q&A

Q. Explain what a full join is.

A. A full join combines the behavior of a left outer join and a right outer join. An example is where you show all customers whether or not they have orders and all orders whether or not they are associated with a customer.

Q. Describe what a subquery does.

A. SQL Server Express evaluates a subquery before it evaluates the main query.

Q. Provide an example of where a self-join is useful.

A. You can use a self-join to determine the name of the supervisor associated with each employee.

Q. Provide an example of where a union query is useful.

A. You can use a union query to combine data from a sales table and a sales history table, displaying the results in a report.

Workshop

Quiz

1. A union query joins two tables (true/false).

2. What operator simulates an inner join?

3. Subqueries are the most efficient way to return rows in one table that do not have associated rows in another table (true/false).

Quiz Answers

1. False. Union queries allow you to combine two tables.

2. INTERSECT.

3. False. Outer joins and the EXCEPT operator are far more efficient techniques to use when you need to return rows in one table that do not have associated rows in another table.

Activities

Create a SQL statement that uses a full join to join the Product and WorkOrder tables. Add some people to the Person table. You will need to create new BusinessEntityIDs in the Person.BusinessEntity table first. Then create a subquery that finds all people in the Person table who do not have records in the PersonPhone table. Build a SQL statement with an outer join that returns the sample people. Finally, accomplish the same task using the EXCEPT operator.

LESSON 10

Modifying Data with Action Queries

Not only can you use T-SQL to select data, you can also use it to update data. T-SQL gives you the ability to update, insert into, and delete data from tables. In this lesson, you learn:

- ▶ How to use the UPDATE statement to update table data
- ▶ How to use the INSERT statement to insert data into an existing table
- ▶ How to use the SELECT INTO statement to insert data into a new table
- ▶ How to use the DELETE statement to selectively delete data from a table
- ▶ How to use the TRUNCATE statement to remove all data from a table

The UPDATE Statement

As its name implies, an UPDATE statement updates table data. The format of the UPDATE statement is as follows:

```
UPDATE tablename SET column1=value1, [column2=value2....]
```

The example that follows updates the contents of the Customers table, changing the city to Venice Beach for all rows in which the city is Westlake Village:

```
UPDATE Person.Address
SET City = 'Venice Beach'
WHERE City = 'Westlake Village'
```

A valuable technique lies in the ability to update data in one table based on the values of data in another table. Here's an example:

```
UPDATE Production.Product
SET Product.ListPrice =
    ProductListPriceHistory.ListPrice
FROM Production.Product
INNER JOIN Production.ProductListPriceHistory
ON Product.ProductID =
    ProductListPriceHistory.ProductID
WHERE GetDate()
BETWEEN ProductListPriceHistory.StartDate
    AND ProductListPriceHistory.EndDate
```

This SQL statement updates the ListPrice in the Product table based on data in the ProductListPriceHistory table. To do this, it joins the two tables on ProductID. It only updates the ListPrice in the Product table where there are corresponding records in the ProductListPriceHistory table and where the current date is between the StartDate and EndDate field values. The results of executing this SQL statement are shown in Figure 10.1.

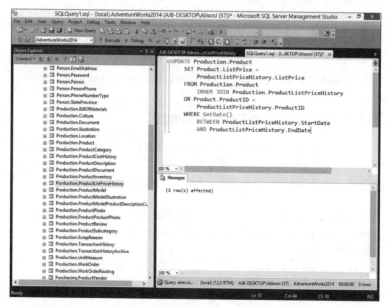

FIGURE 10.1 An UPDATE statement that updates the Product table based on values in the ProductListPriceHistory table.

The INSERT **Statement**

You use the INSERT statement to insert data into an *existing* table. The INSERT statement has the following format:

```
INSERT [INTO] table_or_view [(col1, col2…)] VALUES (value1,
➡ value2)
```

Here's an example:

```
INSERT INTO Person.Address
   (AddressLine1,
   City, StateProvinceID,
   PostalCode,ModifiedDate)
VALUES
   ('34 Elm Street',
   'Venice Beach', 9,
   90291, '1/26/15')
```

In this example, the designated values are inserted into the specified fields in the Address table.

If a column is not provided in the list of values being inserted, one of the following conditions must be true for the omitted column for the record to be inserted successfully:

▶ The column has an Identity property, in which case the next available identity value is used.

▶ The column has a default value, in which case the default value is automatically inserted into the field.

▶ The column has a timestamp data type, in which case the current timestamp value is used.

▶ The column allows nulls, in which case a null value is used.

▶ The column is computed, in which case the computed value is used.

In addition to being able to specify values you want to insert into a record in a table, you can also insert data from another table. Here's an example:

```
INSERT INTO
   [Production].[TransactionHistoryArchive]
   (TransactionID, ProductID,
   ReferenceOrderID,ReferenceOrderLineID,
```

```
TransactionDate, TransactionType,
Quantity, ActualCost,
ModifiedDate)
SELECT TransactionID, ProductID,
ReferenceOrderID, ReferenceOrderLineID,
TransactionDate, TransactionType,
Quantity, ActualCost,
ModifiedDate
FROM Production.TransactionHistory
WHERE TransactionDate < '1/1/2014'
```

In this example, all records from the TransactionHistory table
with a TransactionDate before 1/1/2014 are inserted into the
TransactionHistoryArchive table. The results are shown in Figure 10.2.

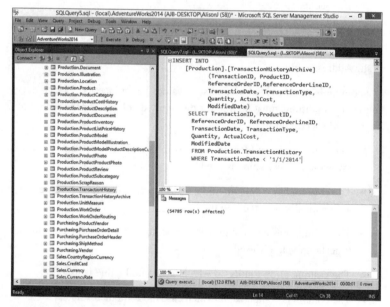

FIGURE 10.2 An INSERT statement that inserts records from the
TransactionHistory table into the TransactionHistoryArchive table.

The SELECT INTO **Statement**

Whereas the INSERT statement inserts data into an existing table, the SELECT INTO statement creates a new table. Here's an example:

```
SELECT
TransactionID, ProductID,
ReferenceOrderID,ReferenceOrderLineID,
TransactionDate, TransactionType,
    Quantity, ActualCost,
    ModifiedDate
INTO Production.TransactionsOld
FROM Production.TransactionHistory
WHERE TransactionDate < '1/1/2014'
```

In this example, all transactions with a TransactionDate before 1/1/2014 are inserted into a new table called TransactionsOld. The resulting table is shown in Figure 10.3.

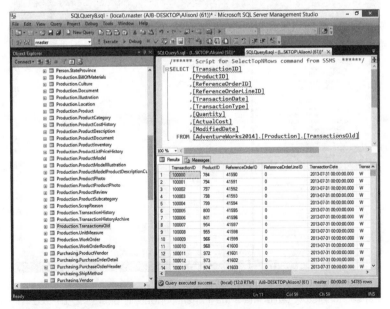

FIGURE 10.3 A SELECT INTO statement that inserts records from the TransactionHistory table into a new table called TransactionsOld.

The DELETE **Statement**

You use the DELETE statement to remove rows from a table. The format of the DELETE statement is as follows:

```
DELETE [FROM] table-name [WHERE search_conditions]
```

Here's an example:

```
DELETE FROM Production.TransactionHistory
WHERE TransactionDate < '1/15/2014'
```

This example removes all rows from the TransactionHistory table in which the TransactionDate is before 1/15/2014. The results of executing the SQL statement are shown in Figure 10.4.

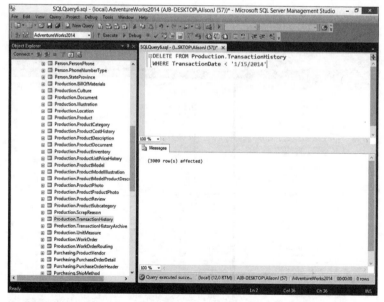

FIGURE 10.4 A DELETE statement that deletes records from the TransactionHistory table where the TransactionDate is prior to 1/15/2014.

The TRUNCATE **Statement**

The TRUNCATE statement removes all rows from a table. It executes more quickly than a DELETE statement that does not contain a WHERE clause. Unlike the DROP statement, which removes a table entirely, the TRUNCATE statement retains the structure of the table while deleting all of its data. It looks like this:

```
TRUNCATE TABLE Production.TransactionsOld
```

Summary

An important use of T-SQL lies in its ability to modify table data. Using T-SQL, you can insert, update, and delete table data. In this lesson, you learned the syntax to perform these important tasks.

Q&A

Q. Explain the difference between INSERT and SELECT INTO.

A. INSERT adds data to an existing table; SELECT INTO creates a new table containing the data you are inserting.

Q. Explain the difference between a DELETE statement and a TRUNCATE statement.

A. A DELETE statement allows you to selectively remove data from a table; the TRUNCATE statement unconditionally removes all rows from a table.

Q. Describe the difference between TRUNCATE and DROP.

A. TRUNCATE removes all data from the table while retaining the table structure; DROP removes the table from the database.

Workshop

Quiz

1. Name the five action keywords available in T-SQL.

2. You can insert data into a view (true/false).

3. What keyword do you use when inserting data into a new table?

4. What statement do you use to *most efficiently* remove all data from the Person.Person table?

Quiz Answers

1. INSERT, SELECT INTO, UPDATE, DELETE, TRUNCATE.

2. True. You can insert data into a view just as you can insert data into a table. The INSERT statement affects all tables underlying the view.

3. INTO.

4. TRUNCATE TABLE Person.Person.

Activities

Write and execute T-SQL that inserts all employees in the HumanResources. Employee table where SupervisorID is equal to 3 into a new table called tblEmployeesSpecial. View the table data to validate that your T-SQL code ran successfully. Insert additional data into the tblEmployeesSpecial table from the HumanResources.Employee table where the SupervisorID is equal to 4. View the table data to validate your T-SQL code. Update all the VacationHours amounts in the tblEmployeesSpecial table, increasing them by eight. Review the table data to make sure that your T-SQL code executed as expected. Delete all rows in the tblEmployeesSpecial table where the SupervisorID is equal to 3. Review the table data to ensure that all the rows with SupervisorID 3 are removed. Truncate the tblEmployeesSpecial table. Open it up and note that the data is unavailable. Finally, DROP the tblEmployeesSpecial table. Note that it is no longer displayed in the list of available tables.

LESSON 11

Getting to Know the T-SQL Functions

The T-SQL language contains numerous functions you can incorporate into the T-SQL statements you build. These functions perform a variety of important tasks. This lesson covers some of the commonly used numeric, string, date/time, and null-related functions. For additional information on the plethora of T-SQL functions available, consult Books Online (online help for SQL Server) or MSDN. To access Books Online from Management Studio, select View Help from the Help menu. In this lesson, you learn:

▶ How to work with some of the numeric functions available in T-SQL

▶ How to work with some of the string functions available in T-SQL

▶ How to work with some of the date/time functions available in T-SQL

▶ How to use T-SQL to work with nulls

Working with Numeric Functions

Important numeric functions include IsNumeric and ROUND. The sections that follow examine these functions and provide examples of their uses.

Using the IsNumeric Function

The IsNumeric function returns information on whether a value is numeric. Here's an example:

```
SELECT City, PostalCode, IsNumeric(PostalCode) FROM
➥ Person.Address
```

The SELECT statement returns each customer's City, PostalCode, and information on whether the postal code is numeric (see Figure 11.1).

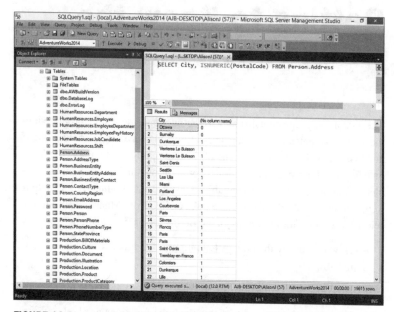

FIGURE 11.1 A SELECT statement that uses the IsNumeric function to determine whether the postal code is numeric.

As you can see in the figure, the postal codes for Ottawa and Burnaby are not numeric, whereas the postal codes for the other cities are numeric.

Exploring the ROUND Function

As its name implies, the ROUND function rounds an expression to a specified length. Here's an example:

```
SELECT ProductID, Name, ListPrice, Round(ListPrice, 0)
➥ FROM Production.Product
```

This SQL statement returns the ProductID, Name, ListPrice, and the ListPrice rounded to whole numbers from the Production.Product table (see Figure 11.2).

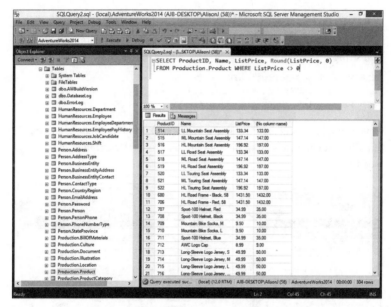

FIGURE 11.2 A SELECT statement that utilizes the SQL ROUND function.

Notice in the figure that the list price of 133.34 is rounded to 133.00, whereas the list price of 196.92 is rounded to 197.00. This is because all values less than .5 are rounded down, and all values .5 and higher are rounded up.

Taking Advantage of String Functions

Important string functions include LEFT, RIGHT, LEN, REPLACE, REVERSE, REPLICATE, STUFF, SPACE, SUBSTRING, LOWER, UPPER, LTRIM, and RTRIM.

Using the LEFT **Function**

The LEFT function extracts a designated number of characters from the left of a string:

```
SELECT ProductDescriptionID,
Description, LEFT(Description, 10)
FROM Production.ProductDescription
```

This example selects the ProductDescriptionID, the Description, and the ten leftmost characters from the Production.ProductDescription table (see Figure 11.3).

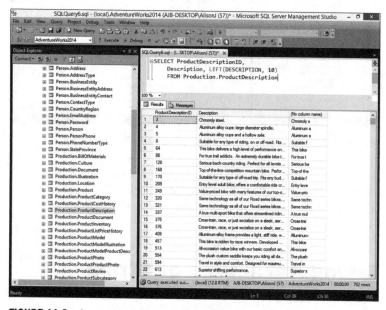

FIGURE 11.3 A SELECT statement that utilizes the LEFT function.

Working with the RIGHT **Function**

The RIGHT function works similarly but extracts the designated rightmost characters from a string. The same example using the RIGHT function looks like this:

```
SELECT ProductDescriptionID,
Description, RIGHT(Description, 10)
FROM Production.ProductDescription
```

This example returns the ProductDescriptionID, Description, and the ten rightmost characters from the Description (see Figure 11.4).

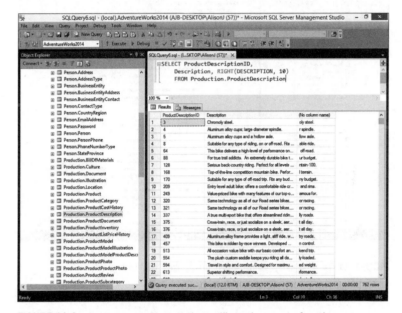

FIGURE 11.4 A SELECT statement that utilizes the RIGHT function.

Exploring the LEN Function

The LEN function returns the length of a string. It looks like this:

```
SELECT ProductDescriptionID,
Description, LEN(Description)
FROM Production.ProductDescription
```

This example returns the ProductDescriptionID, Description, and the length of the description for each row in the ProductDescription table (see Figure 11.5).

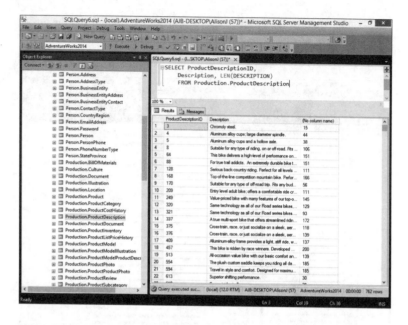

FIGURE 11.5 A SELECT statement that utilizes the LEN function.

Using the REPLACE Function

The REPLACE function replaces all occurrences of one string with another. Here's an example:

```
SELECT ProductDescriptionID,
Description, REPLACE(Description, 'Bike', 'Bicycle')
FROM Production.ProductDescription
```

This example selects the ProductDescriptionID and Description from the ProductDescription table. It includes an additional column that replaces all occurrences of the word Bike in the Description field with the word Bicycle (see Figure 11.6).

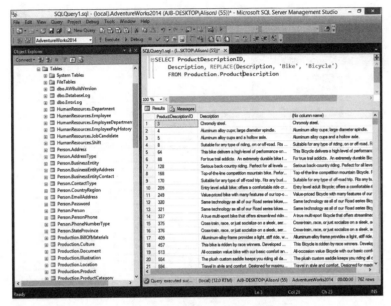

FIGURE 11.6 A SELECT statement that utilizes the REPLACE function to replace all occurrences of the word Bike with the word Bicycle.

Using the REVERSE **Function**

The REVERSE function returns the reverse image of a string. Here's an example:

```
SELECT ProductDescriptionID,
Description, REVERSE(Description)
FROM Production.ProductDescription
```

This example selects the ProductDescriptionID and Description from the ProductDescription table. It includes an additional column that displays the reverse of the characters in the Description field (see Figure 11.7).

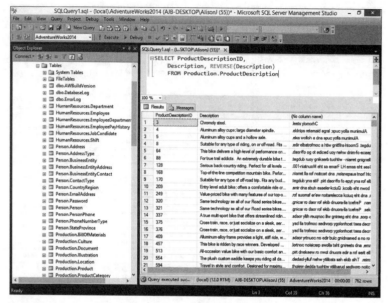

FIGURE 11.7 A `SELECT` statement that utilizes the `REVERSE` function.

Using the `REPLICATE` Function

The `REPLICATE` function replaces all occurrences of one string with another. Here's an example:

```
SELECT ProductDescriptionID,
REPLICATE('0', 5 - DATALENGTH(RTRIM(ProductDescriptionID)))
    + RTRIM(ProductDescriptionID) AS PadZero
FROM Production.ProductDescription
```

This example selects the ProductDescriptionID and the result of an expression that pads the ProductDescription field with leading zeros from the ProductDescription table. It accomplishes this by replicating the correct number of leading zeros based on the length of the trimmed ProductDescriptionID so that all ProductDescriptionID values are five digits in length (see Figure 11.8).

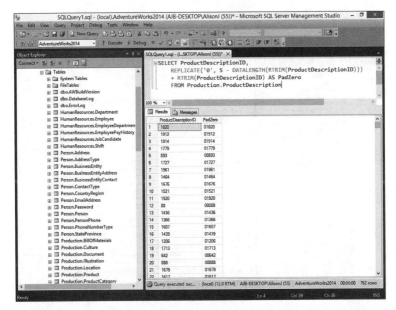

FIGURE 11.8 A SELECT statement that replicates the value 0 so that all ProductDescriptionID values are the same length.

Taking Advantage of the STUFF Function

The STUFF function starts at a specific position and replaces a specified number of characters with other specified characters. Here's an example:

```
SELECT ProductDescriptionID,
    Description,
    STUFF(Description, 5, 10, '**********' ) AS Stuffed
    FROM Production.ProductDescription
```

This example selects the ProductDescriptionID and Description from the Production.ProductDescription table. It includes an additional column that replaces the fifth through fourteenth characters with asterisks (see Figure 11.9).

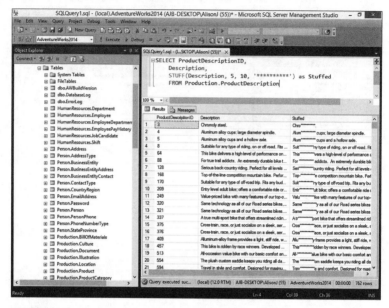

FIGURE 11.9 A SELECT statement that utilizes the STUFF function.

Using the SPACE **Function**

The SPACE function returns a specified number of spaces. Here's
an example:

```
SELECT FirstName + SPACE(1) + LastName
FROM Person.Person
```

This example returns the FirstName and LastName separated by one space
from the Person.Person table (see Figure 11.10).

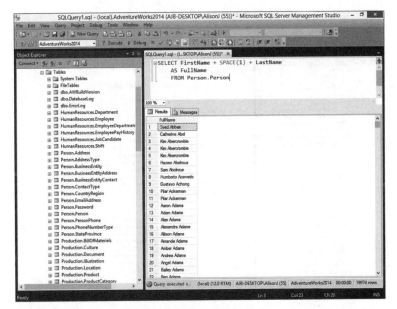

FIGURE 11.10 A `SELECT` statement that utilizes the `SPACE` function.

Using the `SUBSTRING` **Function**

The `SUBSTRING` function extracts specified characters from a string. Here's an example:

```
SELECT ProductDescriptionID, Description,
    SUBSTRING(Description, 6,10)
    AS PartOfDescription
FROM Production.ProductDescription
```

This example returns the ProductDescriptionID, Description, and the sixth through fifteenth characters of the Description field from the Production.ProductDescription table (see Figure 11.11).

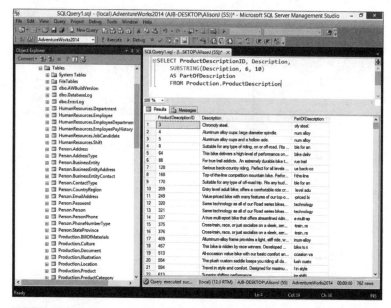

FIGURE 11.11 A `SELECT` statement that returns the ProductionDescriptionID, Description, and the sixth through fifteenth characters of the Description from the ProductDescription table.

Using the `LOWER` Function

The `LOWER` function returns the lowercase version of a string. It looks like this:

```
SELECT ProductDescriptionID, Description, LOWER(Description)
FROM Customers Production.ProductDescription
```

The example returns the contents of the ProductDescriptionID and Description fields and then the lowercase version of the contents of the Description field (see Figure 11.12).

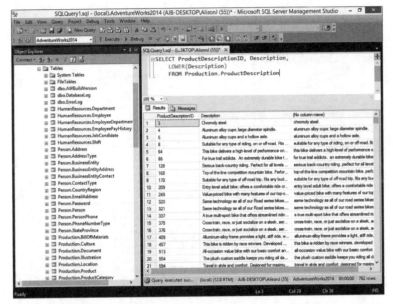

FIGURE 11.12 A `SELECT` statement that returns the lowercase version of the contents of the Description field.

Using the UPPER Function

The UPPER function returns the uppercase version of a string. It looks like this:

```
SELECT ProductDescriptionID, Description, UPPER(Description)
FROM Customers Production.ProductDescription
```

The example returns the contents of the ProductDescriptionID and Description fields and then the uppercase version of the contents of the Description field (see Figure 11.13).

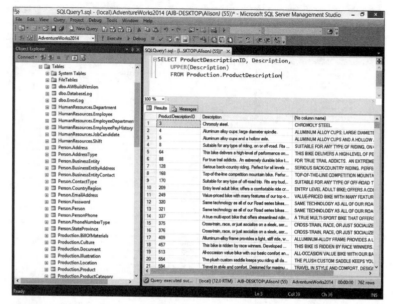

FIGURE 11.13 A SELECT statement that returns the uppercase version of the contents of the Description field.

Working with the LTRIM Function

The LTRIM function returns the string without leading spaces. It looks like this:

```
SELECT ProductDescriptionID, LTRIM(Description)
FROM Production.ProductDescription
```

The example returns the contents of the ProductionDescriptionID field and then the contents of the Description field with any leading spaces removed.

Working with the RTRIM Function

The RTRIM function returns the string without trailing spaces. It looks like this:

```
SELECT ProductDescriptionID, RTRIM(Description)
FROM Production.ProductDescription
```

The example returns the contents of the ProductDescriptionID field and then the contents of the Description field with any trailing spaces removed.

Exploring the Date/Time Functions

Important date/time functions include GETDATE, MONTH, DAY, YEAR, DATEPART, DATENAME, DATEADD, and DATEDIFF. The sections that follow cover these functions.

Using the GETDATE Function

The GETDATE function returns the system date and time. It looks like this:

```
SELECT GETDATE()
```

Learning About the MONTH Function

The MONTH function returns the month portion of a date. It looks like this:

```
SELECT Description, DiscountPct,
    StartDate, MONTH(StartDate)
    FROM Sales.SpecialOffer
```

This SQL statement returns the Description, Discount Percent, Start Date, and the month of the Start Date from the SpecialOffer table (see Figure 11.14).

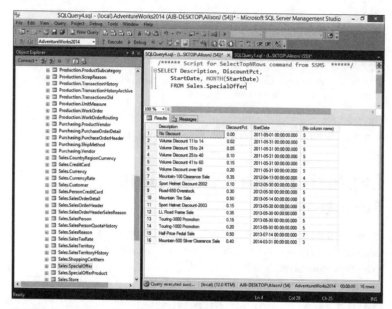

FIGURE 11.14 A SELECT statement that returns the month portion of the start date.

Exploring the DAY Function

The DAY function returns the day portion of a date. It looks like this:

```
SELECT Description, DiscountPct,
    StartDate, DAY(StartDate)
    FROM Sales.SpecialOffer
```

This SQL statement returns the Description, Discount Percent, Start Date, and the month of the Start Date from the SpecialOffer table (see Figure 11.15).

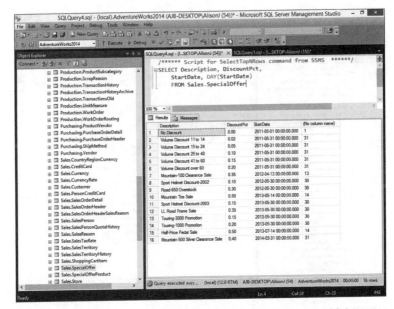

FIGURE 11.15 A SELECT statement that returns the day portion of the start date.

Working with the YEAR Function

The YEAR function returns the year portion of a date. It looks like this:

```
SELECT Description, DiscountPct,
    StartDate, YEAR(StartDate)
    FROM Sales.SpecialOffer
```

This SQL statement returns the Description, Discount Percent, Start Date, and the month of the Start Date from the SpecialOffer table (see Figure 11.16).

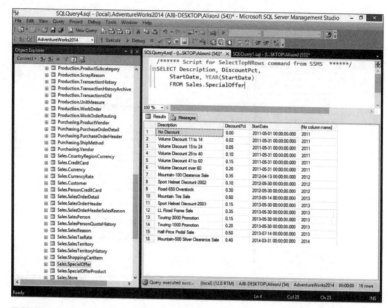

FIGURE 11.16 A `SELECT` statement that returns the year portion of the start date.

Exploring the Powerful `DATEPART` Function

You use the `DATEPART` function to extract a part of a date. The first parameter to the `DATEPART` function is an abbreviation designating the part of the date you want to extract. The second parameter is the date from which you want to extract it. Here's an example:

```
SELECT Description, StartDate,
    DATEPART(qq, StartDate) AS Quarter,
    DATEPART(DAYOFYEAR, StartDate) as DOY
    FROM Sales.SpecialOffer
```

This example selects the Description, the Start Date, the quarter of the Start Date, and the day of the year of the Start Date from the SpecialOffer table (see Figure 11.17).

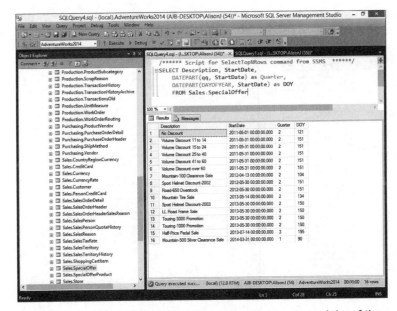

FIGURE 11.17 A SELECT statement that returns the quarter and day of the year of the StartDate from the SpecialOffer table.

Using the DATENAME Function

The DATENAME function returns a string representing a part of a date. It also receives two parameters. The first is the abbreviation indicating the part of the date you want to extract. The second is the date from which you want to extract it. Here's an example:

```
SELECT Description, StartDate,
    DATENAME(dw, StartDate) as DOW
    FROM Sales.SpecialOffer
```

This example returns the Description, the Start Date, and a text description of the day of the week of the Start Date (see Figure 11.18).

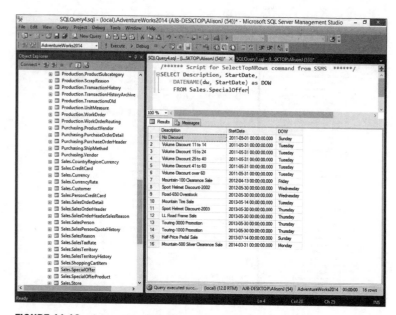

FIGURE 11.18 A SELECT statement that returns a text description of the day of the week of the StartDate.

Working with the DATEADD Function

You use the DATEADD function to add or subtract time from a date. The first parameter is the time period you want to add or subtract (for example, day, month, year). The second parameter is the number of that time period you want to add or subtract (for example, 1 day, 3 months, or 5 years). The final parameter is the date to which you want to add it or from which you want to subtract it. Here's an example:

```
SELECT Description, StartDate,
    DATEADD(mm, 1, StartDate) AS Add1Month,
    DATEADD(dd, -100, StartDate) AS Subtract100Days
    FROM Sales.SpecialOffer
```

This returns the description, the start date, the date one month after the start date, and the date 100 days before the start date (see Figure 11.19).

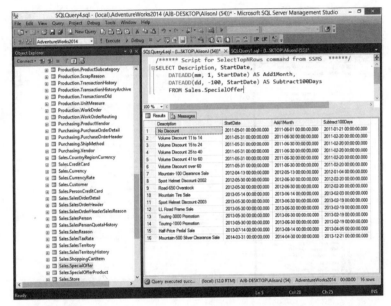

FIGURE 11.19 A `SELECT` statement that returns the dates before and after the StartDate.

Using the DATEDIFF Function

The `DATEDIFF` function returns the difference between two dates. It receives three parameters. The first is the time period in which you want the difference to appear (days, months, and so on). The second and third parameters are the dates whose difference you want to evaluate. Here's an example:

```
SELECT Description, StartDate, EndDate,
    DATEDIFF(dd, StartDate, EndDate) AS DayDiff,
    DATEDIFF(mm, StartDate, EndDate) AS MonthDiff
    FROM Sales.SpecialOffer
```

This example returns the Description, Start Date, End Date, the number of days between the Start Date and the End Date, and the number of months between the Start Date and the End Date (see Figure 11.20).

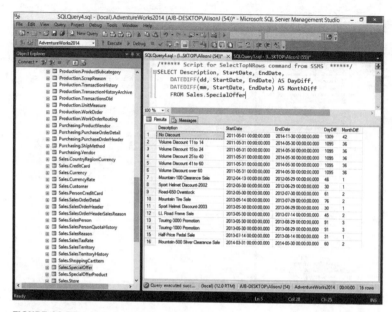

FIGURE 11.20 A SELECT statement that returns the number of days and months between the StartDate and EndDate.

Working with Nulls

Several functions help you deal with nulls in your table data. They include ISNULL, NULLIF, and COALESCE. The sections that follow cover these functions.

Exploring the ISNULL Function

The ISNULL function returns information on whether the value in an expression is null. It receives two parameters. The first parameter is the expression you want to evaluate. The second is the value you want to return if the expression is null. The ISNULL function looks like this:

```
SELECT Description, MinQty,
MaxQty, ISNULL(MaxQty, 100)
FROM Sales.SpecialOffer
```

This example returns the Description, Minimum Quantity, and Maximum Quantity field values. If the Maximum Quantity is null, the fourth column contains the value 100. Otherwise, the fourth column contains the actual Maximum Quantity value for the record (see Figure 11.21).

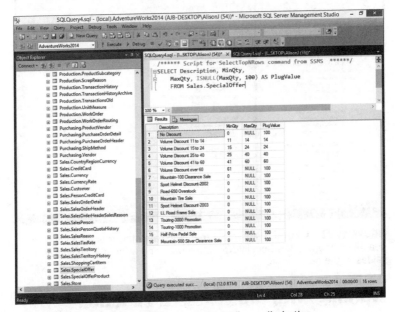

FIGURE 11.21 A SELECT statement that handles nulls in the MaximumQuantity field.

Taking Advantage of the NULLIF Function

The NULLIF function replaces specified values with nulls. It receives two parameters. The first is the name of the expression you want to replace. The second is the value you want to replace with nulls. Here's an example:

```
SELECT AVG(MinQty) AS WithZero,
    AVG(NULLIF(MinQty, 0)) AS NoZero
    FROM Sales.SpecialOffer
```

This example calculates the average Minimum Quantity amount in the SpecialOffer table and then the average Minimum Quantity amount eliminating 0 values from the calculation (see Figure 11.22).

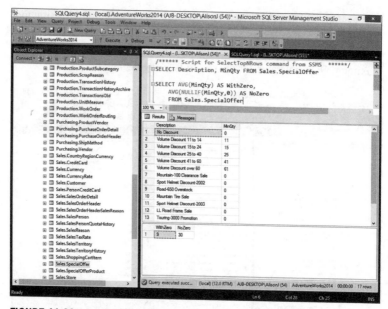

FIGURE 11.22 A SELECT statement that calculates the average minimum quantity amount in the SpecialOffer table, with and without including zero values in the calculation.

Working with the COALESCE **Function**

The COALESCE function returns the first non-null expression in a series of expressions. SQL Server evaluates the first expression. If it is null, it evaluates the second expression. If the second expression is null, it evaluates the third expression. This continues until the function reaches the last expression. Here's an example:

```
SELECT Title, MiddleName, FirstName,
COALESCE(Title, MiddleName, FirstName)
FROM Person.Person
```

This example returns the Title if it is not null. If the Title is null, it evaluates the contents of the MiddleName field. If it is non-null, the contents of the MiddleName field are returned. Otherwise, it evaluates the FirstName field (see Figure 11.23).

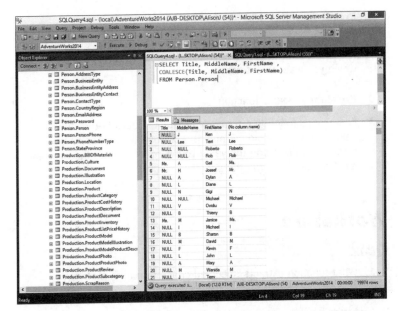

FIGURE 11.23 A SELECT statement that uses the COALESCE function to appropriately handle nulls in the Title and MiddleName fields.

Summary

The T-SQL language provides you with a rich function library. Using this rich library of T-SQL functions, you can manipulate your data in ways you probably haven't even dreamed of. In this lesson, you learned many of the commonly used numeric, string, and date-time functions. You also learned how functions can help you with the process of handling null values in your data.

Q&A

Q. Explain what the STUFF function does.

A. The STUFF function starts at a certain position and replaces a specified number of characters with other specified characters.

Q. Explain what the DATEPART function does.

A. The DATEPART function extracts part of a date. You designate the part of the date you want to extract and the date from which you want to extract it.

Q. Explain the ISNULL function.

A. The ISNULL function returns information about whether the value in an expression is null. It receives the expression you want to evaluate and the value you want to return if the expression is null. It returns the specified value.

Workshop

Quiz

1. What function extracts specified characters from a string?

2. The NOW function returns the system date and time (true/false).

3. Name the two parameters to the DATEPART function.

4. What function finds the difference between two dates?

5. The NULLIF function determines whether a value is null (true/false).

Quiz Answers

1. The SUBSTRING function extracts specified characters from a string.

2. False. The GETDATE function returns the system date and time.

3. The first parameter is an abbreviation designating the part of the date you want to extract. The second parameter is the date from which you want to extract it.

4. The DATEDIFF function.

5. False. The ISNULL function determines whether a value is null.

Activities

Practice executing T-SQL statements that contain functions. First, find the leftmost four characters of each person's LastName in the Person.Person table of the AdventureWorks2014 database. Next, find the fourth through the eighth characters of the AddressLine1 field in the Person.Address table. Find the rightmost four characters of the AddressLine1 field. Next replace all occurrences of the AddressLine1 of "Street" with the word "Court." Find the month of each ModifiedDate in the Person.Person table. Then extract the quarter of each ModifiedDate in the Person.Address table. Find the difference in days between the StartDate and the EndDate in the Production.ProductCostHistory table. Finally, use a SELECT statement to display "No Address2" for all rows in the Person.Address table where the AddressLine2 field is null.

LESSON 12

Working with SQL Server Views

A view is a saved SELECT statement. A view can retrieve data from one or more tables. After you create a view, you can select data from it just as you can select it from a table. In this lesson, you learn:

- ▶ What views are and why you would want to use them
- ▶ How to use the SQL Server Management Studio Query Builder to create a view
- ▶ How to use T-SQL to create or modify a view

An Introduction to Views

Views can only select data. They cannot update it (although you can update the data in the result of a view). For example, a T-SQL UPDATE statement in a stored procedure updates data. Although you cannot use a T-SQL UPDATE statement in a view, you can update the results returned from a SELECT statement.

Views have several advantages. They enable you to

- ▶ Join data so that users can work with it easily.
- ▶ Aggregate data so that users can work with it easily.
- ▶ Customize data to users' needs.
- ▶ Hide underlying column names from users.
- ▶ Limit the columns and rows with which a user works.
- ▶ Easily secure data.

Although a normalized database is easy to work with and maintain from a programmer's viewpoint, it is not always easy for the user to work with. For example, if users look at the HumanResources.Employee table, they see only the BusinessEntityID associated with the employee. If they want to see the employee's name, they must join the HumanResources.Employee table with the Person.Person table. This is not a particularly easy task for users to accomplish. Using a view, you can join the HumanResources.Employee table and the Person.Person table. You provide the view to the user. The user can build forms, queries, and reports that are based on the view without having to understand how to join the underlying tables.

Just as a view can join data, it can also aggregate data. You can very easily create a view that contains the total order amounts for each customer. The user can use the view as the foundation for forms, queries, and reports they build. Once again, it is not necessary for the user to understand the syntax required to aggregate the data.

Another advantage of views is their capability to customize data to the users' needs. For example, a column in a view can combine the first name and last name of a customer, or it can combine the customer's city, state, and ZIP Code. Users do not need to understand how to combine this information. Instead, they use the view as the foundation for the forms, queries, and reports they need.

Developers often use column names that are not particularly intuitive for users. This is another situation where views come to the rescue. You can easily build a view that aliases column names. Users will never see the underlying column names. You simply provide them with access to the view, and they can easily build forms, queries, and reports.

The number of fields in a table can be overwhelming to users. Most of the time, there are certain fields that users need for the majority of the work they do. You can create views containing only the critical fields, which simplifies the process when users build forms, queries, and reports based on the table data.

A major advantage of views is the security they provide. You can grant logins and roles the rights to views *without* granting those logins and roles rights to the underlying tables. An example is an employee table. You can create a view that includes the EmployeeID, FirstName, LastName, Extension, and other nonsensitive fields. You can then grant rights to the view. Although the users have no rights to the Employee table and therefore no access to fields such as the employee salary, they gain rights to the rows and columns included in the view.

SQL Server views are very powerful. Using user-defined functions, you can parameterize views. Using the TOP syntax, you can order view results. All these features make SQL Server views extremely powerful!

Creating a Simple View

A view is actually a SELECT statement with a CREATE VIEW statement that causes SQL Server to save it as a view. You can use a few different methods to create a SQL Server view. This lesson discusses the following methods:

- ▶ You can use the Microsoft SQL Server Management Studio Query Builder to create a view.

- ▶ You can use T-SQL to create a view.

The sections that follow cover each of these options.

Using the Microsoft SQL Server Management Studio Query Builder to Create a View

The Management Studio Query Builder facilitates the process of creating a view. To create a view, follow these steps:

1. Right-click the Views node of the database in which you want the view to appear and select New View. The Add Table dialog box appears (see Figure 12.1).

2. Click each table, view, function, and synonym you want to add to the view and click Add. In the example shown in Figure 12.2, the Sales.Customer and Sales.SalesOrderHeader tables are included in the view.

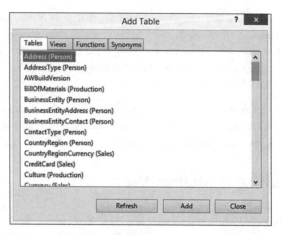

FIGURE 12.1 The Add Table dialog enables you to add tables, views, functions, and synonyms to your view.

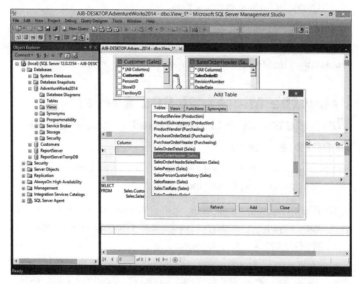

FIGURE 12.2 The Sales.Customer and Sales.SalesOrderHeader tables appear joined in the View.

3. Click Close when you have finished adding objects to the view. Your screen should appear as in Figure 12.3.

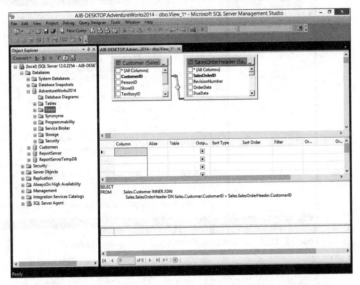

FIGURE 12.3 A new view that includes the Sales.Customer and Sales.SalesOrderHeader tables.

4. Click the check boxes to the left of the field names to select the fields you want to add to the view. If you prefer, you can drag and drop fields to the column list on the query grid. Figure 12.4 shows a view with the CustomerID, AccountNumber, SalesOrderID, OrderDate, and SalesOrderNumber fields included.

5. Specify any criteria that you want to apply to the view. To add criteria, enter the desired criteria in the Criteria column of the appropriate field on the query grid. Adding criteria limits the records returned when you execute the view. Figure 12.5 shows criteria limiting the selected records to those with order date values between 6/1/14 and 6/30/14.

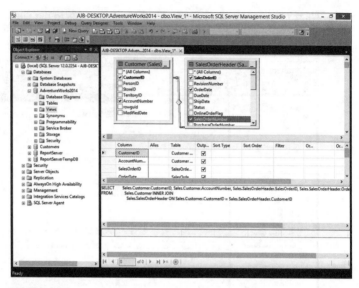

FIGURE 12.4 A View with selected fields and criteria.

FIGURE 12.5 A view that limits the output to orders with order dates between 6/1/14 and 6/30/14.

6. Test the view using the Run button. The output should appear as in Figure 12.6.

7. Attempt to close the view. SQL Server prompts you to save changes to the view.

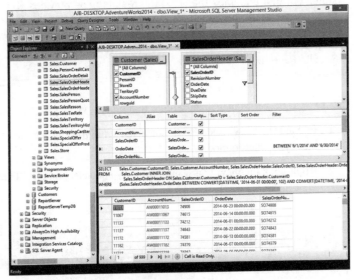

FIGURE 12.6 The results of the view appear in the Output pane.

8. The view appears in the list of views under the Views node. You can treat it much like a table.

NOTE: The views you create do not automatically appear on the Views node. To make them appear, right-click the Views node and select Refresh.

NOTE: The view builder offers four panes: the diagram pane, the grid pane, the SQL pane, and the results pane. The diagram pane shows you the tables included in the view. The grid pane graphically presents you with the columns, aliases, tables, groupings, and criteria for the data in the view. The SQL pane shows you the actual SQL statement that underlies the view. The results pane provides you with the results of executing the view. You can easily hide and show each of these panes with the Show/Hide Diagram Pane tool, Show/Hide Grid Pane tool, Show/Hide SQL Pane tool, and Show/Hide Results Pane tool, respectively.

To use SQL Server Management Studio to modify a view:

1. Expand the Views node for the database until you can see the view you want to modify.

2. Right-click the view you want to modify and select modify. The view appears as in Figure 12.7.

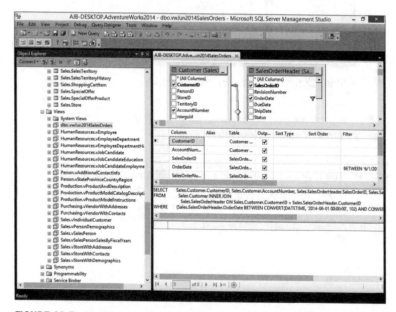

FIGURE 12.7   Modifying a view is similar to building a new view.

3. Make the desired changes and then close and save the view.

> TIP: You can easily drag and drop tables to the diagram pane of the view. Simply resize the View and Object Explorer windows so that you can see both windows simultaneously and then drag and drop the tables from the Tables node of the appropriate database to the diagram pane of the view.

Using T-SQL to Create or Modify a View

In addition to using the Management Studio View Builder to build a view, you can use T-SQL to create a view. Rather than building the view graphically, as outlined in the preceding section, you type the entire CREATE VIEW statement from scratch. The syntax for a CREATE VIEW statement is as follows:

```
CREATE VIEW [DatabaseName] [<owner>] ViewName
       [(column [,…n])]
       [WITH <ViewAttribute> [,…n]]
AS
SelectStatement
[WITH CHECK OPTION]

<ViewAttribute> :: = [ENTCRYPTION|SCHEMASBINDING|VIEW_METADATA]
```

An example of a CREATE VIEW statement is the following:

```
CREATE VIEW vwUSACustomers
AS
SELECT CustomerID, FirstName, LastName, City
FROM Sales.vIndividualCustomer
WHERE CountryRegionName = 'United States'
```

The statement creates a view named vwUSACustomers, which selects the contents of the BusinessEntityID, FirstName, LastName, and City fields from the Sales.vIndividualCustomer view for all customers in the USA.

To type and execute the CREATE VIEW statement, follow these steps:

1. Click the New Query button on the toolbar. Your screen appears as in Figure 12.8.

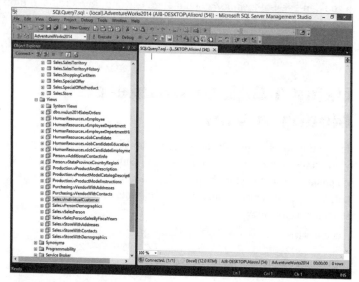

FIGURE 12.8   The screen after clicking the New Query button on the toolbar.

2. Type the SQL statement into the available pane.

3. Click the Execute button on the toolbar. The results should appear as in Figure 12.9.

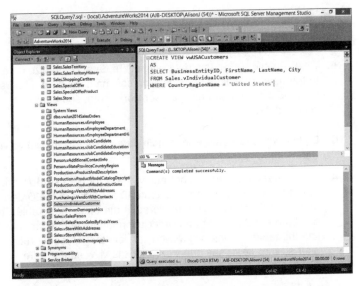

FIGURE 12.9 The results of using the Execute button to create a new view.

If you want use T-SQL to modify a view, you must use an ALTER VIEW statement rather than a CREATE VIEW statement. An example of an ALTER VIEW statement is shown here:

```
ALTER VIEW vwUSACustomers
AS
SELECT CustomerID, FirstName, LastName, City
FROM Sales.vIndividualCustomer
WHERE CountryRegionName = 'Australia'
```

This example modifies the vwUSACustomers view, changing the criteria to return all the customers in Australia.

Summary

Views are a critical part of any application you build. It is therefore important you understand how to create and work with views. In this lesson, you learned how to create and modify simple views, using both the SQL Server Management Studio and T-SQL.

Q&A

Q. Name some advantages of views.

A. Views enable you to join data, aggregate data, customize data to the user's needs, hide underlying column names from users, limit the columns and rows a user works with, and easily secure data.

Q. Explain why you would want to join data so that users can easily work with it.

A. A normalized database is not always easy for the user to work with. For example, only the CustomerID is stored in the Orders table. The Company Name is stored in the Customers table. To see both the Customer and Order information, the user must join the tables. Using a view, you can join the tables for the user so that he or she can work with the view as if it were a single table.

Q. Explain what it means to customize data to a user's needs.

A. Using a view, you can create a column that combines first, middle, and last name of an employee or the city, state, and ZIP Code from an address. This makes it much easier for the user to work with this data.

Q. How do views help you to secure data?

A. You can grant rights to logins and roles to the views you create. It is not necessary to grant rights to the underlying tables. In this way, you can give users access to just desired columns and rows. For example, you can give users rights to name and address data for the sales department in the employee table.

Workshop

Quiz

1. Name two ways you can create a view.

2. What statement do you use to create a view?

3. The result of a view is updateable (true/false).

4. Name the four panes of the view builder.

5. You cannot drag and drop tables onto the diagram pane of the view (true/false).

6. What statement do you use to modify a view?

Quiz Answers

1. Using SQL Server Management Studio and using T-SQL.

2. CREATE VIEW.

3. True.

4. Diagram, grid, SQL, and results.

5. False. You can drag and drop from the Tables node of the appropriate databases to the diagram pane of the view.

6. ALTER VIEW.

Activities

Create a view by using the Microsoft SQL Server Management Studio Query Builder. Include BusinessEntityID, JobTitle, BirthDate, Gender, HireDate, VacationHours, and SickLeaveHours from the HumanResources.Employee table. Sort the result in ascending order and return just the rows where the HireDate is between 1/1/2013 and 12/31/2013. Close and save the view as vw2013Hires. Modify the view and add the LoginID to the view. Create another view by using T-SQL. Include the BusinessEntityID, SalesQuota, Bonus, SalesYTD, and SalesLastYear from the Sales.SalesPerson table. Sort in descending order by SalesYTD and return just the rows where the SalesYTD is greater than 2 million. Close and save the view as vwBigHitters. Modify the view (using T-SQL) and add the CommissionPct field to the view. Change the criteria for the SalesYTD to 3 million.

LESSON 13

Using T-SQL to Design SQL Server Stored Procedures

Stored procedures are at the heart of any client/server application. Using stored procedures, you can guarantee that processing is completed on the server. Stored procedures have many other benefits as well, including the following:

- ▶ Stored procedures help you to separate the client application from the database's structure.

- ▶ Stored procedures help you to simplify client coding.

- ▶ Stored procedures process at the server (reduces required bandwidth).

- ▶ Stored procedures enable you to create reusable code.

- ▶ Stored procedures enable you to perform error-handling at the server.

- ▶ Stored procedures facilitate the security of data.

- ▶ Because stored procedures are precompiled, they execute more quickly.

- ▶ Stored procedures improve the application's stability.

- ▶ Stored procedures reduce network locking.

- ▶ When you build a stored procedure, a query plan is created. This query plan contains the most efficient method of executing the stored procedure given available indexes and so on.

In this lesson, you learn:

▶ The basics of working with stored procedures

▶ How to declare and work with variables

▶ How to control the flow of the stored procedures you write

The Basics of Working with Stored Procedures

Creating stored procedures in SQL Server Management is easy. You can create a stored procedure using the Query Editor or T-SQL.

Designing a Stored Procedure in the Query Editor

Although you may not be able to design an entire stored procedure in the Query Editor, you will probably find it easiest to use the Query Editor to design the T-SQL statement you include in your stored procedure. Take the steps that follow to build the SELECT statement you want to include:

1. Expand the Programmability node of the database you are working with so that you can see the Stored Procedures node underneath it (see Figure 13.1).

2. Right-click the Stored Procedure node and select New, Stored Procedure. A template for a stored procedure appears in the Query Editor (see Figure 13.2).

3. Click and drag over the SELECT statement included in the template and press the Delete key to delete it.

4. Right-click in that same location and select Design Query in Editor. The Add Table dialog box appears (see Figure 13.3).

5. Add the desired tables to the query by selecting each table and clicking Add.

6. Click Close to complete the process. The Query Designer should look similar to Figure 13.4.

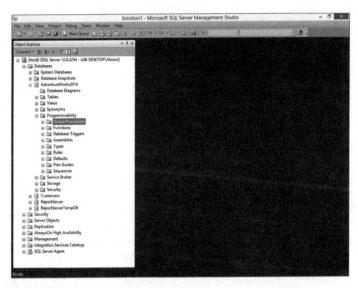

FIGURE 13.1 The Stored Procedures node appears under the Programmability node.

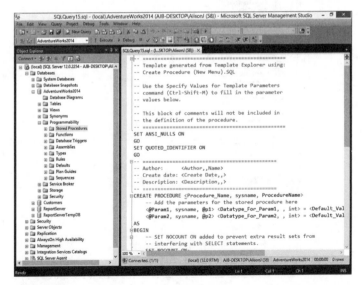

FIGURE 13.2 When you create a stored procedure, Management Studio provides you with a template for that stored procedure.

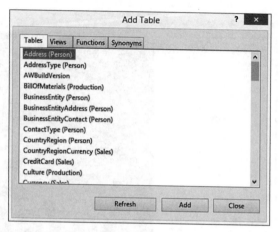

FIGURE 13.3 You replace the template SQL statement with the SQL statement generated by the Query Editor.

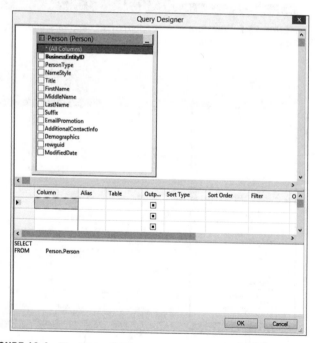

FIGURE 13.4 The Query Designer appears with the selected tables.

7. Click to add the desired fields to the SELECT statement. Click OK when finished. The stored procedure should appear as in Figure 13.5.

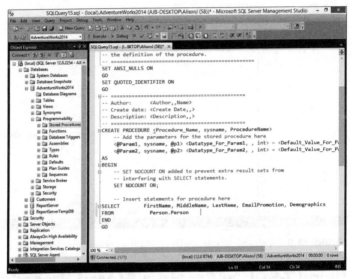

FIGURE 13.5 The generated SQL statement appears within the stored procedure template.

8. Modify the stored procedure, adding all of the functionality you want it to have.

9. After completing the stored procedure, click Execute to execute the CREATE PROCEDURE statement.

10. You only need to save if you want to store the T-SQL behind the stored procedure in an *external* file.

To make the generated stored procedure execute, you must provide the stored procedure with a name and delete all of the superfluous template code, such as the declaration of parameters. An example of a stored procedure that has been modified appears in Figure 13.6.

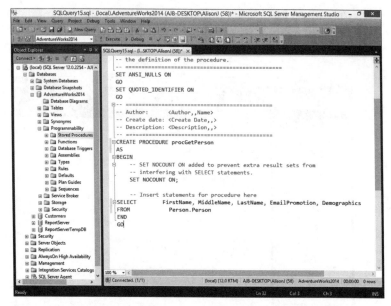

FIGURE 13.6   A stored procedure modified to properly execute.

Using T-SQL to Create a Stored Procedure

Sometimes you might not find it useful to use the Query Editor to get started in creating a stored procedure. In that case, you simply create the stored procedure and begin modifying the template as desired. Here are the steps involved:

1. Expand the Programmability node of the database you are working with so that you can see the Stored Procedures node underneath it.

2. Right-click the Stored Procedure node and select New, Stored Procedure. A template for a stored procedure appears in the Query Editor.

3. Type the body of the stored procedure.

4. After completing the stored procedure, click Execute to execute the CREATE PROCEDURE statement.

5. You only need to save if you want to store the T-SQL behind the stored procedure in an *external* file.

Executing the Stored Procedures You Build

Regardless of the method you use to create a stored procedure, Management Studio creates a new stored procedure, available under the Stored Procedures node, which is part of the Programmability node. Use the following steps to execute a stored procedure:

1. Click to expand the Programmability node.

2. Click to expand the Stored Procedures node.

3. If you don't see the stored procedure you want to execute, right-click the Stored Procedures node and select Refresh.

4. Right-click the stored procedure you want to execute and select Execute Stored Procedure. The Execute Procedure dialog box appears (see Figure 13.7).

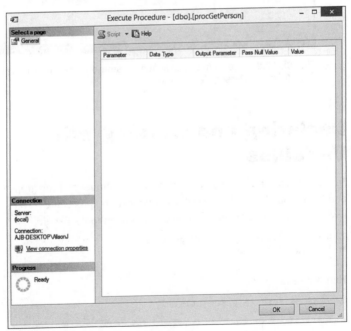

FIGURE 13.7 The Execute Procedure dialog box enables you to supply parameters and execute the stored procedure.

5. Supply the values of any required parameters and click OK to execute the stored procedure. The results appear as in Figure 13.8.

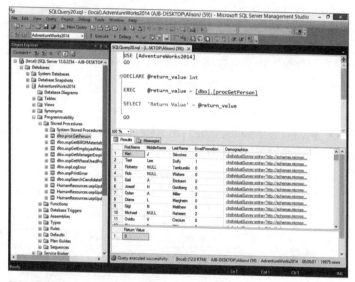

FIGURE 13.8   The result of executing a stored procedure that returns data from the Person.Person table.

Declaring and Working with Variables

Just as you can create variables within the subroutines and functions you build, you can also declare variables in your stored procedures. You use the keyword DECLARE to create a variable. The syntax looks like this:

```
DECLARE @VariableName DataType [(length)], @VariableName
➥ DataType [(length)]
```

Here's an example:

```
DECLARE @FirstName VarChar(35)
```

Uninitialized variables are assigned the value Null. You use a SELECT statement to assign a value to a variable. It looks like this:

```
SELECT @FirstName = 'Alexis'
```

The following is a stored procedure that illustrates the use of a variable:

```
DECLARE @strFirstName nvarchar (50)
SELECT @strFirstName = Upper(FirstName)
FROM Person.Person
WHERE LastName = 'Erickson'
SELECT @strFirstName
```

This example declares a variable called @strFirstName. The code stores the uppercase version of the FirstName associated with the last name Erickson into the variable. The procedure returns the variable using a SELECT statement. Figure 13.9 illustrates the result of executing the sample stored procedure.

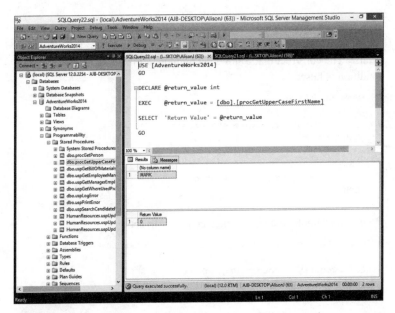

FIGURE 13.9 An example of a variable used in a stored procedure.

Controlling the Flow

Often you want specified statements in your stored procedure to execute only if certain conditions are true. T-SQL contains several constructs that enable you to control the flow of your stored procedures. These include BEGIN...END, IF...ELSE, GOTO, RETURN, CASE, and WHILE. The sections that follow cover each of these constructs.

Using IF...ELSE

You use the IF...ELSE construct to make a decision within the stored procedure. This decision is generally based on parameters supplied to the stored procedure. The IF...ELSE construct works like this:

```
IF (SomeCondition)
    BEGIN
        --Execute multiple statements
    END
```

With this version of the IF...ELSE construct, certain statements execute only if the condition is true. No special statements execute if the condition is false. The construct that follows accommodates the scenario when the condition is false:

```
IF (SomeCondition)
    BEGIN
        --Execute multiple statements
    END
ELSE
    BEGIN
        --Execute multiple statement
    END
```

Here's an example of an IF...THEN construct in action:

```
DECLARE @Locale VarChar(20), @Country VarChar(30)

SELECT @Country = CountryRegionName
    FROM Sales.vIndividualCustomer
    WHERE BusinessEntityID = 1700

IF @Country = 'United States'
    BEGIN
        SELECT @Locale = 'Domestic'
    END
```

```
ELSE
    BEGIN
        SELECT @Locale= 'Foreign'
    END

SELECT BusinessEntityID, @Country, @Locale
    FROM Sales.vIndividualCustomer
    WHERE BusinessEntityID = 1
```

The code begins by declaring two variables: @Locale and @Country. It stores the contents of the CountryRegionName field for the BusinessEntityID 1700 into the @Country variable. It then evaluates the contents of the @Country variable, storing the appropriate locale into the @Locale variable. Finally, it returns the BusinessEntityID, the contents of the @Country variable, and the contents of the @Locale variable for the customer with the BusinessEntityID 1700. Figure 13.10 provides an example of executing the stored procedure.

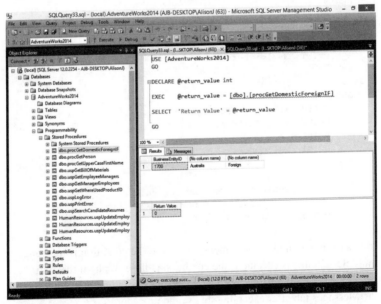

FIGURE 13.10 An example of executing a stored procedure that includes an IF...ELSE construct.

NOTE: It is important to note that if you want to execute more than one statement under a specific condition, you must enclose the statements within the BEGIN...END construct (see the following section).

Working with BEGIN...END

The BEGIN...END construct enables you to group a series of statements together. Without the BEGIN...END construct, only the first statement after the IF or the ELSE executes. Consider the following example:

```
DECLARE @Locale VarChar(20), @Country VarChar(30)

SELECT @Country = CountryRegionName
    FROM Sales.vIndividualCustomer
    WHERE BusinessEntityID = 1700

IF @Country    = 'United States'
    BEGIN
        SELECT @Locale = 'Domestic'
        PRINT 'This is domestic'
        PRINT ' '
        PRINT 'Hello there'
    END
ELSE
    BEGIN
        SELECT @Locale= 'Foreign'
        PRINT 'This is foreign'
        PRINT ' '
        PRINT 'Hello there'
    END

SELECT BusinessEntityID, @Country, @Locale
    FROM Sales.vIndividualCustomer
    WHERE BusinessEntityID = 1700
```

In this example, multiple statements execute if the condition is true, and multiple statements execute if the condition is false. Without the BEGIN... END construct after the IF, the code renders an error. Figure 13.11 shows the Messages tab after executing this stored procedure.

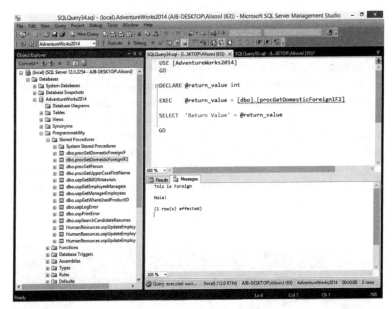

FIGURE 13.11 An example of executing a stored procedure that includes multiple statements between a BEGIN...END construct.

Exploring GOTO, RETURN, **and Labels**

You use the GOTO statement to jump to a label in your stored procedure. Programmers seem to use this statement most commonly in error handling. The RETURN statement unconditionally exits the stored procedure without executing any other statements. These three keywords are covered together because they generally work as a group. Consider the following examples:

```
IF Month(GetDate()) > 6
    BEGIN
        PRINT 'In IF Statement'
        GOTO MyLabel
    END
SELECT FirstName, LastName FROM Person.Person

MyLabel:
    SELECT  Left(FirstName, 1) + '.' +
    Left(LastName, 1) + '.'
    FROM Person.Person
```

This example evaluates to see whether the month associated with the current date is greater than the value six. If it is, the statement In IF Statement appears and code execution jumps to the label MyLabel without executing the first SELECT statement. The procedure then selects the initials from the Person.Person table. If the month associated with the current date is less than or equal to the value six, the procedure first selects the first and last name from the Person.Person table. Code execution then continues at the label where the procedure selects the initials from the Person.Person table. Figure 13.12 shows an example of executing the code when the month associated with the current date is greater than six. Figure 13.13 shows the sample procedure where the month associated with the current date is less than or equal to six.

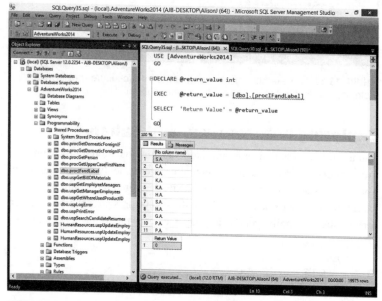

FIGURE 13.12 An example of executing a stored procedure that includes GOTO and a label.

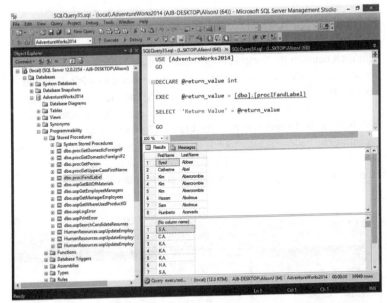

FIGURE 13.13 An example of executing the same stored procedure with a different value for the month of the current date.

As mentioned, a RETURN statement unequivocally exits from the procedure. Take a look at the procedure that follows:

```
IF Month(GetDate()) > 6
    BEGIN
        PRINT 'In IF Statement'
        GOTO MyLabel
    END
SELECT FirstName, LastName FROM Person.Person
RETURN

MyLabel:
    SELECT  Left(FirstName, 1) + '.' +
    Left(LastName, 1) + '.'
    FROM Person.Person
```

In this example, if the month associated with the current date is greater than the value six, the In IF Statement message appears, and then the procedure executes the code in MyLabel, returning the initials associated with each name in the Person.Person table. If the month associated with the current date is less than or equal to the value six, the code selects the first and last name from the Person.Person table and then exits the procedure. Because of the RETURN statement, the procedure does not select the initials from the Person.Person table. Figure 13.14 shows an example of executing the code when the month associated with the current date is less than or equal to six. Figure 13.15 shows the sample procedure where the month associated with the current date is greater than six.

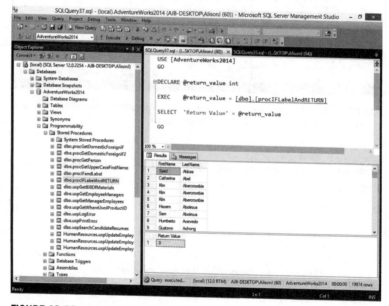

FIGURE 13.14 An example of executing a stored procedure that includes the RETURN statement.

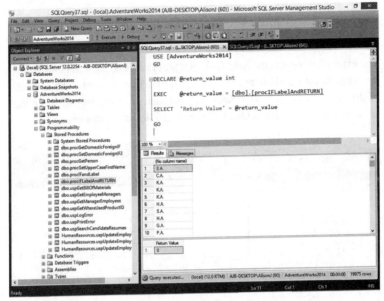

FIGURE 13.15 An example of executing the same stored procedure with a different value for the month of the current date.

Working with the CASE **Statement**

Most developers use the CASE statement to compare a result from a SQL statement against a set of simple responses. The CASE statement returns the appropriate value. The CASE statement looks like this:

```
CASE InputExpression
    WHEN WhenExpression THEN ResultExpression
        [...n]
    [ELSE ElseResultExpression]
END
```

Here's an example of this use of a case statement:

```
SELECT SalesOrderID, ShipDate,
    CASE ShipMethodID
        WHEN 1 THEN 'UPS'
        WHEN 3 THEN 'FedEx'
        WHEN 5 THEN 'U.S. Mail'
    END AS Shipper,
```

```
Freight FROM Sales.SalesOrderHeader
WHERE ShipDate BETWEEN '1/1/13' AND '2/28/13'
AND Freight <= 50
```

The expression selects the SalesOrderID, ShipDate, and Freight fields from the Sales.SalesOrderHeader table. The CASE statement evaluates the contents of the ShipMethodID field. It returns an appropriate string depending on the value in the ShipMethodID field. Figure 13.16 illustrates this example.

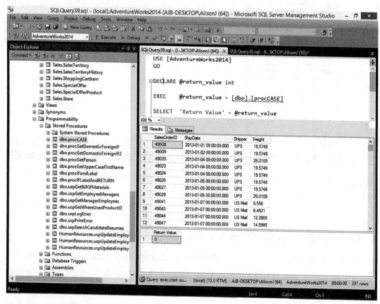

FIGURE 13.16　An example of executing a CASE statement that evaluates a field, returning different values depending on what the field contains.

The second use of the CASE construct looks like this:

```
CASE
    WHEN Expression THEN TruePart
    ELSE FalsePart
END
```

Here's an example:

```
DECLARE @AverageFreight Money
SELECT @AverageFreight = AVG(Freight)
FROM Sales.SalesOrderHeader
```

```
SELECT SalesOrderID, ShipDate, Freight,
    CASE
        WHEN FREIGHT <= @AverageFreight THEN 'Low Freight'
        WHEN FREIGHT = @AverageFreight THEN 'Average Freight'
        ELSE 'High Freight'
    END AS FreightRating
    FROM Sales.SalesOrderHeader
```

The example first declares the @AverageFreight variable. It sets the variable equal to the average freight amount from the Sales.SalesOrderHeader table. The CASE statement evaluates whether the freight of the current row is less than the average freight amount. If so, the statement returns Low Freight. If it is equal to the average freight amount, it returns Average Freight. Otherwise, it returns High Freight. This value is combined with the SalesOrderID, ShipDate, and Freight amounts that are also selected from the table. Figure 13.17 shows this use of the CASE statement in action.

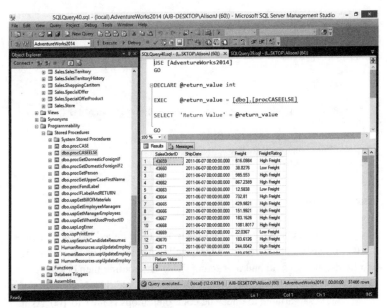

FIGURE 13.17 A CASE statement that uses the ELSE keyword.

Exploring the WHILE Statement

You use the WHILE statement when you want to set up a loop. The loop
continues to execute until the specified condition is met. The WHILE construct looks like this:

```
WHILE BooleanExpression
    (SQLStatement | SQLBlock)
```

Here's an example:

```
IF NOT EXISTS (SELECT * FROM sys.objects
WHERE object_id = OBJECT_ID(N'[dbo].[MyTable]')

CREATE TABLE MyTable
(
LoopID INT,
LoopText VarChar(25)
)

DECLARE @LoopValue INT
DECLARE @LoopText CHAR(25)

SELECT @LoopValue = 1

WHILE (@LoopValue < 100)
BEGIN
    SELECT @LoopText = 'Iteration #' + Convert(VarChar(25), @
➥ LoopValue)
    INSERT INTO MyTable(LoopID, LoopText)
        VALUES (@LoopValue, @LoopText)
    SELECT @LoopValue = @LoopValue + 1
END

SELECT * FROM MyTable
```

The routine first checks for the existence of a table called MyTable, deleting it if it exists. It then creates a table called MyTable. The table contains
two fields: an INT field and a VARCHAR field. The routine then declares
two variables, an INT variable and a VARCHAR variable. It sets the value of
the @LoopValue variable to one. The code then loops from 1 to 100. As it
loops, it sets the VARCHAR variable equal to the text Iteration # combined
with the contents of the @LoopValue variable converted to a VARCHAR.

Next, it inserts the contents of the @LoopValue and @LoopText variables into the table. Finally, it increments the value of the @LoopValue variable. Figure 13.18 shows the results of executing the WHILE statement.

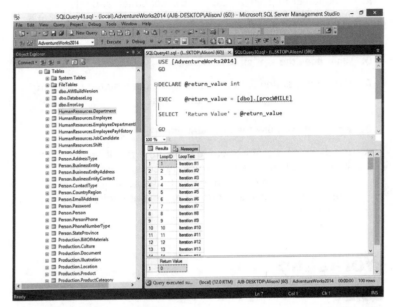

FIGURE 13.18 With a WHILE statement, the loop continues to execute until the specified condition is met.

Summary

Stored procedures have many benefits. In this lesson, you learned the ins and outs of working with stored procedures. You learned the basics of stored procedures and how to declare and work with variables. Finally, you learned numerous ways you can control the flow of the stored procedures you write.

Q&A

Q. What happens if you forget to use BEGIN and END with the IF... ELSE construct?

A. If you forget to place a BEGIN...END construct on the line immediately following the IF statement or the ELSE statement, only the first statement after the IF or the ELSE executes.

Q. What does the RETURN statement do?

A. The RETURN statement unconditionally exits a stored procedure without executing any other statements.

Q. Why would you use the CASE statement?

A. You use the CASE statement to compare a result from a SQL statement against a set of simple responses. For example, a CASE statement might evaluate the contents of the ContactTitle field and return an appropriate string based on those contents.

Workshop

Quiz

1. What is the *main* benefit of stored procedures?

2. What keyword do you use to assign a value to a variable?

3. What construct do you use to group a series of SQL statements together?

4. When is the GOTO statement most commonly used?

5. What does a GOTO statement do?

Quiz Answers

1. You guarantee the code will execute on the server.

2. The SELECT keyword.

3. BEGIN..END.

4. In error handling.

5. Jump to a label in your stored procedure.

Activities

Use SQL Server Management Studio to practice creating a stored procedure. First, use the Query Editor to build a SQL statement that joins the Person.Person, Person.BusinessEntityContact, and Person.ContactType tables. Include the FirstName and LastName from the Person table, the ContactTypeID from the BusinessEntityContact table, and the Name from the ContactType table. Include the resulting SQL statement in a procedure that determines whether the Name field in the ContactType table that is associated with a person is Owner. If the Name is Owner, store Head Hancho into a variable called @TitleName. If the Name is not Owner, store Peon into the @TitleName variable. Finally, return the contents of the FirstName and LastName fields and the @TitleName variable for each record in the Person table.

LESSON 14

Stored Procedure Techniques Every Developer Should Know

The previous lesson covered the basics of working with stored procedures. To really be effective in working with stored procedures, you must learn additional techniques. In this lesson, you learn about:

▶ The SET NOCOUNT statement

▶ How to use the @@ functions in the stored procedures that you build

▶ How to work with input and output parameters

▶ How to add error handling to your stored procedures

The SET NOCOUNT Statement

The SET NOCOUNT statement, when set to ON, eliminates the xx row(s) affected message in the SQL Management Studio window. It also eliminates the DONE_IN_PROC communicated from SQL Server to the client application. For this reason, the SET NOCOUNT ON statement, when included, improves the performance of the stored procedure. Here's an example:

```
CREATE PROCEDURE procPersonGetNoCount AS
SET NOCOUNT ON
SELECT BusinessEntityID, FirstName, LastName
FROM Person.Person
ORDER BY LastName, FirstName
```

If you execute this stored procedure from within SQL Server Management Studio, you'll notice that the xx row(s) affected message does not appear (see Figure 14.1). You might wonder how with SET NOCOUNT ON in effect, you can return the number of rows affected to the client application. Fortunately, this is easily accomplished with the @@RowCount system variable. The following section covers the @@RowCount system variable as well as other system variables.

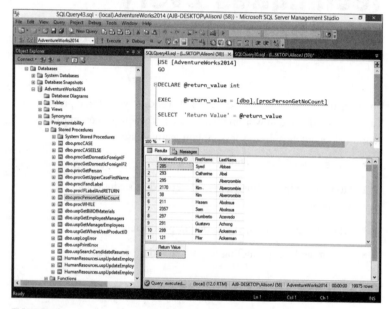

FIGURE 14.1 With a NOCOUNT statement, the xx row(s) affected message does not appear.

Using the @@ Functions

Developers often refer to the @@ functions as global variables. In fact, they don't really behave like variables. You cannot assign values to them or work with them as you would work with normal variables. Instead, they behave as functions that return various types of information about what is going on in SQL Server.

Using the @@RowCount **System Variable**

The @@RowCount variable returns the number of rows returned by a selected statement or affected by a statement that modifies data. It returns zero if no values are returned by the select statement or modified by the action query. Here's an example:

```
CREATE PROCEDURE procPersonGetNoCount AS
SET NOCOUNT ON
SELECT BusinessEntityID, FirstName, LastName
FROM Person.Person
ORDER BY LastName, FirstName
SELECT @@RowCount as NumberOfPeople
```

The example selects all employees who are sales representatives from the Employee table. It returns the number of rows selected (see Figure 14.2).

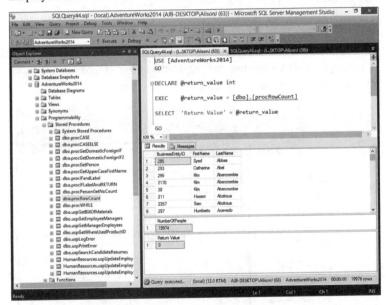

FIGURE 14.2 The @@RowCount variable returns the number of rows returned by a selected statement or affected by a statement that modifies data.

NOTE: You can also see the results of the SELECT @@RowCount statement if you change the query results to display as text rather than as grid. To do this, select Query, Results To, Results to Text.

Using the `@@TranCount` **System Variable**

The `@@TranCount` function is applicable when you are using explicit transactions. Transactions are covered in Lesson 15, "Power Stored Procedure Techniques." The `BEGIN TRAN` statement sets the `@@TranCount` to one. Each `ROLLBACK TRAN` statement decrements `@@TranCount` by one. The `COMMIT TRAN` statement also decrements `@@TranCount` by one. When you use nested transactions, `@@TranCount` helps you to keep track of how many transactions are still pending.

Using the `@@Identity` **System Variable**

The `@@Identity` function retrieves the new value inserted into a table that has an identity column. Here's an example:

```
INSERT INTO Purchasing.ShipMethod
    (Name, ShipBase, ShipRate)
    VALUES ('Speedy Freight', 120, 150)
    SELECT @@Identity
```

The example inserts a row into the ShipMethod table. It returns the identity value of the inserted row (see Figure 14.3).

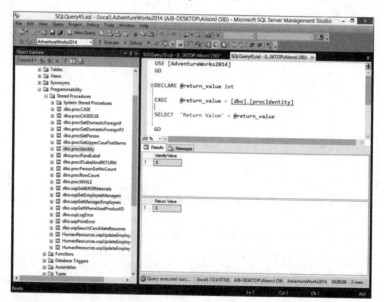

FIGURE 14.3 The `@@Identity` function retrieves the new value inserted into a table that has an identity column.

Using the @@Error **System Variable**

The @@Error function returns the number of any error that occurred in the
statement immediately preceding it. Here's an example:

```
INSERT INTO Sales.SalesOrderDetail
    (CarrierTrackingNumber, OrderQty,
    ProductID, SpecialOfferID,
    UnitPrice, UnitPriceDiscount)
    VALUES (1, 1, 1, 1, 100.00, .05)
    SELECT @@Error
```

This example attempts to insert a row into the SalesOrderDetail table.
If it is successful, @@Error returns zero. If you attempt to insert a sales
order detail record without supplying a value for the SalesOrderID field,
it returns error number 515, an error indicating that you cannot insert a
NULL value into a column (see Figure 14.4).

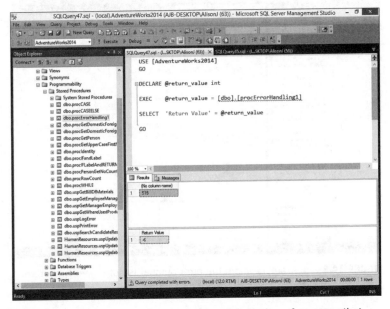

FIGURE 14.4 The @@Error function returns the number of any error that
occurred in the statement immediately preceding it.

It is important to note that @@Error returns the error number associated with the line of code *immediately* preceding it. Consider this example:

```
INSERT INTO Sales.SalesOrderDetail
    (CarrierTrackingNumber, OrderQty,
    ProductID, SpecialOfferID,
    UnitPrice, UnitPriceDiscount)
    VALUES (1, 1, 1, 1, 100.00, .05)
    SELECT @@Identity
    SELECT @@Error
```

Although the INSERT statement renders an error, the @@Error function returns zero (see Figure 14.5) because the SELECT @@Identity statement executes without error.

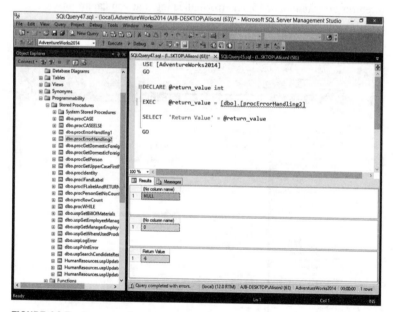

FIGURE 14.5 An example where the error number is not properly reported.

Working with Parameters

Some stored procedures have no interface. They are called, but they do not receive or return anything. Other procedures are input only. These stored procedures have input parameters but no output parameters. A third type of stored procedure has both input parameters and output parameters.

Input Parameters

An example of a stored procedure that has neither input nor output parameters is this one:

```
CREATE PROCEDURE procEmployeeGetYoungSalesReps
AS
SELECT BusinessEntityID, JobTitle,
    BirthDate, HireDate,
    VacationHours
FROM HumanResources.Employee
WHERE JobTitle Like 'Marketing %' AND
    BirthDate >= '1/1/1981'
ORDER BY BirthDate
```

Contrast this stored procedure with the following:

```
CREATE PROCEDURE procEmployeeGetByTitleAndBirthDate
    @JobTitle nVarChar(50),
    @BirthDate DateTime
AS
SELECT BusinessEntityID, JobTitle,
    BirthDate, HireDate,
    VacationHours
FROM HumanResources.Employee
WHERE JobTitle = @JobTitle AND
    BirthDate >= @BirthDate
ORDER BY BirthDate
```

The procedure receives two input parameters, @JobTitle and @BirthDate. The procedure uses these input parameters as variables for the WHERE

clause for job title and birth date. The easiest way to execute this procedure from within SQL Server Management Studio is the following:

1. Right-click the procedure and select Execute Stored Procedure.
   The Execute Procedure dialog box appears. Notice in Figure 14.6
   that the dialog box prompts you for the two parameters.

2. Enter the parameter values in the Value column and click OK.
   The results of executing the stored procedure appear.

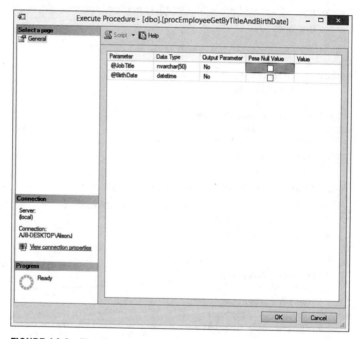

FIGURE 14.6   The Execute Procedure dialog box prompts you for all
parameters.

Another method that you can use to execute the stored procedure is using the New Query toolbar option:

1. Click the New Query toolbar button. A blank query window appears.

2. Type the name of the procedure you want to execute, followed by the parameter values. You must separate each parameter with commas (see Figure 14.7).

3. Click Execute or press F5. The procedure executes.

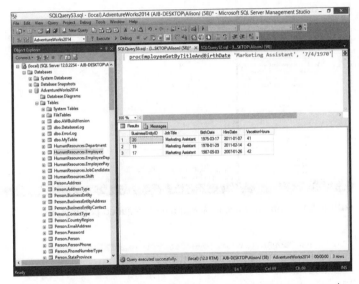

FIGURE 14.7 A parameterized stored procedure that returns records if the criteria are met.

The parameters in this stored procedure are required. If you do not supply them when you call the procedure, an error results (see Figure 14.8). The following is the same procedure with the job title set up as an optional parameter.

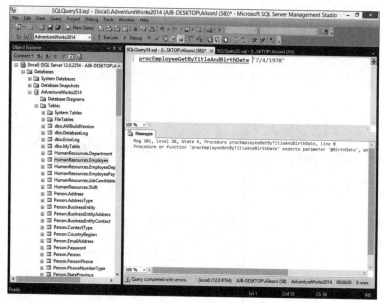

FIGURE 14.8 An error occurs if you omit a required parameter.

```
CREATE PROCEDURE procEmployeeGetByTitleAndBirthDateOpt
    @JobTitle nVarChar(50) = NULL,
    @BirthDate DateTime
AS
IF @JobTitle IS NULL
    BEGIN
    SELECT BusinessEntityID, JobTitle, BirthDate,
        HireDate, VacationHours
    FROM HumanResources.Employee
    WHERE BirthDate >= @BirthDate
    ORDER BY BirthDate
    END
ELSE
    BEGIN
    SELECT BusinessEntityID, JobTitle, BirthDate,
```

```
        HireDate, VacationHours
    FROM HumanResources.Employee
    WHERE JobTitle = @JobTitle AND
        BirthDate >= @BirthDate
    ORDER BY BirthDate
    END
```

You establish an optional parameter by supplying SQL Server with a default value for the parameter. In this example, @JobTitle is an optional parameter, but @BirthDate is required. If you opt to omit the @JobTitle parameter, you would call the stored procedure like this:

```
procEmployeesGetByTitleAndBirthDateOpt @BirthDate = '1/1/1960'
```

Notice that the example supplies the @BirthDate parameter as a named parameter. If you omit the @JobTitle parameter when you call the procedure, the procedure sets its value to Null. The stored procedure evaluates the value of the @JobTitle variable. If it is Null (it wasn't supplied), the WHERE clause omits the title from the selection criteria. If the user of the stored procedures supplies the @JobTitle parameter, the procedure uses the @JobTitle parameter in the criteria for the WHERE clause.

Output Parameters

So far, we have looked only at input parameters—parameters that the user of the stored procedure supplies to the procedure. You can also declare output parameters in the stored procedures you build. SQL Server returns output parameters to the caller (as their name implies). Here's an example:

```
CREATE PROCEDURE procEmployeesGetByTitleAndBirthDateOutput
    @JobTitle nVarChar(50) = NULL,
    @BirthDate DateTime,
    @MyMessage VarChar(50) = NULL OUTPUT
AS
IF @JobTitle IS NULL
    BEGIN
    SELECT BusinessEntityID, JobTitle, BirthDate,
        HireDate, VacationHours
    FROM HumanResources.Employee
    WHERE BirthDate >= @BirthDate
    ORDER BY BirthDate
    SELECT @MyMessage = 'No Title'
    END
```

```
ELSE
    BEGIN
    SELECT BusinessEntityID, JobTitle, BirthDate,
        HireDate, VacationHours
    FROM HumanResources.Employee
    WHERE JobTitle = @JobTitle AND
        BirthDate >= @BirthDate
    ORDER BY BirthDate
    SELECT @MyMessage = 'Job Title Supplied'
    END
SELECT @MyMessage
```

In addition to receiving two parameters, this procedure also has an output parameter called @MyMessage. The IF statement within the procedure sets the value of @MyMessage to the appropriate string (see Figure 14.9). You will see additional examples of OUPUT parameters and their uses as you move through the material. In particular, you will see examples of ADO code that utilize the output parameters within the client/server applications you build.

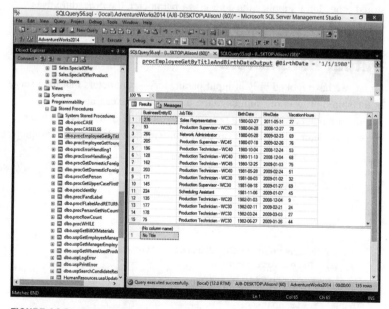

FIGURE 14.9 The IF statement within the procedure sets the value of @MyMessage to the appropriate string.

NOTE: To see the output parameter, you can also change the query results to display as text. To do this, select Query, Results To, Results to Text.

Errors and Error Handling

So far, the examples in this lesson have contained no error handling. This means that they leave what happens when an error occurs up to chance. Although T-SQL provides a means of handling errors, the error handling model in T-SQL is not as powerful as that in many programming languages. Because there's no ON ERROR GOTO statement, you must handle errors as they occur.

Handling Runtime Errors

One alternative to handling errors as they occur is to prevent errors from occurring in the first place. The SalesOrderDetail table in the AdventureWorks database requires that data be entered for the several of the fields. The SalesOrderDetailID field is an IDENTITY column, so this is not of concern. Here's the error that occurs if a value is not supplied for the SalesOrderID field:

```
Msg 515, Level 16, State 2, Line 1
Cannot insert the value NULL into column 'SalesOrderID',
table 'AdventureWorks.Sales.SalesOrderDetail';
column does not allow nulls. INSERT fails.
The statement has been terminated.
```

Here's an example of how you can prevent this error message from ever occurring:

```
CREATE PROCEDURE procOrderDetailAddHandleErrors
@SalesOrderID int = Null,
@CarrierTrackingNumber nvarchar(25) = Null,
@OrderQty smallint = 0,
@ProductID int = Null,
@SpecialOfferID int = Null,
@UnitPrice money = 0,
@UnitPriceDiscount money = 0
AS
```

```
IF @SalesOrderID Is Null
    BEGIN
        PRINT 'SalesOrderID Cannot be Null'
        RETURN
    END

IF @CarrierTrackingNumber Is Null
    BEGIN
        PRINT 'CarrierTrackingNumber Cannot be Null'
        RETURN
    END

IF @ProductID Is Null
    BEGIN
        PRINT 'ProductID Cannot be Null'
        RETURN
    END

IF @SpecialOfferID Is Null
    BEGIN
        PRINT 'SpecialOfferID Cannot be Null'
        RETURN
    END

INSERT INTO Sales.SalesOrderDetail
(SalesOrderID, CarrierTrackingNumber, OrderQty,
ProductID, UnitPrice, UnitPriceDiscount)
VALUES
(@SalesOrderID, @CarrierTrackingNumber, @OrderQty,
@ProductID, @UnitPrice, @UnitPriceDiscount)
```

In the example, several of the parameters are optional. The procedure begins by testing to see whether the value of the @SalesOrderID is Null. If it is, a message is printed, and the RETURN statement exits the procedure. This prevents the error message from ever occurring. The code repeats the process of testing the value and printing a message for both the CarrierTrackingNumber and ProductID parameters. Of course, you could add an output parameter that would report the problem back to the client application.

Returning Success and Failure Information from a Stored Procedure

As discussed in the previous section, it is important for the server to communicate to the client application the success or failure information about what happened within the stored procedure. You can select between two techniques to accomplish this task. The first method involves returning a recordset with status information. Here's an example:

```
CREATE PROCEDURE procOrderDetailAddHandleErrors2
@SalesOrderID int,
@CarrierTrackingNumber nvarchar(25),
@OrderQty smallint,
@ProductID int,
@UnitPrice money,
@UnitPriceDiscount money
AS
DECLARE @SalesOrderDetailID int,
    @LocalError int,
    @LocalRows int

INSERT INTO Sales.SalesOrderDetail
(SalesOrderID, CarrierTrackingNumber, OrderQty,
ProductID, UnitPrice, UnitPriceDiscount)
VALUES
(@SalesOrderID, @CarrierTrackingNumber, @OrderQty,
@ProductID, @UnitPrice,
@UnitPriceDiscount)

SELECT @SalesOrderDetailID = @@Identity,
    @LocalError = @@Error, @LocalRows = @@RowCount
SELECT @SalesOrderDetailID, @LocalError, @LocalRows
```

The procedure first declares three variables: @SalesOrderID, @LocalError, and @LocalRows. It then inserts an order into the SalesOrderDetail table. The statement immediately following the INSERT statement populates the three variables with the identity value, error number (if any), and number of rows affected.

In Figure 14.10, you can see that the @SalesOrderID parameter was not passed to the stored procedure. Notice in the results that the identity value of the inserted row was NULL, the error number was 515, and the number of rows affected was 0. This is because an error occurred and the row was never inserted.

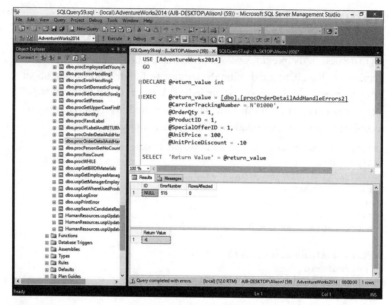

FIGURE 14.10   The results of executing a stored procedure that returns error information.

The alternative to this technique is to use output parameters. Here's an example:

```
CREATE PROCEDURE procOrderDetailAddHandleErrors3
@SalesOrderID int,
@CarrierTrackingNumber nvarchar(25),
@OrderQty smallint,
@ProductID int,
@UnitPrice money,
@UnitPriceDiscount money,
@SalesOrderDetailID int = 0 OUTPUT,
@LocalError int = 0 OUTPUT,
@LocalRows int = 0 OUTPUT
AS
INSERT INTO Sales.SalesOrderDetail
(SalesOrderID, CarrierTrackingNumber, OrderQty,
ProductID, UnitPrice, UnitPriceDiscount)
VALUES
(@SalesOrderID, @CarrierTrackingNumber, @OrderQty,
@ProductID, @UnitPrice, @UnitPriceDiscount)
```

```
SELECT @SalesOrderDetailID = @@Identity,
    @LocalError = @@Error, @LocalRows = @@RowCount
SELECT @SalesOrderDetailID, @LocalError, @LocalRows
```

Notice that the procedure does not declare any variables. Instead, it contains three output parameters: one for the SalesOrderDetailID, another for the error information, and the last for the number of rows affected. The procedure populates the output parameters just as it populated the variables, with a SELECT statement immediately following the INSERT statement.

Summary

You can use many techniques to make your stored procedures more powerful. In this lesson, you learned many of them. You learned about the SET NOCOUNT statement and how to use the built-in @@ functions. You also learned how to pass parameters to the stored procedures you build as well as how to return values from your stored procedures. Finally, you learned how to add error handling to your stored procedures.

Q&A

Q. Why would you use the SET NOCOUNT statement?

A. When it is set to ON, SET NOCOUNT eliminates the xx row(s) affected message in the SQL Express Manager window and the DONE_IN_PROC communicated from SQL Server to the client application. This improves the performance of the stored procedure.

Q. The @@ functions are actually variables (true/false).

A. False. You cannot assign values to them or work with them like normal variables. They are instead functions that return information about SQL Server.

Q. Describe the parameters used when a stored procedure is used to insert data.

A. You generally have one input parameter for each field in the underlying table. It is also common to have output parameters that return error and status information, as well as the identity value of the row that the stored procedure inserted.

Workshop

Quiz

1. What does `@@Identity` do?

2. What keyword do you use to return a value from a stored procedure?

3. You use the `ON ERROR GOTO` statement to write error handling into the stored procedures that you build (true/false).

4. What is the TSQL function you use to determine whether the caller has passed a parameter value to a stored procedure?

Quiz Answers

1. Retrieves the new value inserted into an identity column.

2. The `OUTPUT` keyword.

3. False. The `ON ERROR GOTO` statement is not available in T-SQL stored procedures. You must therefore handle errors as they occur.

4. The `ISNULL` keyword.

Activities

Build a stored procedure that inserts an order into the AdventureWorks Sales.SalesOrderDetail table. Before you attempt to insert the row, write T-SQL to ensure that the SalesOrderID associated with the order detail record is included in the Sales.SalesOrderHeader table. If the sales order associated with the sales order detail is not included in the Sales.SalesOrderHeader table, return an error message to the caller and exit the stored procedure. If the order does exist in the Sales. SalesOrderHeader table, add the order. Return the Identity value of the new row to the caller using an output parameter.

LESSON 15

Power Stored Procedure Techniques

The previous lesson discussed several important stored procedure topics including how to take advantage of @@ functions, parameters, and
error handling. There are several additional techniques that are extremely
beneficial to know when working with stored procedures. In this lesson,
you learn:

- ▶ How to use stored procedures to modify data
- ▶ How to add transaction processing to your stored procedures

Modifying Data with Stored Procedures

Probably the most common use of a stored procedure is to modify the data
in your database. You can easily design stored procedures to insert, update,
and delete data. The sections that follow cover stored procedures that perform each of these tasks.

Inserting Data

Stored procedures are effective at inserting data into your databases.
Stored procedures that insert data generally contain several input parameters, one corresponding with each field in the underlying table. They often
contain output parameters containing status or error information. In fact, in
the coverage of error handling in Lesson 14, "Stored Procedure Techniques

Every Developer Should Know," you are introduced to the process of inserting data into a table. Take a look at the following stored procedure:

```
CREATE PROCEDURE procOrderDetailAdd
@SalesOrderID int,
@CarrierTrackingNumber nvarchar(25),
@OrderQty smallint,
@ProductID int,
@SpecialOfferID int,
@UnitPrice money,
@UnitPriceDiscount money
AS
INSERT INTO Sales.SalesOrderDetail
(SalesOrderID, CarrierTrackingNumber, OrderQty,
ProductID, SpecialOfferID, UnitPrice, UnitPriceDiscount)
VALUES
(@SalesOrderID, @CarrierTrackingNumber, @OrderQty,
@ProductID, @SpecialOfferID, @UnitPrice, @UnitPriceDiscount)
```

The procedure receives seven input parameters, one for each field in the Sales.SalesOrderDetail table into which the procedure inserts data. The INSERT INTO statement uses the input parameters as values to insert into the table. As you can see, the previous example contains no output parameters. The following procedure, which inserts data into the Sales.SalesOrderDetail table, contains an output parameter called @SalesOrderDetailID:

```
CREATE PROCEDURE procOrderDetailAddOutput
@SalesOrderID int,
@CarrierTrackingNumber nvarchar(25),
@OrderQty smallint,
@ProductID int,
@SpecialOfferID int,
@UnitPrice money,
@UnitPriceDiscount money,
@SalesOrderDetailID int = 0 OUTPUT
AS
INSERT INTO Sales.SalesOrderDetail
(SalesOrderID, CarrierTrackingNumber, OrderQty,
ProductID, SpecialOfferID, UnitPrice, UnitPriceDiscount)
VALUES
(@SalesOrderID, @CarrierTrackingNumber, @OrderQty,
@ProductID, @SpecialOfferID, @UnitPrice, @UnitPriceDiscount)
SET @SalesOrderDetailID = @@IDENTITY
```

In addition to receiving six input parameters, this procedure uses the output parameter to house the identity value of the inserted row. Notice

that the code populates the `@SalesOrderDetailID` output parameter
with the value of the system function `@@IDENTITY`. The client application
can use the output parameter via ADO code you write.

Updating Data

Stored procedures are also excellent in their capability to update data.
Here's an example:

```
CREATE PROCEDURE procSalesOrderHeaderUpdate
@SalesOrderID int,
@NewFreight money
AS
UPDATE Sales.SalesOrderHeader
SET Freight = @NewFreight
WHERE SalesOrderID = @SalesOrderID
```

The procedure receives two input parameters. One is for the SalesOrderID
of the order whose freight you want to modify. The other parameter
contains the new value for the freight. Notice that the UPDATE statement
sets the freight to the `@NewFreight` value where the SalesOrderID matches
the customer passed in as the `@SalesOrderID` parameter. Consider this
more complex example:

```
CREATE PROCEDURE procSalesOrderDetailUpdate
@SalesOrderDetailID int,
@SalesOrderID int,
@CarrierTrackingNumber nvarchar(25),
@OrderQty smallint,
@ProductID int,
@SpecialOfferID int,
@UnitPrice money,
@UnitPriceDiscount money,
@ResultCode int = NULL Output,
@ResultMessage varchar(20) = NULL Output
AS
UPDATE Sales.SalesOrderDetail
SET SalesOrderID = @SalesOrderID,
    CarrierTrackingNumber = @CarrierTrackingNumber,
    OrderQty = @OrderQty,
    ProductID = @ProductID,
    SpecialOfferID = @SpecialOfferID,
    UnitPrice = @UnitPrice,
    UnitPriceDiscount = @UnitPriceDiscount
```

```
WHERE SalesOrderID = @SalesOrderID AND
    SalesOrderDetailID = @SalesOrderDetailID

SET @ResultMessage =
    Convert(varchar(20),  @@RowCount) +
    'Records Affected'
SET @ResultCode = 0
```

This example is more similar to the INSERT example. It receives one input parameter for each field in the SalesOrderDetails table that you want to modify. It updates the fields in the SalesOrderDetails table with the values of the input parameters for the customer with the SalesOrderDetailID designated in the @SalesOrderDetailID parameter. It then sets the @ResultMessage output parameter to a string containing the @@RowCount value. Finally, it sets the @ResultCode output parameter to zero. Figure 15.1 illustrates an example of successfully executing the procedure. Notice that the value of @ResultCode is zero, indicating that no error occurred, and @ResultMessage indicates that one record was affected.

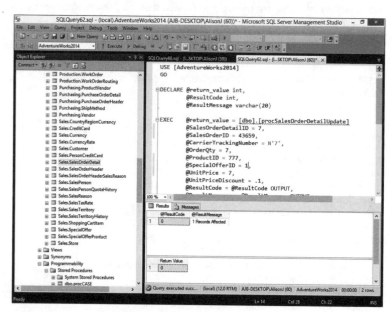

FIGURE 15.1 A stored procedure that updates table data.

Deleting Data

Stored procedures are also very effective at deleting data. Here's
an example:

```
CREATE PROCEDURE procSalesOrderDetailDelete
@SalesOrderDetailID int
AS
DELETE FROM Sales.SalesOrderDetails
WHERE SalesOrderDetailID = @SalesOrderDetailID
```

This example receives one parameter: the SalesOrderDetailID of the sales
order detail row you want to delete. Notice that the DELETE statement
contains a WHERE clause that references the @SalesOrderDetailID
input parameter.

Stored Procedures and Transactions

It is a good idea to place transactions in all the stored procedures you
build. Transactions ensure that a piece of work is completed in entirety or
not at all. One of the classic examples is a banking transaction. You want
all the debits and credits to complete properly or not at all. This is where
transactions come in. When using a SQL Server backend, you should place
all transaction processing inside your stored procedures.

Types of Transactions

Two types of transactions exist: *implicit transactions* and *explicit
transactions*. Implicit transactions happen regardless of what you do in
your programming code. Each time that you issue an INSERT, UPDATE, or
DELETE statement, SQL Server invokes an implicit transaction. If any piece
of an INSERT, UPDATE, or DELETE statement fails, the entire statement is
rolled back. For example, if your DELETE statement attempts to delete all the
inactive customers, and somewhere in the process a record fails to delete
(for example, for referential integrity reasons), SQL Server does not delete
any of the records. Explicit transactions, on the other hand, are transactions

you define and control. Using explicit transactions, you package multiple statements within BEGIN TRANSACTION and COMMIT TRANSACTION statements. In your error handling, you include a ROLLBACK TRANSACTION statement. This ensures that all the statements complete successfully or not at all.

Implementing Transactions

As mentioned, you use the BEGIN TRANSACTION, COMMIT TRANSACTION, and ROLLBACK TRANSACTION statements to implement transactions. The following is a stored procedure that utilizes a transaction:

```
CREATE PROCEDURE procOrderDetailAddTransaction
@SalesOrderID int,
@CarrierTrackingNumber nvarchar(25),
@OrderQty smallint,
@ProductID int,
@SpecialOfferID int,
@UnitPrice money,
@UnitPriceDiscount money
AS
SET NOCOUNT ON
DECLARE @SalesOrderDetailID int, @LocalError int, @LocalRows int

BEGIN TRANSACTION

INSERT INTO Sales.SalesOrderDetail
(SalesOrderID, CarrierTrackingNumber, OrderQty,
ProductID, SpecialOfferID, UnitPrice, UnitPriceDiscount)
VALUES
(@SalesOrderID, @CarrierTrackingNumber, @OrderQty,
@ProductID, @SpecialOfferID, @UnitPrice, @UnitPriceDiscount)
SELECT @LocalError = @@Error, @LocalRows = @@RowCount

IF @LocalError <> 0 or @LocalRows = 0
    BEGIN
    ROLLBACK TRANSACTION
    SELECT SalesOrderDetailID = Null,
    Error = @LocalError,
    NumRows = @LocalRows
    END
ELSE
    BEGIN
    COMMIT TRANSACTION
```

```
SELECT @SalesOrderDetailID = @@Identity
SELECT SalesOrderDetailID = @SalesOrderDetailID,
Error = 0,
NumRows = @LocalRows
END
```

In the example, the BEGIN TRANSACTION starts the transaction. The procedure attempts to insert a row into the Sales.SalesOrderDetail table. It populates the @LocalError variable with the value returned from the @@Error function and the @LocalRows variable with the value returned from the @@RowCount function. An IF statement evaluates whether either @LocalError is non-zero or @LocalRows is zero. If either condition is true, the procedure was unsuccessful at inserting the row. The ROLLBACK TRANSACTION statement is used to terminate the transaction, and the procedure returns error information to the caller. If the error number equals zero, and the @LocalRows variable is non-zero, you can assume that the process completed successfully. The COMMIT TRANSACTION statement commits the changes, and the procedure returns the status and identity information to the caller (see Figure 15.2).

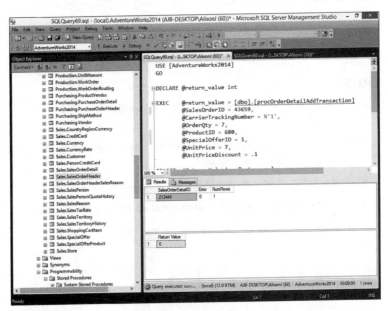

FIGURE 15.2 A stored procedure that utilizes transactions and returns status information.

Summary

You can use many techniques to make your stored procedures more powerful. In this lesson, you learned a few of them. You first learned how you can use stored procedures to modify data. Then you learned how you can add transaction processing to the stored procedures you build.

Q&A

Q. What are three keywords that you can use to modify table data?

A. You can use INSERT, UPDATE, and DELETE to modify table data.

Q. What keywords do you use when working with transactions?

A. BEGIN TRANSACTION, COMMIT TRANSACTION, ROLLBACK TRANSACTION.

Q. Why would you use transactions?

A. You want a procedure to execute in entirety or not at all.

Workshop

Quiz

1. What keyword do you use to determine the identity value of the inserted row?

2. What keyword do you use to determine how many rows were inserted, updated, or deleted?

3. You use the EDIT keyword to modify table data (true/false).

4. What keyword do you use to limit the data you update or delete?

5. What keywords do you use to start a transaction?

Quiz Answers

1. @@Identity.

2. @@RowCount.

3. False. You use the UPDATE keyword to modify table data.

4. The WHERE keyword.

5. The BEGIN TRANSACTION keywords.

Activities

Build a stored procedure that updates the TaxRate field in the AdventureWorks Sales.SalesTaxRate table for all rows where the TaxType field equals 1. Then build a stored procedure that deletes all rows from Sales.SalesOrderDetail WHERE SalesOrderID = 43892. Finally, modify the first stored procedure so that it contains transaction processing. If any errors occur or no rows are affected, the procedure should return error information and roll back the transaction. If the procedure executes successfully, commit the transaction.

LESSON 16

Stored Procedure Special Topics

You should be aware of some special topics when writing your stored procedures. In some cases, understanding these topics can help you provide a more efficient solution to a problem. In other cases, these topics address functionality available only with the techniques covered during this lesson. In this lesson, you find out:

- ▶ How to work with stored procedures and temporary tables
- ▶ How to utilize cursors in the stored procedures you build
- ▶ How stored procedures interact with the security of your database

Stored Procedures and Temporary Tables

SQL Server creates temporary tables in a special system database called TempDB. SQL Server creates TempDB each time it starts and destroys it each time it shuts down. SQL Server uses TempDB to house many temporary objects that it needs to run. You can use TempDB to share data between procedures or to help you to accomplish complex tasks. You often will need to incorporate temporary tables into the stored procedures that you write. Here's an example of how you create and use a temporary table:

```
CREATE PROCEDURE procEmployeesGetTemp AS
BEGIN
CREATE TABLE #TempEmployees
```

```
(BusinessEntityID int NOT NULL PRIMARY KEY,
JobTitle varchar(50),
HireDate datetime,
VacationHours int)
INSERT INTO #TempEmployees
(BusinessEntityID, JobTitle, HireDate, VacationHours)
EXEC procEmployeesGetByJobTitleAndHireDate '1/1/2009',
➥ 'Production Technician - WC20'
SELECT BusinessEntityID, JobTitle, HireDate, VacationHours
FROM #TempEmployees
ORDER BY HireDate DESC
END
```

This procedure uses a second procedure called procEmployeesGetByHire-DateAndJobTitleAndHireDate. It looks like this:

```
CREATE PROCEDURE procEmployeesGetByJobTitleAndHireDate
    @HireDate DateTime,
    @JobTitle varchar(50)
AS
SELECT BusinessEntityID, JobTitle, HireDate, VacationHours
FROM HumanResources.Employee
WHERE HireDate >= @HireDate AND
JobTitle = @JobTitle
ORDER BY HireDate DESC
```

The procEmployeesGetByHireDateAndJobTitleAndHireDate procedure receives two parameters. It uses those parameters for the WHERE clause for HireDate and JobTitle. The procEmployeesGetTemp procedure creates a temporary table that holds customer information. It inserts into the temporary table the results of executing the procEmployeesGetByHireDateAndJobTitle procedure, passing it 1/1/2009 and Design Engineer as the hire date and job title values. Finally, the procedure selects data from the temporary table, ordering the result by HireDate in descending order. The results appear in Figure 16.1. Notice that only employees with the title Production Technician – WC20 and a hire date on or after 1/1/2009 appear.

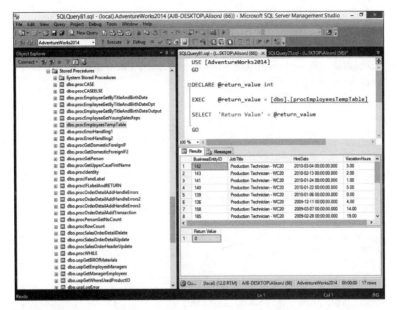

FIGURE 16.1   The stored procedure outputs data contained in a temporary table that is populated by the results of executing a second stored procedure.

Stored Procedures and Cursors

A SQL Server SELECT statement outputs a complete result set. There are times when you will want to process one row at a time, performing some operation on each row. Opening a cursor on a result set allows you to process each row in the result set independently.

You use the DECLARE CURSOR statement to define a SQL Server cursor. The parameters to the DECLARE CURSOR statement allow you to determine the behavior of the cursor. For example, you can designate a cursor as read-only or as forward-only.

The OPEN statement populates the cursor with the data in the result set.
FETCH returns a single row from the result set. You use CLOSE to release the
result set associated with the cursor and DEALLOCATE to release all resources
associated with the cursor. The following example illustrates the process of
working with a cursor:

```
CREATE PROCEDURE procEmployeesGetCursor
AS
BEGIN
DECLARE @BusinessEntityID int,
    @HireDate datetime,
    @JobTitle varchar(5)

DECLARE EmployeeCursor CURSOR FOR
SELECT BusinessEntityID, JobTitle, HireDate
FROM HumanResources.Employee
WHERE HireDate >= '1/1/2009'
ORDER BY HireDate DESC

OPEN EmployeeCursor

FETCH NEXT FROM EmployeeCursor INTO
    @BusinessEntityID, @JobTitle, @HireDate

--As long as there are more rows to fetch
WHILE @@FETCH_STATUS = 0
BEGIN
    PRINT 'BusinessEntityID: ' +
    CONVERT(varchar(10), @BusinessEntityID) +
    ' - ' + UPPER(@JobTitle) +
    ' Hire Date = ' + CONVERT(varchar(10), @HireDate)
    FETCH NEXT FROM EmployeeCursor
END

CLOSE EmployeeCursor
DEALLOCATE EmployeeCursor
END
```

The procedure procEmployeesGetCursor first declares variables used by
the cursor. It then retrieves data from the Employee table. After opening
the EmployeeCursor cursor, it uses the FETCH NEXT statement to retrieve
the first row from the result set, placing its data into the three variables.
The @@FETCH_STATUS determines if there are more rows to fetch from the
cursor. If there are, the code prints data from the cursor. It then fetches

the next row from the cursor. Finally, the code closes and deallocates the cursor, freeing the resources associated with it. Figure 16.2 provides an example of executing the stored procedure.

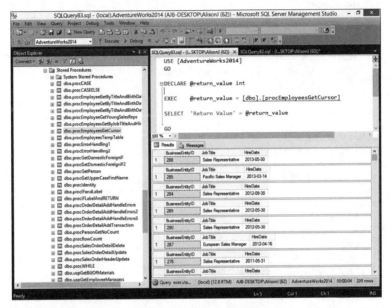

FIGURE 16.2 The stored procedure utilizes a cursor to loop through the Employee table, outputting data from each row in the table.

The stored procedure used in the previous example provided a simple illustration of how you can use a cursor to loop through records in a result set. The stored procedure that follows shows how you can use a cursor to solve a real-life data problem. Specifically, it allows you to search for a specific string with any text-type columns in a table. It looks like this:

```
CREATE PROCEDURE procGetString
@FindString varchar(8000)
AS
BEGIN
-- SET NOCOUNT ON added to prevent extra result sets from
-- interfering with SELECT statements.
SET NOCOUNT ON;
DECLARE @SQLCommand varchar(8000)
DECLARE @Where varchar(8000)
```

```
DECLARE @ColumnName sysname
DECLARE @Cursor varchar(8000)

SET @SQLCommand = 'SELECT * FROM Person.Address'
SET @Where = ''
SET @Cursor = 'DECLARE FindCursor CURSOR FOR SELECT COLUMN_NAME
    FROM ' + DB_NAME() + '.INFORMATION_SCHEMA.COLUMNS
    WHERE TABLE_SCHEMA = ' + '"Person"' + ' AND
    TABLE_NAME = ' + '"Address"' + ' AND
    DATA_TYPE IN ("char", "nchar", "ntext",
    "nvarchar", "text", "varchar")'

EXEC (@Cursor)

OPEN FindCursor
FETCH NEXT FROM FindCursor INTO @ColumnName

WHILE @@FETCH_STATUS = 0
BEGIN
IF @Where <> ''
    BEGIN
    SET @Where = @Where + ' OR '
    END
SET @Where = @Where + ' [' + @ColumnName +
'] LIKE "'+ @FindString + '"
FETCH NEXT FROM FindCursor INTO @ColumnName
END

SET @SQLCommand = @SQLCommand + ' WHERE ' + @Where
EXEC (@SQLCommand)

CLOSE FindCursor
DEALLOCATE FindCursor
END
```

This procedure is designed to accept a string as a parameter. It then searches for that string in all text-type columns within the Person.Address table.
After declaring four variables, the procedure uses a SET statement to assign
the beginning of a SELECT statement to the @SQLCommand variable. The SET
statement is an alternative way (the other being SELECT) to assign a value
to a variable.

Probably the most complex statement in the procedure is the SET statement that creates the DECLARE CURSOR statement and assigns it to the @Cursor variable. This statement sets the @Cursor variable equal to a string that declares a cursor that is responsible for looping through all the text-type columns (char, nchar, ntext, nvarchar, text, and varchar) in the Person.Address table. The EXEC (@Cursor) statement executes the contents of the @Cursor variable, thereby creating the FindCursor cursor.

As the code loops through the result set, it builds a WHERE clause containing all of the text-type fields and the contents of the @FindString variable. Finally, it sets the @SQLCommand variable equal to the SELECT clause concatenated with the WHERE clause. Figure 16.3 provides an example of the results of executing the stored procedure passing the parameter %Wood%. Notice in the results that rows that contain Wood in either the AddressLine1 field or the City field appear in the output.

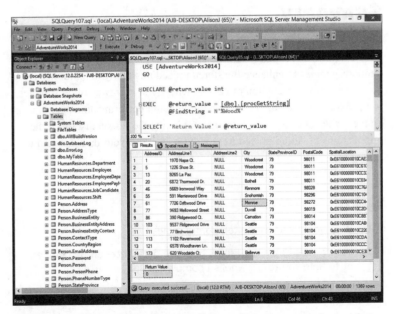

FIGURE 16.3 The stored procedure utilizes a cursor to search for a string within any text-type field in the Address table.

Stored Procedures and Security

Like views, stored procedures provide an excellent tool for securing your application's data. You can grant rights to a stored procedure without providing any rights to the underlying table(s). Consider the following scenario. Imagine you create an unbound Access form where users can select various customers. You then execute stored procedures to insert, update, and delete data. In this scenario, you can grant users view rights to the Customers table. You do not need to grant them insert, update, or delete rights to the table. Instead you grant them execute rights to the appropriate stored procedures. In this way, you can allow your users to easily create queries and reports that use the Customer data (you granted them view rights to the table). They can only insert, update, and delete data via the stored procedures that you call from your application code.

Summary

There are some special topics you should be aware of when working with stored procedures. This lesson began by talking about how you can use temporary tables to enhance the stored procedures that you build. It then continued with a discussion of cursors where you saw two solid examples of how you can use cursors to loop through and perform some operation on the result set of a SELECT statement. Finally, the lesson discussed the implications of stored procedures on the security of your database and the data contained within it.

Q&A

Q. Why would you create temporary tables?

A. You create temporary tables to share data between procedures or to help you to accomplish complex tasks.

Q. What does a cursor do?

A. A cursor allows you to loop through a result set, performing some operation on each record individually.

Q. **What role do stored procedures take in allowing you to secure your table data?**

A. Using stored procedures, you can grant rights to the stored procedure without granting any rights to the underlying tables.

Workshop

Quiz

1. What database does SQL Server use for temporary tables?

2. With stored procedures, the user must have rights to the tables that are affected by the stored procedure (true/false).

3. What keywords do you use to create a cursor?

Quiz Answers

1. TempDB.

2. False. They need rights to only the stored procedure.

3. `DECLARE mycursor CURSOR FOR`.

Activities

Build a stored procedure that creates a temporary table containing PurchaseOrderID, EmployeeID, OrderDate, ShipDate, and Freight. Execute a second stored procedure that selects those fields from the Purchasing.PurchaseOrderHeader table, ordering by EmployeeID and OrderDate. The first stored procedure should pass the second stored procedure a parameter for the freight amount. The second stored procedure receives the parameter for the freight amount. It selects all fields from the Orders table where Freight is greater than the parameter value, ordering by EmployeeID and Freight. It returns the result into the temporary table in the first stored procedure. Finally, have the first stored procedure display the contents of the temporary table. For help, consult the example in the "Stored Procedures and Temporary Tables" section of this lesson.

LESSON 17

Building and Working with User-Defined Functions

SQL Server user-defined functions add power and flexibility slightly different than that available with views and stored procedures. SQL Server user-defined functions accept parameters, perform one or more actions, and return a result. Three types of user-defined functions exist: scalar, inline table-valued, and multi-statement table-valued. The sections that follow cover each of these types of user-defined functions in detail. Used properly, SQL Server user-defined functions enhance your ability to create powerful client/server applications. This lesson covers:

▶ How to create and work with scalar functions

▶ How to take advantage of inline table-valued functions

▶ How to utilize multi-statement table-valued functions

Scalar Functions

Scalar functions return a single value of the type defined in the RETURNS clause. The body of the function is between a BEGIN and END block. Scalar functions can return any data type *except* text, ntext, image, cursor, or timestamp. Here's an example of a scalar function:

```
CREATE FUNCTION dbo.FullName
    (@FirstName nVarChar(10),
    @LastName nVarChar(20))
RETURNS nVarChar(35)
BEGIN
    RETURN (@LastName + ', ' + @FirstName)
END
```

This function receives two parameters: `@FirstName` and `@LastName`. It returns an `nVarChar(35)` value. The return value is the combination of the `@LastName` and `@FirstName` input parameters combined with a comma and a space. You could call the function like this:

```
SELECT FirstName, LastName, dbo.FullName(FirstName, LastName) as
➡ FullName
FROM Person.Person
```

The example displays the `FirstName`, `LastName`, and result of the `FullName` function (see Figure 17.1).

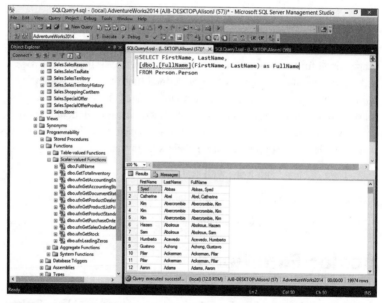

FIGURE 17.1   Scalar functions return a single value of the type defined in the RETURNS clause.

The next example of a scalar function is more complex. It calculates the total quantity for a specific ProductID in the ProductInventory table. It looks like this:

```
CREATE FUNCTION ?.[GetTotalInventory](@ProductID int)
RETURNS int
```

```
AS
-- Returns the stock level for the product.
BEGIN
    DECLARE @return int
    SELECT @return = SUM(Quantity)
    FROM Production.ProductInventory
    WHERE ProductID = @ProductID
    IF (@return IS NULL)
        SET @return = 0
    RETURN @return
END
```

The GetTotalInventory function receives an integer parameter called
@ProductID and returns an int. After declaring a variable called @return, it
sums the contents of the Quantity field in the Production.ProductInventory
table where the ProductID equals the integer value passed as a parameter
to the function. It then returns the total quantity value for that ProductID.
You call the function like this:

```
SELECT DISTINCT ProductID, ?.[GetTotalInventory](ProductID)
FROM Production.ProductInventory
WHERE ProductID BETWEEN 1 AND 4
```

This SELECT statement returns each unique combination of ProductIDs and
return values from the ProductInventory table for all the rows where the
ProductID is between 1 and 4. Notice that each ProductID found in the
result is passed to the function. The results appear in Figure 17.2.

The DISTINCT keyword prevents the contents of the ProductID field from
repeating over and over again for each row with a particular ProductID.
Repeating the ProductID is not necessary because the GetTotalInventory
function sums the contents of the Quantity field for a given ProductID.
If you omit the DISTINCT keyword, the results are as they appear in
Figure 17.3.

The advantage of placing database functionality in a scalar function
is that you write the logic once and then you can call it from multiple SQL statements, views, and stored procedures. This is quite
valuable if you will use the functionality over and over again throughout
your database.

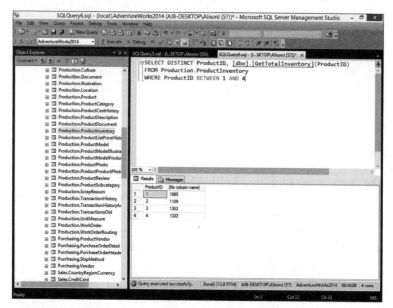

FIGURE 17.2 The results of executing the scalar function
GetTotalInventory with the DISTINCT keyword in the calling SQL
statement.

The disadvantage of using scalar functions lie in the effect they have on
the performance of the database. If you call a scalar function in a SELECT
clause or a WHERE clause of a SQL statement, the function executes once
for each row in the result set.

In conclusion, scalar functions can greatly simplify the use of complex
expressions in your SQL statements, views, and stored procedures.
However, it is important that you evaluate the performance implications
they impose to ensure their benefits outweigh the costs.

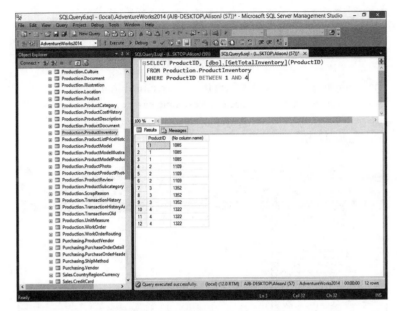

FIGURE 17.3 The results of executing the scalar function GetTotalInventory without the DISTINCT keyword in the calling SQL statement.

Inline Table-Valued Functions

As their name implies, inline table-valued functions return a table. Inline table-valued functions have no body. They simply return the result of a simple SELECT statement. Here's an example:

```
CREATE FUNCTION dbo.EmpGetByTitle
    (@Title nVarChar(30))
RETURNS Table
AS
RETURN SELECT FirstName, LastName,
JobTitle, VacationHours, HireDate
FROM vwEmployee WHERE JobTitle = @Title
```

This example receives a parameter called @Title. It returns a table containing selected fields from the vwEmployee view where the

`ContactTitle` equals the `@Title` parameter value. You would call the function like this:

```
SELECT * FROM dbo.EmpGetByTitle('Design Engineer')
```

The example selects all fields from the table returned from the `EmpGetByTitle` function. Because the example passes `Design Engineer` as a parameter, only the design engineers are included in the result set (see Figure 17.4).

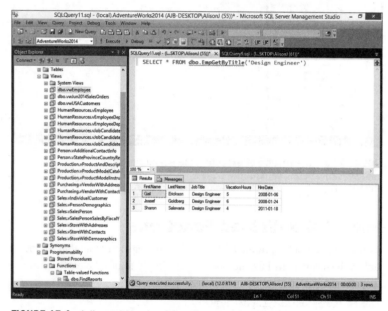

FIGURE 17.4   Inline table-valued functions return a table.

Multi-Statement Table-Valued Functions

Multi-statement table-valued functions are similar to inline table-valued functions. The main difference is that like scalar functions, they have a body defined by a `BEGIN...END` block. Like inline table-valued functions, they return a table. Here's an example:

```
CREATE FUNCTION ?.[FindReports] (@EmpID INTEGER)
RETURNS @FindReports TABLE
(
```

```
    EmployeeID int primary key NOT NULL,
    FirstName nvarchar(255) NOT NULL,
    LastName nvarchar(255) NOT NULL,
    JobTitle nvarchar(50) NOT NULL,
    RecursionLevel int NOT NULL
)
AS
BEGIN
WITH EMP_cte(EmployeeID, OrganizationNode, FirstName, LastName,
    JobTitle, RecursionLevel) -- CTE name and columns
    AS (
    -- Get the initial list of Employees for Manager n
    SELECT e.BusinessEntityID, e.OrganizationNode,
        p.FirstName, p.LastName, e.JobTitle, 0
        FROM HumanResources.Employee e
            INNER JOIN Person.Person p
            ON p.BusinessEntityID = e.BusinessEntityID
        WHERE e.BusinessEntityID = @EmpID
        UNION ALL
        SELECT e.BusinessEntityID, e.OrganizationNode,
            p.FirstName, p.LastName, e.JobTitle,
            RecursionLevel + 1 -- Join recursive member to
            anchor
        FROM HumanResources.Employee e
            INNER JOIN EMP_cte
            ON e.OrganizationNode.GetAncestor(1) =
            EMP_cte.OrganizationNode
                INNER JOIN Person.Person p
                ON p.BusinessEntityID = e.BusinessEntityID
        )
    INSERT @FindReports
    SELECT EmployeeID, FirstName, LastName, JobTitle,
    RecursionLevel
    FROM EMP_cte
    RETURN
END
```

This example is fairly complex. It uses a built-in function called GetAncestor to return a result set that lists all the employees who report to a specific employee directly or indirectly. It is not necessary for you to understand the intricacies of the TSQL within the function. What is important to understand is that after building a recordset with a list of all employees that report to the employee whose EmployeeID is passed as a parameter to the function, the function returns the results in a table. You call the function like this:

```
SELECT * FROM ?.[FindReports](2)
```

The results of calling the GetReports function appear in Figure 17.5. All employees who report to EmployeeID 2 appear in the result set.

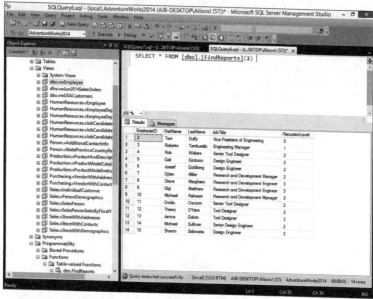

FIGURE 17.5 The results of using a multi-statement table-valued function to return all employees that report to the specified employee.

Summary

This lesson introduced you to an alternative to stored procedures: user-defined functions. User-defined functions are a close relative to stored procedures. They enable you to encapsulate complex functionality into a reusable component. User-defined functions can return either a single value (scalar functions) or a table (table-valued functions). Although scalar functions can help to simplify the SQL statements you build, they can negatively impact performance. It is up to you to determine whether their benefits outweigh their limitations. There are two types of table-valued functions. The first simply returns a table. The second allows you to perform complex logic, which determines what data is returned in its result set.

Q&A

Q. What are the two main categories of user-defined functions?

A. Scalar functions and table-valued functions.

Q. Why can a scalar function cause performance problems?

A. The function executes for each record in the SELECT statement.

Q. What are the two types of table-valued functions?

A. Inline table-valued functions and multi-statement table-valued functions.

Workshop

Quiz

1. You can pass parameters to user-defined functions (true/false).

2. What type of function returns a single value?

3. What type of function allows you to perform multiple operations before returning a result set?

4. The statements in an inline table-valued function are between a BEGIN clause and an END clause (true/false).

Quiz Answers

1. True.

2. Scalar functions return a single value.

3. Multi-statement table-valued functions allow you to perform multiple operations.

4. False. The statements between scalar functions and multi-statement table-valued functions are between a BEGIN clause and an END clause.

Activities

Build a scalar function that combines the contents of the ProductNumber and Name fields from the Production.Product table. Combine the fields by outputting the ProductNumber, a colon followed by a space, and the Name (for example, BA-8327: Bearing Ball). The function should contain a parameter that limits the output to those rows with a designated Color value.

Build an inline table-valued function that returns the ProductID, Name, ProductNumber, Color, SafetyStockLevel, and ReorderPoint. Have the function use the same expression as just described to concatenate the ProductNumber, a colon, a space, and the contents of the Name field. Include a parameter that limits the output to those rows with a designated Color value.

LESSON 18

Creating and Working with Triggers

A *trigger* is specialized type of stored procedure, which functions like an event procedure and that runs when data changes. You can create triggers that execute in response to inserts, updates, and deletes. Developers use triggers to enforce business rules and even to perform tasks such as inserting data into an audit log. This lesson explains:

▶ How to create triggers

▶ How to work with Insert, Update, and Delete triggers

▶ What an Instead Of trigger is and why you'd want to use one

▶ Downsides of triggers

Creating Triggers

Use the following steps to create or modify a trigger:

1. Click to expand the node for the table to which you want to add the trigger. The Triggers node appears (see Figure 18.1).

2. Right-click the Triggers node and select New Trigger. A new query window appears, enabling you to type the text for the trigger (see Figure 18.2).

3. Type the T-SQL that comprises the trigger.

4. Execute the CREATE TRIGGER statement (see Figure 18.3). After refreshing the list of triggers, it appears under the list of triggers associated with that table (see Figure 18.4).

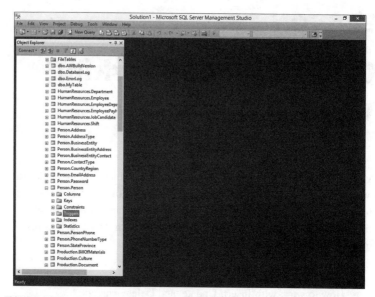

FIGURE 18.1   The Triggers node shows you the existing triggers associated with a table.

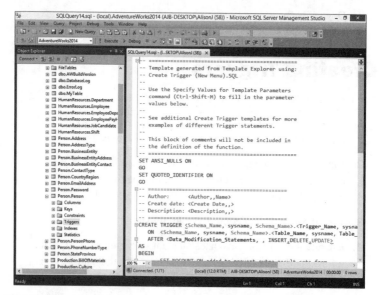

FIGURE 18.2   The new query window allows you to type the T-SQL that comprises the trigger.

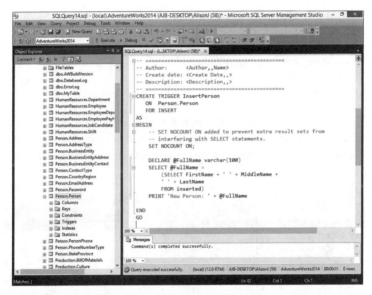

FIGURE 18.3 You must execute the T-SQL to create the trigger.

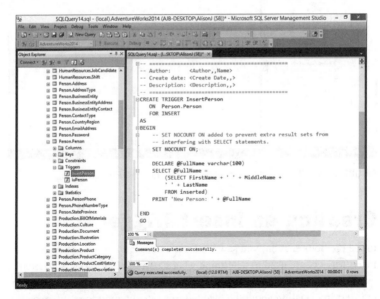

FIGURE 18.4 Once created, a trigger appears under the list of triggers available for that table.

The syntax for a trigger is as follows:

```
CREATE TRIGGER TriggerName
    On TableName
    FOR [INSERT], [UPDATE], [DELETE]
    AS
    --Trigger Code
```

The trigger shown in Figure 18.4 prints the full name associated with the person who was added to the table. Figure 18.5 shows the results of executing an `INSERT INTO` statement that inserts data into the Person table.

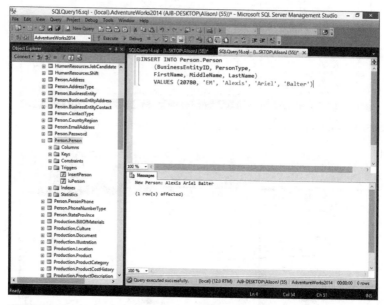

FIGURE 18.5 The results of inserting a row into the Person table.

Creating an Insert Trigger

In the previous section, you saw a simple example of an insert trigger. Insert triggers are used to determine what happens after a row is inserted into a table. Insert triggers are often used to validate data being inserted or to insert information about the inserted row into an audit log.

The example we are going to explore inserts information into an audit log every time a row is inserted into the Person table. To work with this example, you first need to create the audit log table. The TSQL statement that follows creates this table:

```
CREATE TABLE tblAuditLog
(
BusinessEntityID int,
EmployeeName varchar(100),
AuditAction varchar(100),
AuditTimeStamp datetime
)
```

The insert trigger looks like this:

```
CREATE TRIGGER InsertPerson
    ON  Person.Person
    FOR INSERT
AS
BEGIN
    -- SET NOCOUNT ON added to prevent extra result sets from
    -- interfering with SELECT statements.
    SET NOCOUNT ON;
    DECLARE @BusinessEntityID int
    DECLARE @FullName varchar(100)
    DECLARE @AuditAction varchar(100)
    SELECT @BusinessEntityID = BusinessEntityID
        FROM inserted
        SELECT @FullName =
            (SELECT FirstName + ' ' + MiddleName +
            ' ' + LastName
            FROM inserted)
        SELECT @AuditAction = 'Row Inserted'
        INSERT INTO tblAuditLog
            (BusinessEntityID, EmployeeName,
            AuditAction, AuditTimeStamp)
            VALUES
            (@BusinessEntityID, @FullName,
            @AuditAction, GetDate())
    END
```

This trigger is a more sophisticated and utilitarian version of the trigger introduced in the first section of the lesson. It first declares variables that will be populated with information about the inserted row. It then establishes the values of those variables based on the data being inserted. Finally, it inserts the contents of the variables, along with the current date and time, into the tblAuditLog table. Figure 18.6 shows the TSQL used to insert rows into the Person table. Figure 18.7 shows the resulting data added to the audit log.

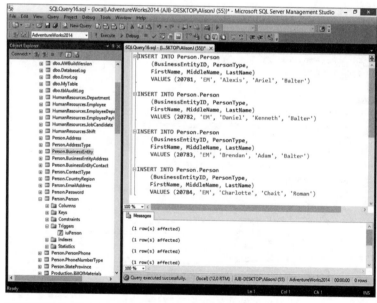

FIGURE 18.6   New rows inserted into the Person table.

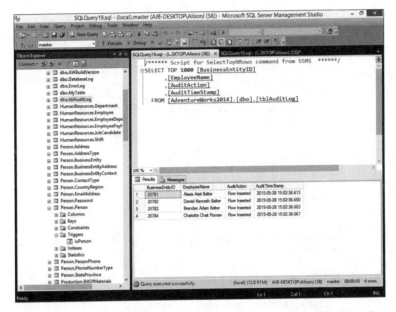

FIGURE 18.7 Records added to tblAuditLog reflecting data inserted into the Person table.

Creating an Update Trigger

Whereas an Insert trigger executes when data is inserted into a table, an Update trigger executes any time data in an existing row is modified. The following is an example of a trigger that inserts data into an audit log whenever the user updates a row:

```
CREATE TRIGGER [Person].[UpdatePerson]
    ON  [Person].[Person]
    FOR UPDATE
AS
BEGIN
    SET NOCOUNT ON;

    DECLARE @BusinessEntityID int
    DECLARE @FullName varchar(100)
    DECLARE @AuditAction varchar(500)
```

```
If UPDATE(FirstName)
    BEGIN
        SELECT @AuditAction = 'First Name Updated, '
    END

If UPDATE(MiddleName)
    BEGIN
        SELECT @AuditAction = @AuditAction + 'Middle Name
        ➥ Updated, '
    END

If UPDATE(LastName)
    BEGIN
        SELECT @AuditAction = @AuditAction + 'Last Name
        ➥ Updated, '
    END

    SET @AuditAction = LEFT(@AuditAction, LEN(@AuditAction)
    ➥ - 1)

    INSERT INTO tblAuditLog
        (BusinessEntityID, EmployeeName,
        AuditAction, AuditTimeStamp)
        SELECT i.BusinessEntityID,
        i.FirstName + ' ' + i.MiddleName +
        ' ' + i.LastName,
        @AuditAction,
        GetDate()
        FROM inserted i, deleted d
        WHERE i.BusinessEntityID = d.BusinessEntityID

END
```

This example inserts data into an audit log whenever the user modifies data in the Person table. The trigger uses the UPDATE function to determine which data was modified. While doing so, it builds a string that indicates which fields were updated. Finally, the trigger inserts the BusinessEntityID, the full name, the string containing the fields that were updated, and the current date into the tblAuditLog table. Figure 18.8 shows the TSQL used to update rows in the Person table. Figure 18.9 shows the resulting data added to the audit log.

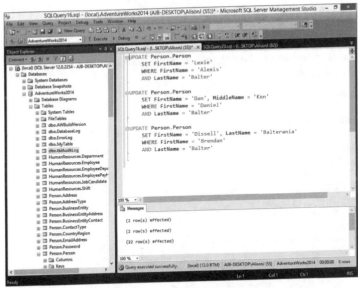

FIGURE 18.8 UPDATE statements that invoke the UPDATE trigger.

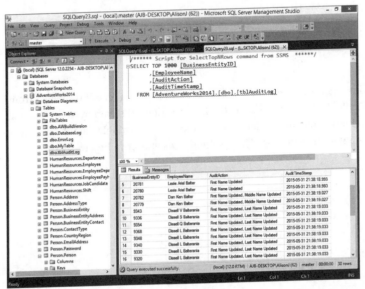

FIGURE 18.9 Records added to tblAuditLog reflecting data updated in the Person table.

Creating a Delete Trigger

A Delete trigger executes in response to a record being deleted. The following is an example of a trigger that inserts data into an audit log when a row is deleted:

```
CREATE TRIGGER [Person].[DeletePerson]
    ON [Person].[Person]
    AFTER DELETE
AS
BEGIN
    DECLARE @BusinessEntityID int
    DECLARE @FullName varchar(100)
    DECLARE @AuditAction varchar(500)

    SET @AuditAction = 'Record Deleted'

    INSERT INTO tblAuditLog
        (BusinessEntityID, EmployeeName,
        AuditAction, AuditTimeStamp)
        SELECT d.BusinessEntityID,
        d.FirstName + ' ' + d.MiddleName +
        ' ' + d.LastName,
        @AuditAction,
        GetDate()
        FROM deleted d

END
```

This example inserts data into an audit log when a record is deleted from a table. Notice that it inserts the BusinessEntityID, employee first, middle, and last name, the contents of the AuditAction variable, and the current date into the audit log. The resulting rows appear in Figure 18.10.

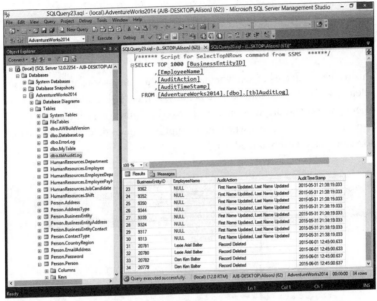

FIGURE 18.10 Records added to tblAuditLog reflecting data deleted from the Person table.

Another use of a Delete trigger is to abort a deletion when certain conditions are met. Here's an example:

```
CREATE TRIGGER [Production].[NoDeleteActive]
ON [Production].[Product]
FOR DELETE
AS
BEGIN

    SET NOCOUNT ON;
    DECLARE @ErrorMessage varchar(100)
    SELECT @ErrorMessage = 'Active Product Cannot be Deleted'

    DECLARE @Discontinued datetime
    SELECT @Discontinued =
        (SELECT DiscontinuedDate FROM deleted)

    IF @Discontinued IS NULL
        BEGIN
            ROLLBACK TRAN
```

```
        RAISERROR (@ErrorMessage,
        16, 1)
    END
END
```

This trigger evaluates to see whether the product the user is attempting to delete is active (DiscontinuedDate is null). If it is, SQL Server aborts the delete process and displays an error message. Figure 18.11 illustrates the error message that occurs when an attempt is made to delete a record with no value in the DiscontinuedDate.

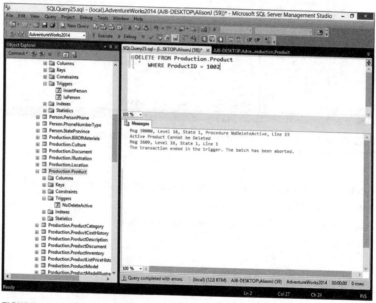

FIGURE 18.11   Error message that occurs when a record without a value in the DiscontinuedDate field is deleted.

Downsides of Triggers

Many developers avoid triggers entirely. Probably the biggest disadvantage of triggers is that although they appear as a node under the table that they are associated with, they get buried in your database and are difficult to debug and troubleshoot. Triggers also slow down database operations. Furthermore, they often lock data for relatively long periods of time, increasing the chance of concurrency problems. For these reasons, many developers opt to utilize stored procedures and functions to replace the role of triggers in the applications that they build. In reality, triggers have their place. The examples shown in this lesson provide practical uses of triggers.

Summary

Triggers are cousins of stored procedures. They are "special" stored procedures that execute automatically in response to data being inserted, updated, or deleted. Although they do have their limitations, triggers are an excellent tool to use when you want to insert data into an audit log when a table's data is in any way modified. You can also use triggers to control the insert, update, and delete processes.

Q&A

Q. Explain what a trigger is.

A. A trigger is like an event procedure that runs when data changes. You create triggers that respond to inserts, updates, and deletes.

Q. Explain why developers use triggers.

A. Developers use triggers to enforce business rules and even to perform tasks such as inserting data into an audit log.

Q. Describe some disadvantages of triggers.

A. Triggers can be difficult to troubleshoot, can increase locking conflicts, and can degrade performance when modifying data.

Workshop

Quiz

1. List three types of triggers.

2. You can use a trigger to cancel the deletion of a record (true/false).

3. You can use a trigger to increment and decrement a value such as an inventory balance when a process modifies data (true/false).

4. Triggers only execute when the user of a database modifies its data (true/false).

Quiz Answers

1. Insert, Update, Delete.

2. True.

3. True.

4. False. One of the benefits of triggers is that they execute regardless of how the data is modified. In other words, a trigger executes even as the result of a stored procedure modifying data.

Activities

Create three triggers on the Sales.SalesOrderDetail table. Have all three triggers (Insert, Update, and Delete) add data to a table called tblSalesAuditLog. First create tblSalesAuditLog. Include SalesOrderID, SalesOrderDetailID, CarrierTrackingNumber, OrderQty, ProductID, UnitPrice, and LineTotal. When any process inserts data into the SaleOrderDetail table, add data from the appropriate fields into the audit log. When any process updates data within the SalesOrderDetail table, add the *modified* values (not the original values) into the tblSalesAuditLog table. Finally, when a process deletes table data, insert the deleted data into the tblSalesAuditLog table.

LESSON 19

Authentication

Security is a critical aspect of a server database. It ensures that the data you enter into the database is protected. This lesson covers:

- ▶ The basics of security
- ▶ The types of authentication available
- ▶ How to create logins
- ▶ How to create roles

The Basics of Security

Security is necessary to prohibit access by unauthorized users and to ensure that authorized users have only the rights you want them to have. SQL Server security is robust and offers you several alternatives for your security model.

Let's begin by contrasting SQL Server security to that of a desktop database such as Microsoft Access. Access security is very limited and does not provide you with a lot of protection. You must grant read, write, and delete permissions to the users of an Access database for the network share on which the database resides. This makes the database vulnerable to hackers as well as the inadvertent actions of users (for example, accidentally moving or deleting a file). Furthermore, user-level security is not available in recent versions of Access. This means that you must "home-grow" Access security using VBA code, and users must log on to both the operating system and Microsoft Access. Finally, operating system features such as password aging, the logging of user activity, and the logging of invalid login attempts are all unavailable with Microsoft Access.

On the other hand, SQL Server offers a robust and flexible security model. SQL Server security is tightly integrated with Windows security. This means that SQL Server can utilize the users and roles you set up at the operating system level. Within SQL Server, you determine the rights the users and roles have for the various SQL Server objects. Not only are Windows users and roles available, but you can also take advantage of operating system features such as password expiration and the logging of login attempts and database activities.

The process of validating a user is known as *authentication*. The process of determining what a user can do is called *permissions validation*. This lesson covers authentication. Lesson 20, "SQL Server Permissions Validation," covers permissions validation.

Types of Authentication

Authentication involves ensuring that a user is who he says he is. After SQL Server authenticates a user, the user can perform any actions specifically granted to his login, as well as actions granted to any roles of which the user is a member.

Two types of authentication exist:

- ▶ SQL Server and Windows (Mixed authentication)
- ▶ Windows only

With SQL Server and Windows authentication, SQL Server supports both SQL Server and Windows logins. With Windows-only authentication, SQL Server supports only Windows logins. When you install SQL Server, you can configure the type of authentication that SQL Server uses. To modify the type of authentication you want to use, follow these steps:

1. Launch SQL Server Management Studio.

2. Right-click the server whose authentication mode you want to modify and select Properties. The Server Properties dialog box appears.

3. Click the Security node.

4. Modify the Server authentication, as shown in Figure 19.1.

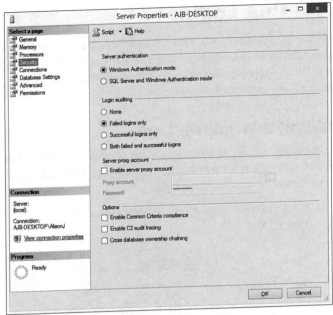

FIGURE 19.1 The Security tab of the SQL Server Properties dialog box enables you to modify the authentication type of the server.

Windows Only authentication has several advantages over SQL Server and Windows (Mixed) authentication. These advantages include the following:

▶ Requirement for the user to log on only once

▶ Central administration of logins

▶ Enforceable minimum password length

▶ Account lockout after unsuccessful login attempts

▶ More secure validation

▶ Encryption of passwords

▶ Auditing features

The main advantage of SQL Server and Windows (Mixed) authentication is that SQL Server and Windows (Mixed) authentication enables you to support non-Windows users such as Novell users.

Creating Logins

If you select Windows authentication, SQL Server assumes a trust relationship with your Windows server. It assumes that the user has already successfully logged in. Regardless of the authentication mode you select, you must still create SQL Server logins.

Adding a Windows Login

To begin, we're going to take a look at the process of creating a Windows login; the process is somewhat different from creating a SQL login. Follow these steps to create a Windows login:

1. Click to expand the Security node for the server (see Figure 19.2).

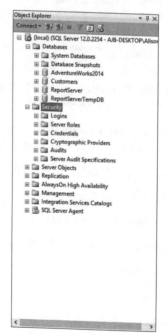

FIGURE 19.2   To add a Windows login, click to expand the Security node for the server.

2. Right-click Logins and select New Login. The Login – New dialog box appears (see Figure 19.3).

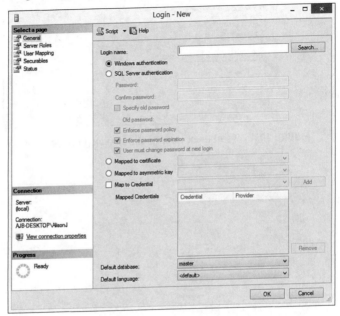

FIGURE 19.3   The Login – New dialog box is where you to enter information about the new login.

3. Type the name for the login or click Search to locate the login.

4. If you click Search, the Select User or Group dialog box appears (see Figure 19.4). Make sure that the object type and location are correct and then type the name of the user or group.

5. Click Check Names to verify that the user or group exists.

6. Click OK to close the Select User or Group dialog box.

7. Make sure that Windows authentication is selected.

8. Specify the default database for the user (refer to Figure 19.3).

9. Click the Server Roles node to grant the user membership to server roles (see Figure 19.5).

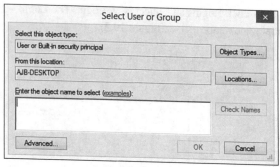

FIGURE 19.4 The Select User or Group dialog box enables you to search for a login.

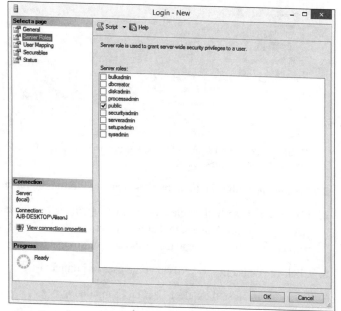

FIGURE 19.5 You use the Server Roles node to grant the user membership to server roles.

10. Click the User Mapping node to designate to which databases the user has rights. The "Granting Database Access to Logins" section of this lesson covers database access.

11. Click OK to close the dialog box and add the user.

Adding a SQL Server Login

When adding a SQL Server login, you are adding a login that does not exist anywhere else. The login is independent of the operating system and its logins. Follow these steps to create a SQL Server login:

1. Click to expand the Security node for the server.

2. Right-click Logins and select New Login. The Login – New dialog box appears.

3. Type the name for the login.

4. Make sure you select SQL Server authentication.

5. Type a password for the user (see Figure 19.6). This case-sensitive password can contain from 1 through 128 characters, including letters, symbols, and digits.

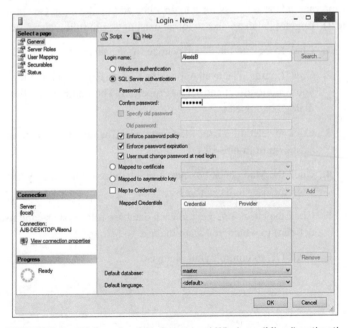

FIGURE 19.6 When using SQL Server and Windows (Mixed) authentication, the SQL Server Login – New dialog box prompts you to type a password for the user.

6. Confirm the password.

7. Specify the default database for the user.

8. Click the Server Roles node to grant the user membership to server roles.

9. Click the User Mapping node to designate to which databases the user has rights. The "Granting Database Access to Logins" section of this lesson covers database access.

10. Click OK to close the dialog box.

Granting Database Access to Logins

Whether you use Windows Only authentication or SQL Server authentication, you need to determine to which databases the user has rights and to which fixed database and user-defined database roles the user belongs. You can grant database access for a login when adding the login (see previous text). To grant database access for an existing login, follow these steps:

1. Click to expand the Security node for the server.

2. Click Logins. The available logins appear. Right-click the login you want to affect and select Properties. The Login Properties dialog box appears.

3. Click to select the User Mapping node. The dialog box appears, as shown in Figure 19.7.

4. Click the Map check box next to each database to which you want the user to have access.

5. Click the check box next to each database role (system- and user-defined) to which you want the user to belong.

6. Click OK to commit your changes.

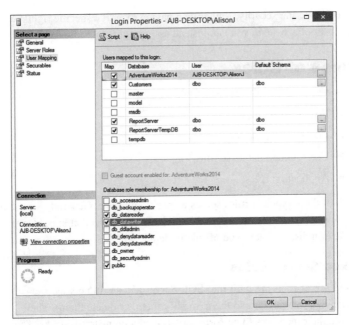

FIGURE 19.7   The User Mapping tab of the SQL Server Login Properties dialog box enables you to designate the databases to which you want the user to have access.

Understanding the SA Login

The SA Login is a special login within the SQL Server environment. If you install SQL Server in mixed mode (Windows and SQL Server authentication), the SA login has unlimited powers. With mixed-mode authentication, there is no way to modify or delete the SA account. It is therefore *imperative* you assign a password to the SA account. Failure to do so renders any other security you apply to the server futile.

Creating Roles

Roles are the equivalent of Windows groups. You create roles and then grant users membership to those roles. Users who are members of a role inherit the permissions assigned to that role. The process of creating roles and assigning permissions to those roles greatly facilitates the process of administering security. Rather than having to assign specific rights to each user of a system, you can instead assign rights to groups of users.

Types of Roles

SQL Server offers four types of roles:

- ▶ Fixed server roles
- ▶ Fixed database roles
- ▶ User-defined database roles
- ▶ Application roles

Each of these types of roles serves a specific purpose. Generally you will use several types of roles in combination. The sections that appear later in the lesson discuss each type of role in detail.

Fixed Server Roles

Fixed server roles are built into SQL Server and are in no way user-definable (you cannot add them, modify them, or delete them). They enable their members to perform server-level administrative tasks. The fixed server roles are the following:

- ▶ **Bulk Insert Administrators (bulkadmin)**—Can execute bulk insert statements.
- ▶ **Database Creators (dbcreator)**—Can create and alter databases.
- ▶ **Disk Administrators (diskadmin)**—Can manage disk files.
- ▶ **Process Administrators (processadmin)**—Can manage SQL Server processes.
- ▶ **Security Administrators (securityadmin)**—Can manage server logins.
- ▶ **Server Administrators (serveradmin)**—Can configure server-wide settings.
- ▶ **Setup Administrators (setupadmin)**—Can install replication and can manage extended properties.
- ▶ **System Administrators (sysadmin)**—Can perform *any* activity on that SQL Server instance. This includes all activities of the other roles. In fact, if a user is a member of the sysadmin role, you cannot prohibit him from performing *any* tasks on the server.

Server roles greatly facilitate the process of managing security. They accomplish this by allowing you to compartmentalize the administrative tasks that users can perform and to grant them rights to perform only those specific tasks.

> NOTE: When you install SQL Server, the installation process adds the Windows Administrators group to the sysadmin role. This means that all members of the Administrators group instantly become members of sysadmin. Fortunately, you can remove this mapping from Administrators to the sysadmin role. To remove the mapping, you must deny the Administrators group from logging on to the SQL Server. You then grant the individual users membership to the sysadmin role.

To assign a user to a fixed server role, follow these steps:

1. Expand the Security node until you can see the Server Roles subnode (see Figure 19.8).

FIGURE 19.8   The Server Roles subnode of the Security node enables you to assign users to a fixed server role.

2. Right-click the role to which you want to grant users member-ship and select Properties. The Server Role Properties dialog box opens (see Figure 19.9).

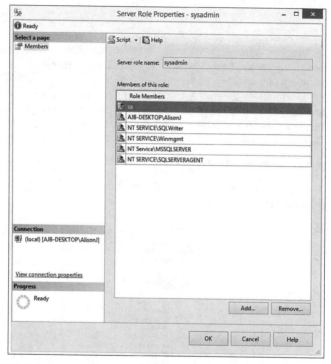

FIGURE 19.9 The Server Role Properties dialog box enables you to add users to a role.

3. Click Add to add a user to the role. The Select Server Login or Role dialog box appears (see Figure 19.10).

4. Click Browse to select the logins you want to add. The Browse for Objects dialog box opens (see Figure 19.11).

5. Click to check the objects you want to add to the role.

6. Click to close the Browse for Objects dialog box.

7. Click OK. SQL Server adds the selected users to the role.

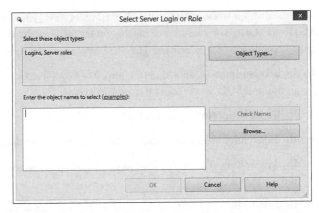

FIGURE 19.10 The Select Server Login or Role dialog box is where you add logins to a role.

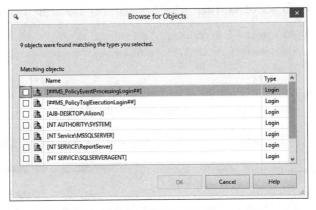

FIGURE 19.11 The Browse for Objects dialog box enables you to select the users you want to add to a role.

Fixed Database Roles

Whereas fixed server roles enable you to assign rights to users that apply at the server level, fixed database roles enable you to assign rights at the database level. Because fixed server roles apply at the server level, they are found under the Security node. Because fixed database roles apply at a database level, they are located under the specific database node of the database to which they apply.

As with fixed server roles, you cannot add, remove, or modify the rights granted to fixed database roles. Fixed database roles facilitate the process of assigning permissions for a database. The fixed database roles are as follows:

- **db_accessadmin**—Can add and remove Windows users and groups and SQL Server users for the database.

- **db_backupoperator**—Can back up the database.

- **db_datareader**—Can view data in all user tables in the database.

- **db_datawriter**—Can add, edit, and delete data in all user tables in the database.

- **db_ddladmin**—Can add, modify, and drop database objects.

- **db_denydatareader**—Cannot see any data in the database.

- **db_denydatawriter**—Cannot modify any data in the database.

- **db_owner**—Can perform the activities of any of the other roles. Can also perform all database maintenance and configuration tasks.

- **db_securityadmin**—Can manage role membership and statement and object permissions for the database.

To assign a user to a fixed database role, perform these steps:

1. Expand the Database node of the desired database until you can see the Security subnode.

2. Click to expand the Roles node for the database.

3. Click to expand the list of Database Roles (see Figure 19.12).

4. Right-click the role to which you want to grant users membership and select Properties. The Database Role Properties dialog box appears (see Figure 19.13).

5. Click Add to add a user to the role. The Select Database User or Role dialog box appears (see Figure 19.14).

6. Click Browse. The Browse for Objects dialog box appears (see Figure 19.15).

FIGURE 19.12 The Database Roles subnode enables you to work with roles for that database.

FIGURE 19.13 The Database Role Properties dialog box enables you to add users to a database role.

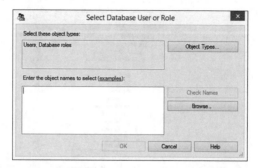

FIGURE 19.14   The Select Database User or Role dialog box enables you to add users to a role.

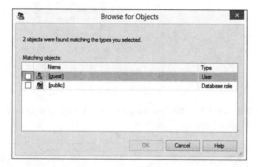

FIGURE 19.15   The Browse for Objects dialog box enables you to select the users you want to add to a role.

7. Click to select the logins you want to add and click OK. Click OK to close the Select Database User or Role dialog box. SQL Server adds the selected users to the role.

The Public role is a special built-in fixed database role. Every user is a member of it. When you grant a user access to a database, SQL Server adds the user to the Public database role. You can't remove the Public role, nor can you remove users of a database from the Public role. Any rights that you grant to the Public role are automatically granted to all users of the database. The Public role therefore provides an excellent means of easily granting all users rights to a particular object. On the other hand, if you accidentally grant the Public role rights, those rights apply to all users of the database.

User-Defined Database Roles

At a database level, you are not limited to the predefined roles. In addition to the predefined roles, you can add your own roles. SQL Server offers two types of user-defined roles. They are the following:

▶ **Standard role**—Custom role that you use to facilitate the task of assigning rights to users of the database.

▶ **Application role**—Role used by an application.

To create a user-defined role, follow these steps:

1. Expand the Database node of the desired database until you can see the Roles subnode (see Figure 19.16).

FIGURE 19.16 The Roles subnode of the Database node enables you to create and work with user-defined database roles.

2. Right-click the Roles subnode, select New, and then select New Database Role. The Database Role – New dialog box appears, prompting you to enter the name of the new role (see Figure 19.17).

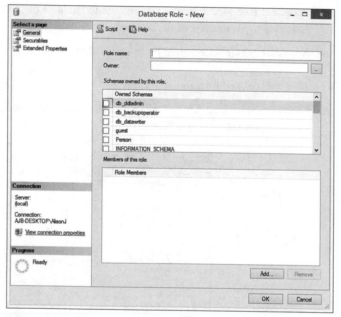

FIGURE 19.17 The Database Role – New dialog box enables you to enter the name of the new role.

3. Type the name of the role in the Role name text box.

4. Designate the schemas owned by the role.

5. Click Add to add a user to the role. The Select Database User or Role dialog box appears.

6. Select the logins you want to add (clicking Browse if necessary) and click OK. SQL Server adds the selected users to the role and the role to the database.

Ownership

It is important to understand what ownership is and what the implications of ownership are. SQL Server designates the creator of an object as its owner. The owner of an object has *full* permissions for that object. Furthermore, the name of the object is actually `owner.objectname`—for example, `alexis.tblCustomers`.

You cannot remove a user from a database as long as he owns objects within it. Ownership of an object is implied. This means you cannot directly administer an object's owner.

dbo is a special user account within each database. SQL Server maps the dbo to the sysadmin fixed server role. This means that if you are a member of the sysadmin group and you create an object, SQL Server flags the object as owned by dbo, not by you. You can refer to the object as `dbo.objectname`.

The `sp_changeobjectowner` system-stored procedure enables you to change an object's owner. Only members of the sysadmin fixed server role, the db_owner fixed database role, or a member of *both* the db_ddladmin and db_securityadmin fixed database roles can execute the `sp_changeobjectowner` stored procedure. It looks like this:

```
EXEC sp_changeobjectowner 'tblCustomers', 'Brendan'
```

When you change an object's owner, SQL Server drops all permissions for the object. To change the owner back to dbo, you must fully qualify the owner name and object name. The syntax looks like this:

```
EXEC sp_changeobjectowner 'Brendan.tblCustomers', 'dbo'
```

Summary

You can create the best application and database in the world, but if it is not properly secured, someone can easily sabotage it. This lesson explained the basics of security. You read about the types of authentication available and about logins and roles. Lesson 20, "SQL Server Permissions Validation," covers security in additional detail.

Q&A

Q. Explain the difference between Windows Only authentication and SQL Server and Windows (Mixed) authentication.

A. With Windows authentication, the user does not need to log on to the server more than one time. Users you add to the SQL Server then gain the specified access to the server. With Windows authentication, you also get all the benefits of the operating system login process. For example, you can enforce minimum password length.

With SQL Server and Windows (Mixed) Authentication you can use SQL Server logins. You do not have to have organized Windows domains, and finally, SQL Server and Windows (Mixed) authentication enables you to support non-Windows users such as Novell users.

Q. Explain the SA Login and what it can do.

A. The SA Login is available only with Mixed Authentication and has unlimited powers! There is no way to modify or delete the SA account. It is therefore imperative that you assign a password to the SA account. Otherwise, any other security measures you take will be futile.

Q. Explain the interaction between sysadmin and the Windows Administrators group.

A. All members of the Windows Administrators group are added automatically to the sysadmin role upon installation of SQL Server. Remember that sysadmin is all-powerful in working with your server. Fortunately, you can remove this mapping. You must first deny the Administrators group from logging on to the SQL Server. You then grant the individual users membership to the sysadmin role as required.

Workshop

Quiz

1. Name four types of roles.

2. The SA user is available with both SQL Server and Windows authentication (true/false).

3. Name some benefits of Windows authentication.

4. If a login exists in Windows and you want them to be able to access the SQL Server, you don't have to do anything special (true/false).

5. You find fixed database roles under the database node of the database with which they are associated (true/false).

6. What user is automatically the owner of an object?

7. Name the stored procedure that enables you to change an object's ownership.

Quiz Answers

1. Server, Database, User-Defined, Application.

2. False. Only with Mixed authentication.

3. Single login, password expiration, central administration, more secure validation, password encryption, account lockout after a certain number of attempts.

4. False. You still have to create them as a user in SQL Server.

5. True.

6. The user that creates the object.

7. `sp_changeobjectowner`.

Activities

Set up a server with Windows-Only authentication. Add three new logins. Grant each login access to the AdventureWorks database. Assign one user to the Process Administrator fixed server role. Assign another user to the db_datareader role of AdventureWorks. Create a user-defined role as part of the AdventureWorks database. Assign all three logins to that role.

LESSON 20

SQL Server Permissions Validation

Lesson 19, "Authentication," discussed SQL Server authentication, which is the process of ensuring that only valid users work with your database. After users gain access to a database, it is important that they have specific rights to objects within the database. This lesson covers:

- ▶ The types of permissions available
- ▶ How to work with table permissions
- ▶ How to work with view permissions
- ▶ How to work with stored procedure permissions
- ▶ How to work with function permissions
- ▶ How to implement column-level security

Types of Permissions

When a user logs in to the server, SQL Server first authenticates him to ensure that he is a valid user. SQL Server then grants the user permission to perform any task assigned to the user or to any roles of which the user is a member.

SQL Server offers three types of permissions:

- ▶ **Object permissions**—Permissions set for objects such as tables and views. These include SELECT, INSERT, UPDATE, and DELETE permissions.
- ▶ **Statement permissions**—Permissions applied to statements such as the CREATE VIEW statement. These permissions define what rights the user has to the specified statement.

▶ **Inherited or implied permissions**—These permissions refer to rights that a user has to an object because he is a member of a role that has rights to that object or because the user is the owner of the object.

Adding Database Users

If you want a user to have access to a database, you must first create a user account in the database by following these steps:

1. Expand the Database node of the desired database until you can see the Users subnode (see Figure 20.1).

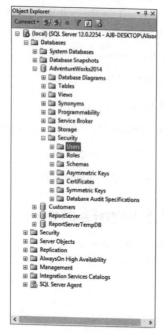

FIGURE 20.1 The Users subnode enables you to manage a database's users.

2. Right-click the Users subnode and select New User. The Database User – New dialog box opens, prompting you to enter the login name of the new user (see Figure 20.2).

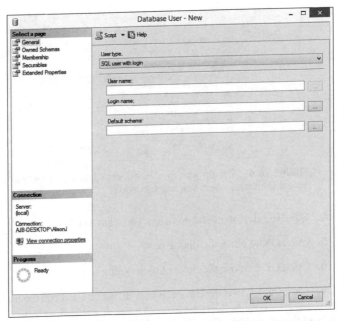

FIGURE 20.2 The Database User – New dialog box prompts you to enter the new user's login name.

3. Type the login name or click the ellipsis. If you click the ellipsis, the Select Login dialog box appears (see Figure 20.3). Here you can type login names or click Browse. If you click Browse, the Browse for Objects dialog box appears (see Figure 20.4).

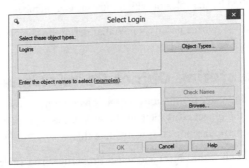

FIGURE 20.3 The Select Login dialog box enables you to type login names.

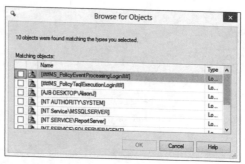

FIGURE 20.4 The Browse for Objects dialog box enables you to select database users you want to add.

4. Click to select the database users you want to add.

5. Click OK to close the dialog box.

6. Click OK to close the Select Login dialog box.

7. Click OK to close the Database User dialog box and add the user(s).

Working with Permission Statements

You can execute three different permission statements for the objects in your database:

▶ GRANT—Grants permission.

▶ WITH GRANT—Revokes permission. If you revoke permission for a user to an object, the user still possesses any permissions implied by the roles of which the user is a member.

▶ DENY—Revokes permission so that permission for that object cannot be inherited.

Administering Object Permissions

You can administer permissions for an object in one of two ways. The first way is via the object. This method shows you the rights for all users and roles for a particular object. It works like this:

1. Right-click the object and select Properties. The Table Properties dialog box opens.

2. Click to select the Permissions page. The rights established for the selected object appear (see Figure 20.5). Here you can assign users and roles rights for the object.

FIGURE 20.5 The Permissions page enables you to assign users and roles rights for the object.

3. Click Search to begin the process. The Select Users or Roles dialog box appears (see Figure 20.6).

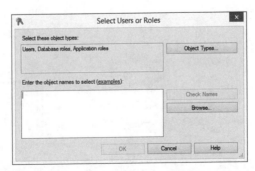

FIGURE 20.6 The Select Users or Roles dialog box enables you to enter users or roles to which you want to designate permissions.

4. Enter user and role names or click Browse to select the users and roles to which you want to grant rights (see Figure 20.7).

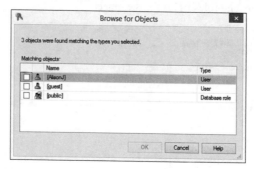

FIGURE 20.7 The Browse for Objects dialog box enables you to select the users and roles for which you are setting rights.

5. Click OK to close the Browse for Objects dialog box.

6. Click OK to close the Select Users or Roles dialog box. The Permissions page of the Table Properties dialog box should look like what's shown in Figure 20.8.

FIGURE 20.8 The Permissions page after selecting the users and roles to which you want to assign rights.

7. Select a user or role in the list of users and roles.

8. For each type of permission, designate whether you want to Grant, With Grant, or Deny permissions to the user or role, for that object. For example, in Figure 20.9, the user named AlisonJ has been granted Insert rights to the HumanResources. Department table but has been denied Delete rights.

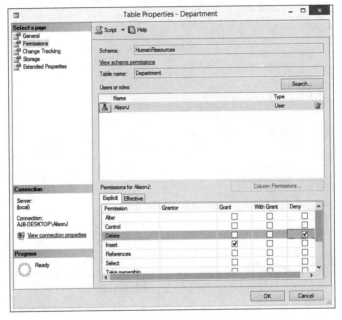

FIGURE 20.9 The Permissions page enables you to assign users and roles rights for the object.

9. After granting all desired rights to all users and roles, click OK to close the Table Properties dialog box. SQL Server applies the designated rights.

As an alternative, you can assign rights for all objects to a *database* user or role. Follow these steps:

1. Right-click the user or role and select Properties. The Database User dialog box appears.

2. Click to select the Securables page (see Figure 20.10). Here you can see a particular user or role and manage rights to all objects for the user or role.

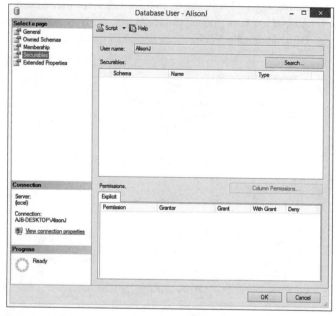

FIGURE 20.10 The Securables page enables you to select a user or role and then manage rights for its objects.

3. Click Search to add the objects you want to secure. The Add Objects dialog box appears (see Figure 20.11).

4. Indicate whether you want to secure specific objects, all objects of specific types (for example, tables), or all objects belonging to the schema. Make your selection and click OK.

5. If you click Specific Objects and click OK, the Select Objects dialog box opens (see Figure 20.12).

6. Click Object Types. The Select Object Types dialog box opens (see Figure 20.13).

FIGURE 20.11 The Add Objects dialog box enables you to designate the types of objects you want to secure.

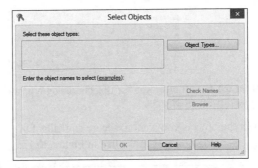

FIGURE 20.12 The Select Objects dialog box initiates the process of allowing you to select the types of objects you want to secure.

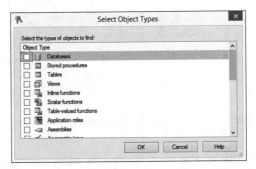

FIGURE 20.13 The Select Object Types dialog box enables you to select the types of objects you want to secure for that user or role.

7. Click to select the types of objects you want to secure for that user. Click OK.

8. Click OK to return to the Select Objects dialog box.

9. Click Browse to locate the object names you want to secure. The Browse for Objects dialog box opens, showing only the selected types of objects (see Figure 20.14).

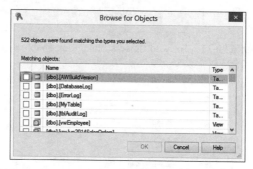

FIGURE 20.14   The Browse for Objects dialog box shows you the selected types of objects.

10. Select the objects you want to secure and click OK. The Select Objects dialog box now looks like in Figure 20.15.

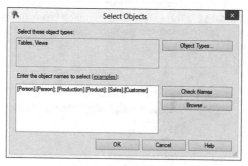

FIGURE 20.15   The Select Objects dialog box appears with the types of objects you want to secure.

11. Click OK to close the Select Objects dialog box. The Securables page of the Database User dialog box looks like in Figure 20.16. You are ready to assign rights to the selected objects.

FIGURE 20.16 The Securables page of the Database User dialog box appears with all the objects you want to secure.

NOTE: If you select all objects of the types in Step 4, the Select Object Types dialog box opens. Here you select the types of objects you want to find. You are then ready to assign rights to the selected objects.

Getting to Know Table Permissions

You can grant ALTER, CONTROL, DELETE, INSERT, REFERENCES, SELECT, TAKE OWNERSHIP, UPDATE, and VIEW DEFINITION rights for a table. These are each described as follows:

▶ ALTER **permissions**—Allow the user to alter all properties of a table except ownership. Include the capability to create, alter, and drop tables.

▶ CONTROL **permissions**—CONTROL permissions confer ownership-like capabilities for an object. The user can administer the object (assign rights, and so on) and has permissions for all objects within it. For example, users who have CONTROL permissions to a database can fully manage that database.

▶ DELETE **permissions**—Allow the user to delete table data.

▶ INSERT **permissions**—Allow the user to add data to the table.

▶ REFERENCES **permissions**—Allow the user to create a foreign key constraint.

▶ SELECT **permissions**—Allow the user to view the data in a table.

▶ TAKE OWNERSHIP **permissions**—Allow the user to take ownership of the table on which it is granted.

▶ UPDATE **permissions**—Allow the user to update the data in the table.

▶ VIEW DEFINITION **permissions**—Allow the user to access metadata for the table.

To assign permissions for a table, follow these steps:

1. Right-click the table for which you want to assign permissions and select Properties. The Table Properties dialog box opens.

2. Click the Permissions page. The Table Properties dialog box appears as in Figure 20.17.

3. Click Search to view the users and roles to which you want to assign rights for that table. The Select Users or Roles dialog box opens.

4. Click Browse. The Browse for Objects dialog box opens.

5. Click to select the users and roles you want to affect.

6. Click OK. SQL Server returns you to the Select Users or Roles dialog box.

7. Click OK to close the Select Users or Roles dialog box and return to the Table Properties dialog box. It should now look like Figure 20.18.

FIGURE 20.17 The Permissions page of the Table Properties dialog box before the users and roles to which you are assigning rights have been designated.

FIGURE 20.18 The Permissions page of the Table Properties dialog box after the users and roles to which you are assigning rights have been designated.

8. Click to Grant, With Grant, or Deny ALTER, CONTROL, DELETE, INSERT, REFERENCES, SELECT, TAKE OWNERSHIP, UPDATE, and VIEW DEFINITION rights as required.

9. Click OK when done. SQL Server applies the designated permissions.

> NOTE: EXEC permissions are not applicable to a table. They are applicable only for stored procedures and are therefore covered in the "Getting to Know Stored Procedure Permissions" section of this lesson.

Getting to Know View Permissions

Permissions for a view override those for the underlying tables. Using views, you can easily apply both row-level and column-level security. You can achieve column-level security by limiting the columns included in the view. You can implement row-level security by adding a WHERE clause to the view. Because the results of most views are updateable, the process of applying security for a view is similar to that for a table. Follow these steps:

1. Right-click the view for which you want to assign permissions and select Properties. The View Properties dialog box opens.

2. Click the Permissions page of the View Properties dialog. The View Properties dialog box should look like Figure 20.19.

3. Click Search to add the users and roles who will gain rights to the view. The Select Users or Roles dialog box opens.

4. Click Browse to designate the users and roles to which you want to assign rights. The Browse for Objects dialog box opens.

FIGURE 20.19 The View Properties dialog box enables you to assign ALTER, CONTROL, DELETE, INSERT, REFERENCES, SELECT, TAKE OWNERSHIP, UPDATE, and VIEW DEFINITION permissions for a View as required.

5. Select the users and roles to which you want to assign rights for the view.

6. Click OK to close the Browse for Objects dialog box.

7. Click OK to close the Select Users or Roles dialog box. The Permissions tab of the View Properties dialog box appears as shown in Figure 20.20.

8. Click the check boxes to assign ALTER, CONTROL, DELETE, INSERT, REFERENCES, SELECT, TAKE OWNERSHIP, UPDATE, and VIEW DEFINITION rights as required.

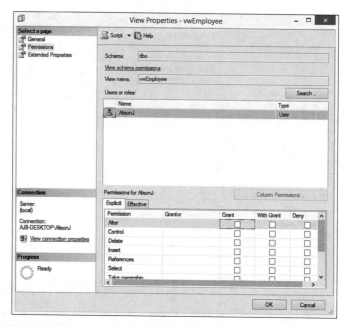

FIGURE 20.20   The View Properties dialog box after giving a user rights to the vwEmployee view.

9. Click OK when finished.

Getting to Know Stored Procedure Permissions

As with rights for a view, rights assigned for a stored procedure override rights assigned for the underlying tables and views. This is the case as long as the stored procedure has the same owner as the tables referenced with it. Stored procedures have only five permissions: ALTER, CONTROL, EXECUTE, TAKE OWNERSHIP, and VIEW DEFINITION. The most commonly assigned right, the EXECUTE right, determines whether the user or role can execute the stored procedure.

Getting to Know Function Permissions

As with rights assigned for views and stored procedures, rights assigned for a user-defined function that returns a table override rights assigned for the underlying tables and views. This is the case as long as the function has the same owner as the tables referenced with it. Functions have the same permissions as tables. The main limitation of functions is that they return read-only results.

Implementing Column-Level Security

SQL Server enables you to assign column-level permissions easily for tables and views. Column-level permissions enable you to determine on a column-by-column basis whether the user has SELECT and UPDATE rights for that particular column. INSERT and DELETE rights cannot be assigned at a column level because they affect the entire row. To assign column-level permissions for tables and views, follow these steps:

1. Right-click the table for which you want to assign permissions and select Properties. The Table Properties dialog box opens.

2. Click the Permissions page to select it. You see the Permissions page of the dialog box.

3. Click Search to add the users and roles to which you want to apply column-level permissions. The Select Users or Roles dialog box opens.

4. Click Browse to designate the users and roles to which you want to apply column-level permissions.

5. Click to select your choices.

6. Click OK to close the dialog box.

7. Click OK to close the Select Users or Roles dialog box.

8. Click to grant SELECT or UPDATE rights to the selected user or role for that table or view. The Column Permissions command button becomes enabled (see Figure 20.21).

9. Click the Column Permissions button. The Column Permissions dialog box opens (see Figure 20.22). Indicate the SELECT or UPDATE rights for the individual columns as desired.

10. Click OK to close the Column Permissions dialog box and return to the Table Properties dialog box.

11. Click OK to apply the permissions.

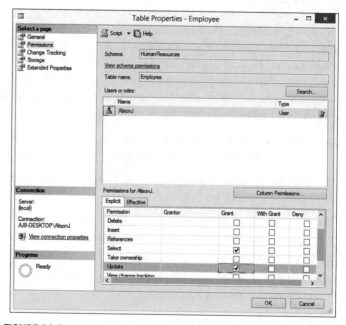

FIGURE 20.21 The Column Permissions command button becomes enabled after you grant SELECT or UPDATE rights to the selected user or role.

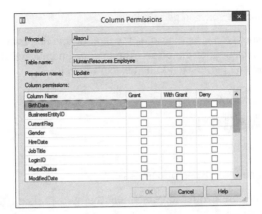

FIGURE 20.22 The Column Permissions dialog box lets you determine on a column-by-column basis whether the user has SELECT and UPDATE rights for that particular column.

Summary

After a user gains access to a database, you must then determine what rights the user has to objects within the database. This lesson explained permissions validation, the process of determining what a user can do after gaining access to the database. You were shown how to designate permissions for the various types of objects in the database, and you were introduced to the types of permissions available. Finally, you walked through how to apply table and view security at a column-level.

Q&A

Q. Explain inherited permissions.

A. Inherited permissions refer to rights that a user has to an object because he is a member of a role that has rights to that object or because he is the owner of the object.

Q. Explain the difference between WITH GRANT **and** DENY **permissions.**

A. WITH GRANT permissions revoke permission for an object unless that user is a member of a role that has rights to that object. DENY permissions revoke permission so that permission for an object cannot be inherited.

Q. Describe CONTROL **permissions.**

A. With CONTROL permissions, the user or role has ownership-like capabilities for the object. The user can administer the object and has permission to all objects within it.

Workshop

Quiz

1. Name three types of permissions.

2. Name the permission statement that gives a user rights to an object.

3. Describe VIEW DEFINITION permissions.

4. Permissions for a view override those for the underlying table (true/false).

5. How can you implement row-level security with a view?

6. The results of views are not updateable (true/false).

7. What is the most commonly assigned right for a stored procedure?

Quiz Answers

1. Object, Statement, and Inherited or Implied.

2. GRANT.

3. VIEW DEFINITION permissions allow the user to access metadata for the table.

4. True.

5. By using a WHERE clause.

6. False. The results of most views are updateable.

7. EXECUTE.

Activities

Add three roles to the AdventureWorks database. Name one staff, another managers, and another system administrators. Apply permissions for the HumanResources.Department table in the AdventureWorks database. Give staff SELECT and INSERT rights to the table. Give management SELECT, INSERT, UPDATE, and DELETE rights to the table. Give system administrators CONTROL permissions for the table. Add three users, assigning each user to one of the three roles. Practice logging in as each user and note what you can do within the HumanResources.Department table.

... ...

LESSON 21

Configuring, Maintaining, and Tuning SQL Server

The most attractive application can be extremely frustrating to use if its performance is less than acceptable. As a developer, you must take precautions to try to assure that the SQL Server is as lean and efficient as possible. This lesson explains:

▶ How to select and tune your hardware

▶ How to configure and tune SQL Server

▶ How to maintain your databases

▶ How to maintain your tables and other objects

Selecting and Tuning Hardware

Your choice of hardware can greatly affect the performance of your server. Areas of particular concern are the amount of memory, processor speed, and hard disk configuration. The network architecture is also an important factor. The sections that follow cover the details of each of these items.

Memory—The More RAM, the Better!

SQL Server uses memory (RAM) to hold all data pages, index pages, and log records. It also uses memory to hold compiled queries and stored procedures. Needless to say, that memory is vital to the performance of the server.

Clients are always asking me how much memory they should purchase for their server. My answer is, the more, the better. In fact, RAM is the best investment you can make for your SQL Server. That aside, here are some guidelines. A bare minimum amount of RAM for SQL Server Express is 512MB. Although all other editions require 1GB of RAM, at least 4GB is recommended. SQL Server 2014 Express can take advantage of 1GB. SQL Server 2014 Standard can utilize 128GB. Finally, SQL Server 2014 Enterprise can utilize the operating system maximum!

Processor

Although it's not as important as RAM, more processing power never hurts. SQL Server 2014 Express can take advantage of one processor. SQL Server 2014 standard can take advantage of up to four processors, and SQL Server 2014 Enterprise can take advantage of the operating system maximum. Despite the advantages of multiple processors, if limited funds force a choice between more RAM and multiple processors, more RAM is the most cost-effective choice.

Storage

Because SQL Server stores all of your data on disk, the type, configuration, and throughput of the storage media you use are important factors. Today, there are three common interfaces for disk storage: Serial AT Attachment (SATA), Serial Attached Small Computer System Interface (SAS), and Fibre Channel (FC). SATA disks are prevalent on laptop and desktop computers because they are less expensive than SAS drives. Rotational speed on the platters within each disk also have a significant effect on the speed of data access. SATA drives commonly come in speeds of either 5,400RPM or 7,200RPM (Revolutions per Minute). SAS drives commonly come in speeds of either 10,000RPM or 15,000RPM, which is part of the reason why SAS drives can generally access data faster than SATA drives. Higher speeds are better.

SATA disks work well on individual computers because single users rarely need the advanced throughput of multiple Input/Output (I/O) paths for accessing data on the disk. Servers for small offices might also use SATA disks when there are not many users and those users do not constantly access very large files or continuously access numerous small files on the server. Generally speaking, you should only store SQL Server data on SATA disks for development, testing, or for a very small number of users.

SAS disks improve on the performance of the old SCSI standard. Simultaneous multiple I/O gives SAS disks a large performance advantage over SATA disks in addition to their higher rotational speeds. The FC standard is used primarily in enterprise environments for high capacity and highly available Storage Area Network (SANs). SANs employ multiple disks that are configured as storage volumes (drive letters). The multiple disks that comprise a SAN provide redundancy and resiliency from disk failures as part of a Redundant Array of Independent Disks (RAID) configuration.

A data protection RAID configuration can and should be used whenever downtime needs to be avoided due to disk failure. For example, RAID Level 1 consists of two disks where one disk mirrors its data onto the second disk. If one of the disks fail, the system can still operate normally using the other disk. You can also employ disk duplexing, which is the same concept as disk mirroring, but each disk has its own disk controller so that the disk controller is not a single point of failure. RAID Level 5 uses between 3 and 32 disks. The more disks, the higher capacity of the storage array. In a RAID Level 5 configuration, one disk can fail, and the system continues to operate normally. If more than one disk fails at the same time, data is lost. Ideally, SQL Server system and transaction log files should both be mirrored or duplexed. This means that they should be mirrored and on separate disk controllers wherever possible. At a minimum, all SQL Server database and transaction log files should be stored in a data protection RAID configuration, such as RAID Levels 1, 5, 6, or 10.

A new breed of data storage has emerged recently, which greatly speeds up data access over conventional "hard disks." Solid State Disks (SSDs) are all electronic, similar to Random Access Memory (RAM) used in all computers. The main difference between RAM and SSDs is that SSDs do not lose data when powered off. Unlike conventional hard disks, SSDs have no mechanical parts, so data retrieval and recording is significantly faster, and SSDs have no moving parts to wear out. Eventually, SSDs will be the standard for data storage on all computers because the pricing on SSDs has come down dramatically from a few years ago. However, SSDs still cost significantly more than conventional drives. In the coming years, when SSDs will cost about the same as conventional disks, computer manufacturers will install SSDs as standard equipment on all machines.

SSDs come in the same variety of interfaces as conventional drives, including SATA, SAS, and FC. SSDs can also be used in RAID configurations just like conventional disks. Besides much faster performance, SSDs are manufactured in the smaller 2.5-inch form factor, the same form factor as laptop drives. SSDs generally do not come in the 3.5-inch desktop drive size; you can purchase adapters so that a 2.5-inch SSD will fit into a 3.5-inch hard disk slot on a desktop or server computer.

Network

Both the network card in the SQL Server machine and the network bandwidth are important factors in the performance of your application. The server should contain a 64-bit network card, which is usually standard in today's computers that run Microsoft's 64-bit operating systems, such as Windows 7/8/8.1/10 and Windows Server 2008/2012/2016. You should use Gigabit (1GB) Ethernet network adapters versus legacy 10MB/100Mb Ethernet network adapters whenever possible. Use 10GB network adapters if your local area network (LAN) supports it! The bottom line is that the best hardware and the best designed database do you no good on a slow, overtaxed network.

Configuring and Tuning SQL Server

If you do not configure the server properly, all of the hardware in the world and the best designed database mean nothing. Processor options, memory options, I/O options, and query and index options all allow you to designate the most appropriate server configuration for you. Although most of the time you will leave these options at their default values, it is useful to know what configuration options are available to you.

Memory Options

You can designate the minimum and maximum memory used by SQL Server. You can also specify the minimum memory allocated to each user for each query run. You should generally not modify any of the memory options. This is because SQL Server does an excellent job of allocating and deallocating memory on its own. The only time you would want to modify these options is if you are running SQL Server on the same machine as another highly memory-intensive application, such as Microsoft Exchange Server. I recommend running SQL Server on a dedicated machine where this is not a problem. If you must modify the SQL Server memory options, here's the process:

1. Right-click the server you want to affect and select Properties. The Server Properties dialog box opens (see Figure 21.1).

FIGURE 21.1 The Server Properties dialog box contains pages that enable you to modify various properties of your SQL Server.

2. Click to select the Memory page (see Figure 21.2).

3. Modify the options as desired.

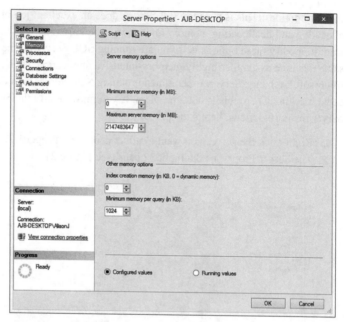

FIGURE 21.2 The Memory page of the SQL Server Properties dialog box enables you to set memory options.

Processor Options

You can configure the way in which SQL Server uses your server's processors. The configuration options available include the following:

▶ You can configure the relative priority of the SQL Server process.

▶ You can determine which of the server's CPUs SQL Server will use.

▶ You can designate the total number of operating system threads that SQL Server can use on your computer.

▶ You can set the maximum number of CPUs used by parallel query operations.

To modify the processor-related properties:

1. Right-click the server you want to affect and select Properties.

2. The Server Properties dialog box appears.

3. Click to select the Processors page. The dialog box appears as in Figure 21.3.

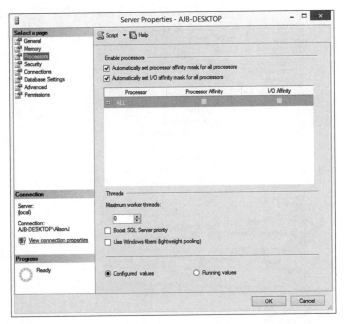

FIGURE 21.3 The Processors page of the Server Properties dialog box enables you to modify processor-related properties of your SQL Server.

4. Modify the options as desired.

Security Options

You will usually work with Security options when establishing a SQL Server. Options available include the type of authentication you want on the server (Windows Authentication or SQL Server and Windows Authentication) and the type of login auditing you want to perform when user logins are unsuccessful.

Use the following steps to modify Security options for the server:

1. Right-click the server you want to affect and select Properties.

2. The Server Properties dialog box appears.

3. Click to select the Security page. The dialog box appears as in Figure 21.4.

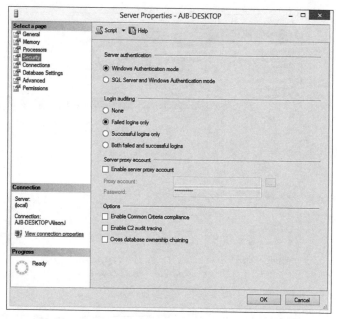

FIGURE 21.4 The Security page of the Server Properties dialog box enables you to modify security-related properties of your SQL Server.

4. Modify the options as desired.

Connections Options

The Connections options enable you to determine the maximum number of concurrent connections that the server will allow, as well as whether the server will allow remote connections. Other options are available as well.

Use the following steps to modify Connections options for the server:

1. Right-click the server you want to affect and select Properties.

2. The Server Properties dialog box appears.

3. Click to select the Connections page. The dialog box opens as in Figure 21.5.

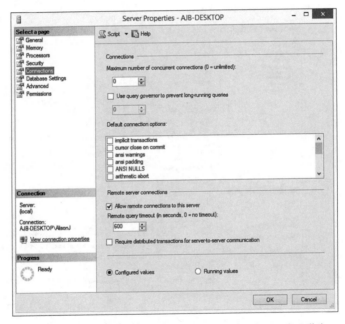

FIGURE 21.5 The Connections page of the Server Properties dialog box enables you to modify connection-related properties of your SQL Server.

4. Modify the options as desired.

Database Settings Options

The Database Settings page of the Server Properties dialog box enables you to alter settings that affect the databases on that server. For example, you can set the default locations for database and log files, and you can set the default index file factor.

To modify Database Settings options for the server:

1. Right-click the server you want to affect and select Properties.

2. The Server Properties dialog box opens.

3. Click to select the Database Settings page. The dialog box appears as shown in Figure 21.6.

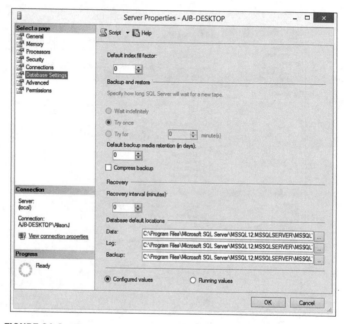

FIGURE 21.6 The Database Settings page of the Server Properties dialog box enables you to modify database-related properties of your SQL Server.

4. Modify the options as desired.

Advanced Options

The Advanced page of the Server Properties dialog box enables you to configure various server options. These include where triggers can fire other triggers, the two-digit year cutoff, and much more.

Use the following steps to modify Advanced options for the server:

1. Right-click the server you want to affect and select Properties.

2. The Server Properties dialog box appears.

3. Click to select the Advanced page. You see the dialog box in Figure 21.7.

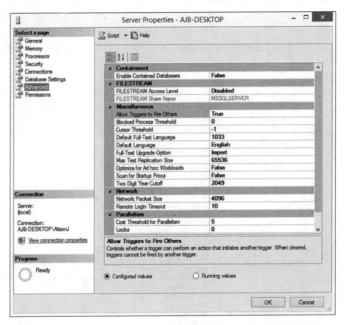

FIGURE 21.7 The Advanced page of the Server Properties dialog box enables you to modify various properties of your SQL Server.

4. Modify the options as desired.

Permissions Options

The Permissions page of the Server Properties dialog box enables you to modify permissions that relate to the server (not to a particular database). Here you can add and remove logins and roles to and from the server. You can also Grant, With Grant, and Deny server-related rights to logins and roles. Server-related rights include whether the user or role can alter any database, whether the user or role can alter any login, and much more.

Use the following steps to modify Permissions options for the server:

1. Right-click the server you want to affect and select Properties.

2. The Server Properties dialog box appears.

3. Click to select the Permissions page. You see the dialog box in Figure 21.8.

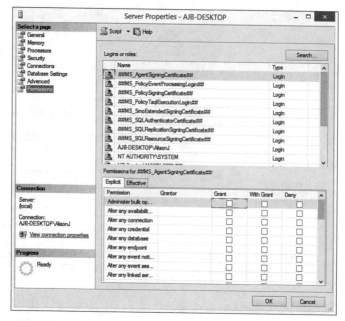

FIGURE 21.8 The Permissions page of the Server Properties dialog box enables you to modify permission-related properties of your SQL Server.

4. Modify the options as desired.

Summary

The best-designed system will fail to meet users' needs if it performs poorly. The first line of attack when attempting to optimize performance is to ensure that the hardware on which SQL Server runs is adequate for the job at hand. After all the proper hardware is in place, you must determine that you have properly configured the SQL Server software. After you configure your hardware and the SQL Server software, you must make sure you take all of the steps to properly maintain the server. In case things go awry, you must implement and test a backup and restore procedure.

Q&A

Q. Why is memory so important to a SQL Server?

A. SQL Server uses memory to hold all data pages, index pages, and log records. It also uses memory to hold compiled queries and stored procedures.

Q. Explain some of the security options available.

A. Using the Security page of the Server Properties dialog box, you can change the type of authentication you want to allow (Windows only versus Windows and SQL Server). You can also determine what type of logging SQL Server will perform when logins are unsuccessful.

Workshop

Quiz

1. Name four things you can do to your hardware to improve performance of your SQL Server.

2. Using the Memory options page of the Server Properties dialog box, you can configure the relative priority of the SQL Server process (true/false).

3. Using the Processor options page of the Server Properties dialog box, you can determine which of the server's CPUs SQL Server will use (true/false).

4. The Permissions page of the Server Properties dialog box enables you to modify database permissions (true/false).

Quiz Answers

1. More memory, more processors, RAID array, faster network.

2. False. Using the Processor options page of the Server Properties dialog box, you can configure the relative priority of the SQL Server process.

3. True.

4. False. The Permissions page of the Server Properties dialog box enables you to modify server-related permissions.

Activities

View the various pages of the Server Properties dialog box. When you are finished, back up the AdventureWorks database and then restore the database.

LESSON 22

Maintaining the Databases You Build

Just as you need to maintain your SQL Server, you also need to maintain the databases you build. If you fail to properly maintain your databases, not only can performance be affected, you can also lose your data. This lesson explains:

- ▶ How to back up your databases
- ▶ How to restore your databases
- ▶ How to utilize the Database Tuning Advisor
- ▶ How to create and work with maintenance plans

Backing Up Your Databases

Most companies store mission-critical information on their SQL Servers. If your data is important to you, it is imperative that you back up your databases.

Think of backing up your database like brushing your teeth. It is something that you don't think about; you just do it unequivocally each and every day, *without exception*! Two types of backups are available:

- ▶ **Full database backups:** Back up the entire database and portions of the log.
- ▶ **Differential database backups:** Back up data modified since the last backup.

You need to decide which backup option is appropriate for you. The right choice depends on how much information is changed each day as well as how critical the information is to you. For example, if the data is changed throughout the day and is mission-critical, you want to perform a full database backup daily and then back up the transaction log hourly.

SQL Server offers three recovery models:

- ▶ **Full:** Offers full protection. With this option, you are able to restore all committed transactions. The database and the log are both backed up.

- ▶ **Bulk Logged:** Offers *minimal* data recovery. With this option, logging is minimal. You get the best performance and use the least amount of memory.

- ▶ **Simple:** In the case of failure, this option loses all data modified since the last backup. With this option, you can recover data only as of the last backup.

Use the following steps to select a recovery model:

1. Right-click the database for which you want to establish the recovery model and select Properties. The Database Properties dialog box appears.

2. Click the Options page.

3. Open the Recovery Model drop-down list and select the appropriate recovery model (see Figure 22.1).

4. Click OK to close the Properties dialog box and save your changes.

Use the following steps to perform a backup:

1. Right-click the database that you want to back up and select Tasks|Back Up. The Back Up Database dialog box appears (see Figure 22.2).

2. Designate which database you want to back up, the name for the backup, and an optional description for the backup.

3. Use the Backup Type drop-down to indicate whether you want to perform a full or a differential backup.

FIGURE 22.1 The Recovery Model drop-down list on the Options page enables you to select the appropriate recovery model.

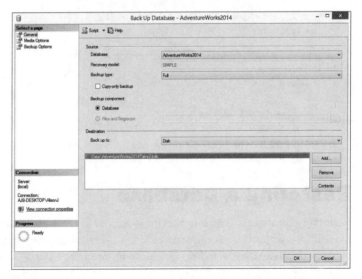

FIGURE 22.2 The Back Up Database dialog box enables you to designate information about the backup.

4. Click Add or Remove to designate the filename and location for the backup.

5. Click the Backup Options page to designate additional backup options (see Figure 22.3). For example, you can designate whether you want SQL Server to verify the backup on completion.

6. Designate whether you want to append to or overwrite the existing media.

7. Click OK to complete the process.

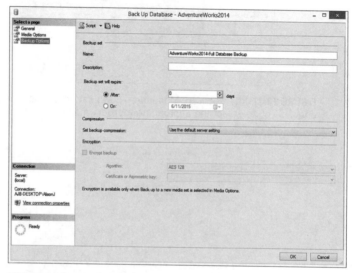

FIGURE 22.3 The Backup Options page of the Back Up Database dialog box enables you to designate additional backup options.

Restoring a Database

Restoring a database is similar to backing it up. You can restore a database to itself (overwrites the existing database), to another existing database, or to a new database. Use the following steps to restore a database:

1. Right-click the database that you want to restore and select Tasks|Restore|Database. The Restore Database dialog box appears (see Figure 22.4).

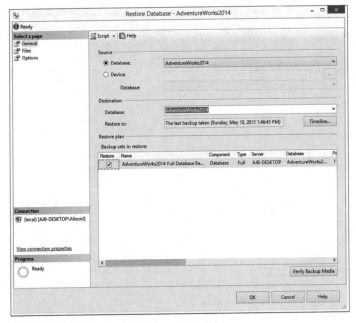

FIGURE 22.4 The Restore Database dialog box enables you to designate information about the restore process.

2. Designate whether you want to restore from a database or you want to restore from a device.

3. If you click Device and then click the ellipsis (...), the Select Backup Devices dialog box, shown in Figure 22.5, appears. Here you can designate the backup location.

4. Click Add to specify the file you want to restore from. The Locate Backup File dialog box displays.

5. Select a file and click OK.

6. Click OK to close the Select Backup Devices dialog box. You return to the Restore Database dialog box.

7. Click the Options page to designate the restore options (see Figure 22.6).

FIGURE 22.5 The Select backup devices dialog allows you to designate the backup location.

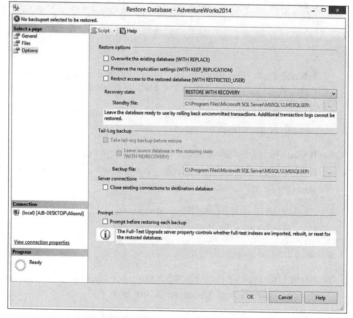

FIGURE 22.6 The Options page of the Restore Database dialog box enables you to designate additional restore options.

8. Designate whether you want to overwrite the existing database. If you do not select this option and you attempt to restore to an existing database, SQL Server returns an error.

9. Designate the logical and physical filenames for the database and the log file. If you are restoring from one machine to another and the machines have different directory structures, you need to change the physical filename to reflect the appropriate directory structure.

10. Indicate the recovery completion state.

11. Click OK to perform the restore process.

The Database Engine Tuning Advisor

As its naming implies, the Database Engine Tuning Advisor provides you with the information you need to optimize the performance of your databases. You access the Database Engine Tuning Advisor within the Performance Tools folder underneath SQL Server on the Start menu (see Figure 22.7).

FIGURE 22.7 You can find the Database Engine Tuning Advisor within the Performance Tools folder on the Start menu.

After launching the Database Engine Tuning Advisor, the Connect to Server dialog box displays. Supply the connection information and click Connect. The Database Engine Tuning Advisor opens as shown in Figure 22.8.

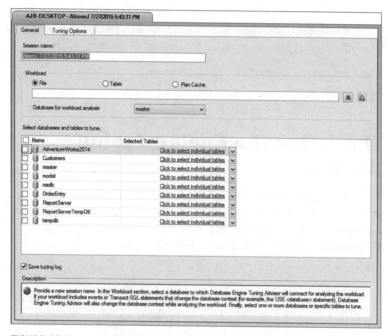

FIGURE 22.8 The Database Engine Tuning Advisor enables you to designate options for tuning the tables in one or more databases.

To tune a database, take the following steps:

1. Type a name for the session in the Session name text box.

2. Indicate where you want to store the Workload analysis. You can select File, Table, or Plan Cache (see the section "Creating a Workload" later in this lesson).

3. Select the databases and tables you want to tune. Note that you can tune all tables in a database or tune only selected tables.

4. Click Start Analysis to perform the analysis.

5. After performing an analysis, the results appear as in Figure 22.9. Notice in the figure that the Database Engine Tuning Advisor has suggested the indexes that would help to improve the performance of the database.

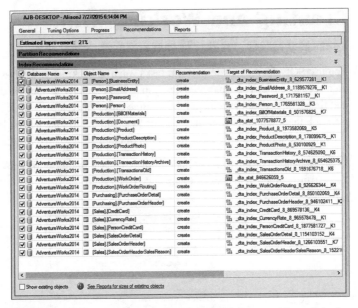

FIGURE 22.9 The Database Engine Tuning Advisor provides a list of recommendations for indexes you should create.

Creating a Workload

A *workload* is a set of T-SQL statements that execute against a database you want to tune. The Database Engine Tuning Advisor analyzes the workloads in order to recommend strategies you can use to improve performance.

You can create a workload using one of three methods:

▶ Use the plan cache as a workload. This prevents you from having to manually create a workload.

- ▸ Use the Query Editor in Management Studio to create a workload.

- ▸ Use SQL Server Profiler to create a trace file or trace table workloads.

Creating and Working with Database Maintenance Plans

You use SQL Server jobs to perform tasks, such as backing up databases, on a regular basis. You can schedule a job to run regularly at specific days and times, or you can execute a job one time only. The easiest way to create a job that maintains your databases is by using the Maintenance Plan Wizard. Use the following steps to run the Maintenance Plan Wizard:

1. Expand the Management node in the Object Explorer until you can see the Maintenance Plans node (see Figure 22.10).

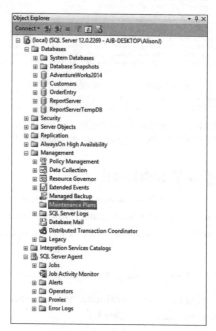

FIGURE 22.10 The Maintenance Plans node enables you to create and manage maintenance plans.

2. Right-click the Maintenance Plans node and select Maintenance Plan Wizard. The Maintenance Plan Wizard opens (see Figure 22.11).

3. Click Next. The Select Plan Properties portion of the wizard displays (see Figure 22.12). Here you provide a name for the plan. You also indicate the user the plan will run as and whether you need a separate schedule for each task.

FIGURE 22.11 The Maintenance Plan Wizard greatly facilitates the process of creating maintenance plans.

FIGURE 22.12 The Plan Properties page of the wizard enables you to designate basic settings for the maintenance plan.

4. Click Change to designate the schedule for the maintenance plan. The New Job Schedule dialog box appears (see Figure 22.13).

5. Designate the frequency and other properties of the schedule. In Figure 22.13, the job is scheduled to run daily at 2am starting 7/27/2015 and with no end date.

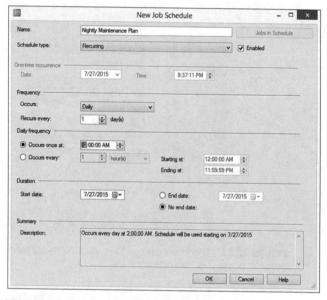

FIGURE 22.13 The New Job Schedule dialog box enables you to designate when the maintenance plan will execute.

6. Click OK to close the New Job Schedule dialog box and return to the wizard.

7. Click Next. The Select Maintenance Tasks step of the wizard displays (see Figure 22.14). Here you select the tasks you want the plan to perform. For example, you can have the plan update database statistics and back up the database.

8. Click Next. The Select Maintenance Task Order step of the wizard displays (see Figure 22.15). Here you can order the tasks you selected in the Select Maintenance Tasks step.

FIGURE 22.14   The Select Maintenance Tasks step of the wizard enables you to specify what operations the maintenance plan will perform.

FIGURE 22.15   The Select Maintenance Task Order step of the wizard enables you designate the order in which the task operations will execute.

9. Click Next. This step differs depending on what tasks you have opted for the plan to perform. In this example, the Define Back Up Database step appears (see Figure 22.16), prompting you for information about the backup that the plan will perform.

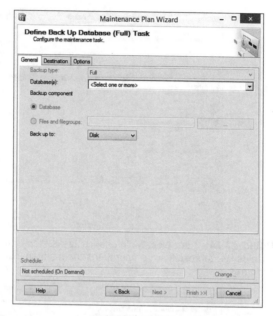

FIGURE 22.16 The Define Back Up Database step enables you to designate specifics about the backup the maintenance plan will perform.

10. Continue to click Next until you have supplied information for all tasks the plan will perform.

11. The Select Report Options step displays. You can write the report to a text file and optionally email it to a designated email address.

12. Click Next. The Complete the Wizard step displays, providing you with a summary of the options you selected (see Figure 22.17).

13. Click Finish. The wizard creates the steps and jobs necessary to complete the maintenance processing.

The process that the wizard just went through created a maintenance plan with the name specified in the wizard (see Figure 22.18). To modify the maintenance plan, right-click the name of the maintenance plan and select Modify. The plan appears (see Figure 22.19).

FIGURE 22.17 The Complete the Wizard step provides you with a summary of the options you selected.

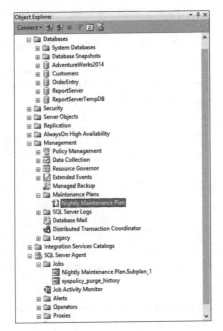

FIGURE 22.18 The wizard creates a maintenance plan that appears with the name that you specified in the wizard.

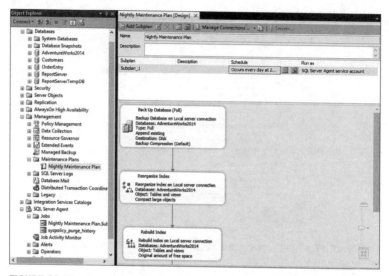

FIGURE 22.19 You can easily modify the maintenance plan you created.

If you want to modify one of the steps, use the following steps:

1. Double-click the step you want to modify. You see the dialog box that's appropriate for the step you selected. As in Figure 22.20, the Reorganize Index Task dialog box displays.

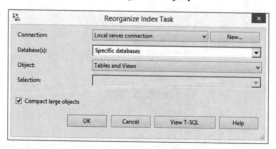

FIGURE 22.20 Double-clicking a step brings up the appropriate dialog box.

2. When you are finished designating the desired values for the step, click OK to close the dialog box.

3. Continue editing steps as desired.

4. Click the Save toolbar tool and then close the plan.

The process of running the wizard also created a job that executes the maintenance plan at designated intervals. To view the job that the wizard created, use these steps:

1. Expand the SQL Server Agent node.

2. Expand the Jobs node.

3. Right-click the job that the Maintenance Plan Wizard created.

4. Select Properties. The Job Properties dialog box displays (see Figure 22.21).

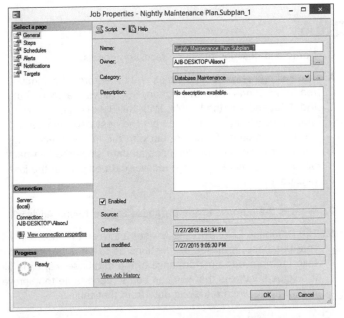

FIGURE 22.21   The Job Properties dialog box enables you to modify attributes of the job that the Maintenance Wizard created.

5. Click the appropriate tab to modify the desired properties. For example, the Schedules page enables you to easily modify the schedule associated with the job.

6. Click OK to close the dialog box and return to Management Studio.

Summary

The best-designed system will fail to meet users' needs if it performs poorly. The first line of attack when attempting to optimize performance is to ensure that the hardware on which SQL Server runs is adequate for the job at hand. After all the proper hardware is in place, you must determine that you have properly configured the SQL Server software (see Lesson 24, "Installing and Upgrading SQL Server"). After you configure your hardware and the SQL Server software, you must make sure that you take all of the steps to properly maintain the server. In case things go awry, you must implement and test a backup and restore procedure.

Q&A

Q. Name and describe the three recovery models.

A. The Full recovery model enables you to restore all committed transactions. With this option, SQL Server backs up both the database and the log file. With the Bulk Logged recovery model, logging is minimal. You get the best performance with the least amount of memory, but with the minimal recovery. The Simple recovery model loses all data since the last backup. With this model, you can recover data only as of the last backup.

Q. What is the purpose of the Database Engine Tuning Advisor?

A. The Database Engine Tuning Advisor analyzes the tables in your database. It makes suggestions as to what steps you can take to improve the performance of the database. For example, it suggests indexes that you can add to each table to improve performance when retrieving data from that table.

Workshop

Quiz

1. Name two types of database backups.

2. You can overwrite an existing database when restoring a database (true/false).

3. What is a workload?

4. You do not need to specify a workload when utilizing the Database Engine Tuning Advisor (true/false).

5. The Database Maintenance Plan Wizard only enables you to specify when backups are performed (true/false).

Quiz Answers

1. Full database backups and differential database backups.

2. True. This is an option that you can designate when restoring a database.

3. A workload is a set of T-SQL statements that execute against a database you want to tune.

4. False. A workload is required.

5. False. The Database Maintenance Plan Wizard enables you to specify a plethora of tasks that you can include in the maintenance plan.

Activities

Back up and then restore the AdventureWorks2014 database. Then run the Database Maintenance Plan Wizard. Practice including different tasks within the maintenance plan. When you are finished, take a look at the job the maintenance plan created.

LESSON 23

Performance Monitoring

It is important you build SQL statements that will execute efficiently. Fortunately SQL Server Management Studio provides you with the tools to analyze your SQL statements and ensure you have built them as efficiently as possible. This lesson introduces you to:

▶ How to execute queries in SQL Server Management Studio

▶ How to display and analyze the estimated execution plan for a query

▶ How to add indexes to allow queries to execute more efficiently

▶ How to set query options

▶ How to use the SQL Server Profiler to diagnose performance bottlenecks

Executing Queries in SQL Server Management Studio

By executing a query within SQL Server Management Studio, you can easily troubleshoot performance problems and tune your SQL statements. Use the following steps to execute a query:

1. Click the New Query button on the toolbar (see Figure 23.1). A new query window appears where you can type a SQL statement (see Figure 23.2).

2. Type the desired SQL statement (see Figure 23.3).

3. Click the Execute button on the toolbar to execute the query. The results appear as in Figure 23.4.

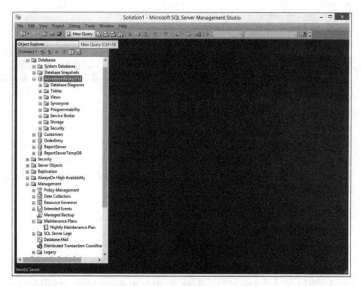

FIGURE 23.1 Click the New Query button on the toolbar to create a new query.

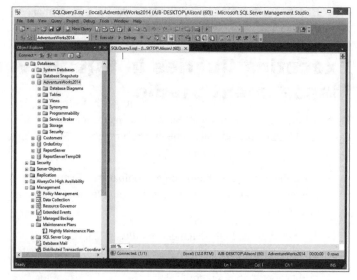

FIGURE 23.2 You use the query window to type the SQL statement you want to execute.

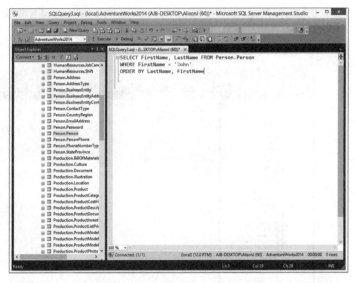

FIGURE 23.3 Type the desired SQL statement in the Query window.

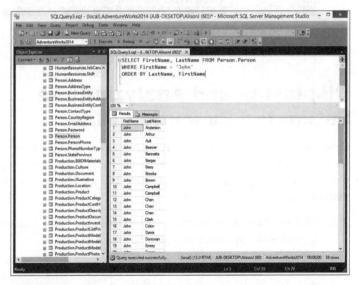

FIGURE 23.4 After executing the query, the results appear in the Results pane of the query window.

4. Click the Messages tab to view any messages associated with the execution of the query (see Figure 23.5).

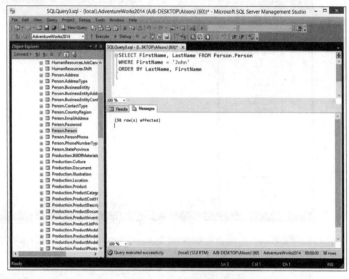

FIGURE 23.5 The Messages tab of the Results pane shows you any messages associated with the execution of the query.

Displaying and Analyzing the Estimated Execution Plan

Generally, you will not want to simply execute queries in SQL Server Management Studio. You will also want to analyze those queries to see if they are executing as efficiently as possible. Use the following steps to analyze a query:

1. Click the New Query button on the toolbar. A new query window appears where you can type a SQL statement.

2. Type the desired SQL statement.

3. Click Display Estimated Execution Plan. Your screen appears as in Figure 23.6.

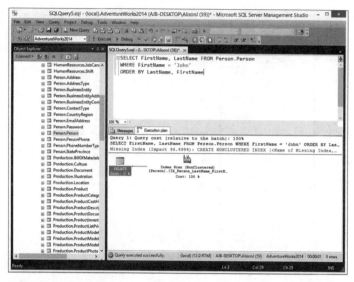

FIGURE 23.6   After clicking the Display Estimated Execution Plan toolbar button, you can see the execution plan for the query.

4. Hover your mouse pointer over the various steps in the execution plan. You will get more information about each step (see Figures 23.7 and 23.8).

5. If you want to display the execution plan each time you execute the query, click the Include Actual Execution Plan button on the toolbar. The Execution Plan tab displays each time you execute the query (see Figure 23.9).

6. To include client statistics each time you execute the query, click the Include Client Statistic button on the toolbar. After executing the query, the Client Statistics tab appears as in Figure 23.10. Here you can receive valuable statistical information about the execution of the query. For example, you can determine the number of roundtrips SQL Server made to the server in executing the query.

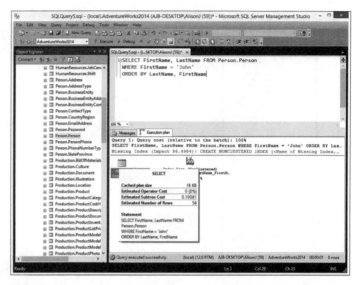

FIGURE 23.7 If you hover your mouse pointer over each step of the execution plan, you see information about that step.

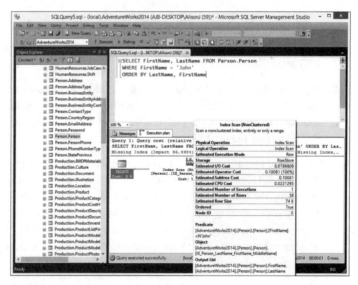

FIGURE 23.8 Notice in the example, SQL Server is using a clustered index scan when executing the SQL statement.

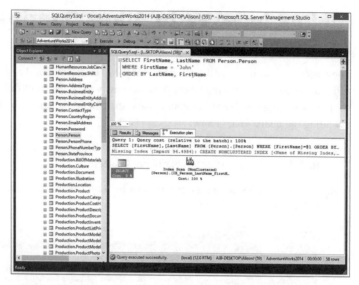

FIGURE 23.9 If you click the Include Actual Execution Plan button on the toolbar, the Execution Plan tab displays each time you execute the query.

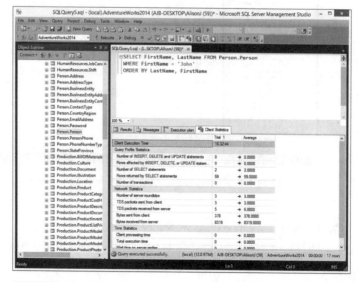

FIGURE 23.10 If you click the Include Client Statistics button on the toolbar, the Client Statistics tab appears each time you run a query.

Adding Indexes to Allow Queries to Execute More Efficiently

The easiest way to improve the efficiency of the queries you build is to add indexes to the underlying tables. You can easily view the results of your efforts using the Execution Plan tab and the Client Statistics tab after executing the query. Here's how:

1. Make sure you have both the Include Actual Execution Plan and Include Client Statistics toolbar buttons selected.

2. Execute a query and apply criteria to a field on which there is no index (see Figure 23.11).

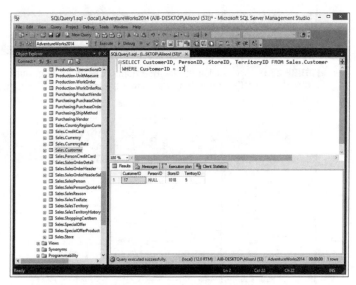

FIGURE 23.11 This query is querying by ClientID for which there is no index.

3. Click the Execution Plan tab. Notice that the execution plan includes a sort (see Figure 23.12). A sort is very inefficient when executing a query.

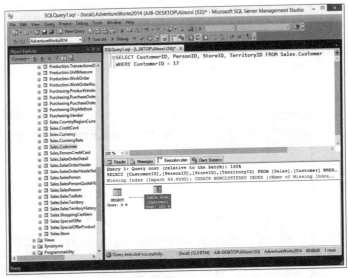

FIGURE 23.12 Notice that the execution plan for the query includes a sort.

4. Click the Client Statistics tab and note the Total execution time so you can compare it to your optimized query.

5. Create an index on the field by which you are searching (see Figure 23.13).

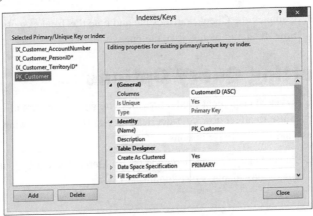

FIGURE 23.13 Create an index based on ClientID.

6. Execute the query again.

7. Compare the Execution Plan tab. Notice that the execution plan no longer includes a sort and instead includes a clustered index scan (see Figure 23.14).

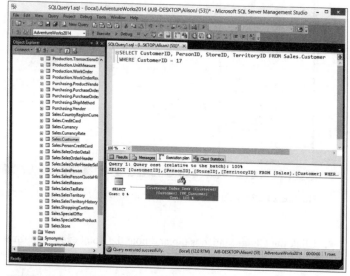

FIGURE 23.14 After creating the index, the Execution Plan no longer includes a sort.

8. Compare the Client Statistics tab and note the Total execution time. It should be less than the one without index.

Setting Query Options

SQL Server Management Studio provides you with a plethora of options you can use to affect how your queries process. Use the following steps to access and modify these options:

1. Select Query Options from the Query Menu. The Query Options dialog box displays (see Figure 23.15).

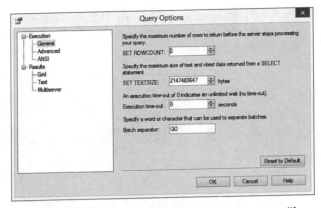

FIGURE 23.15 The Query Options dialog enables you to modify options that affect how your queries process.

2. Using the General page, you can set options, such as determining the maximum number of rows that SQL Server returns before stopping. This valuable setting ensures that you don't accidentally execute a query that returns millions of rows.

3. Using the Advanced page (see Figure 23.16), you can set additional options. An example is the SET NOCOUNT setting. When turned on, SQL Server refrains from returning the number of rows processed. This improves the performance of your queries.

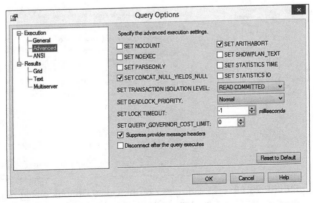

FIGURE 23.16 The Advanced page of the Query Options dialog box enables you to set additional query options.

4. The ANSI page (see Figure 23.17) enables you to set some of the SQL-92 standard query execution behavior. An example is how SQL Server handles nulls.

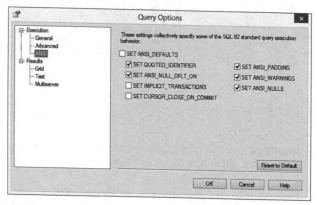

FIGURE 23.17 The ANSI page of the Query Options dialog box enables you to set some of the SQL-92 standard query execution behavior.

5. The Grid page (see Figure 23.18) of the Query Options dialog box enables you to affect how SQL Server displays the output from the query.

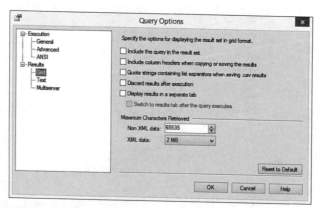

FIGURE 23.18 The Grid page of the Query Options dialog box enables you to affect how SQL Server displays the output from the query.

6. The Text page (see Figure 23.19) of the Query Options dialog enables you to set the options that apply when you opt to display the result set in text format or to redirect it to an output file.

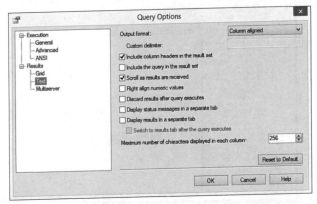

FIGURE 23.19 The Text page of the Query Options dialog enables you to set options that affect you when you display the result set as text.

SQL Server Profiler

A helpful tool when monitoring and analyzing performance is the SQL Server Profiler. Using the SQL Server Profiler, you can monitor the SQL Server environment to determine which SQL statements are negatively affecting performance. The SQL Server Profiler enables you to

▶ Step through problem queries.

▶ Find and diagnose slow-running queries.

▶ Capture a series of SQL statements that are causing a performance bottleneck.

The steps that follow cover both how to launch the Profiler and how to create a new trace.

1. To launch the SQL Server Profiler from SQL Server Management Studio, select Tools, SQL Server Profiler (see Figure 23.20). The Profiler opens and prompts you to connect to the server.

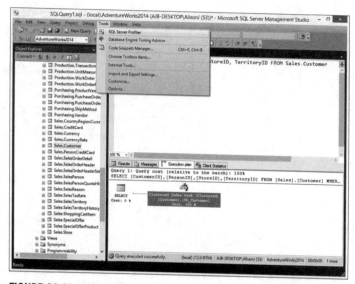

FIGURE 23.20 While in Management Studio, select Tools, SQL Server Profiler to launch the Profiler.

2. Enter the required connection information and click Connect. The Profiler appears as in Figure 23.21. You are now ready to designate the properties of the trace you are creating.

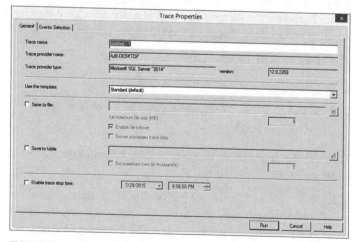

FIGURE 23.21 After you have launched the Profiler, you are ready to set properties of your trace.

3. Enter a name in the Trace name text box.

4. By default, the trace information displays in a window. You can opt to instead save the trace information to a file or to a table. These options enable you to easily analyze the trace information at a later time.

5. Click the Events Selection tab. The Trace Properties dialog box appears as in Figure 23.22. This is where you designate the types of events you want to capture as the trace runs.

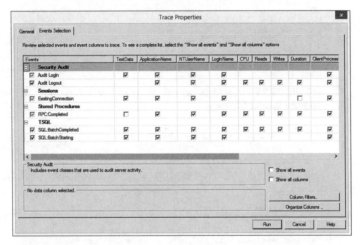

FIGURE 23.22 The Trace Properties dialog box enables you to determine the behavior of the trace.

6. The Events listed by default do not include many of the events you will probably want to capture. To show all available events, click the Show All Events check box. The dialog box now appears as in Figure 23.23.

7. Expand and collapse the event groupings to view the various events you want to capture. Figure 23.24 shows the TSQL group expanded with five events selected.

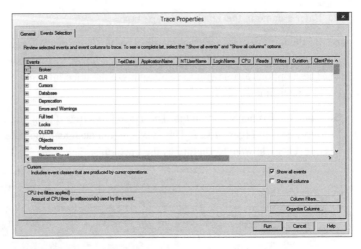

FIGURE 23.23   Use Show all events to view all the events you can capture in your trace.

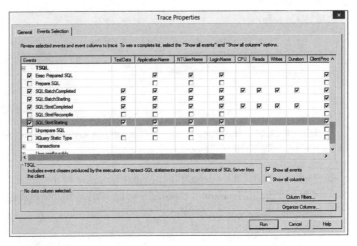

FIGURE 23.24   You can select as many events from as many groupings as you would like.

8. Select all the events you want to capture.

9. You will probably want to filter the database whose events you want to trace. To do that, click Show All Columns. The Trace Properties dialog box opens as in Figure 23.25.

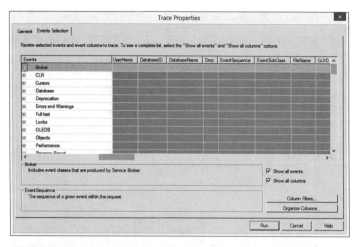

FIGURE 23.25 You must show all columns if you want to filter the trace to activity in a specific database.

10. Click any one of the column headings. The Edit Filter dialog box appears.

11. Click DatabaseName.

12. Enter the name of the database whose events you want to view (see Figure 23.26).

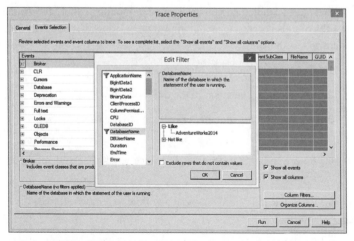

FIGURE 23.26 To filter the trace to activities occurring in a specific database, enter the name of the database.

13. Click OK to close the dialog box.

14. When you are ready, click Run to run the trace. The running trace appears as in Figure 23.27.

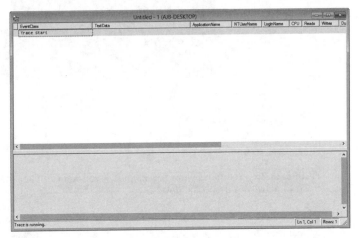

FIGURE 23.27 When you run your trace, it starts capturing the designated events.

It is easy to see the effects of the actions you take within your database on the trace output. If, for example, you execute a SQL statement in Management Studio and you have opted to monitor T-SQL events, the results of those events appear in your trace window. Use the following steps to test this out:

1. Create a new query in Management Studio.

2. Enter a SQL statement in the query window.

3. With your trace running, execute the SQL statement (see Figure 23.28).

4. Return to the SQL Profiler. The trace window should appear as in Figure 23.29.

5. Click Clear Trace Window at any time to remove all trace information.

6. Click Stop Selected Trace to terminate the trace process.

FIGURE 23.28 After you have filtered your events, you must do something that triggers the events you have selected.

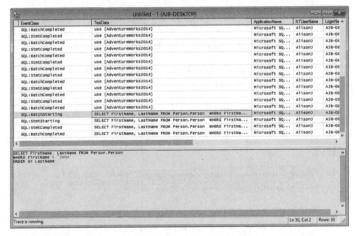

FIGURE 23.29 The effects of executing your SQL statement show up in the Trace window.

Summary

Learning how to create queries can be moderately difficult. Learning to create efficient queries is even more difficult. In this lesson, you learned how you can use SQL Server Management Studio to design and test the queries you will include in your stored procedures, triggers, functions, and other objects that use T-SQL. You saw how you can use the tools built into Management Studio to display and analyze the estimated execution plan for a query. You learned how to add indexes to enable queries to execute more efficiently and how to set query options. Finally, you saw how you can use the Query Analyzer to see exactly what is happening when you execute a T-SQL statement.

Q&A

Q. Explain why you will probably want to analyze the queries you include in your stored procedures, functions, and so on.

A. Using the analysis tools built into SQL Server Management Studio, you can analyze your T-SQL statements to ensure that they execute as efficiently as possible. You can modify your queries at will and observe the effect those changes have on performance.

Q. Describe what the SQL Profiler is used for.

A. You use the SQL Profiler to trace selected events that occur when a query, view, stored procedure, or function executes.

Workshop

Quiz

1. Name the tool on the toolbar that enables you to run the query you type into the query window.

2. Name the tool on the toolbar that enables you to view the execution plan each time you run a query.

3. Name the tool on the toolbar that enables you to view client statistics when you run your queries.

4. What is the most important thing you can do to improve query execution?

Quiz Answers

1. New Query

2. Include Actual Execution Plan

3. Include Client Statistics

4. Add indexes

Activities

Build a query based on the Sales.SalesOrderDetail table. Display the SalesOrderID, OrderQty, UnitPrice, and LineTotal, ordering the data by LineTotal. Execute the query. Notice the number of rows affected on the Messages page. Indicate that you want to view both the execution plan and the client statistics. Run the query again. View the results in both the Execution Plan tab and the Client Statistics tab. Add an index based on LineTotal. Finally, re-execute the query, noting the differences in the execution plan and client statistics.

LESSON 24

Installing and Upgrading SQL Server

Although you can use the material in this book with most versions of SQL Server, SQL Server 2014 is the most commonly used version of SQL Server at the time of this writing. This lesson explains:

- ▶ How to launch the SQL Server installation process
- ▶ How to configure the various installation options
- ▶ How to launch SQL Server Management Studio

Installing SQL Server 2014 Enterprise Edition

Although installing SQL Server is a fairly simple process, there are a few questions you are asked during the installation process that might need some clarification. The text that follows walks you through the process of installing the SQL Server 2014 database engine and provides an explanation of the various options available to you. Here's the process:

1. Before launching the setup program, you must first locate and mount the ISO file. Right-click the ISO file and select Mount (see Figure 24.1). This opens the ISO file so you can view its contents (see Figure 24.2).

2. Double-click setup.exe.

3. When prompted to allow the program to make changes to your computer, click Yes.

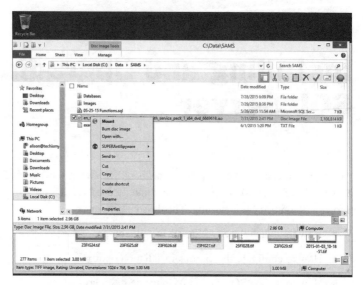

FIGURE 24.1   Mount the ISO file so that you can view its contents.

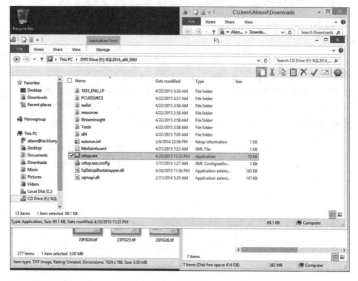

FIGURE 24.2   The contents of the ISO file contain setup.exe.

4. After a short delay, the SQL Server Installation Center appears. Here you can opt to perform a variety of operations.

5. Click Installation. The dialog box displays as in Figure 24.3.

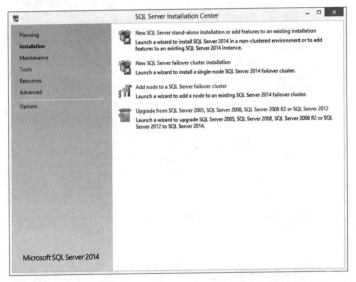

FIGURE 24.3   After clicking Installation, you can select the type of installation you want to perform.

6. Click New SQL Server Stand-alone Installation or Add Features to an Existing Installation. The installation process goes through a series of steps that might take quite a bit of time to execute (see Figure 24.4).

7. After quite some time, the installation wizard prompts you to indicate whether you want to perform a new instance of SQL Server or add features to an existing instance of SQL Server (see Figure 24.5).

8. Click Perform a New Installation of SQL Server 2014 and click Next.

9. Indicate whether you are installing a free edition or if you have a product key that you will be using. Click Next.

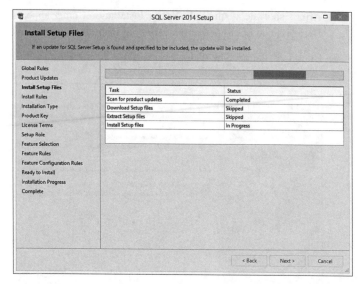

FIGURE 24.4   It is important to be patient as the installation process executes.

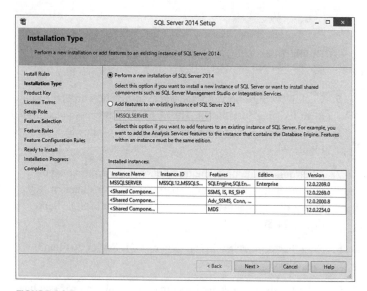

FIGURE 24.5   You can either create a new SQL Server instance, or add features to an existing instance.

10. Accept the license terms and click Next.

11. Select SQL Server Feature Installation and click Next.

12. As its name implies, the Feature Selection step of the installation process enables you to easily designate the features you want to include in your instance of SQL Server (see Figure 24.6). Select the desired features and click Next.

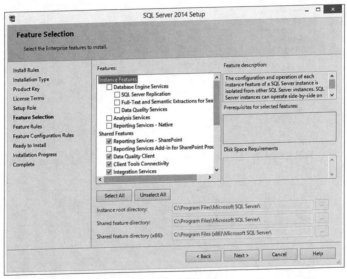

FIGURE 24.6   You can customize SQL Server to include only the features you need.

13. If you have multiple instances of SQL Server installed on your computer, each one must be identified by a unique instance name. Provide a name for the instance that you are creating (see Figure 24.7) and click Next.

14. With the Server Configuration step of the installation process, you can create accounts for the various server processes and indicate when the operating system starts each service (see Figure 24.8). Make your selections and click Next.

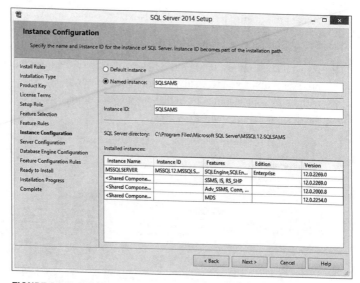

FIGURE 24.7 Provide a unique name for the SQL Server instance.

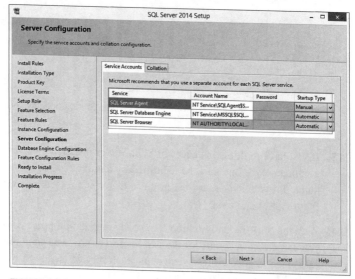

FIGURE 24.8 You can designate account information for each process.

15. In the Database Engine Configuration step, you designate the type of authentication you prefer, information about administrators, and details about data directories. In Figure 24.9, Windows authentication mode is designated, and AlisonJ has been designated as an Administrator.

16. On the Data Directories tab, shown in Figure 24.10, you can view and modify the directories within which SQL Server will store the various files utilized by the server (for example, databases).

17. After designating all desired features, click Next. The Ready to Install step displays, reflecting all features you installed (see Figure 24.11). Review the settings carefully.

18. Click Install to complete the process. After several minutes, you should receive a message indicating that you need to reboot your computer. After rebooting your computer, you will be ready to start working with SQL Server.

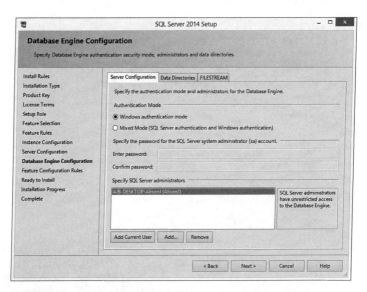

FIGURE 24.9   Select the authentication mode and any system administrators.

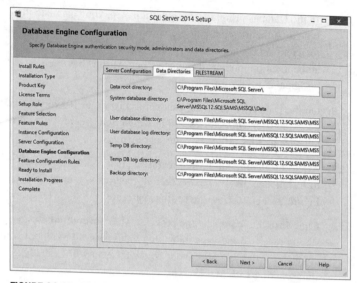

FIGURE 24.10 You can easily customize where the various SQL files will reside.

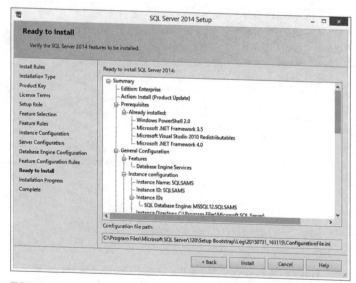

FIGURE 24.11 It is important to review the settings you have selected before you click Install.

Installing SQL Server Management Studio

SQL Server Management Studio is a separate download and a separate installation process. Use the following steps to install SQL Server Management Studio:

1. Download the file and run the executable file (.exe).

2. Double-click the executable and click Yes, allowing the program to run.

3. Choose a directory for the extracted files and click OK.

4. When the SQL Server Installation Center launches, click the link to select New SQL Server Stand-alone Installation or Add Features to an Existing Installation.

5. Accept the license terms and click Next.

6. Select Add Features to an Existing Instance of SQL 2014 (see Figure 24.12).

7. Click Next. The Feature Selection portion of the installation appears. Select all the desired features. Note that in Figure 24.13, Management Tools is selected. This includes Management Studio.

8. Click Next.

9. Complete the installation. Management Studio is now ready to use.

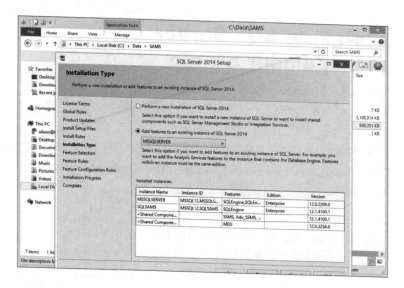

FIGURE 24.12   To install Management Studio, you must add features to your existing instance of SQL Server.

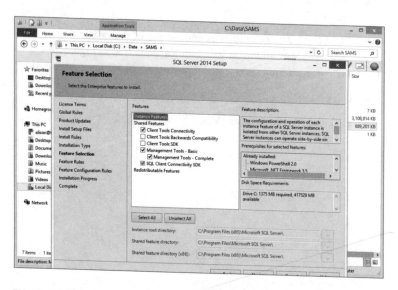

FIGURE 24.13   Add Management Tools to your SQL Server instance so that you can use Management Studio.

Summary

Although Microsoft makes it fairly easy to install SQL Server, it prompts you for information that you might not be familiar with. This lesson walked you through the installation process, covering the available options.

Q&A

Q. **What is the difference between the SQL Server Database Engine and Management Studio?**

A. The SQL Server Database Engine is the application that provides the processing for the database. This processing includes the execution of T-SQL, whether from the Query window, views, stored procedures, functions, or triggers. SQL Server Management studio provides a means of graphically managing database servers, databases, and their objects.

Workshop

Quiz

1. You are prompted for the authentication model during the installation of the SQL Server 2014 database engine (true/false).

2. Name the management tool you use to manage SQL Server 2014 databases.

Quiz Answers

1. True

2. SQL Server Management Studio

Activities

Download SQL Server. Install both the database engine and SQL Server Management Studio. Launch Management Studio and practice expanding and contracting the nodes of the Object Explorer. Select different nodes and view the summary information.

Index

J-K

processor options, 326-327

security options, 327-328

Perform a New Installation of SQL Server 2014 option, 379-380

permissions options (SQL Server), 331-332

permission statements, 302

permissions validation, 299

    column-level permissions, 315-316

    database users, adding, 300-302

    definition of term, 278

    function permissions, 315

    inherited/implied permissions, 300, 317

    object permissions

        assigning for particular objects, 302-305

        assigning to users or roles, 305-309

        explained, 299

    permission statements, 302

    statement permissions, 299

    stored procedure permissions, 314

    table permissions, 309-312

        assigning, 310-312

        types of, 309-310

    view permissions, 312-314

plans, Estimated Execution Plan, 358-359

populating cursors, 246

primary key constraints, 51, 65

procedures, stored. *See* stored procedures

procEmployeeGetByTitleAndBirthDateOpt stored procedure, 224-225

procEmployeeGetByTitleAndBirthDate stored procedure, 221

procEmployeeGetYoungSalesReps stored procedure, 221

procEmployeesGetByJobTitleAndHireDate stored procedure, 244

procEmployeesGetByTitleAndBirthDateOutput stored procedure, 225-226

procEmployeesGetCursor stored procedure, 246

procEmployeesGetTemp stored procedure, 243-244

processadmin, 286

Process Administrators (processadmin), 286

processors, 322, 326-327

procGetString stored procedures, 247-248

procOrderDetailAddHandleErrors2 stored procedure, 229

procOrderDetailAddHandleErrors3 stored procedures, 230-231

procOrderDetailAddOutput stored procedure, 234

procOrderDetailAdd stored procedure, 234

procOrderDetailAddTransaction stored procedure, 238

procSalesOrderDetailDelete stored procedure, 237

procSalesOrderDetailUpdate stored procedure, 235-236

procSalesOrderHeaderUpdate stored procedure, 235

Profiler, 16-17, 367-373

    analyzing trace output, 372-373

    creating traces, 367-372

    when to use, 374